THE 100 BEST STOCKS

YOU CAN BUY

2010

PETER SANDER
AND
JOHN SLATTER, CFA

BUSINESS

AVON, MASSACHUSETTS

Copyright © 2009 by F+W Media, Inc.
All rights reserved. This book, or parts thereof, may not be
reproduced in any form without permission from the publisher;
exceptions are made for brief excerpts used in published reviews.

Published by Adams Business,
an imprint of Adams Media, a division of F+W Media, Inc.
57 Littlefield Street
Avon, MA 02322
www.adamsmedia.com

ISBN 10: 1-59869-780-3
ISBN 13: 978-1-59869-780-3

Printed in the United States of America.

J I H G F E D C B A

Library of Congress Cataloging-in-Publication Data
is available from the publisher.

This book is available at quantity discounts for bulk purchases.
For information, please call 1-800-289-0963.

Contents

Dedication

I dedicate this book to all of you active investors who have the sense of purpose and independence of thought to make your own investing decisions, or at least, to ask the right questions. You're all wise enough—and inquisitive enough—to realize that not all the answers can be found in one place, and smart enough to seek the convenience of a good place to start.

Acknowledgments

Two pairs of eyes are better than one, and so for this tenth edition I must thank my research partner and long time friend and colleague J. Scott Bobo for his prescient analysis and hard work. I must also recognize the good work of Value Line Inc. and their investment survey, which does more than any other investment service I know of to turn piles of facts and figures into a simple readable page. Next, no book happens without the added value of exercise to keep my body in shape and my mind clear, and to that end I offer my thanks to my exercise companions. And of course I must thank my family—wife Jennifer and boys Julian and Jonathan—for taking care of business while I engaged in this enterprise.

PART I

THE ART AND SCIENCE OF INVESTING IN STOCKS

By Peter Sander

The Art and Science of Investing in Stocks

Peter Sander

Congratulations on your purchase of the 2010 edition of *The 100 Best Stocks You Can Buy*.

If you bought this book, you're probably an astute and experienced individual investor who invests in individual stocks in individual companies. Now, that might not seem so profound, but with the some 10,000 mutual funds, 8,000 hedge funds, and countless Exchange Traded Funds (ETFs) and index funds out there, it's not inconceivable that the individual stock investor is becoming an endangered species.

But that's just not so. For the better, not only for your own wealth but for the efficient allocation of capital to businesses and ideas that work best, millions still engage in this sort of "pure" investing for all or part of their wealth.

Even if you buy just a few shares of one company, you're an individual investor. You're participating actively in the economy, and you're buying your share of the company with hopes of participating in its success. Like a homeowner choosing to take part in the work of owning a home as a "do-it-yourselfer" you're participating in the individual satisfaction, responsibility, and control that comes with doing it yourself.

If you succeed, you accept the benefits of increased wealth (and reduced fees) along with the satisfac-tion and sense of accomplishment of doing it yourself. If you fail, true, you'll have no one else to blame but yourself. But at least you won't be forced to drink the poison of having someone else lose your money for you. In the entrepreneurial spirit that so characterizes America and much of the Western world, you'll pick your-self up, dust yourself off, learn from the mistakes, and go out and do it again.

The 2010 edition of *The 100 Best Stocks You Can Buy* is intended to be a core tool for the individual investor. Sure, it's hardly the only tool avail-able. Today's explosion of Internet-based investing tools has made this book one of hundreds of choices for investing information. With the speed of cyberspace our book will hardly be the most current source. So instead, it is intended as a handy guide and core reference for your investing; not as a be-all end-all investing source. Thus, as much as a source of facts and num-bers itself, *100 Best Stocks* is intended as a *model* for selecting the best com-panies and stocks to invest in.

To that same point, *100 Best Stocks* goes well beyond just being a stock screen or a "study" of stocks to invest in. Analysis forms the base of *100 Best Stocks*, but it isn't the rigid, strictly numbers-based selection and analysis so often found in published "best stocks" lists. Sure, we look at earnings, cash flow, balance sheet strength, and so forth, but we'll also look far beyond those things. We'll look at the intangible and often subtle factors that make truly great businesses—that is, companies—great.

Great companies have good business fundamentals, but what makes them really great is the presence of intangibles and subtleties that will *keep* them great—or make them greater—in the future.

So the selection of the *100 Best Stocks* goes far beyond being a simple numbers-based stock screen. It's a selection and analysis of really good businesses you would want to buy and own, not just for past results but for future outcomes. Now, does "future" mean "forever?" No, not hardly, not anymore. Nothing is really forever these days—as those who invested in GM or Eastman Kodak or AIG or Bank of America can attest. So while the *100 Best Stocks* list correlates well with the notion of "blue chip" stocks, the discussion proceeds with the harsh reality that "blue chip" no longer means "forever."

As the book title suggests, I feel that the 100 companies listed and analyzed in the pages that follow are the best companies to own for 2010. That said, the word "own" has become a more active concept these days. Gone are the days of "own forever," like the halcyon days of my parents Jerry and Betty Sander, who bought their 35 shares of General Motors and lovingly placed the stock certificate in their safe deposit box and henceforth bought nothing but GM cars. Today,

there is no forever; the economy, technology, and consumer tastes simply change too fast, and the businesses that participate in the economy by necessity change with it. Ownership is a more active concept than it was even ten or twenty years ago.

So going forward, I offer the 100 best companies to own now and in 2010, and that have the best chances of not only surviving but evolving with—or even ahead of—the economy based on their current market position and approach to doing business. But as we all found out during the past two years, nothing is sacred in the business world and things can fall apart with astounding speed. What does that mean?

Simply this: You can't take anything you read in the following as "investment advice" or as hard, unwavering truths. The world simply changes too fast, and the analysis of a business and especially the *value* of a business is not a precise science, it is inherently a combination of science and art. True business value is subject to different interpretations and different opinions, and further, we must layer in the pace and effects of change.

What that means is simple and straightforward: You'll have to take the information presented, do your own assessment, reach your own conclusions, and take your own actions. Anything else would go beyond my intentions, and more importantly, stop short of the mark for you.

With that in mind, make the most of what follows, and good luck with your investing!

So Why Buy an Investing Book These Days?

The Internet is great: anything you want at your fingertips, practically real time, latest news, latest analysis, latest numbers. News and numbers are great, and they will inevitably help you take the latest facts into consideration and add points and counterpoints to your investment decision. But is the Internet enough?

Consider what a book, like *The 100 Best Stocks You Can Buy*, has to offer. It gives not just facts and figures, but also a mindset. A thought process you can browse through, one you can see applied repeatedly to different situations.

You might not align to the set of 100 stocks I offer here because they are too expensive or don't appeal to your tastes or just don't suit your needs or interests at the moment. That's okay. Even if you don't choose from the 100 stocks offered here, you can follow the thought processes, the choices and decisions made, as a model.

Being an individual investor is rather like being an airplane pilot. You are ultimately in control of your aircraft, you are in control of your finances. And that means taking responsibility for your own decisions, regardless of the information sources—the gauges, charts, and ground control folks you have helping you out. So you must develop your own mindset and set of investment knowledge and tools—that's where books come in.

Remember, in investing, like life, it's the thought—or, more precisely, the thought process—that counts.

Passing the Baton: 2010

Those of you loyal and faithful readers of previous editions of *100 Best Stocks* may have noticed something different about this year's edition. There is a new author, a different and perhaps unfamiliar name on the cover.

Yes, John Slatter has turned the reins over to me, and an introduction is in order. I am Peter Sander, and I am most grateful for the opportunity to assume this franchise. I enter this new phase not in the manner of a hostile takeover, not with a "let's clean house and start fresh" mentality, but instead with the idea of preserving the essence and core values of Mr. Slatter's previous work. I will use his work and approach and add a few ideas and concepts of my own.

First, a few words about me. I am an independent professional researcher, writer, and journalist specializing in personal finance, investing and location reference, as well as other general business topics. I have written twenty-one books on these topics, done numerous financial columns and independent privately contracted research and studies. I come from a background in the corporate world, having experienced a twenty-one-year career with a major West Coast technology firm.

I am an individual investor. And have been since the age of twelve, when my curiosity at the family breakfast table got the better of me. I started reading the stock pages with my parents. I had an opportunity during a one-week "project week" in the seventh grade to read about, and learn about, the stock market. I read Louis Engel's *How to Buy Stocks*, then the pre-eminent—and one of the only—books about investing available at the time (it first appeared in 1953; I think I read a 1962 paperback edition). I read Engel, picked stocks, and made graphs of their performance by hand with colored pens on real graph paper. I put my hard-earned savings into buying five shares of each of three different companies. I watched those stocks like a hawk and salted away the meager dividends to reinvest. I've been investing ever since, and in combination with twenty-six years of home ownership and a rigorous, almost sacrificial savings regimen, I, along with my wife Jennifer, have accumulated a net worth exceeding the total *gross* income I received in twenty-one years in the corporate job.

Yes, I have an MBA from a top-rated university (Indiana University, Bloomington), but it isn't an MBA in finance. I also took the coursework and certification exam to become a Certified Financial Planner (CFP). But I have never worked in the financial profession. That is by design and choice. My goal has always been to share my knowledge and experience in an educational way, a way helpful for the individual as an investor and a personal financier to make their own decisions.

And so I have never made money giving investment advice or managing money for others, nor do I intend to.

An Eye for Value

A few years ago it dawned on me that I really make my living finding value, and helping others or teaching others to find value. Not just in stocks, but other things in business and in life. And what do I mean by value? Simply, the current and potential *worth* of something (or someone) as compared to its price or cost. As it turns out, I've made a career out of assessing the value of people, places, and companies.

My last assignment at the high tech firm was to find value in customers. *People*. My title: Customer Valuation Manager. At the time, around the turn of the millennium, we were building a "customer relationship management" platform, and my job was to segment millions of customers by value, and to assign values to each one to help target messaging and so-called "one-to-one" marketing campaigns. A tricky enterprise, no doubt, because no company can really know what a customer is truly worth, down to the penny, especially going forward. It became an exercise in looking at previous buying behavior, considering other known customer attributes internal and external to the business, assessing the customer's cost (marketing and support costs) making some assumptions, and testing results.

At the time I did not really grasp that the same exact process really

applied to investing, too. But a sharp editor at John Wiley & Sons' "Dummies" division put two and two together and hired me to write *Value Investing for Dummies*. The light went on. Whether it's people or stocks, the thought process is the same. Take what you know (fundamentals), add some intuition (intangibles), make some assumptions, proceed carefully, and evaluate the results.

The same publisher—different division—gave me another chance two years later, this time to write a complete reference guide to places to live. Hundreds of places to live appraised for value and ranked top to bottom, best to worst. Value is extremely important in deciding where you would want to live. Sure, the "best" places to live might include Greenwich, Connecticut; Jupiter, Florida; or Palo Alto, California. But most of us can't afford them. So the true "best places" for most of us anyway are the places that deliver the most value for the money, now and in the future. The resulting book, *Cities Ranked & Rated—More Than 400 Metropolitan Areas Evaluated in the U.S. and Canada*, and the sister publication *Best Places to Raise Your Family*, finally went beyond the "study" and short list to truly answer the question most of us have—what's the best place to live *for my money*.

The same value approach works in the world of business and stock investing. It isn't just the biggest nor the richest corporations that we should be putting our hard-earned money into. If that were the case, we'd simply buy GE or ExxonMobil and move on.

But do these companies represent the best *value* for your investing dollar? Maybe, but maybe not.

Just like customers or places to live, we want companies that produce the greatest return, the highest value, *per dollar invested*. And *for the amount of risk taken*. The amount of risk taken translates into additional dollars an investment might cost, analogous to living in a great place rampant with crime or with questionable schools that might cost you more in the long run. The companies I will identify as among the 100 best have, in my assessment, the greatest long-term *value*, and if you can buy these companies at a *reasonable price* (a factor which I leave out of this analysis because this is a book and prices can change considerably) these investments deliver the best prospects.

Later I'll come back to describe some of the attributes of value that I look for.

A Two-Man Team

Meanwhile, enough about me. I have help. Help to execute the thought process to identify, analyze, and describe the 100 best stocks crisply and in plain English so that you can make the best use of the list. Help so that you get the combined wisdom and observations of two people, not just one, where hopefully one plus one equals something greater than two.

An engineer by training and profession, J. Scott Bobo and I have been buddies for some thirty-seven years. We sat next to each other in an American Government class in high school,

became college roommates and later coworkers at that technology company, and the rest is history.

Scott adds a strong analytical touch. But he is most at home as an applications engineer, explaining how a company's products work and how they apply to a customer's needs. As a consequence, and in addition to analytical legwork, Scott really adds an extraordinary and very real-world sense of how a company's products "fit" in the marketplace. Determining whether a company's products are relevant and best-in-class and have a competitive advantage over others is an oft-overlooked core skill for a value investor. Scott brings this skill to the table in a big way.

What's Changed, What's Stayed the Same

So while I owe a lot to the original structure and theme of *The 100 Best Stocks You Can Buy*, and to the structure of Mr. Slatter's excellent work, I will adapt it to the times. I will also add a stronger "intangibles" component to Mr. Slatter's already demonstrated value-oriented investing approach.

Here's a high-level summary of what's changed and what's stayed the same:

What's Stayed the Same

- *Focus on fundamentals.* Mainly, business results and business health. Mr. Slatter placed strong emphasis on sales, earnings, and dividends; I agree these are all important, and a company with flat or declining sales, poor earnings results, and little to no dividend must have something else very strong speaking for it, or it doesn't become part of the list. I've kept these fundamentals in sight but have added emphasis on some new ones; see "What's Changed."

- *Long-term horizon.* Mr. Slatter had a long-term approach to investing; so do I. However, that said, again for reasons mentioned shortly, the definition of "long-term" is evolving and is a relative thing. Faster business change means that no investment is forever, and even though a company has long-term appeal, it is dangerous to lock it away forever as an investment. "Long-term" may be as little as three to five years in some industries.

- *Reasons to buy/not to buy.* This is the bottom line, after all—should we buy, or not? I've always done this in my other value analyses; for example with cities—that is, to list the strongest "pros" and "cons" about the place which bubble up from the analysis. It helps me as the reader focus on the few really important factors, and it should help you as the reader to do the same. That happens here, too, as reasons to buy and reasons to be cautious or concerned about the company.

What's Changed

- *Fundamentals that count the most.* While earnings and dividends are important value drivers for an investment, in tune with the times I place a little less emphasis on them. Instead I focus more on some of the real business differentiators like cash flow, profitability, and balance sheet strength, including debt and working capital health. The reasons will become clear as you read on. This shift in emphasis did not result in many changes to the 100 best list, as companies excellent on the "old" fundamentals tend to perform well with the new ones, but I believe it brings a stronger evaluation to the company and its prospects for generating true shareholder value.

- *Greater weight on intangibles*— Fundamentals mainly reflect past results. I truly believe prospects for strong future fundamentals (which is what we really invest for) lie in the intangibles—brand, brand strength, customer loyalty, product excellence, market leadership, management quality. Another way to look at it—intangibles are the things that make good companies "great."

- *Shift toward value-add.* Previous editions of this book highlighted many companies currently "in favor" because of the business cycle—for example, energy, materials suppliers, and industrials in the 2009 edition. True, some of these companies are great in their marketplace, but some are simply undifferentiated commodity producers riding the times. I tend to focus more on long-term business value and business value-add, factors more likely to create longer term "greatness."

Further below I'll go into more specifics on my "value" approach. First, I want to circle back to explain why today's investing climate has shifted, and why it's important to adapt the investing approach to the current climate.

Today's Investment Climate: Changed Forever?

The markets, as measured by the major indexes, lost some 50 percent of their value in 2008 and the early part of 2009.

Who could have predicted that? Turns out, not many people did or could have. Most market participants, including—no, *especially*—the professionals offering investment advice, running major mutual finds, pension funds, and so forth—didn't see it coming. The conventional wisdom, of course, was that "corrections" were signaled by 10 percent pullbacks and "bear markets" by 20 percent pullbacks.

And when these levels were hit, surely the cycle would be done, new buyers would be attracted, and we'd all go on our merry way. These "rules" and their accompanying psychology were so pervasive that they actually became a self-fulfilling prophecy. Complacent investors eyeing the 10 percent mark would step in, saying "correction done" and buy, thus boosting the market to recover new losses and eventually move on to new highs.

It didn't happen that way this time.

What did happen is that years of excessive lending and leverage, large and unsustainable profits in the financial sector, and the resulting consumer consumption boom—overconsumption, really—fueled by numbers one and two, finally caught up with us. We entered a period of profound corporate instability and uncertainty, wiping out trillions in current and future value of American companies, and it was reflected in stock prices.

This is oversimplifying the case, for sure. Many other factors were involved, including the unwinding of the commodity boom and the pain caused to speculators and hedge fund managers that so counted on persistent gains in commodity prices (China would continue to grow forever and put pressure on commodity prices, right?). And financial services firms, which make most of their money by moving money around without creating a lot of value in the process, reaped some 40 percent of all the profits made in corporate America, again signaling something was quite wrong.

I don't want to go into all of the factors contributing to the bust, but it was large and painful, to be sure. Aside from the 1929 stock market crash and the Great Depression that followed, no stock market collapse has caused so much pain nor was it so widespread. Even damage from the dot.com bust, as the name implies, was largely although not wholly contained in the tech sector. The causes of the 2008–2009 bust were many and varied, and largely related to individual and corporate balance sheets (translation: debt) so the effects lasted longer.

But—aside from the periodically relearned lessons of keeping debts under control—there were other changes in the air which all investors, large and small, need to be aware of, and build into their investing mentality. Some of these forces directly affect companies and company performance, some have more effect on the stock markets, but not necessarily the business performance of the companies themselves. You as a sharp investor must separate the two and keep closer tabs on the forces that affect companies. That said, you cannot ignore the forces that increase market volatility, if for no other reason than they mean that investments will need to be re-evaluated more frequently.

Following are some fundamental forces causing permanent change to the investing landscape.

Shorter Business Cycles

The birth, technological evolution, and eventual death of any business is inevitable, just as birth, life, and death must happen for all as individuals. But the speed of that cycle is increasing. Consider railroads, which started as a commercially viable entity in the 1840s and boomed for the next eighty years to reach a peak in the 1920s, only then to start a slow decline after World War II. Or radio, coming alive in the 1920s to reach maturity in thirty years, then, a long, slow decline. And now the PC, moving to maturity in less than twenty years, and the In-

ternet, in ten to fifteen years. A railroad investor in the late 1800s could count on a long future for the industry and the business. But what about someone in the PC business? Sure, Microsoft has made billions, but how long until its technology is replaced by something else? That, in fact, was much of their defense in their celebrated antitrust cases.

The point is—a company cannot become complacent in its technology nor its market position. Change happens faster. Technology and changing consumer preferences drive that change, and companies must adapt to it or perish. Eastman Kodak is a poster child for what happens when technological change—digital photography—changes faster than the company expected or could adapt to. They've been behind the curve ever since, watching their traditional business disappear. Same story for the entire newspaper industry—first complacency, then concern, now sheer panic as the Internet took most of their revenue generating business while they continued to do business as usual.

As an investor, you must observe how companies keep up with—or even lead—this kind of change. Apple Computer has done an excellent job of leading change in the digital entertainment world, but any investor must carefully watch for the next new thing that might come along and pass Apple by. And it isn't just the product itself—Dell Computer made the mistake of allowing its once-leading edge direct sales model to become passé—as computer prices dropped and people wanted to see their printers and laptops in person at their local retailer, and customization became less important.

Great companies know that change happens faster, and they work hard to stay ahead of change. They change their products and their marketing strategies at least in pace with the market, if not ahead of it. The landscape is littered with companies that failed to keep up—GM, Chrysler, Eastman Kodak, Sun Microsystems, Circuit City, to name a few—with changes in technology and consumer tastes.

The World Is Flat

Borrowing liberally from Thomas Friedman's excellent book by this name, no investor can ignore the global forces affecting today's businesses. In today's "flat" world, competition can strike from almost anywhere for any product. That is both a problem and an opportunity for today's corporations. The problem, of course, is the competition itself; again the auto industry is a perfect example of where foreign competition has changed the competitive landscape forever, and investors must beware.

But the "flat" world, in which information and even goods can travel anywhere cheaply and in virtual real time, businesses quick to take advantage of competitive advantages available in other countries stand to stay ahead of the pack. "Offshoring" is not only a buzzword but an essential component of the business strat-

egy of many companies. Those that get it right will succeed; those who go too slow may fail, and some who go too fast and send too much of their work—and their souls—overseas may also fail. Smart investors look for companies that can become more efficient, and they look for companies that use the flat world to their advantage—to sell their products overseas. The Hewlett-Packards and Procter & Gambles and Boeings of the world sell more than half of their product overseas and have emerged as truly global corporations.

The point: Today's truly great businesses stay in front of technology and geographic specialization and use it to their advantage. Others continually play catch-up.

The Increasing Speed of Information

The Internet has made news a truly real-time phenomenon; the latest news flash can be read on your PC or your BlackBerry or iPhone almost as it happens. The result is a generally faster speed of business and speed of markets. Businesses can react faster to changing marketplaces; that's generally a good thing at least for the companies set up to make fast change. They can change production schedules or redirect inventory or employees to where they are needed most. The ability of businesses to respond to change separates good from bad businesses.

Beyond the businesses themselves, the securities markets will react almost instantaneously to news as it hits the world stage in real time, creating considerable volatility. And with so much news hitting so many market players at once, these news flashes can cause overreaction, which can panic people into or out of a stock. As an investor, you must keep a finger on the pulse of the news, but learn to react only when necessary and not to follow crowds to the exits or entrances all at once.

The good news: It's easier to keep tabs on what's going on with the businesses you invest in.

New, Bigger, Faster Players in the Game

At one time the markets were primarily geared to long-term institutional investors, high commissions, relatively archaic communication tools, and a poor public understanding of the stock market which combined to make buying and selling a pretty big deal for the average investor, cost effort and comfort wise. But that's all changed, starting with broker deregulation in 1975 allowing highly discounted commissions, and carried forward in a big way by computers, the Internet, and electronic trading. Active stock and commodity trading used to be a specialty engaged in only by a few with direct contact to the NYSE and other exchange floors. Now anyone can do it with electronic markets real-time electronic execution available at the stroke of a keyboard. Many, many more players can and have entered the game.

The new technology and low transaction costs have allowed individuals of all stripes to enter and trade the markets, not just typical core investors looking for long-term asset growth. So-called "day trading" came into vogue in the late 1990s, where individuals could buy and sell within the trading day, actually, within seconds, functioning more as a dealer than a retail customer in the market. This wasn't all bad. It added to market volume, price transparency, and liquidity, as there were more visible buyers and sellers at any given price point, making the market less subject to manipulation. But it also allowed for gamesmanship among professional traders, and it gave rise to very active trading by private equity funds, or *hedge* funds.

Hedge funds are private funds with very limited regulation dealing only with who qualifies to invest in them and how they can promote themselves. Once they have investor funds, they can do what they please with them. Many are solid investment vehicles run by name-brand investment houses like Merrill Lynch and Goldman Sachs, but many others are fast-buck propositions managed by high-rolling fund managers and compensated richly on a "2-and-20" basis—that is, 2 percent of assets invested *plus* 20 percent of net annual gains. That compensation structure drove many of these hedge fund managers to take big risks to try to score big by reaping larger fees—and to lock in gains quickly and sell short for more when things went south. At one time during the 2008 crisis, hedge funds accounted for more than half of all shares traded.

Many of these hedge fund managers, looking for fast profits, jumped onto whatever big trends were in play. When oil started to move up and China demand became an irresistible story, funds jumped with both feet into oil futures, as well as oil and oil service stocks. They drove up other resource stocks, fertilizer stocks, and even mining machinery stocks, anticipating demand, and creating more demand as others saw the prices rise. It all came to a halt in 2008, and hedge funds started selling everything that wasn't nailed down to handle redemptions, and jumped into short selling bets with both feet.

Enough about hedge funds. If you invest in or with hedge funds, you probably don't need this book. The point is this: Hedge funds, the ease and rapidity of trading, and the existence of more players in the market all serve to increase volatility, create overreactions (like $147 oil) and magnify trends—upward and downward. Such overcooked trends in the market, and especially in certain sectors of the market, have become more common. As an individual investor and stock picker, you must stay aware of these "über" trends and avoid becoming victimized by them.

As Warren Buffett once famously put it: "The worst reason to buy a stock is because it's going up." I'm not sure I'll go that far—if your choice among the 100 best stocks in this book is going up, that's probably a good sign, a sign that other people like it, too. But be careful—if it is going up because it's part of a mania, if every stock in the sector is going nuts and rising at unsustainable rates, far beyond any reasonable assessment of sales or earnings growth, watch out. You might be able to buy the stock at a better price.

Think of it like playing poker— the worst reason to bet is because everybody else at the table is betting.

Is Long-Term Investing Under Siege?

With the recent volatility and the speed of change noted above, many financial journalists and pundits have recently announced the demise of long-term investing, specifically the so-called "buy-and-hold" strategy. Indeed, one wonders when such stalwarts as Citigroup and AIG and such long-term growth favorites as Whole Foods and Starbucks run into trouble. The speed of change—change in technology and consumer tastes—does indeed bring some concern to the idea of buying shares and locking them away in your safe deposit box. More than ever, you need to stay on your toes and watch for change.

What it really means is that you need to select companies that adapt well to change and can stay in front of changing markets. And it means that a periodic review of your investments—all of your investments—is more important than ever. Every stock you own should be evaluated from scratch—as though you were going to buy it again—at least once a year.

But that doesn't mean that long-term investing is dead. Great companies respond to change and find ways to continue to satisfy customers and make money, regardless of the mood and change of the day. Companies like Procter & Gamble reinvent themselves constantly, and not with a big housecleaning and restructuring every few years. They get into cosmetics like Olay as the population ages and people become more conscious of their appearance, and as competitive pressure and lack of consumer interest drives profit margins on peanut butter steadily downward. As aging men become more concerned about their appearance, Procter develops Olay lines for men. You get the idea.

Some companies respond better to changes in the wind than others. Starbucks sailed in front of a huge tailwind, opening store after store until they had so many stores that they cannibalized each other and worse, lost their agility and brand cachet. I feel, however, that they learned from this mistake, and have included them in this book on the basis of brand strength, management excellence, balance-sheet strength and core business profitability. A fault once in a while is okay, but I tend to avoid companies that seem to be "restructuring" or "reinventing themselves" continuously.

Value—Now More Than Ever

The bottom line is this: For intelligent investors, chasing the latest fad doesn't work, nor does buying something and locking it away forever. Investors must make intelligent choices based on true value and follow those choices through time and change. It all points to taking a "value" oriented approach to investing, and to staying modestly "active" with your investments.

The next obvious task is to define what I mean by a "value" approach. Essentially, it is to think of buying shares in a company as buying the company itself; it is about putting yourself in an entrepreneurial frame of mind, not just an investment frame of mind. Would you want to own that business? Why or why not? That's the first and biggest question that must be answered.

Fundamentally, whether or not you want to own the business depends on two factors: first, the returns you expect to receive on your investment in the near and long-term future and second, the risk you'll take in generating those returns. Fortunately, the third factor the prospective entrepreneur must consider—"Do I have the time for this?"—isn't typically a consideration.

So you are looking for tangible value—tangible worth—for your precious, scarce and hard-earned investment capital. Now that return doesn't have to be immediate in the form of dividends or a share of the assets, as many in the traditional "value school"

suggest. It can come in the form of growth for the longer term. If you realize your return in the form of owning a share of a larger company eventually, that's still a legitimate return. Cash flow received later in the form of a higher share price or a takeover is still cash return, it is just less certain because of the forces of change that may take place in the interim. It is also theoretically worth less because of the nature of discounting—a dollar received tomorrow is worth more than a dollar received twenty years in the future.

The point: Many investment experts distinguish between "value" and "growth" investing; in fact, mutual funds are often classified as being one or the other. I dismiss this separation; growth can be an essential component of a firm's value. Indeed, this is the key difference between the original 1930s Benjamin Graham school of value and the more evolved Warren Buffett take.

Value also implies safety. The safety comes in three forms. First is the fundamental quality and soundness of the firm's financial fundamentals, that is, income, cash flow, and the balance sheet. Value companies have plenty of reserves, and a large enough "margin of safety," to weather downturns and unforeseen events in the marketplace. Second, they have strong enough intangibles—brands, market position, supply chain strength, etc.—to maintain their position in that marketplace and generate future returns.

Thirdly, if you're really practicing value investing principles, you buy these companies at reduced prices, when the markets are down, when the company is out of favor. You're looking for situations where the price is less than what you perceive to be the value, although calculating the value that precisely is difficult. When you "buy cheap" you provide another margin of safety, that makes it less likely that the stock will drop further. It gives you room for error if you turn out to be wrong about a choice. Again, it's much like buying a business of your own—you want to pay as little as possible in case things don't turn out as you expected.

So taking a value approach provides greater confidence and safety, and is more likely to get you through today's volatile business and investing cycles.

You Don't Need to Be a Math Genius

Calculating "value" can be a daunting task, especially if one goes into the nuances of compounding, discounting, and all that business school stuff. Today's value investor doesn't ignore the numbers, but shuns complex mathematical formulas, which in the recent bust, tended not to work anyway; greater forces overtook almost all statistical and mathematical models for stock analysis, leaving many a "quant" scratching his or her head.

Buying companies is not a math-driven process, just like you can't evaluate a school based on its test scores alone. Warren Buffett and Charlie

Munger have made this clear over the years and came back to the point with emphasis in the 2009 Berkshire Hathaway shareholders meeting. Buffett mused: "If you need to use a computer or a calculator to make the calculation, you shouldn't buy it." Reading between the lines: The story should be simple and straightforward enough to be obvious without detailed calculations.

Munger, Buffett's relatively more intrepid sidekick, added: "Some of the worst business decisions I've ever seen are those with future projections and discounts back. It seems like the higher mathematics with more false precision should help you, but it doesn't. They teach that in business school because, well, they've got to do something."

No need to read between the lines there.

Indeed, while the numbers are important, savvy value investors try to see where the puck is going. And that means a clear-eyed assessment of the intangible things that make companies great.

This Year's 100 Best: A Few Comments

Before going further into the whys and wherefores of investing technique, it's as good a place as any to stop and talk about this year's list of 100 best stocks, and what you'll see as you move forward into Part II.

For now, the Part II presentation takes largely the same form as in previous editions. And so far as content is concerned, the 100 best stocks list, not surprisingly, is with a few exceptions what you might call a "blue chip" list of stocks—venerable favorites like IBM and General Mills and Kellogg and Boeing and so forth. But there are also new names on the block like Perrigo and CarMax and Iron Mountain—names you might have run across as an active follower of stocks and new companies, or as customers of these companies, but they are far from household names, at least so far.

This year's list starts with financial strength and fundamental solidarity, but goes farther into the "intangibles"—the not-so-quantifiable factors that make good companies great and portend strong *future* profits, rather than just measuring past ones. Put simply, the 100 best stocks are companies you'd really want to own and be proud to own; you couldn't replicate their businesses if you had to.

With every edition of this book, a handful of stocks have been replaced. This year's replacement list is larger than usual—there are some 26 new names among the 100 stocks presented, that is, 26 companies that weren't on the 2009 list. There are two reasons for that. First, we've been through a major economic crisis, and that crisis has changed the fortunes of many companies, some temporarily, some more permanently. While we're tolerant of a short period of weak performance in such a crisis, companies that might suffer long term impairment are no longer on the list. Several companies in the financial services and industrial sector "bit the dust" in

this regard. Also, the 2009 list was probably overweighted in energy stocks due to the boom underway at the time; the current list is down to 8 from 10 energy companies (see Table 3 on p. 19).

The second reason for so many changes is that, quite simply, no two people see a company or a stock exactly alike. New analysis from a new author is bound to bring some changes; I'd have to say the current list is biased to companies with stronger forward, not just current, prospects. Intangibles such as brand, market dominance, management competence, information systems application, and others play a slightly stronger role; that's why you see companies like Starbucks or CarMax on the list.

With these thoughts in mind, it's time to look at what new companies made the list (Table 1), what companies fell off the list from 2009 (Table 2), and the distribution of companies among major business sectors and how that changed for this edition.

TABLE 1: NEW COMPANIES FOR 2010

COMPANY	SYMBOL	CATEGORY	SECTOR
Alexander & Baldwin	ALEX	Growth and Income	Transportation
Apple	AAPL	Aggressive Growth	Consumer Discretionary
Archer Daniels Midland	ADM	Conservative Growth	Consumer Staples
Baxter	BAX	Aggressive Growth	Health Care
CarMax	KMX	Aggressive Growth	Retail
Diebold	DBD	Growth and Income	Industrials
eBay	EBAY	Aggressive Growth	Consumer Discretionary
Fair Isaac	FIC	Aggressive Growth	Business Services
Fluor	FLR	Aggressive Growth	Heavy Construction

COMPANY	SYMBOL	CATEGORY	SECTOR
Google	GOOG	Aggressive Growth	Information Technology
Heinz	HNZ	Growth and Income	Consumer Staples
Iron Mountain	IRM	Aggressive Growth	Information Technology
Kraft Foods	KFT	Growth and Income	Consumer Staples
Marathon Oil	MRO	Growth and Income	Energy
Monsanto	MON	Aggressive Growth	Industrials
Nike	NIKE	Aggressive Growth	Consumer Discretionary
Nucor	NUE	Aggressive Growth	Materials
Peet's	PEET	Aggressive Growth	Restaurant
Perrigo	PRGO	Aggressive Growth	Health Care
Ross Stores	ROST	Aggressive Growth	Retail
Southern Co.	SO	Growth and Income	Utilities
Starbucks	SBUX	Aggressive Growth	Restaurant
Tractor Supply	TSCO	Aggressive Growth	Retail
United Health Corp.	UNH	Aggressive Growth	Health Care
Valmont	VMT	Aggressive Growth	Industrials
Verizon	VZ	Growth and Income	Telecommunications Services

COMPANY	SYMBOL	CATEGORY	SECTOR
Gentex	GNTX	Growth and Income	Consumer Discretionary
IDEX	IEX	Conservative Growth	Industrials
Ingersoll-Rand	IR	Aggressive Growth	Industrials
Intel	INTC	Aggressive Growth	Information Technology
KIMCO Realty	KIM	Growth and Income	Financials
McGraw Hill	MHP	Growth and Income	Consumer Discretionary
MDU Resources	MDU	Growth and Income	Utilities
Meredith	MDP	Conservative Growth	Consumer Discretionary
Nabors Industries	NBR	Aggressive Growth	Energy
Nordson	NDSN	Aggressive Growth	Industrials
Omnicon	OMC	Conservative Growth	Consumer Discretionary
Oshkosh	OSK	Aggressive Growth	Industrials
Parker Hannefin	PH	Aggressive Growth	Industrials
Rohm & Haas	ROH	Growth and Income	Materials
T. Rowe Price	TROW	Aggressive Growth	Financials

TABLE 3: SECTOR ANALYSIS AND CHANGE BY SECTOR

	NUMBER OF COMPANIES		
SECTOR	ON 2010 LIST	ADDED FOR 2010	CUT FROM 2009
Business Services	1	1	0
Consumer Discretionary	4	3	-6
Consumer Staples	13	3	0
Energy	8	1	-3
Financials	2	0	-3
Health Care	14	3	0
Heavy Construction	1	1	0
Industrials	18	3	-10
Information Technology	6	2	-1
Materials	9	1	-1
Restaurant	3	2	0
Retail	10	3	0
Telecommunications Services	2	1	0
Transportation	4	1	-1
Utilities	5	1	-1

TABLE 2: COMPANIES REMOVED FOR 2010

COMPANY	SYMBOL	CATEGORY	SECTOR
Alcoa	AA	Aggressive Growth	Industrials
Canadian National	CNI	Conservative Growth	Transportation
Carnival Corp.	CCL	Aggressive Growth	Consumer Discretionary
Cash America Int'l	CSH	Aggressive Growth	Financials
Coach	COH	Aggressive Growth	Consumer Discretionary
CONSOL Energy	CNX	Aggressive Growth	Energy
Devon Energy	DVN	Aggressive Growth	Energy
Donaldson	DCI	Conservative Growth	Industrials
Eaton Corp.	ETN	Growth and Income	Industrials
Emerson Electric	EMR	Growth and Income	Industrials
Fastenal	FAST	Aggressive Growth	Industrials

Tenets, Anyone?
The Essentials of Successful Investing

To start off, I do not intend to give a complete course on investing, or value investing, here. That probably wasn't the purpose you had in mind when you bought this book, and there isn't space here for a complete discussion anyway. For a more complete treatment of the topic, refer to my title *Value Investing for Dummies* (second edition, Wiley, 2008).

At the risk of sounding "corporate," what makes sense here is to give a high level overview of key investing "tenets" to keep top of mind and back of mind as you sift through the thousands of investment choices. By absorbing these principles, you'll gain a better understanding of the 100 best stocks list and take away ideas to help with your own investment choices outside the list.

Buy Like You're Buying a Business

Already covered this one but it's worth repeating: By buying shares of a corporation you are really buying a share of a business. The more you can approach the decision as if you were buying the entire business yourself, the better.

Buy What You Know and Understand

Two of the most widely followed investment "gurus" of our age, Peter Lynch and Warren Buffett, have stressed the idea of buying businesses you know about and understand. This idea naturally follows the entrepreneurial idea of buying stocks as if you were buying a business; if you didn't understand the business, would you be comfortable buying it?

Peter Lynch, former manager of the enormous Fidelity Magellan fund and author of the well known 1989 bestseller *One Up on Wall Street*, gave us the original notion of buying what you know. He suggests that the best investment ideas are those you see—and can learn about and keep track of—in daily life, on the street, on the job, in the mall, in your home. A company like Starbucks makes sense to Lynch because you can readily see the value proposition and how it extends beyond coffee, and can follow customer response and business activity at least in part just by hanging around your own neighborhood edition.

Buffett has famously stuck with businesses that are easy to understand—paint, carpet, electric utilities—with his investments (though he deals with the fantastically complicated businesses of casualty insurance and re-insurance in his core Berkshire Hathaway business). He has shunned technology investments because he doesn't understand them, and more than likely, because their value and consumer preference shifts too fast for him to keep up.

Both approaches make sense, and especially in hindsight, would have kept us farther from trouble in the 2008 crash. Many, many investors didn't understand financial firms as well as they should have; the preponderance of evidence suggests that they didn't even understand themselves!

Clearly, you won't understand everything about the businesses you invest in—there's a lot of complexity and detail even behind the cooking and serving of hamburgers at McDonald's! Further, a sizeable amount of good knowledge is confidential so you likely won't ever get your hands on it. So you need to go with what you know and realize that a lot of the devil is in the details. When you analyze a company, if you can say "the more you know the better" instead of "the more you know the more you don't know," you'll be better off.

Greater Trends Are Important

Popular expressions abound about the idea of staying in touch with the big picture when you make any sort of decision: *Don't lose the forest for the trees, keep your eye on the prize,* and so forth. These phrases enjoy no finer hour than tied in with the subject of investing.

We already covered the notion that technologies and consumer tastes change, and with them so do businesses—at least the good ones. Add to this idea of change brought on by demographic trends (the aging of the population, for instance) and changes in law and policy (toward "green," for instance) and you end up with a wide assortment of "forest" influences that can affect your stock picks.

John Slatter placed a lot of emphasis on sector investing; that is, choosing the right sectors or industries in which to invest. That probably makes sense, but buying a stock just because it's in the right "sector" doesn't make sense to me. The best maker of buggy whips or silver halide photo film simply isn't going to succeed.

Where sector analysis does make sense is in capturing and correctly assessing the larger trends in that sector or industry. The sector thus becomes the arena in which to appraise those trends, often by reading sector analyses published in the media or in trade publications in that sector. One can, and should, learn about the construction industry or health care industry before investing in a company in that industry.

Once the sector trends are understood, a selection of a company, or companies, in that sector can make more sense. A good example is offered by PC makers Hewlett-Packard (a *100 Best Stocks* choice) and Dell Computer. Dell was the darling of the sector for years, achieving high margins and return on equity, market share growth, and popular marketplace preference for years. The direct sales model seemed unbeatable as a way to reduce costs and avoid obsolescence, and with the just-in-time supply chain model, using accounts payable as a primary financing mechanism, all seemed strategically right.

But change was in the air for the PC industry. Lower prices, greater standardization, and the migration to laptops all pointed to HP's retail-centric model. No longer was it necessary, or even advantageous, for customers to order direct from Dell. With more standardized computing applications and inexpensive technology, there was less need to customize computers. With laptops, displays, size, and look and feel are more important than simple "speeds and feeds" and people wanted to see what they were buying. Finally, as costs came down, a PC, laptop or otherwise, was simply something to pick up at a local store. I predict PCs will soon sell in Walgreens, and if you don't believe that, consider that VCRs and DVD players also followed that thought-to-be-impossible path.

So HP ended up in the right place with their emphasis on the retail channel (Dell struggles as a late-comer) and further, was strategically correct in their emphasis on printers and high margin consumables that go with them, and in their emphasis on international markets. Dell has fallen by the wayside on all counts, hence their 80 percent price drop from 2000 and 70 percent drop from their 2005 price peaks, respectively.

So again the lesson, or tenet, is to understand the greater trends in the economy, in the market, in the sector, and in the industry. If you buy a business, you want to know about the industry, right? Who the competitors are, how they compete, about the market and customer needs and cus-tomer tastes, and how companies do business in that market. Right? You want to understand the *future* of that industry and market, right? It's no different when you buy shares.

One more thing to add: Most of the time I try to buy what I think to be the best company in the sector—best based on past, current, and expected future performance. But sometimes it makes sense, from an opportunity viewpoint, to "play the Avis game;" that is, to buy a more nimble, more aggressive, and less arrogant or complacent number two competitor. Such a company is leaner, meaner, hungrier, and likely sells for a more reasonable price. Sometimes I'll buy both if I feel the industry or sector is large enough to support two strong competitors, and if there are large enough or strong enough niches available so they won't become cutthroat competitors.

For example, I own Starbucks (a 100 Best Stock) and Caribou Coffee, a much smaller competitor located largely in the upper Midwest. There are two reasons for this choice. One, I felt that the Caribou brand cachet would work well in Minnesota and similar places. Second, and more importantly, I liked Caribou's franchising model as a contrast to Starbucks' company-owned model (which now may be starting to change with the announcement of franchising for their own subsidiary Seattle's Best). Caribou just might do well capturing business with ambitious franchisees doing the work and understanding local markets best.

Niche and Get Rich

In understanding sectors, industries, and markets it's important to consider success opportunities for niche players. A "niche" is a small captive market segment, usually too small for the biggest competitors to profitably consider, but still lucrative for a smaller, more nimble player. Niche players can define and play smaller markets based on product, location or geography, distribution channels, or other differentiators like language. Caribou is an example, capturing the franchising niche. Or McCormick & Co. (a 100 Best Stock) capturing the spice niche in a larger food and beverage industry.

For more on niche marketing, see *Niche and Grow Rich—Practical Ways to Turn Your Ideas Into a Business* (Entrepreneur Press), a book I did with my wife Jennifer back in 2003. It is aimed at small business, but (not by design) offers useful material for investing, too.

Is It Time to Go Green?

Much has been made in the news media about the green movement and the profound effects it will have on the business world and the everyday marketplace. The case has been made rather poignantly about the steady march of global warming, and it doesn't take a rocket scientist to realize that full scale consumption of and dependence on fossil fuels can't go on forever.

So does that mean it's really time to invest in the green movement? Is it the wave of the future? Will companies that supply green goods and services make a fortune just as mainframe computer companies did in the 1960s and PC companies did in the 1980s and (some) Internet companies did in the 1990s? Are there potent niches in the green world for a company with the right technology to clean up (pardon the pun) as Microsoft did in the PC boom?

The answer is "yes, probably." But that said, from my point of view, it's still too early to judge which companies out there will truly prosper with the green movement. Another way to put it: Like the gold in them thar' hills, there is value out there, but the trouble is in finding it.

There are three basic approaches to investing in the green movement. The first and most traditional approach is to invest in companies that are involved in providing or maintaining clean air, clean water, and effective waste management—companies like Nalco, in water treatment chemicals, or Stericycle in the medical waste recycling business. The second approach, far more at the cutting edge, is to invest in companies providing new technologies, particularly in the alternative or renewable energy field; so solar, wind power, and biomass conversion all apply. Some, like solar or new battery technologies are more cutting edge than others, like ethanol.

The third approach is to invest in mainstream companies that seem to "get" the green movement. Those companies sell products or have implemented substantial operations programs consistent with green principles and philosophy. The trick here is to separate the reality from the marketing message; it is easy to tout green principles in an ad or on a label, but is the product or process truly green? In a distinguishable way? Or is it merely a marketing message?

In my view, it is still too early in the green "game" to distinguish truly successful businesses and business models. That's why there are currently no "green" companies in the 100 best stocks list. Sure, there are a lot of small companies to invest in, and some bigger ones like General Electric that have sizeable green product lines (wind turbines). There are some good products. But like the PC business twenty-five years ago, a good product that is still too expensive and not generally accepted by the market does not usually support a good business model. As I always say, when I can buy solar panels at Home Depot and install them on my roof myself, we're there. I don't think we're close at this point, but investing is about seeing where the puck is going, right? So when a product or approach seems to gain some traction, it's time to take note, as one might have done with the first IBM PC and the DOS operating system.

For now, while some green stocks might be worth an opportunistic play, I think the best approach is to invest in funds targeted toward certain green technologies. With a fund you get diversification and will benefit if the entire group prospers,

which is probably a safer bet given the current imperatives to go green. To that end, here's a list of Exchange Traded Funds (ETFs) built around green ideas:

- Claymore Global Solar Energy ETF (TAN)
- Claymore S&P Global Water Index ETF (CGW)
- Claymore/LGA Green ETF (GRN)
- First Trust ISE Global Wind Energy Index Fund (FAN)
- First Trust NASDAQ Clean Edge ETF (QCLN)
- Global Warming ELEMENTS ETN (GWO)
- PowerShares Cleantech Portfolio ETF (PZD)
- PowerShares Global Clean Energy Portfolio ETF (PBD)
- PowerShares Global Nuclear Energy Portfolio ETF (PKN)
- PowerShares Nasdaq OMX Clean Edge Global Wind Energy ETF (PWND)
- PowerShares Water Resources Portfolio ETF (PHO)
- PowerShares Global Water Portfolio ETF (PIO)
- PowerShares WilderHill Clean Energy Portfolio ETF (PBW)
- PowerShares WilderHill Progressive Energy Portfolio ETF (PUW)
- Van Eck Market Vectors Environmental Services ETF (EVX)
- Van Eck Market Vectors Global Alternative Energy ETF (GEX)
- Van Eck Market Vectors Nuclear Energy ETF (NLR)

So, do your research and commit a small amount to green plays, and you'll probably do well in the long term. It's a potentially lucrative market well worth keeping an eye on.

Stick to the Real Stuff

If you're familiar with accounting or the accounting profession, contrary to public perception, accounting for business assets and activity is not always a precise science. In fact, there can be quite a bit of art involved in accounting, especially for business assets and business income.

Why? Because, while the purchase *price* for most "physical" assets is known, the *value* of those assets over time is a subjective calculation. And there are many assets, like intellectual property, that elude precise evaluation altogether. How much is a patent worth? How much is an acquired business worth? Just like a stock you buy, you know what you paid for it, but how much is it really worth in terms of future returns to the acquiring company? It's a subjective number.

Likewise, reported net income can be fairly subjective, too. How much depreciation expense was taken against assets, and thus against income? How much "expense" was taken to write down intangible assets like patents and other intellectual property? How much "restructuring" expense was incurred? The rules give the accountants and corporate management quite a bit of flexibility to "manage" reported earnings, and asset values as well: What you see may not always be what you get.

The bottom line is this: While assets and income have at least some subjectivity in their valuation, debts are quite real, and so is cash. Debts must be paid sooner or later; there is no subjectivity or "art" to their valuation. Likewise, cash is cash, the stuff in the proverbial drawer, and is a take-it-or-leave-it, like-it-or-not fact of life or death for a business.

Thus, as value investors, we look at assets and income as important measures of business activity, but know that there's some subjectivity in those measures. At the same time, we look at debts and cash and cash flow in and out of the business as absolute; neither cash nor debt lie. So we hang our valuation hats on cash and debt where we can.

Now, in particular, cash isn't an absolute measure of business success, either, for there are timing issues. Suppose you are running an airline, and decide this is the year to buy an airplane. This creates a huge cash outflow, possibly matched by a cash inflow from borrowing. Are this year's cash flow statements fully representative of the firm's success or failure? No, because the airplane will be used over a number of years, and the cost of the airplane must be divvied up among those years and matched to airfares collected and other costs to truly understand performance. So that's where conventional income accounting comes in—it helps to do that.

All that said, sharp value investors learn to look for companies that, over time, *produce* capital, in contrast to companies that *consume* it. As judged by the statement of cash flows, a company that produces more cash from operations than it consumes in investing activities (capital equipment purchases mainly) and in financing activities (repaying debt, dividends etc.) is producing capital. When a company must always go to the capital markets to make up for a deficit in operating or investing cash flow, that's a sign of trouble, which is incidentally borne out by the other absolute measure—debt. If debt is high and especially increasing and especially if it is increasing faster than the business is growing—look out. Or at least, look for a story, like company XYZ is going through a known, understood, and rational expansion that needs to be funded. Going to the capital markets to fund operational cash deficits is an especially bad thing to do.

Thus, as an investor, you should always pay attention to assets and income, but even closer attention to cash and debt. This tenet was used in identifying the 100 best stocks.

What Makes a Best Stock Best?

So now we get down to brass tacks. Now, the rubber meets the road. Just exactly what is it that separates the wheat from the chaff, the cream from the milk, the great from the merely good? What is it that defines excellence—sustainable excellence—among companies? That's been a topic of considerable debate for years, and with all the study that's gone into it, it's amazing that nobody has hit upon a single formula for deciphering undeniable excellence in a company.

That's largely because it isn't as scientific as most of us would like or expect it to be. It defies mathematical formulas. Take the square of net profits, multiply by the cosine of the debt-to-equity ratio, add the square root of the revenue-per-employee count, and what do you get? Some nice numbers, but not a clear picture of how it works together nor how a company will sell its products to customers and prosper going forward.

Business and financial analysts study such fundamentals, and well they should. Fundamentals such as profitability, productivity, and asset efficiency tell us how well a company has done and by proxy, how well it is managed and how well it has done in the marketplace. Fundamentals are about what the company has already achieved, and where it stands right now, and if a company's current fundamentals are a mess, stop right now, there isn't much point in going any farther.

But in most cases, what really separates great from good are the intangibles, the "soft" factors of market position, market acceptance, customer "love" of a company's products, its management, its aura. These features create competitive advantage, or "distinctive competence," as economists would put it, that cannot be valued. Furthermore and most importantly, they are more about what a company is set up to achieve in the future.

Buffett put it best: "Give me $100 billion, and I could start a company. But I could never create another Coca-Cola."

What does that mean? It means that Coke has already established a worldwide brand cachet, the distribution channels, and the product development expertise that cannot be duplicated at any cost. When companies have competitive advantages that cannot be duplicated at any cost, they have an enduring grip on their markets. They can charge more for their products. They have a "moat" which insulates them from competition, or makes it much more expensive for competitors to participate. They're perceived by loyal customers as being top-line products worth paying more for.

A company with exceptional intangibles can control price and in many cases, can control its costs.

LUV—A Great Experience, But Is It a Good Investment?

One way to learn a principle is to examine what happens when the principle does not apply. One industry where most of the fundamentals and almost all the intangibles work against it is the airline industry. Airlines cannot control price, because of competition, and because an airplane trip is an airplane trip. Aside from serving different snacks or offering better schedules, there is little an airline can do to differentiate their product, and almost nothing they can do to justify charging a higher price. Further, they have no control over costs—like fuel prices, union contracts, and airport landing fees. While some airlines offer good service, there is almost nothing they can do to distinguish themselves as excellent companies or excellent investments. Southwest Airlines (ticker symbol LUV) came closest by offering simplicity, efficiency, a loyal customer base, and excellent management, and was rewarded for many years with a market cap greater than all other U.S. airlines combined, but because of the industry it's in, it lands short of being an excellent company to invest in.

Strategic Fundamentals

Without any further ado, let's examine a list of "strategic fundamentals" that define, or keep score of, a company's success. This list can be used as a checklist, although it's hard to find a company that shows excellence in all of these areas.

Are gross and operating profit margins growing?

I like profitable companies; who doesn't? But what really counts is the size of the margin and especially the growth. If a company has a gross margin (sales minus costs of goods sold) exceeding that of its competitors, that shows that it's doing something right, probably with its customers and/or with its costs. But competitive analysis is elusive; there is no dependable source of "industry" gross margins, and comparing competitors can be difficult because no two companies are exactly alike; it's easy to mix apples and oranges.

So I like to see what direction gross margin is moving in—up or down. A growing gross margin also signals that the company is doing something right. That isn't perfect either; as the economy moved from boom to bust many excellent companies reported declines in gross and especially operating margins (sales minus cost of goods sold minus operating expenses) as they laid off workers and used less capacity. Still, in a steady state environment, it makes

sense to favor companies with growing margins. In a declining market, companies that can *protect* their margins will come out ahead.

Does a company produce more capital than it consumes?

Make no mistake about it—I like cash. And pure and simple—I like it when a company produces more cash than it consumes.

At the end of the day, cash generation is the simplest measure of whether a company is being successful, especially over the long term. Sure, if a company buys an airplane or opens a factory or a bunch of stores in a given quarter, it will be cash-flow negative. But that should be a temporary thing; over the long haul, it should produce, not consume cash. Companies that continually have to borrow or sell shares to raise enough cash to stay in business are on the wrong track.

So how do you determine this? You'll have to become familiar with the Statement of Cash Flows or the equivalent in a company's financial reports. "Cash flow from operations" is usually positive and represents cash booked from sales less cost of goods sold, with adjustments for noncash items like depreciation and for increases or decreases in working capital. In simple terms, it is the cash going into the cash register from the business.

"Cash used for investing purposes" or something similar is a bit of a misnomer, and represents net cash used to "invest" in the business—usually for capital expenditures but also for short-term noncash investments like securities and a few other smaller items usually beyond scope. This figure is typically negative unless the company sells some part of its infrastructure. Over the long haul, cash generated from operations should well exceed cash used to invest in the business.

Companies in expansion mode may not show this surplus, and that's where "cash from financing activities" comes in. That's the cash generated from issuing debt or selling securities—or paying off debt or repurchasing shares, if things are going well, and dividends are included here as well. Again, a successful company will produce more cash—capital—from the business than it consumes, just as a successful household does the same, else it goes into debt. Smart investors track this surplus over time.

Are expenses under control?

Again, just like your household, company expenses should be under control, and anything else, especially without explanation, is a red flag.

The best way to test this is to check whether "Selling, General and Administrative" expenses—so called "SG&A" are rising, and more to the point, rising faster than sales. If so, that's a yellow, not necessarily a red, flag, but if it continues, it suggests that something is out of control, and it will catch up with the company sooner or later. In the recent downturn, companies that were able to reduce their expenses to match revenue declines score more points, too.

Is noncash working capital under control?

Working capital is a hard concept to grasp—even for small entrepreneurs who live with its ups and downs on a daily basis. Insufficient working capital is one of the biggest causes of death for small businesses, and working capital and especially changes in working capital can signal success or trouble.

Using a simplistic analogy, working capital is the circulatory lifeblood of the business. Money comes in, money goes out, working capital is what circulates in the veins in between. In its purest sense, it is cash, receivables, and inventory, less short term debts. It's what you own less what you owe aside from fixed assets like plant, stores, and equipment.

If receivables are increasing, that sounds like a good thing—more people owe you more money. But if receivables are rising and sales aren't, that suggests that people aren't paying their bills, or worse, the business has to finance more to achieve the same level of sales. Similarly, a rise in inventory without a rise in sales means that it costs the business more money—more working capital—to do the same amount of business. That costs twice, because unless the firm is lucky, more inventory means more obsolescence and potentially more writeoffs down the road.

So a sharp investor will check to see that major working capital items—receivables and inventory—aren't growing faster than sales; indeed, a company that generates more sales with a decrease in working capital is becoming more productive.

Is debt in line with business growth?

Like many other "fundamentals" items, you can tear your hair out looking at debt figures and trying to decide whether they're in line with asset levels, equity levels, and industry norms. A simpler test is to check and see whether long-term debt is increasing or decreasing, and in particular, whether it is increasing faster than business growth. Gold stars go to companies with little to no debt, and to companies able to grow without issuing mountains of long-term debt.

Is earnings growth steady?

I enter the danger zone here, because the management of many companies have learned to "manage" earnings to provide a steady improvement, always "beating the street" by a penny or two. So stability is a good thing for all investors, and companies that can manage toward stability get extra points, and it's worth checking for, but with the proverbial grain of salt.

Still, a company that is able to manage its sales, earnings, cash flow, and debt levels more consistently than competitors, and perhaps more consistently than what would be suggested by the ups and downs of the economy is desirable—or at least more desirable than the alternatives.

Is return on equity steady or growing?

Return on equity (ROE) is another of those hard to grasp concepts, and another measure prone to subjectivity in valuing assets and earnings. But at the end of the day, it's what all investors really seek, that is, returns on their capital investments.

And like many other figures derived from income statements and balance sheets, a pure number is hard to interpret—does a 26.7 percent ROE mean, in itself, that a company is excellent? The figure sounds healthy, to be sure—it's a heck of a lot better than investing your money in a CD or T-Bill. But because earnings and asset values are subjective, it may not represent true success. In fact, a company can increase ROE simply by borrowing money (yes!) and investing it into the business, even if it isn't invested as productively as other previous funds invested. The math is complicated; I won't go into it here.

So the true test of ROE success is to check whether it is steady or increasing. Increasing—that makes sense. Why *steady*? Because if a company makes profits in a previous period and reinvests them in the business, that amount of money becomes part of equity ("retained earnings"). If the company reinvests productively, it will produce more returns, and ROE will at least keep up. If the company can't reinvest those earnings productively, ROE will drop—and perhaps it should be paying the earnings to you as dividends instead of investing them unproductively in the business.

So if ROE is steady, the company still has good investments to make, and management is probably doing the right thing.

Does the company pay a dividend?

Different people feel differently about dividends. After all, save for the eventual sale of the company to someone else, a dividend is the only true cash that an investor will realize from buying a stock in a corporation, other than by selling the stock. And, at least in theory, investors should receive some compensation for their investments once in a while.

Yet, most companies tend not to pay dividends, or don't pay dividends that compete very effectively with fixed income yields. So why do investors put up with this? Because, in theory anyway, a company in a good business should be able to reinvest profits more effectively than the investor can (else why would the investor have bought the company in the first place?). And, investors trust that reinvested profits will eventually bring the growth in company value that will be reflected in the share price or eventual takeover or an eventual payment of a dividend or growth in that dividend.

That's the theory, anyway. But there are still lots of companies that get away with paying no dividend at all. Can we tolerate this? Yes, if a company is really doing a great job. But I favor companies that offer at least something to their investors in the short term, some return on their hard-earned and faithfully commit-

ted capital. If nothing else, it keeps management teams honest, and shows that management understands that shareholder interests are up there somewhere on the list of priorities.

A dividend is a plus. Lack of a dividend isn't necessarily a showstopper, but it suggests a closer look. A dividend reduction—and there were many in the past year—suggests poor financial and operational health, because the dividend is usually the last thing to go, but in some cases reflects management prudence and conservatism. Best question to ask yourself: Would you have reduced the dividend if you were running the company? And down the road, does the company bring back the dividend as times get better? A "no" to either of these questions is troubling.

Are valuation ratios in line?

One of the most difficult tasks in investing is determining the true value—and per-share value—of a company. If this were easy, you'd just determine a value, compare it to the price, and if the price were lower than the value, push the buy button.

Professional investors try to determine what they call the "intrinsic value" of a company, which is usually the sum of all projected future cash flows of a company, discounted back to the present (remember, money received tomorrow is both less predictable and less valuable than money received now). They use complex math models, specifically, "discounted cash flow" (DCF) models, to project, then discount, earnings flows. But those models—especially for the individual investor, depend too much on the crystal-ball accuracy of earnings forecasts, and the so-called discount rate is a highly theoretical construct beyond the scope of most individual investors. DCF models require a lot of estimates and number-crunching, especially if multiple scenarios are employed as they should be. They take more time than it's worth for the individual investor. If you're an institutional investor buying multimillion-share stakes, I would conclude otherwise.

Valuation ratios are a shorthand way to determine if a stock price is acceptable relative to value. By far and away the most popular of these ratios is the so-called "price-to-earnings" or P/E, ratio, a measure of the stock price usually compared to "ttm," or trailing twelve months' earnings, but also sometimes compared to future earnings.

The P/E ratio correlates well to your expected return on an investment you might make in the company. For instance, if the P/E is 10, the price is 10 times the past, or perhaps expected, annual earnings of the company. Take the reciprocal of that—1 divided by 10—and you get 0.10, or 10 percent. That's known as "earnings yield," the theoretical yield you'd get if all earnings were paid to you as dividends as an owner. Ten percent is pretty healthy compared to returns on other investments, so a P/E of 10 suggests success.

But of course, the earnings may not be consistent or sustainable, or there may be substantial risk from fac-

tors intrinsic to the company, or there may be exogenous risk factors, like the total meltdown of the economy. The more risk, the more instability, the lower the expected P/E should be, for the earnings stream is less stable. If you think the earnings stream is solid and stable in the face of the risk, then the stock may be truly undervalued. Look for P/Es that (1) suggest strong earnings yield and (2) are favorable compared to competitors and the industry.

Apart from P/E, the price-to-sales ratio (P/S), price to cash flow (P/CF), and price-to-free cash flow (P/FCF) are often used as fundamentals yardsticks. Like P/E, these measures also have some ambiguities, and it's best to think about them in real-world, entrepreneurial terms. Would you pay three times annual sales for a business and sleep well at night? Probably not—unless its profit margins were exceptionally high. So if a P/S ratio is 3 or above, look out; and opt for a business with a P/S of 1 or less if you can. Similarly, the price-to-cash-flow ratios can be thought of as true return going into your pocket for your investment; is it enough? Is it enough given the risk? And about the difference between "cash flow" and "free cash flow:" the difference is mostly cash laid out for capital expenditures, so it's worth making this distinction, although the lumpiness of capital expenditures makes consistent application of this number elusive. Incidentally, I don't regard price-to-book value (P/B) ratios as that helpful, because the book value of a company can be very elusive and arbitrary unless most of a company's assets are in cash or other easy-to-value forms.

Companies with high P/E, P/S, P/B, and P/CF ratios aren't necessarily bad investments, but you need to have good reasons to look beyond these figures if they suggest truly inadequate business results.

Strategic Intangibles

When you look at any company, perhaps the bottom line question follows the Buffett wisdom: If you had a hundred billion to spend (and we'll assume, the genius intellect to spend it right), could you recreate that company?

If the answer is "yes," it may still be a great company, but it may not be great enough to fend off competition and keep its customers forever. If the answer is "no," the company truly has something unique to offer in the marketplace, difficult to duplicate at any cost. That distinctive competence, that sustainable competitive edge—whatever it is, a brand, a trade secret, a lock on distribution or supply channels—may be worth more than all the factories and high rise office buildings and cash in the bank it could ever have.

What we're talking about are the intangibles, the "soft" factors that make companies unique, that add up to more than the sum of their parts, the factors that ultimately drive future revenues. Intangibles not only define excellence, they define the future, while fundamentals mainly define the past. Seven key intangibles follow, although you'll think of more, and some indus-

tries may have some unique ones of their own, like technology and intellectual property.

Does the company have a moat?

A business "moat" performs much the same role as the medieval castle equivalent—it protects the business from competition. Whatever factors, some discussed below, create the moat, ultimately those are the factors that prevent you, with your $100 billion, from taking their business. Moats are usually a combination of brand, product technology, design, marketing and distribution channels, and customer loyalty all working together to protect a company. A moat doesn't just protect the existence of a company, it helps it command higher prices and earn higher profits.

Whether a company has a "narrow" moat, a "wide" moat, or none at all is a subjective assessment for you to make. However, you can get some help at Morningstar (*www.morningstar.com*) whose stock ratings include an assessment of the moat.

Coca-Cola has a moat because of the sheer impossibility of surpassing its brand and brand recognition worldwide. CarMax has a moat because it is farther along in putting retail-style dealerships on the ground and applying management information technologies to its business than anyone else; it would take years for a competitor to catch up.

Does the company have an excellent brand?

It's hard to say enough about brand, especially in today's fast-moving, highly packaged, highly national and international culture. A strong brand means consistency and a promise to consumers, and consumers sold on a brand will prefer it over any other, almost regardless of price. People still buy Tide, and although there's been a slowdown lately, Starbucks is still synonymous with a high quality and ambience. Good brands command higher prices and foster loyalty and identity and even customer "love." Again, using the Starbucks example, websites appeared soliciting customer appeals to not close stores during the recent store-closing initiative; when has anyone (other than a worker) offered so much resistance to closing a U.S. auto plant? Once a company has created a dominant brand (or brands, in the case of P&G) in the market-place, aside from some major faux pas, they will endure and continue to create value for shareholders for years to come; a good brand is one of the most valuable (yet hard to value) long term assets around.

Ask yourself if a company has a sought-after brand, a brand customers would pay extra to buy or align with, a brand that would be difficult to duplicate at any cost. Would customers rather fight than switch? Think about Starbucks, Coca-Cola, Heinz, Nike, or the brands within a house, like Frito-Lay (Pepsi) or Tide (P&G).

Is the company a market leader?

Market leadership usually—but not always—goes hand in hand with brand. The trick is to decide whether a company really leads in its industry. Often—but not always—that's a factor of size. The market leader usually has the highest market share, and the important point is that it calls the shots with regards to price, technology, marketing message, and so forth—other companies must play catch-up and often discount their prices to keep up. Apple is a market leader in digital music, Intel is the market leader in microprocessors, and Toyota is emerging as the market leader in automobiles.

Excellent companies tend to be market leaders, and market leaders tend to be excellent companies. But this relationship doesn't always hold true—sometimes the nimble but smaller competitor is the excellent company—and will likely assume market leadership eventually. Examples like CarMax, Nucor, Perrigo, and Peet's Coffee and Tea can be found on our list.

Does the company have channel excellence?

"Channels" in business parlance means a chain of players to sell and distribute a company's products. It might be stores, it might be other industrial companies, it might be direct to the consumer. If a company is considered a top supplier in a particular channel, or a company has especially good relations with its channel, that's a plus.

Excellent companies develop solid channel relationships and become the preferred supplier in those channels. Companies like Dentsply, Patterson,

Fair Isaac, McCormick, Nike, Pepsi, Procter & Gamble, and Sysco could all have excellent relationships with their channels through which they sell their product.

Does the company have supply chain excellence?

Like distribution channels, excellent companies develop excellent and low cost supply channels. They are seldom caught off guard by supply shortages and tend to get favorable and stable prices for whatever they buy. This is often not an easy assessment unless you know something about a particular industry.

Does the company have excellent management?

Well, it's not hard to grasp what happens if a company *doesn't* have good management; performance fails and few inside or outside the company respect the company. It's not easy for an investor to determine if a management team does a good job or acts in shareholder interests. Clues can include candor and honesty and the ability of company management to speak in accessible, easily understood terms about the company and company performance (it's worth listening to conference calls as a resource). A management team that admits errors and eschews other forms of arrogance and entitlement (i.e., luxury perks, office suites, aircraft) is probably tilting their interests toward shareholders, as is the management team that can cough up some return to shareholders once in a while as a dividend.

This may be the most subjective and elusive assessment of all, as few investors work with these folks on a daily basis. Still, over time, you can garner a strong hunch about whether a management team is effective and on your side.

Are there signs of innovation excellence?

This question seems pretty obvious, but it's not just about the products that a company sells. True, if the company is leading the industry in innovation, that's usually a good thing, for "first to market" definitely offers business advantages.

The less obvious part of this question is whether the company makes the best *use* of technology to make operations and customer interfaces as efficient and effective as possible. Again, Southwest Airlines didn't make our list because of the sheer impossibility of achieving excellence in an industry where players can't control prices or costs. But they do make our list in terms of innovation excellence. Why? Simply because, after all of these years, amazingly, they still have the best, simplest, easiest-to-use flight booking and checking flight in the industry. Sometimes these sorts of innovations mean a lot more than bringing new fancy products and bells and whistles to the market. And one can also look to Apple, Google, and eBay on our list for more obvious examples.

It Pays to Find a Smart Friend in the Business

Most publicly traded companies are required to report their fundamentals on a quarterly and an annual basis, which involves income statement, balance sheet, and statement of cash flows. That's good, because we as investors can easily see how the company is performing; we don't need to get on the phone with the CFO to check the progress of our investment.

But what about the intangibles? Companies are required to report exactly nothing of their brand strength, market position, new product pipeline, or management style. Sure, you may read a lot in an annual report, but it's as much a spin, a marketing message to investors, as it is the real "scoop" about what is or what's going to be.

So how do you fill this information gap? One way is to keep up with the trade press and trade publications of the industry you invest in. Like technology stocks? Read technology magazines and websites and the technology sections of the *Wall Street Journal* and the *New York Times*. But if you really want the inside scoop, make friends with people who work in the industry. They are (or should be) experts in their business. They know the products and the competition. It's not so much that they'll divulge trade secrets about the company they work for; that isn't the point. Instead, they'll help you see where the puck is going for the industry, their company, and other players in their industry. The thousand words you get from a friend in the business can be worth far more than the picture in the annual report.

Signs of Value

Following are a few signs of value to look for in any company. Not an exhaustive list by any means, but a good place to start:

- Gaining market share
- Can control price
- Loyal customers
- Growing margins
- Producing, not consuming, capital (free cash flow)
- Steady or increasing ROE
- Management forthcoming, honest, understandable

Signs of Unvalue

. . . and signs of trouble, or "unvalue":

- Declining margins
- No brand or who-cares brand
- Commodity producer, must compete on price
- Losing market dominance or market share
- Can't control costs
- Must acquire other companies to grow
- Management in hiding, off message, or difficult to understand

Choosing the 100 Best

So with all of this in mind, just how were this year's 100 best stocks list actually chosen? It's probably about time, after pages and pages, to get to that.

The answer is a little more subtle than you might think. If we could give you a precise formula, you wouldn't need this book. You'd be able to do it yourself. In fact, investors would be able to do it on their own. Our book would simply be the result of yet another stock screener. And every investor would invest in the same stocks. Is that a feasible or practical solution? Hardly. Everyone would scramble to buy the same 100 best stocks. The prices would be sky high, and the price of other stocks would melt to nothing.

Fortunately or unfortunately, however you want to look at it, it isn't that simple. There are too many fundamentals and too many intangibles and too many unknown and unknowable weighting factors to combine the fundamentals and intangibles that—well—it just wouldn't work. No screener could recreate the subtle judgment that gets applied to the hard, cold facts. It's that judgment, the interpretation of the facts and intangibles, that makes it worth spending money on a book like this.

While we didn't apply a specific formula or screener to the universe of stocks, we did take a few measur-able factors into account to narrow the list from thousands to a few hundred issues. Those factors came from several sources, but at this point we must tip our cap to Value Line and the research and database work they do as part of the Value Line Investment Survey. If you aren't familiar with Value Line, it's worth a look for any savvy individual investor, either online at *www.valueline.com* or, in many cases, at your local library. It is an excellent resource.

Anyway, here are some of the measured factors we looked into, most of which go beyond individual facts or items and instead are measures of strength or performance compiled from a number of factors. In this way, we gain some leverage for not having to deal with lots of little bits of individual data. Here are 6 metrics we used to select and sort stocks for further review:

- *Standard & Poor's (S&P) Rating* is a broad corporate credit rating reflecting the ability to cover indebtedness, in turn reflecting business levels, business trends, cash flow, and sustained performance. It's a bit like the credit score you might use or might have used to determine your own personal credit risk.
- *Value Line Financial Strength Rating* is used much like the

S&P rating except that it goes further into overall balance sheet and cash flow strength. It should be noted that several companies with "B" ratings were selected; these are typically newer companies that will grow into A companies or that may have been hit harder by the recession than others.

- *Value Line Earnings Predictability* is what it sounds like; a calculated tendency of companies to deliver consistent and predictable earnings without surprises.
- *Value Line Growth Persistence* is again what it sounds like—the company's ability to consistently grow even in weaker economic times.
- *Value Line Price Stability* reflects the stability and relative safety of a company. Again, we did not reject a company out of hand due to volatility, rather, if stability was low, we tried to make a case that the business, business model, and intangibles were worth the risk.
- *Dividends and yield*: Companies that pay something are held in

higher regard; however, again, it is not by any means an absolute criterion.

With these facts and figures in mind, the evaluation proceeded with a close eye on the "signs of value" and intangibles mentioned above. Some consideration was also given to diversification; we did not want to overweight any sector or industry but instead to give you a healthy assortment of stocks to pick from across a variety of industries.

With these thoughts in mind, you can make more sense of the companies we picked. And of course, full disclosure and full disclaimer—we didn't do *all* the analysis. We couldn't have. It wouldn't have made any sense anyway, for things would have changed from the time we did it, and it might not match your preferences. So it is of utmost importance for you to take our selections and analysis and make them yours—that is, do the due diligence to further qualify these picks as congruent with your investment needs.

The Surgeon General would label this book as "hazardous to your wealth" if you didn't.

Strategic Investing

Although this book is designed to help you pick the best stocks to buy, investing by nature goes well beyond simply buying stocks, just like owning an automobile goes far beyond buying it. Just as clearly, this book isn't about investing strategy, nor about the personal financial strategies necessary to ensure retirement or a prosperous future. That said, I think a few words are in order.

I find that a lot of investors lose the forest in the trees, spending all of their energy trying to find individual stocks or funds without putting enough consideration into their overall investing framework. If they look at the big picture at all, they look at the formulaic covenants of asset allocation, a favorite subject of the financial planning and advisory community, as though the difference between 50 percent equities and 60 percent equities makes all the differece in the world. Sure, it might in the world of pension funds and other institutional investments, where a 10 percent adjustment could move millions into or out of a particular asset class and more or less toward safety, but what about a $100,000 portfolio? Does $10,000 more or less in stocks, bonds, or cash make that much difference?

Perhaps not. And of course there's more to that story—doesn't it matter more which equities you invest in than just the fact that you're 60 per-cent in equities? So while asset allocation models make for nice pie charts, I prefer to approach big-picture portfolio constructs differently.

Start with a Portfolio in Mind

First, I'll make an assumption. That assumption is simply this: You are not a professional investor. You have other things to do with your time, and time is of the essence. You cannot spend forty, fifty, sixty hours a week glued to a computer screen analyzing your investments.

To that assumption I'll add another: that, as an individual investor, you're looking to beat the market. Not by a ton—20 percent sustained returns simply aren't possible without taking outlandish risks. But perhaps if the market is up 4 percent in a year, you'd like to achieve, 5, 6, perhaps 7 percent without taking excessive risks. Or if the market is down 20 percent, perhaps you cut your losses at 5 or 10 percent. You're looking to do *somewhat* better than the market.

Because of time constraints, and owing to your objective to do slightly better than averages, I suggest taking a tiered approach to your portfolio. The tiers aren't based on the type of assets; they're based on the amount of activity and attention you want to pay to different parts of your portfolio. It's a strategic portfolio approach you would probably take if you were managing a small business—put most of your focus on the products and customers who might bring the greatest new return to your business; let the rest of your slow and steady customer base function as it has for the long term.

I suggest breaking up your portfolio into three tiers, or segments. This can be done by setting up specific accounts; or less formally by simply applying the model as a thought process.

We can't go much further without defining the three segments:

The Foundation Portfolio

In this construct each investor defines and manages a cornerstone foundation portfolio, which is long-term in nature and requires relatively less active management. Frequently the foundation portfolio consists of retirement accounts (the paradigmatic long-term investment) and may also include your personal residence or other long-lived personal or family assets, such as trusts, collectibles, and so forth. The typical foundation portfolio is invested to achieve at least average market returns through index funds, quality mutual funds, and some income-producing assets like bonds held to maturity. A foundation portfolio may contain some long-term plays in commodities or real estate to defend against inflation, particularly in such commodities as energy, precious metals, and real estate trusts. The foundation portfolio is largely left alone, although as with all investments it is important to check at least once in a while to make sure performance—

and managers if involved—are keeping up with expectations.

The Rotational Portfolio

The second segment, the rotational portfolio, is managed fairly actively to keep up with changes in business cycles and conditions. It is likely in a set of stocks or funds that might be rotated or remixed occasionally to reflect business conditions or to get a little more offensive or defensive. More than the other portfolios, this portfolio follows the rotation of market preference among different kinds of businesses and business assets. The portfolio is managed to redeploy assets among market or business sectors, between aggressive and defensive business assets, from "large cap" to "small cap" companies from companies with international exposure to those with little of same, from companies in favor versus out of favor, from stocks to bonds to commodities, and so forth. Sector-specific exchange-traded funds are a favorite component of these portfolios, as are cyclical and commodity-based stocks like gold mining stocks.

Is this about "market timing"? Let's call it "intelligent" or "educated" market timing. Studies telling us that it is impossible to effectively time market moves have been around for years. It is impossible to catch highs and lows in particular investments, market sectors, or even the market as a whole. Nobody can find exact tops or bottoms. But by watching economic indicators and taking the pulse of business and the marketplace, long-term market performance can be boosted by well-rationalized and timely sector rotation. The key word is "timely." The agile active investor has enough of a finger on the pulse to see the signs and invest accordingly.

While the idea isn't new, the advent of "low-friction" exchange traded funds and other index portfolios makes it a lot more practical for the individual investors. What does "low-friction" mean? They trade like a single stock—one order, one discounted commission. You don't have to liquidate or acquire a whole basket full of investments on your own to follow a sector. We should note that it's been possible to rotate assets in mutual fund families for years with a single phone call, but most funds in these families are less "pure" plays in their sector, and most families do not cover all sectors.

The Opportunistic Portfolio

The opportunistic portfolio is the most actively traded portion of an active investor's total portfolio. The opportunistic portfolio looks for stocks or other investments that seem to be notably under- or overvalued at a particular time. The active investor looks for shorter-term opportunities—perhaps a few days, perhaps a month, perhaps even a year—to wring out gains from undervalued situations.

The opportunistic portfolio also may be used to generate short-term income through covered option writing. Options are essentially a cash-based risk transfer mechanism whereby a possible, but low probabil-

ity investment outcome is exchanged for a less profitable but more certain outcome. A fee or "premium" is paid in exchange for transferring the opportunity for more aggressive gain to someone else. You collect this fee. Effectively, you as the owner of a stock can convert a growth investment into an income investment, paying yourself a dividend for the ownership of the stock by selling an option. Is this risky? Actually, it is less risky than owning the stock without an option.

Curiously, the main objective of this short-term portfolio is to generate income, or cash. Most traditional investors look at the long-term, more conservative components of a portfolio to generate income through bonds, dividend-paying stocks, and so forth. In this framework, the short-term opportunistic portfolio actually does the "heavy lifting" in terms of generating cash income. An active investor might look to trade those stocks with varying degrees of frequency or to sell some options to generate cash. These "swing" trades usually run from a few days to a month or so, and may be day trades if things work out particularly well and particularly fast. It should be emphasized again that day trades are not the active investor's goal nor his or her typical practice.

Are Retirement Accounts Always Part of the Foundation?

The long-term objectives and nature of retirement accounts suggest normal inclusion as part of the foundation portfolio. In fact, retirement assets can be deployed as part of either the rotational or opportunistic portfolio. And in fact, it might make a lot of sense. Why? Because returns generated are tax free, at least until withdrawn. Tax-free returns can compound much faster. Because of the importance of these assets, one should only commit a small portion to an actively managed opportunistic portfolio, but it can be a good way to "juice" the growth of this important asset base.

100 Best Stocks and the Segmented Portfolio

The next natural question is: "So how do I use *The 100 Best Stocks* to construct my portfolio tiers?" The answer is really that selections from the 100 best list can be used in all tiers, depending on your time horizon and current price relative to value. If you see a stock on the 100 best list take a nosedive, and feel that nosedive is out of proportion to the real news and near-term prospects of the company, it may be a candidate for the opportunistic portfolio. If the stock makes sense as a long-term holding (as many on our list do) it's a good candidate for the foundation portfolio. Likewise, if you feel that, say, energy stocks are, as a group, likely to be in favor and are undervalued now, you can pick off the energy stocks on the 100 best list as a rotational portfolio pick. Similarly, if you feel that large-cap dividend paying stocks will do well, again you can use the 100 Best list to feed into this hunch.

Not surprisingly, I feel the 100 best stocks are of the highest quality, and can be used with relatively less risk than most other stocks to achieve your objectives.

Ten Ways to Reduce Investment Risk

My predecessor John Slatter offered twenty ways to reduce investment risk. I have chosen to adapt some of his and add a few of my own, and to condense the list to a more manageable ten ways.

- *Diversify, but don't overdiversify.* As Warren Buffett put it, for some, diversification is a substitute for not knowing what you're doing. It does make sense to diversify your holdings into different kinds of companies in different sectors, for it does take some of the risk away of being wrong about a business or about an industry. But too much diversification cuts your opportunity and makes your "best case scenario" one of achieving only market returns, and may increase your investing costs by having more, smaller transactions. Avoid the temptation to own more than 5–10 different companies.
- *Know what you're doing and why.* Remember, you're buying a business. Keep track of why you're doing it and why you did it, and if the assumptions change or were incorrect in the first place, do something about it. Fortunately it's much easier to sell a bad investment than to sell a bad business.

- *Stay focused on cash and debt.* Sounds like we're talking about your own personal finances, right? Well, yes, but also no. We're talking about the finances of the companies you plan to buy. As pointed out above, cash is real and debt is real; neither are vulnerable to the ambiguities of the accounting process nor management discretion. If Company A generates a lot of cash and doesn't have a lot of debt, it probably is better than Company B, although it isn't the whole story—just like you're probably better off than your neighbor if you have a lot of cash, earn a lot of cash, and generate no debt, while he or she has an erratic income, a large mortgage, and a boat in the driveway.
- *Favor long-term performance.* I mean company performance, not necessarily stock price performance—although they should go hand-in-hand to some degree. And long-term, sustained performance is far better than a brilliant quarter here and there. Of course, with excellent new companies in an up-and-coming industry, like digital entertainment or solar energy or medical records technology, you might not have much of a track record; you'll have to go on intuition.

But this section is about reducing risk, so . . . pick the pitcher that can go nine full innings rather than the one who can strike out the side in the first, then throw like who knows what.

- *Favor where the puck is going.* Perhaps this sounds contradictory to *"Favor long-term performance,* but instead of long-term performance, now we're talking about reducing risk by favoring companies that get—or are even defining—the future. The reality is—both are best. A company with a solid track record and that gets the future is probably the least risky. Eastman Kodak had a solid past but didn't see the future. Jamba Juice saw the future of refreshing, nutritious drinks but had no past. There's nothing worse than betting on a company that does well today but fades into the sunset starting the day after you buy it—especially with today's rapid business change and evolution, make sure they have the future right, too.

- *Learn not to overreact or over-commit—up or down.* You can't know everything about a company, and you can't know everything about the future. So logically, it's ill advised to "go for broke" and make a huge upfront investment in a company. Buy in small increments—it isn't that much more expensive with today's discount commissions. You'll get a better average price if you happen to be wrong the

day you make the first purchase. Similarly, don't overreact on the sell side—many an investor has panicked at bad news and sold—at a daily, monthly, or all-time low. Not that you shouldn't sell if you've decided that a company is no longer a fit—but to do it all at once in panic mode makes the whole transaction more risky.

- *Don't put it all in stocks.* At the end of the day, corporate America is truly the driver of the economy, in not only what is produced, sold and consumed but also what is innovated and brought to market. Investing in stocks is investing in the growth and prosperity of America. Investing in bonds or other fixed income securities is investing for a fixed return with regard to safety but not to the success of the issuer; investors in commodities are making bets on supply and demand, not the prosperity of anyone in particular. That said, it's a mistake, as many found out in 2008, to bet too heavily on stocks. Prosperity can turn into poverty very quickly as spending drops, sales dry up, and costs escalate. I don't prescribe what percentage of your assets should be put into stocks or stock funds, but it clearly shouldn't be everything—it should be what you can reasonably afford to risk on the ups and downs of the U.S. and international economies.

And that varies from person to person.

- *Get at least some current returns.* If a company is wildly successful and can invest every dime of existing and new capital in lucrative venture, by all means, it probably should. But most companies don't have such a set of incredible opportunities in front of them. Some good ones, yes. But I prefer a company that can give you some current return, some bit of "thank you" for the capital you have provided, some contrition and admission that just maybe, yes, you have some good ideas for how to invest capital, too. I realize that many of our top companies pay no dividend, and that's okay, they've chosen to do your investing for you. But if you're stuck between choosing two companies, the one that recognizes that you, too, want to realize some returns, that company would get my nod, all else being equal.

- *Re-evaluate every year (or more often).* I can't say it often enough. The speed of business, and the speed of business change, is getting faster and faster. You must re-evaluate each of your investments each year—as though you were going to "buy" your stocks again—to make sure your assumptions are still valid. Or else the risk of change and obsolescence is bound to swamp your investing boat sooner or later.

- *Keep track of the big picture.* I see a lot of investors become overly focused on what made their stock selection great, and why even though it's down, the future is probably still bright "if only we can get through this." Again, in line with my comments on business change, the environment can change too, and change very quickly. As an investor you should keep up with world events, new technologies, and new business and consumer trends, not just companies and stocks. If you aren't reading the *Wall Street Journal*, *The Economist*, the *New York Times*—print or online version, it doesn't matter—you may not be getting a clear-eyed view of the bigger economic and corporate picture. It's also important to keep track of trends in the sectors or industries you invest in. That can be done by reading the press and trade news in those industries—or if nothing else, by keeping track of the prices and business levels in the markets your company serves. Buying energy stocks? At the least, you should keep track of oil, natural gas, and refinery blend prices; geopolitical turmoil; driving behavior; and so forth. Again, those who keep track of the forest, not just the trees, are bound to come out ahead, especially in today's volatile and changing economic times.

When to Buy? Consider When to Sell

If it's hard to figure out when to buy a stock, it's even harder to figure out when to sell. People "get married" to their investment decisions, feeling somehow that if it isn't right, maybe time will help, and things will get better. Or they're just too arrogant to admit that they made a mistake. There are lots of reasons why people hold on to investments for too long a time.

Here's the fundamental truth: Buying and selling should be much the same process. Let's look at it from the point of view of selling. When should you sell? Simply, when there's something else better to buy. Something else better for future returns, something else better for safety, something else better for timeliness or synchronization with overall business trends. That something else can be another stock, a futures contract, or a house. It can also be cash—sell that stock when . . . when what? When cash is a better investment. Or when you need the money, which is another way of saying that cash is a better investment.

Similarly, if you think of a buy decision as a best-possible deployment of capital, as a buy because there's no better way to invest your money, you'll also come out ahead. It really isn't that hard, especially if you've done your homework. And it's also made easier if you avoid rash overcommitments; that is, you avoid buying all at once in case you've made a mistake or in case better prices come later down the road.

Investing for Retirement

Most of us don't invest just for the sake of investing. We're not so much like players at a poker table who not only enjoy winning money but the process of winning. We're more interested in the result of investing than the process. We may like to invest, like to do research, like to see things come out the way we had in mind. But the main reason we do it is to make money.

And why do we want to make money? Well, for some of us, it's about buying homes, paying for college, or just having a little extra spending money. But for a great many of us, especially those of us for whom there's no defined-benefit pension awaiting us when we retire, we invest because we want a more secure, comfortable retirement years down the road.

So how should one invest for retirement? Should one invest any differently than they would for any of the other objectives I just mentioned? Mostly, investing is investing, and the goal is to make money over the intended period of time one invests. Retirement investing isn't that much different, except there is a greater emphasis on the long term, and for many, a greater need for safety.

The retirement planning process starts with creating a goal, that is, estimating what you will need during retirement to live on. The "what you'll need" is referred to euphemistically as your "number": an amount that will, with carefully planned withdrawals, service your needs net of government (Social Security) and other pensions until you and your spouse die. There are many ways to calculate this "number," and financial advisers have a bag of tricks and fancy spreadsheets. I like to use a permanent withdrawal rate rule of thumb—that is, you can draw down 4 percent of your asset base each year in retirement. So if you need $2,000 a month (plus Social Security) to live, that's $24,000 a year; $24,000 a year is 4 percent of what number (multiply by 25)—that's $960,000 you'll need in your retirement account on Retirement Day 1. This number, however, assumes that you want to live strictly off of income, not principal, and that you want to leave the principal intact. Of course, this is a conservative assumption. You can see how complex the calculation can become.

But that's not the point of reading *100 Best Stocks*—the point is to get some tips on where and how to invest to achieve the number. I offer the following:

- *Stay diversified.* You've read about how Enron shareholders had their entire retirement tied up in company stock. If the company fails, you fail twice. It's probably best to not even invest most of your retirement assets in the same industry you work in. A good portfolio of stocks or funds (seven or so different stocks, three or so different funds) is probably optimal. But don't overdiversify—you can achieve the same returns at a lot less cost by simply buying an index fund.

- *Think long term.* Obvious, right? Well, today's market can bring some serious surprises to those who think they can simply buy and hold forever and capitalize on the growth of the American Way. The trick here is to buy individual companies that you think will not only be around when you retire, but will be better than they are today. Try to visualize your company ten, twenty, or thirty years from now. And be prepared to bail out when things start to not look like you expected. There are a lot of GM shareholders and bondholders who wish they had done just that.

- *Get at least some dividends.* Future appreciation is nice for retirement, but I believe that a bird in hand is worthwhile, especially if you can reinvest it in the stocks or funds held in your retirement accounts.

- *Dollar cost average.* If you keep reinvesting dividends and/or adding funds to your accounts consistently, you'll buy more shares when prices are low, bringing your average cost down. For most people it's best to keep retirement contributions—and investments—as consistent as possible.

- *Use a portfolio strategy.* As in the ones outlined above, these create a strong, steady "foundation" and add some opportunistic investments. The opportunistic investments can be used to stretch returns a bit, and they work better in retirement accounts because capital gains taxes are deferred or avoided altogether. That said, you should opportunistically invest only what you can afford to lose. Most of the 100 best stocks are suitable for foundation investments, and a few of the "aggressive growth" entries are good for opportunistic investments as well.

So good luck, and I'll come visit you at your beach house.

When and How to Use an Adviser

To use a professional adviser? Or not to use a professional adviser? That is the question almost all individual investors ask themselves at one time or another.

Individual investors are independent, self-starting, self-driven folks largely capable of accepting responsibility for their own decisions and actions. That's good, and I assume that if you're reading this book, you have at least some of that character. However, the world isn't so simple, and your time isn't so plentiful, and maybe business and investing stuff just isn't your cup of tea, anyway. You don't want to throw everything over the wall to a professional adviser (and pay the fees and lose control and all that) but you may want some help from time to time.

Just remember this—you, you only, and ultimately you are responsible for your own finances, just like a pilot flying an airplane is ultimately responsible for what happens to that airplane and its passengers. You are in charge. You are in charge whether or not you have someone else, like a broker or professional adviser, helping you out. You can (and should) think of an adviser as more like a co-pilot, navigator, or air traffic controller who will give you information and suggestions and help you interpret the information and remind you of the rules when necessary—but ultimately you're in charge.

Financial advisers come in many forms, and I won't go into the details here. What's important is to realize that no matter how much you outsource, you're still at the helm. You need to develop a good, two-way relationship with the adviser where he or she can bring value and can help you bring value to the investment decisions and investment strategy. Advisers shouldn't tell you what to do, and they shouldn't just be the "yes man" for everything you want to do. A lively, point-counterpoint discussion of any financial move with an adviser is healthy; two heads are better than one. Remember, if two people think the exact same way, you don't need one of them.

Don't be snowed by fancy terminology and concepts. Investing is a complex subject, but if the explanation sounds more complex than the task itself, look out below. Find an adviser that speaks your language, that is, plain English. Smart, experienced people make things simple, not complex, for others.

Also be clear what you want and what you expect from advisers. If you aren't, they'll give you the "standard" product, and it may be the same standard product they gave their last client. If you want help constructing your portfolio and learning about, say, the tech and health care sectors, which you don't know enough about, ask them to help you understand the headlines and what's important about them for the banking industry. And so forth.

And of course, as Bernard Madoff has made so clear for so many—make sure you understand what they're doing, if they're managing anything on your behalf. There is nothing worse than thinking everything is okay—when in fact it's completely off in the weeds.

Bottom line, an investment adviser should be a great partner, someone you'd hire into your business if you were trying to create a partnership in the investing business. Look for common sense, look for the adviser to help you most with the things you're least comfortable with. Learn what he or she does (and has done) with other clients; if it sounds too good to be true, it probably is.

Here's another bottom line: Your adviser should make you sleep better at night. If you're waking up at 3 A.M. thinking about your investments, that's bad. If you're waking up at 3 A.M. thinking about your adviser, that's worse. In both cases, they're too risky for you.

Individual Stocks vs. Funds and ETFs

As long as I'm sharing opinions on things like financial advisers and other help you can get with your investing, it makes sense to take a short detour into the world of managed investments. What are managed investments? Simply, they are individual investments where some intermediary buys and repackages individual investments, and sells you pieces of that package.

Intermediaries can be investment companies with professional managers choosing specific investments and otherwise looking after the portfolio. They can also be indexes, where groups of like stocks are accumulated into an index according to some sort of generally fixed formula. Either way, by buying into one of these intermediaries, you're giving up picking individual investments in favor of a packaged and sometimes professionally managed approach.

Of course, like any value proposition, you're giving up something in the interest of gaining something else. The "something else" you're trying to gain by using the packaged approach is usually a combination of the following:

- **Time**—You don't have the time to research individual stocks, or to research individual stocks for 100 percent of your portfolio.
- **Expertise**—In the case of managed funds, you're getting a

trained, experienced, investment professional. Some also prefer to hire others to do the work to take the emotion out of investing decisions.

- **Diversification**—By definition, both managed and index funds spread your investments so that you don't have too much wrapped up in a single company; this is generally good unless they diversify away any chance of outperforming the markets. Funds and ETFs also allow you to play in markets otherwise difficult to play in for lack of knowledge or time, e.g., Asian stocks, European currencies, etc.
- **Convenience**—It takes work to build and manage an investment portfolio. With funds you can move in and out of the markets with a single transaction, and the administrative work is taken care of.

Of course, with any value proposition comes a downside, and the downsides of fund and index investing are often underappreciated by prospective clients:

- **Fees**—Not surprisingly, funds, and especially managed funds, charge money for the packaging and services they provide. Actively managed funds can take a half to over two percent of your asset value each year, whether they do well or not. If you understand compounding, you know that the difference between a 6 percent return and a 4 percent net return over time is huge. Index funds and ETFs are better in this regard, usually charging 0.25 to 0.75 percent, but it still puts a drag on your outcomes.

- **Tax efficiency**—When ordinary mutual funds sell shares, any gains flow through to you (unless you hold them in a tax-free or tax-deferred retirement account). You cannot control when this happens, and many "active" funds may roll their portfolios frequently, producing adverse tax consequences. Also, you need to watch when you enter the fund—you should buy in after capital gains are paid out, not before, else you'll be paying for someone else's gains. Index funds and ETFs are far less likely to produce "unwanted" gains, for they tie their investments to the indexes, which don't change much.

- **Control**—With funds of any sort, you lose control, and as we said at the outset, there are few things more painful than having someone else lose your money for you. Particularly with managed funds, it is almost impossible to know what they are really doing with your money except in hindsight; I would support any initiative requiring funds to give you more real time accounting for what they do with your funds.

- **Tendency toward mediocrity**— One of the biggest criticisms of funds over time is the tendency for managers to follow each other and to follow standard business-school investing and risk management formulas. The result you tend to get is a herd instinct, known in the trade as an "institutional imperative." You can see this in many funds—pick almost any fund and the top 10 holdings are GE, Microsoft, ExxonMobil; you get the idea. Worse—and this is the biggie from my perspective—when you buy a fund and especially an index fund, you're getting all the companies in the industry—the mediocre players, the weak hands—not just the best ones.

So I suggest using funds where it makes sense to get some exposure to an industry or a segment of the market otherwise difficult to access or outside your expertise. Use funds to round out a portfolio or build a foundation or rotational portfolio, and to save yourself the time and bandwidth to focus more closely on other more "opportunistic" investments.

Basic Terminology

If you are new to the investment arena, you may not be familiar with some of the terms used this book. To get you over the rough spots, I have listed some common expressions that appear frequently in investing books and media, including the *Wall Street Journal*, *Forbes*, *BusinessWeek*, and analysis you'll read in *Value Line* and other sources.

Annual Report 10-K

If you own a common stock, each year you'll receive an annual report shortly after the close of the company's fiscal year, either by mail or, increasingly, by e-mail. Annual reports are legally required summaries of a company's business and business results. They take two forms: the glossy "consumer" version which reads more like a magazine about the company; and the more official "10-K" version, not usually glossy but incorporating more information for regulators and other investment analysts. As a cost cutting move, many companies have blended the two. As a serious investor, you should be more interested in the 10-K version.

Annual reports can give a good view of how a company perceives itself, albeit usually with a positive spin. You can usually get a pretty good idea how things are going and what the near and long term risks are for the company. In particular, financial highlights and the president or CEO's letter will give a good summary of current directions and challenges, and it is usually written in language you can understand.

If you want detailed information on the company's various businesses, the annual report will often overwhelm you with details that may be difficult to fathom. If you are really curious about what they are trying to say, feel free to use other sources or even call the investor contact, listed on the annual report or available through the phone numbers listed with each stock. Investor contacts are usually quite personable and helpful.

Asset Allocation

Asset allocation refers to a strategy of allocating your investment funds among different types of investments, such as stocks, bonds, or money-market funds. In the long run, studies show you're normally better off with all of your assets concentrated in common stocks. In the short run, this may not be true, since as we know the stock market occasionally experiences sharp downturns. A severe one, such as the recent 2008–2009 episode, can cause your common stock holdings to decline in value by 50 percent or more. To protect against this, most investors spread their money around. They may, for instance, allocate 50 percent to stocks, 40 percent to bonds, and

10 percent to a money-market fund. A more realistic breakdown might be 70 percent in stocks, 25 percent in bonds, and 5 percent in a money-market fund.

Allocation depends on a lot of factors, including your risk tolerance and age—if you are approaching retirement, for instance, you want a greater portion of your nest egg in safe and steady investments like bonds, especially Treasury bonds. A popular formula holds that your common stock percentage should equal (100 − your age), so if you're thirty, your allocation is 70 percent stocks; if you're sixty, it is 40 percent stocks. There are many ways to allocate a portfolio, for example the "strategic investing" framework I advocate on page 40 in Part I.

Balance Sheet

Publicly traded corporations are required to release a set of financial statements. Most companies must file annual and quarterly financial statements, including a *balance sheet*, an *income statement*, and a *statement of cash flows*. The balance sheet is a financial snapshot of the company on a specific date, such as December 31 or at the end of a quarter.

On the left hand side of the balance sheet are the company's assets—loosely translated, properties or things *owned*—which include cash, receivables, inventories, buildings and equipment, and intangible assets like patents and other intellectual property. On the right hand side are its liabilities, or amounts *owed*, including

accounts payable and short and long-term debt. Also on the right hand side is shareholders' equity, which represents total assets less liabilities, which in turn is the owners' net interest in the company. The right hand side of the balance sheet adds up to the same value as the left hand side, which is why it is called a balance sheet.

Most corporations give figures for the current year and the prior year. By examining the changes, you can get an idea of whether the company's finances are improving or deteriorating.

Beta Coefficient

The beta coefficient, as used in this book, is a single-figure measure of the relationship, or *correlation*, between the price of a stock and the financial markets as a whole. The best way to explain is by example: a stock with a beta of 0 means that its price doesn't correlate at all with the market. A positive beta means that the stock tends to move in the same direction as the market as a whole (which most stocks do), and the larger the beta, the more closely the stock tracks the market. A stock with a beta of 1 moves exactly with the market; a beta greater than one indicates that the stock moves in the same direction as the market but more sharply, as a percentage. A stock with a negative beta tends to move in the opposite direction as the market, so would be considered a "defensive" stock. In general, the higher the beta the more risky the stock, but correspondingly, the potential returns are higher. A beta coefficient can also be calculated for a portfolio of stocks, but that is outside the scope and framework of this book.

"Blue Chip" Stock

The term "blue chip" is commonly used to describe the stock of an established company of substantial size with stable earnings and relatively little risk compared to other stock choices. The term comes from casino gambling where blue gambling chips once were used as the highest denomination. Stocks in the Dow Jones Industrial Average and other prominent indexes are considered blue chips, and most, but not all, stocks in this book would also be described that way.

Bonds

A bond is a security representing a loan made to a company or entity; unlike a stock, is not a form of ownership. A bond is a contractual agreement to pay the money back at some future date (maturity) and to pay you a certain sum of money (interest) typically every six months until that bond matures. At maturity, you will also get back the money you originally invested—no more, no less. Most bonds are issued in $1,000 denominations. The safest bonds are those issued by the U.S. government. The two advantages of bonds are safety and income. If you wait until the maturity date, you will be assured of getting the face value of the bond. In the meantime, however, the bond will fluctuate, because of changes in interest rates, inflation or inflation fears, or the perceived creditworthiness of the corporation. Long-term bonds, moreover, fluctuate far

more than short-term bonds. Stocks, rather than bonds, are the focus of this book, but bond investors can use the information presented to assess the success and safety of a corporation under consideration for a bond investment.

Capital Gains

When you buy common stocks, you expect to make money in two ways: capital gains and dividends. Capital gains represent the growth in value of the investment over time vis-à-vis what you paid for it. If the stock rises in value and you sell it above your cost, you are enjoying a capital gain. Capital gains are taxed differently than ordinary income; currently long term capital gains enjoy a reduced maximum tax rate of 15 percent.

Common Stock

Common stocks are the basis for this book. All publicly owned companies—those that trade their shares outside of a small group of executives or the founding family—are based on common stocks. A common stock represents a partial ownership in a corporation. Most of the stocks described in this book have millions, even billions, of shares outstanding. As common stock represents an ownership interest, there are no guarantees. If the company is successful, the stock will grow in price, and it may in addition pay a dividend as much as four times a year. Better yet, these dividends may be raised periodically, perhaps even annually. If, however, the company has problems, it may cut or eliminate its dividend, and its share value may decline as well. This can happen even to a major company, such as Citigroup, Eastman Kodak, or, worse, General Motors. Again, there are no guarantees.

Most common stocks are *liquid*; that is, investors who own common stock can sell their shares at any time almost instantly by pushing the right button on a keyboard.

Compound Earnings Per Share Growth

This "compound" or complex term actually includes a few ideas. First is earnings per share, the popular common-denominator measure of corporate performance. Second is the idea of earnings per share *growth*, a measure of the relative progress of the company and how it turns into a return for shareholders. A company may grow earnings, but if the number of shares increases at the same rate, shareholders haven't gained at all. Investors should look for growth, especially *sustained* per share earnings growth. Finally, the *compounded* growth rate represents the truest and most conservative measure of return over a sequence of years. Think of it this way—buy a house and it doubles in value in ten years from 4100,000 to $200,000. One hundred percent return, right? Well, yes, but only 10 percent nominal annual return. But the money was left in the home to compound, that is, returns earned returns, over the years. So to calculate the compounded return, take the doubled return (2) and take the 10th root of it to deconstruct the ten years of return. You get 1.072 using a calculator, of course—that's a 7.2 percent compounded annualized return. By illustration, if you had invested $100,000 in a CD paying 7.2 percent it would have returned the same amount in ten years. The point: compounded annualized returns—in earnings or dividends as presented in this book—are the most conservative way to measure returns and the most effective way to compare different investments over the long term.

Diversification

Since investments are inherently risky, it pays to spread the risk by diversifying. If you don't, you are too vulnerable if an individual investment turns sour.

Most investment professionals advise not investing more than 5 percent of your portfolio in a single investment, and similarly you don't want to put too much into a single sector, like semiconductors or retailers. Many professionals advise investing no more than 12 percent in a single sector.

The counterpoint, however, is that many investors are tempted to over-diversify. If you buy 50 different stocks, some will gain, some will lose, and at the end of the day, you won't do much better or worse than buying the overall market, that is, an index fund. The more you diversify, the more your returns converge onto overall market returns, and the more likely you'll add bad stocks to the good stocks in your portfolio. Warren Buffett famously said, "Diversification is for those who don't know what they're doing." Bottom line: diversify where it makes sense, but if you have the knack for picking winners, less diversification can produce better returns.

Dividends

Unlike bonds, which pay interest, common stocks may pay a dividend. Most dividends are paid quarterly, but there is no set date that all corporations use. Most companies like to pay the same dividend every quarter until they can afford to increase it, and most only increase it when business prospects are likely to support the higher dividend for the long term. For that reason, stocks with a consistent track record of dividend increases gain even more favor. However, the 2008–2009 crises brought on a lot of dividend cuts—remember that dividends are neither contractual nor permanent.

Dividends are nice to have and a good indication not only of financial health but of a management that is willing to share returns with shareholders. That said, many companies have excellent business prospects and choose to reinvest their earnings in the business. This is often a good decision but as an investor, you should work to confirm this judgment. At the end of the day, dividends are nice but not an essential characteristic of a good stock.

Dividend Payout Ratio

If a company earns $4 a share in a twelve-month period and pays out $3 to shareholders in the form of dividends, it has a payout ratio of 75 percent. However, if it pays only $1, the payout ratio is 25 percent. In the past, many investors looked favorably on a low payout ratio. The thinking was that such a company was plowing back its earnings into such projects as research, new facilities, acquisitions, and new equipment. It sounds logical.

Now, there is evidence that you are better off buying a company with a higher payout ratio. Mark Hulbert, who writes frequently for the Sunday *New York Times*, has come up with some studies that focus on this concept. According to work done by Michael C. Jensen, currently an emeritus professor of business administration at the Harvard Business School, "The more cash that companies have now (beyond what is needed for current projects), the less efficient they will be in the future."

Two other scholars concur that a higher payout ratio serves investors better than a low one. They are Robert D. Arnott of First Quadrant and Clifford S. Asness of AQR Capital Management. For one thing, they found that "For the overall stock market between 1871 and 2001, corporate profits grew fastest in the ten years following the calendar year in which companies had the highest average dividend payout ratio." Mr. Hulbert concludes that "The common theme that emerges from these various studies is a very unflattering portrait of corporate management: give executives lots of rope and they too often end up hanging themselves. It would appear that a high dividend payout ratio is an effective way to reduce the length of that rope."

Dividend Reinvestment Plans

To achieve greater wealth from the shares you own, you might like to reinvest your dividends in more shares. Many companies have a dividend reinvestment plan (also known as a DRIP) that will allow you to do this, and the charge for this service is often minimal. Most of these companies also allow you to mail in additional cash, which will be used to purchase new shares, again at minimal cost.

Companies with such plans include ExxonMobil, McDonald's, Procter & Gamble, and Southern Company.

DRIPs are a good way to build your savings, and they can also be a good way to avoid paying brokerage commissions, but there are some drawbacks to bear in mind. For one thing, you can't time your purchases, since it may be a week or more before your purchase is made.

Even worse is calculating your cost basis for tax purposes. By the time you sell, you may have made scores of small investments in the same stock, each with a different cost basis. Make sure you keep a file for each company so that you can make these calculations when the time comes. Or, better still, don't sell.

Dollar-Cost Averaging

Dollar-cost averaging is a systematic way to invest money over a long period, such as ten, fifteen, or twenty years. It entails investing the same amount of money regularly, for example, each month or each quarter. If you do this faithfully, you will be buying more stock when the price is lower and less stock when the price is higher. This tends to smooth out the gyrations of the market. Dollar-cost averaging is often used with a mutual fund, but it can almost as easily be done with an individual company.

Income Statement

A corporate income statement is analogous to your own "statement" of income and expenses. Investors are interested in net earnings, or earnings per share (EPS) but also the items that got them there. The income statement lists such items as net sales, cost of sales, interest expense, and gross profit. As with the balance sheet, change is important—it makes sense to compare this year's numbers with those of the prior year.

Investment Adviser

Investors who do not have the time or inclination to manage their own portfolios may elect to employ an investment adviser. Most fee-based or fee-only advisers charge 1 percent of a portfolio value each year. Thus, if you own stocks worth $300,000, your annual fee would be $3,000. If an adviser is "fee-based" (as opposed to fee-only) they may also get paid a commission for selling certain investment products, i.e. funds. Brokers, on the other hand, are subject to a different level of regulation, and make most of their money charging commissions for transactions— which will tend to bias them towards making more transactions. Advisers stand to gain when your portfolio increases, and additionally, assume fiduciary responsibility to act in your best interests. If you choose to use an adviser (see discussion in Part I), make sure you know how they're paid.

Moving Average

Some investors use the moving average to time the market. Designed to filter out random variations and show a bigger-picture look at the overall direction of a stock, there are many different kinds of moving averages. One popular strategy is to buy a stock when it is selling above its moving average and sell when it falls below. Many investors look at a 200-day moving average for this purpose. A dotted line is drawn, taking the average price of the stock over the previous 200 days. The actual price of the stock is plotted on the same graph. Studies show that this method of timing the market does not work on a consistent basis.

Mutual Fund

Mutual funds are a popular form of investment company established by the Investment Company Act of 1940 specifically to offer individual investors a managed, more diversified way to participate in the stock market. Mutual funds collect cash from investors and build a stock portfolio with the cash; investors then participate in the returns according to the size of their individual investments. The unique structure of mutual funds allows them to pass gains on without being taxed at the fund level; additionally 90 percent of such gains must be paid out to investors.

Open-ended mutual funds have no limits to the amount of funds that can be paid in; new cash is simply invested to expand the portfolio—unless the fund decides to close itself because it is becoming too big. The share price reflects the current value, or "Net Asset Value" (NAV) of the fund's holdings at the end of each trading day. Most shares are bought directly from the fund. Closed end funds have a fixed number of shares that themselves are traded on an exchange, and the price of those shares reflect supply and demand for the fund and may not exactly match asset value, selling at a premium or discount. There are thousands of funds to choose from to meet almost any investment need, but be careful, as many funds charge a lot in fees and tend not to outperform the market. Morningstar (*www.morningstar.com*) is a good further resource to learn about mutual funds.

PEG Ratio

The PEG, or Price Earnings to Growth, ratio is a helpful measure to evaluate the price of a stock. It relates the price/earnings ratio (see definition below) to the growth rate of the stock; the idea being that a higher growth rate justifies a higher P/E, that is, a more expensive stock. It is calculated by dividing the price-earnings ratio by the expected earnings growth rate. A PEG ratio of 1 or less suggests an attractive stock price, while PEG over 3 is considered expensive.

Preferred Stock

A preferred stock is much like a bond, typically paying the same dividend year in and year out. The yield is usually higher than a common stock. It is stock, but generally does not participate in the growth of the company but rather earns through the dividend (exception: *convertible* preferreds, which under some conditions are convertible to common stock). If the company issuing the preferred stock does well, your dividend becomes secure; if it does poorly, however, you may suffer, since the dividend could be cut or eliminated. Also, preferred stock owners sit behind bond holders in priority in a bankruptcy situation.

Price-Earnings Ratio (P/E)

An important valuation measure, the P/E ratio is sometimes referred to as "the P/E" or "the multiple."

The P/E ratio tells you whether a stock is cheap or expensive. It is usually calculated by dividing the price of the stock by the company's earnings per share over the most recent twelve months, although some prefer to calculate a "forward" P/E based on the *next* twelve months' earnings.

A high P/E ratio tends to indicate a stock with good prospects for the future—or it may just be too expensive. Investors should compare P/E's with other stocks in similar industries and with the market overall, and against the risk of the investment. They should also consider the inverse of the P/E, or earnings yield, corresponding roughly to the percentage return on

investment—i.e. a P/E of 20 implies a return of 5 percent (1/20).

Profit Margins

Profit margins describe the amount, or percentage, of profit being made per dollar of sales. At least three profit margin figures are observed by investors when analyzing a stock. The first is gross profit margin, that is, sales less the direct "cost of goods sold" used to produce a product. The second is operating profit margin, capturing not only cost of goods sold but also expenses. The third is net profit margin, which is sales less all costs and expenses, including taxes. Net profit is usually the first measure investors look at and is the "standard" way to compare companies, but sharp-eyed investors look at other margins for relative size and growth compared to other companies.

Statement of Cash Flows

While most investors focus on earnings, it also makes sense—sometimes more sense—to focus on cash flows. Cash is king these days, and just like you, when you run your own business, the amount of cash in the register, and the amount of cash coming into your business (less the amount going out) determines whether you can pay yourself and survive to another day.

The Statement of Cash Flows comes with the balance sheet and income statement as one of the "big three" financial statements. It tells you as an investor what is happening with cash in the company. Typically you'll see it summarized as follows:

- *Cash Flow from Operations* is the first component, and tells on a net basis how much cash was generated (or used) in the daily course of business. Normally this figure is positive—if a company is consuming more than it produces just in delivering its base product, that's a problem—although sometimes it reflects a change in inventory or receivables or some other cash generating or cash consuming activity. Over the long haul, cash flow from operations should be positive, because the business needs to use that cash to fund investments (next category) or to pay down debt or return money to shareholders (the third category).
- *Cash from Investing Activities* tells us how much cash was invested in the business, usually for capital goods like plant or equipment. Typically this figure is negative indicating a net outflow, but sometimes if an asset is sold it may actually generate net cash.
- *Cash from Financing Activities* tells how much cash was sourced by selling stock or bonds or used to pay off bonds, to pay dividends, etc. A positive figure indicates more cash was brought into the company by selling such securities than was consumed by paying them off (or buying them back as in the case of stock).

Bottom line: you want to invest in companies that produce more cash than they consume. So over the long haul, cash flow from operations should exceed that spent for investments, and should not have to be supplemented by cash generated by financing.

Stock Split

Corporations believe investors prefer buying lower priced stocks, because they can buy more shares for the same amount of money, and it's easier to buy the standard "round lot" of 100 shares. Thus, when the price of the stock gets to a certain level, some companies may choose to split the stock. For instance, if the stock is $75, they might split it three-for-one. Your original 100 shares now become 300 shares. Unfortunately, your 300 shares are worth exactly the same as your original 100 shares. What it amounts to is this: Splits please small investors, but they don't make them any richer. Berkshire Hathaway has never been split, and is now worth over $90,000. On the other hand, the recent stock market plunge caused some companies to do reverse splits to build their stock prices back up to minimally acceptable levels for stock exchanges and some fund investors. A reverse split might be 1 for 10, bringing a $1 stock to a $10 level with a corresponding 90 percent decrease in the number of shares owned. Again, no real value has changed; it is a matter of perceptions. Generally speaking a reverse split is a sign of bigger problems and the have a tendency to resume their fall once the split takes effect.

Technical analysis

There are two basic ways to analyze stocks: *fundamental analysis and technical analysis.*

Fundamental analysts examine the numbers and key characteristics of a company, including its management, sales and earnings potential, research capabilities, new products, competitive strength, balance sheet strength, dividend growth, extrinsic or marketplace developments, and industry conditions.

Technicians, by contrast, rarely consider any of these fundamental factors. They rely on charts and graphs and a host of other statistical factors, such as point-and-figure charts, breadth indicators, head-and-shoulders formations, relative strength ratings, and the 200-day-moving average. The technician is looking for patterns reflecting aggregate behavior of traders and investors in the marketplace. This book focuses on fundamental, not technical, factors as analysis tools.

Value Investing

Value investing is a fundamentals-based approach which seeks to place a value on the business, much as you would a small business you'd like to buy. That value is compared to the price, and if the price is attractive relative to value, the stock is attractive to buy. If the stock appears to sell at a substantial discount to value, that provides a *margin of safety* against error, recognizing that valuing a company is far from an exact science. Some investors and invest-ment professionals classify stocks as being "value" or "growth" stocks. I believe this distinction is invalid, because growth is part of a value occasion.

Value Line Investment Survey

Value Line is an investment analysis service geared towards individual investors. The popular *Value Line Investment Survey* provides one-page reports on about seventeen hundred stocks. For an individual it costs about $600 per year to subscribe, but it is normally available in brokerage houses and libraries. This book draws a lot of data and some analysis from *Value Line.*

Working Capital

Working capital is the difference between current assets, like cash, inventory, and receivables, and current liabilities, like payables and short-term debt. Working capital provides the basic "lifeblood" of the business, paying the payroll and putting inventory on the shelves to sell. Companies must raise funds to finance working capital; and in periods of tight credit, this can be difficult. Well-managed companies have sufficient working capital to fund their business—but keep non-cash working capital items like inventory to a minimum required to service a given business level. When working capital is growing faster than a business is, that's a problem—unless it's a deliberate strategy to grow the business and increase market share.

Yield

If your company pays a dividend, you can relate this dividend to the price of the stock in order to calculate the yield. A $50 stock that pays a $2 annual dividend (which amounts to 50 cents per quarter) will have a yield of 4 percent. (Divide $2 by $50). Actually, you don't have to make this calculation, since the yield is given to you in the stock tables of the *Wall Street Journal and in financial portals like Yahoo!Finance.* Although the yield is of some importance, you should not judge a stock by its yield without looking at many other factors.

PART II

THE 100 BEST STOCKS YOU CAN BUY

Index of Stocks by Category

Index of Stocks by Category (continued)

Company	Symbol	Industry	Sector	Category
—E—				
eBay	EBAY	ECommerce	Cons Discre	Aggr Gro
Ecolab	ECL	Specialty Chem.	Materials	Con Grow
EnCana Corporation	ECA	Oil & Gas Energy	Energy	Aggr Gro
Energen	EGN	Oil & Gas	Energy	Aggr Gro
Entergy	ETR	Energy	Utilities	Grow Inc
ExxonMobil	XOM	Petroleum	Energy	Grow Inc
—F—				
Fair Isaac	FIC		Business Svcs	Aggr Gro
FedEx Corporation	FDX	Air Freight	Transportation	Aggr Gro
Fluor	FLR	Engineering	Heavy Constr	Aggr Gro
FMC Corporation	FMC	Feeding World	Materials	Aggr Gro
FPL Group	FPL	Elect. Power	Utilities	Grow Inc
—G—				
General Dynamics	GD	Aerospace	Industrials	Con Grow
General Mills	GIS	Packaged Foods	Cons Staples	Grow Inc
Goodrich	GR	Aerospace	Industrials	Aggr Gro
W. W. Grainger	GWW	Supplies	Industrials	Con Grow
—H—				
Harris Corp.	HRS	Communications	Inform Tech	Aggr Gro
Heinz	HNZ	Food	Cons Staples	Grow Inc
Hewlett-Packard	HPQ	Computer	Inform Tech	Aggr Gro
Honeywell	HON	Aerospace	Industrials	Aggr Gro
Hormel Foods	HRL	Packaged Foods	Cons Staples	Con Grow
—I—				
Illinois Tool Works	ITW	Machinery	Industrials	Con Grow
Int'l Business Mach.	IBM	Computers	Inform Tech	Con Grow
International Paper	IP	Packaging	Materials	Con Grow
Iron Mountain	IRM	Data Mgmt.	Inform Tech	Aggr Gro
—J—				
Johnson & Johnson	JNJ	Med Supplies	Health Care	Grow Inc
Johnson Controls	JCI	Elect. Equip.	Industrials	Con Grow

Index of Stocks by Category (continued)

Company	Symbol	Industry	Sector	Category
—K—				
Kellogg	K	Packaged Foods	Cons Staples	Grow Inc
Kraft Foods	KFT	Packaged Foods	Cons Staples	Grow Inc
—L—				
Lowe's Companies	LOW	Retail	Retail	Aggr Gro
Lubrizol	LZ	Specialty Chem	Materials	Grow Inc
—M—				
Marathon Oil	MRO	Gas & Oil	Energy	Aggr Gro
McCormick & Co.	MKC	Spices	Cons Staples	Con Grow
McDonald's	MCD	Food	Restaurant	Aggr Gro
Medtronic	MDT	Med. Devices	Health Care	Aggr Gro
Monsanto	MON	Food	Industrials	Aggr Gro
—N—				
NIKE	NIKE	Clothing	Cons Discret	Aggr Gro
Norfolk Southern	NSC	Railroads	Transportation	Con Grow
Northern Trust	NTRS	Bank	Financials	Con Grow
—P—				
Patterson Companies	PDCO	Dental	Health Care	Aggr Gro
Paychex	PAYX	Payroll Services	Inform Tech	Aggr Gro
Peet's	PEET	Beverages	Restaurant	Aggr Gro
PepsiCo	PEP	Beverages	Cons Staples	Con Grow
Perrigo	PRGO	Pharmacy	Health Care	Aggr Gro
Piedmont Nat'l Gas	PNY	Nat'l Gas	Utilities	Grow Inc
Praxair	PX	Indust. Gases	Materials	Con Grow
Procter & Gamble	PG	Household Products	Cons Staples	Con Grow
—R—				
Raytheon	RTN	Defense	Industrials	Aggr Gro
Ross Stores	ROST	Clothing	Retail	Aggr Gro
—S—				
Schlumberger	SLB	Oilfield Services	Energy	Aggr Gro
Sigma–Aldrich	SIAL	Life Science	InformTech	Aggr Gro
Southern Co.	SO	Elec. Serv.	Utilities	Gro Inc
St. Jude Medical	STJ	Medical Devices	Health Care	Aggr Gro

Index of Stocks by Category (continued)

Company	Symbol	Industry	Sector	Category
Staples	SPLS	Office Products	Retail	Aggr Gro
Starbucks	SBUX	Beverages	Restaurant	Aggr Gro
Stryker	SYK	Medical Sup.	Health Care	Aggr Gro
Sysco Corporation	SYY	Food Distrib.	Cons Staples	Con Grow
—T—				
Target Corporation	TGT	Gen. Merchandise	Retail	Aggr Gro
Teva Pharmaceutical	TEVA	Pharmaceuticals	Health Care	Aggr Gro
3M Company	MMM	Diversified	Industrials	Con Grow
TJX	TJX	Retailer	Retail	Aggr Gro
Tractor Supply	TSCO	Industrial Mach.	Retail	Aggr Gro
—U—				
UnitedHealth	UNH	Med. Insur.	Health Care	Aggr Gro
United Parcel	UPS	Expr. Carrier	Transportation	Con Grow
United Technologies	UTX	Aircraft Eng.	Industrials	Grow Inc
—V—				
Valmont	VMT	Equipment	Industrials	Aggr Gro
Varian Medical	VAR	Med. Devices	Health Care	Aggr Gro
Verizon	VZ	Communication	Telecomm Svcs	Grow Inc
Vulcan Materials Co.	VMC	Construction	Materials	Con Grow
—W—				
Walgreen	WAG	Drug Stores	Cons Staples	Aggr Gro
Wells Fargo	WFC	Divers Bank	Financials	Grow Inc

Abbott Laboratories

100 Abbott Park Road □ Abbott Park, IL 60064–6400 □ Phone: (847) 937–3923 □ Website: www.abbott.com
□ Ticker symbol: ABT □ Listed: NYSE □ S&P rating: A– □ Value Line financial strength rating: A++

Financial Highlights, Fiscal Year 2008

Net revenues for calendar 2008 rose 14 percent over 2007 to $19.4B against an earnings increase of 6.9 percent. Net margins, even at 16 percent, were at a ten-year low due primarily to acquisitions, litigation, and internal initiatives. Recent guidance from Abbott, however, has been for renewed double-digit increases in EPS throughout 2009, and indeed its 2008Q4 EPS was up 14 percent over the previous quarter.

The company grew cash flow by 6 percent while buying back over $1B worth of stock and reducing net debt. The company also initiated the purchase of eye surgery equipment maker Advanced Medical Optics and began construction of a $300M manufacturing facility in Singapore for the production of nutritional products. International sales revenues exceeded domestic revenues in 2008.

Dividends were up 11 percent on a largely flat share base, somewhat lessening the blow of a total net return of -18.3 percent due to general market weakness.

Company Profile

Abbott Laboratories, currently ranked at 80 in the *Fortune* 500, is one of the most diverse health-care manufacturers in the world. The company was founded in 1888 by Dr. Wallace C. Abbott and is headquartered in Chicago, Illinois. The company's products are sold in more than 130 countries, with about 40 percent of sales derived from international operations. ABT has paid consecutive quarterly dividends since 1924.

Abbott's major business segments include Diagnostic Products (laboratory and molecular diagnostics, diabetes and vision care), Vascular Products (stents and closure devices), Nutritional Products (infant, adult, and special needs), and Pharmaceuticals (particularly in immunology, cardiology, and infectious diseases).

The company's leading brands are:

- AxSym PRISM (blood analysis and screening)
- Freestyle (diabetes monitoring)
- Depakote (bipolar disorder; epilepsy; migraine prevention)
- Depakote ER (migraine prevention)
- Ensure (adult nutritionals)
- Humira (rheumatoid arthritis)
- Isomil (soy-based infant formula)
- Kaletra (HIV infection)
- MediSense glucose monitoring products
- PRISM (blood screening)
- Similac (infant formula)

- Synthroid (hypothyroidism)
- Tricor (a lipid-control agent)
- Vision / Xience V (bare and drug-releasing stents)

Reasons to Buy

Abbott's 17 percent increase in earnings compares very nicely against a sector where 2008 earnings overall were flat. They experienced growth in all four of their major markets, with highlights such as their line of stents, where sales increased 78 percent to $1.2B in 2008. Sales of their vascular products were up nearly 35 percent with very strong growth in the United States in particular.

Abbott has a very strong patent position, with only Depakote having recently gone off patent. Their blockbuster product, Humira, which saw sales up 48 percent in 2008 (to $4.5B) isn't due to come off patent until 2016. This is a product that addresses inflammatory diseases such as arthritis and which has recently shown great promise against Crohn's disease, which bodes well for continued sales into an aging demographic.

Their pipeline is in good shape, according to the CEO, with a number of products showing "breakthrough potential" in areas including oncology, neuroscience, and immunology. An asthma treatment and a drug for the treatment of psoriasis are both expected to hit approval phase in 2009.

Abbott has stated that they are planning to scale back on mergers and acquisitions and plan to generate a larger percentage of their growth going forward through internal development initiatives. Their most recent acquisition

of Advanced Medical Optics has given them a strong position in cataract treatment. Previous acquisitions brought Humira and their stent business into the fold, but Abbott feels they no longer need to pay a premium on acquisitions in order to meet their commitments.

Finally, Abbott has been one of the most reliable and stable growth stocks in the last twenty years. They have raised their dividend every year for the last thirty-six years while producing long-term (if somewhat cyclical) growth. They are particularly well-positioned at the moment, and especially so when compared to the overall sector, where several of their competitors are scheduled to lose patent protection on one or more of their star products.

Reasons for Caution

Looking at Abbott's near-term prospects, Neil A. Martin of *Barron's* writes, "(It) doesn't mean that double-digit growth is in the bag. The key will be to keep Humira hot. After all, that mainstay product been growing an average of 30 percent annually in recent years, nearly triple the growth of the rest of Abbott. There's some concern on Wall Street that the sales growth is unsustainable, that it will have to level off and then decline. It would certainly be hard to replicate Humira's recent growth with another product."

A number of lawsuits are ongoing against several major pharmaceutical manufacturers regarding what the plaintiffs perceive to be predatory pricing and artificial availability problems. The potential impact to the company is generally considered to be minor.

SECTOR: **Health Care**
BETA COEFFICIENT: **.55**
10-YEAR COMPOUND EARNINGS PER SHARE GROWTH: **7.5%**
10-YEAR COMPOUND DIVIDENDS PER SHARE GROWTH: **9.0%**

		2008	2007	2006	2005	2004	2003	2002	2001	2000
Revenues (Mil)		29,528	25,914	22,476	22,337	19,680	19,681	17,684	16,285	13,745
Net Income (Mil)		4,734	4,429	3,841	3,908	3,522	3,479	3,242	2,944	2,768
Earnings per share		3.03	2.84	2.52	2.50	2.27	2.21	2.06	1.88	1.78
Dividends per share		1.44	1.30	1.18	1.10	1.04	0.98	0.94	0.82	0.74
Price:	high	61.1	59.5	49.9	50.0	47.6	47.2	58.0	57.2	56.3
	low	45.8	48.8	39.2	37.5	38.3	33.8	29.8	42.0	29.4

AGGRESSIVE GROWTH

Air Products and Chemicals, Inc.

7201 Hamilton Boulevard □ Allentown, PA 18195–1501 □ Phone: (610) 481–5775 □ Website: www.
airproducts.com □ Listed: NYSE □ Fiscal year ends September 30 □ Ticker symbol: APD □ S&P rating: A □
Value Line financial strength rating: A

Financial Highlights, Fiscal Year 2008

APD's sales were up 14 percent to $10.4B, while income rose 16 percent to $1.1B. Growth was led by their merchant gases and tonnage gases segments, which were up 21 and 13 percent respectively. A fire in their electronics plant as well as a weak fourth quarter negatively impacted revenues from that operation. Dividends rose 15 percent to $1.70, and the company repurchased 2.8 percent of its shares. Income and diluted earnings per share from continuing operations increased 7 percent and 9 percent, respectively.

On January 3, 2008, Air Products sold its high-purity chemicals business to KMG chemicals for $75 million. The unit generated $87 million in sales in 2007.

On July 1, APD announced the final sale of its polymer emulsions business to Ashland Oil of Covington, Kentucky, for $92 million. The unit generated sales of $126 million in 2007.

Also in July, the company took a total charge of $329 million ($1.12/share) related to the impairment of its health-care segment, anticipating its eventual sale at a realizable value.

Company Profile

Air Products and Chemicals sells gases such as hydrogen, helium, nitrogen, and oxygen to industrial manufacturers and commercial end-users worldwide. Gases are vital inputs to many manufacturing processes, and APD is one of the largest global bulk gas sellers. For large customers, APD will put one of its own plants next to the customers' factory and supply gas directly via pipeline. The company operates in over 40 countries and now derives nearly 60 percent of its sales from outside the United States.

After the Q1 2008 divestiture of the Chemicals business, APD reports revenues in four segments:

- Merchant Gases—Industrial and medical customers throughout the world use oxygen, nitrogen, argon, helium, hydrogen, and medical and specialty gases for a wide array of applications. APD supplies most merchant gas in liquid form to small and larger customers delivered via tanker trucks and rail cars. APD provides smaller quantities of "packaged" gases in cylinders and dewars for customers who require smaller quantities for their processes.
- Tonnage Gases—Air Products supplies hydrogen, carbon monoxide, synthesis gas, nitrogen, and oxygen via large on-site facilities or pipeline systems to meet the needs of large-volume, or "tonnage" industrial gas users. AP either constructs a gas plant adjacent to or near the customer's facility or delivers product through a pipeline from a nearby location. They also design and manufacture cryogenic and gas processing equipment for air separation, hydrocarbon recovery and purification, natural gas liquefaction (LNG), and helium distribution equipment.
- Electronics and Performance Materials—This segment spe-

cializes in delivery of products relevant to the electronics industry. APD's products in this segment enable the manufacture of silicon, semiconductors, displays, and photovoltaic devices. They specialize in low-k dielectrics, which play a big part in shrinking semiconductor geometries. The segment also provides performance chemical solutions for the coatings, inks, adhesives, civil engineering, personal care, institutional and industrial cleaning, mining, oil field, polyurethane, and other industries.

- Equipment and Energy—Designs and sells equipment for energy production, and also partially owns and operates several small energy plants around the world. Equipment is sold worldwide to customers in a variety of industries, including chemical and petrochemical manufacturing, oil and gas recovery and processing, and steel and primary metals processing. Energy markets are served through the company's operation and partial ownership of cogeneration and flue gas treatment facilities. The company is developing technologies to continue to serve energy markets in the future, including gasification and alternative energy technologies.

Reasons to Buy

APD's business has been more diversified and less tied to the steady delivery of gas than some of the competition, and their liquidation of several of their business segments over the last few years has created some setbacks. Now that the company is finding its focus, we expect them to recover more quickly than they might have otherwise.

The company remains committed to its goal of achieving 17 percent margin by 2010, and is taking various cost-cutting steps to get there.

Incremental project starts in 2009 should add $500M in top-line growth, or an estimated $.35/share.

Reasons for Caution

The first half of 2009 has been a rough start, with earnings down 22 percent. Look for improvement in this key measure before considering the turnaround to have begun.

SECTOR: **Materials**
BETA COEFFICIENT: **1.10**
10-YEAR COMPOUND EARNINGS PER SHARE GROWTH: **8.0%**
10-YEAR COMPOUND DIVIDENDS PER SHARE GROWTH: **10.0%**

		2008	2007	2006	2005	2004	2003	2002	2001	2000
Revenues (Mil)		10,415	10,038	8,850	7,768	7,411	6,297	5,401	5,858	5,467
Net Income (Mil)		1,091	1,036	723	712	604	397	525	466	533
Earnings per share		4.97	4.40	3.18	3.08	2.64	1.78	2.42	2.12	2.46
Dividends per share		1.70	1.52	1.34	1.25	1.04	0.88	0.82	0.78	0.74
Price	high	106.1	105.0	72.4	65.8	59.2	53.1	53.5	49.0	42.2
	low	41.5	68.6	58.0	53.0	46.7	37.0	40.0	32.2	23.0

Alexander & Baldwin

822 Bishop Street □ Honolulu, HI 96813-3924 □ Phone: (808) 525–6611 □ Fax: (808) 525–6652 □ Website: www.alexanderbaldwin.com □ Listed: NASDAQ □ Ticker symbol: ALEX □ S&P Rating: BBB+ □ Value Line financial strength rating: B+

Financial Highlights, Fiscal Year 2008

Helped by sales in the company's Keola La'I condominium project, 2008 operating revenue increased 14 percent, or $229 million, to $1,898 million. However, that figure overstates the current economic picture, which is hurt by the global recession in real estate and shipping. Shipping volumes and pricing are down, although off of their lows. Net income was flat from 2007 and is expected to decline again in 2009 but should rebound in 2010. The company's vast Hawaiian sugar plantations are selling sugar at a loss because of draught and market conditions; the future of this relatively smaller business segment is unclear.

Cash flow remains strong at some $5.68 per share vs. $3.19 in earnings per share in 2008; the implied price to cash flow ratio is a healthy 6.7 based on projected 2009 cash flow and the mid-2009 share price of $23.40. The dividend of $1.24 gives a healthy yield of 5.3 percent.

Company Profile

An old Hawaiian company with origins dating back to the missionary days of the 1830s, Alexander & Baldwin, Inc., together with its subsidiaries, operates in ocean transportation, real estate, and agribusiness. The company offers container ship freight services primarily between the ports of the U.S. Pacific Coast, Hawaii, Guam, China, and other Pacific Islands, the most apparent of which is under the wholly owned subsidiary Matson Lines.

The company operates some of the fastest container ships in the Pacific Rim; it also has subsidiaries specializing in logistics, stevedoring, and port services in Hawaii but also in China and on the U.S. mainland. The transportation business accounted for 72 percent of revenue, 49 percent of profit, and 52 percent of assets in 2008.

The real estate subsidiaries develop and sell residential and commercial property primarily in Hawaii, currently owning over 89,000 acres in the state. In 2008 the real estate business accounted for 23 percent of revenue, 56 percent of profit, and 40 percent of assets. The agribusiness segment specializes in sugar and the production, marketing, and distribution of coffee, and represents a relatively small share of the company's business at 6 percent of revenue.

Reasons to Buy

Alexander & Baldwin is a long-term play on the continued growth and importance of trans-Pacific shipping, combined with the growth and value of Hawaiian real estate and agriculture. An economic recovery, apparently already underway, should bode well for transportation, logistics, and eventually, real estate operations. The company, while hardly in recession- or competition-proof businesses, has well defined niches both in its transportation and Hawaiian real estate activities.

The strong cash flow thrown off by all three operations bode well for investors interested in cash returns and dividends. Looking at historical share prices, 2009 seems to build in the worst of recessionary scenarios; the company could rebound well with the economy; the dividend and cash flow are pluses.

Reasons for Caution

The global downturn has hurt pricing, revenues, margins, and profits in the transportation business. Additionally, competition is fierce in most of the transportation markets the company serves. The real estate business is also soft and dependent on the more-or-less cyclical Hawaiian economy. As of mid-2009, S&P had a negative credit watch on the company.

SECTOR: **Transportation**
BETA COEFFICIENT: **1.46**
10-YEAR COMPOUND EARNINGS PER SHARE GROWTH: **4.0%**
10-YEAR COMPOUND DIVIDENDS PER SHARE GROWTH: **8.0%**

	2008	2007	2006	2005	2004	2003	2002	2001	2000
Revenues (Mil)	1,898	1,681	1,607	1,606	1,494	1,232	1,089	1,064	1,069
Net Income (Mil)	132.0	142.0	122.0	118.7	101.0	81.0	58.2	67.6	78.3
Earnings per share	3.19	3.30	2.81	2.70	2.33	1.94	1.41	1.44	1.91
Dividends per share	1.24	1.12	0.90	0.90	0.90	0.90	0.90	0.90	0.90
Price high	53.5	59.4	54.9	56.1	44.7	34.6	29.3	29.6	28.3
low	20.6	44.2	39.3	36.8	29.0	23.5	20.5	20.5	17.9

Apache Corporation

One Post Oak Central □ 2000 Post Oak Boulevard □ Suite 100 □ Houston, TX 77056–4400 □ Phone: (713) 296–6662 □ Website: www.apachecorp.com □ Listed: NYSE □ Ticker symbol: APA □ S&P rating: A- □ Value Line financial strength rating: A

Financial Highlights, Fiscal Year 2008

Apache's 2008 was another in a six-year run of record earnings, up 24.1 percent over 2007 to $12.4B, while earnings also hit record levels of $3.91B, up 39.1 percent. The company ended the year with over $1.8B in working capital.

Capital spending increased by 21.8 percent on a per-share basis to a record-high $15.81 as the company has leveraged the recent record commodity prices into increased production capability and exploration. The company also exited the year with a 20 percent increase in long-term debt, and lower energy prices reduced operating margins approximately 30 percent compared to the most recent five-year trend.

Company Profile

Established in 1954 with $250,000 of investor capital, Apache Corporation has grown to become one of the world's top independent oil and gas exploration and production companies with $155 billion in assets.

Apache's domestic operations are focused in some of the nation's most important producing basins, including the Outer Continental Shelf of the Gulf of Mexico, the Anadarko Basin of Oklahoma, the Permian Basin of West Texas and New Mexico,

the Texas-Louisiana Gulf Coast, and East Texas.

In Canada, Apache is active in British Columbia, Alberta, Saskatchewan, and the Northwest Territories. The company also has exploration and production operations in Australia's offshore Carnarvon, Perth, and Gippsland basins; Egypt's Western Desert; the United Kingdom sector of the North Sea; China; and Argentina.

Apache's strategy is built on a portfolio of assets that provide opportunities to grow through both grassroots drilling and acquisition activities. The company has seven core areas—two in the United States, and in Canada, Egypt, the United Kingdom sector of the North Sea, Australia, and Argentina.

The company's portfolio also is balanced in terms of gas versus oil, geologic risk, reserve life, and political risk.

Natural gas now represents 53 percent of production, while oil is 47 percent—a balanced product mix that provides upside potential in either market. Each core area has significant producing assets and large undeveloped acreage to provide running room for the future, but no single region contributes more than 25 percent of production or reserves. In each core area, the company's goal is to build critical mass that supports sustainable, lower-risk, repeatable drilling opportunities, balanced by higher-risk, higher-reward exploration.

Apache has increased reserves in each of the last twenty-one years and production in twenty-seven of the last twenty-eight years. Management believes the company's portfolio of assets provides a platform for profitable growth through drilling and acquisitions across the cycles of the industry.

Reasons to Buy

After several years of stellar growth, 2009 projects to be a dismal year for Apache. Revenues will likely be off as much as 45 percent versus 2008, with earnings down as much as 75 percent. We like the stock's potential in 2010, however, as the company is still in a strong cash position and has continued to explore and develop new oil and gas finds throughout 2008 and early 2009.

The company has leveraged the revenues from the run-up in the commodities to develop a large number of quality exploration projects, including one of the largest gas-shale deposits in North America.

The oil exploration and production sector overall is expected by many analysts to rebound in the second half of 2009 and even more strongly in first-half 2010. Apache appears to be well positioned to capitalize on a healthier worldwide economy with its well-balanced portfolio of businesses and its significant holdings in natural gas.

Reasons for Caution

Looking out to 2011, there is potential for oversupply in the world natural gas market. Apache's largest revenue stream is in gas and liquefied natural gas (LNG) products, so any significant reduction in margins in this sector will have a real impact on Apache's bottom line.

SECTOR: **Energy**
BETA COEFFICIENT: **1.15**
10-YEAR COMPOUND EARNINGS PER SHARE GROWTH: **32%**
10-YEAR COMPOUND DIVIDENDS PER SHARE GROWTH: **15%**

	2008	2007	2006	2005	2004	2003	2002	2001	2000
Revenues (Mil)	12,389	9,978	8,289	7,584	5,333	4,190	2.560	2,791	2,291
Net Income (Mil)	3,912	2,812	2,552	2,618	1,670	1,246	566	764	721
Earnings per share	11.65	8.39	7.64	7.84	5.03	3.74	1.84	2.50	2.48
Dividends per share	0.60	0.60	0.50	0.36	0.26	0.22	0.19	0.17	0.09
Price high	149.2	109.3	76.2	78.2	52.2	41.7	28.9	31.5	32.1
low	57.1	63.0	56.5	47.4	36.8	26.3	21.1	16.6	13.9

Apple Inc.

1 Infinite Loop □ Cupertino, CA 95014 □ Phone: (408) 996–1010 □ Website: www.apple.com □ Listed: NASDAQ □ Ticker symbol: AAPL □ Value Line financial strength rating: A++

Financial Highlights, Fiscal Year 2008

Apple turned in another year of stellar numbers, with net sales up 35 percent, gross margin up 30 basis points or 0.3 percent to 34.3 percent, net income up 38.2 percent to $4.83B, and net margin also up 30 basis points to 14.9 percent.

At first glance, one might think that the ubiquitous iPods and iPhones led the charge in 2008, but in fact the iMac was the boss in unit growth, up 38 percent versus the iPod's 35 percent. In fact, the best overall unit growth was in Mac units sold at retail, up 47 percent. This helps to explain the profitability of the business, as earnings per Mac sold are higher than the retail price of many iPods. The iPod still leads in total revenue, with just over $9B in total sales.

Company Profile

Apple Inc. designs, manufactures, and markets personal computers, portable music players, cell phones, and related software, peripherals, and services. It sells these products through its retail stores, online stores, its sales force, and third-party and value-added resellers. The company also retails a variety of third-party compatible products such as printer, storage devices, and other accessories through its online and re- tail stores, and digital content through its iTunes store.

The company's products have become household names: iMac, iPhone, iPod, and MacBook are some of the company's hardware products, and while the software may be less well known, iTunes, QuickTime, and OSX are important segments of the business with their own revenue streams.

The company was incorpo- rated in 1977 by Steve Wozniak and Steve Jobs as Apple Computer, Inc. Thirty years later, Apple Computer, Inc. officially changed their name to Apple Inc., but by that time they had already sold their 100 millionth iPod, and iTunes was doing $1.2 billion in revenue with an estimated 10 per- cent operating margin. Their days as a computer company were certainly not over, but the name change was a tacit acknowledgment that the com- pany had fundamentally changed its business.

Prior to the release of the origi- nal iMac in 1998, the company had differentiated its computer products from the more popular Windows- based PCs by touting their ease of use and the stability of their proprietary operating system. The iMac, how- ever, marked a significant change in Apple's overall product strategy with its emphasis on industrial design. Whereas the PCs of the time were, by-and-large, dull beige boxes, the iMac was a bulbous, rounded shape that came only in colors never seen in the computer business before—neon orange, blood red, and mint green, among others. And ten years later, ever since the introduction of the iMac, every successful Apple product has been characterized by a compelling and state-of-the-art industrial design. This is what sets Apple apart, and makes them perhaps the only "luxury" brand in the consumer electronics business.

Reasons to Buy

In 1997, many people didn't think much of Apple's prospects. Michael Dell, CEO of Dell Computer said that if he ran Apple he would "shut it down and give the money back to the shareholders." Ten years later, Apple's market cap exceeded that of Dell, who had had a pretty good decade themselves. Never discount the value of "cool."

It's hard to put a price on "cool," but Apple has certainly been able to probe the limits of the concept with $300 MP3 players, $600 phones, and, even now, $5000 personal computers. There seems to be very little that Apple cannot charge hefty premiums for, as long as customers feel they're getting the coolest product on the planet for the task at hand.

Make no mistake, the numbers here are great—net margins that a pharmaceutical company would envy, skyrocketing EPS, zero debt, and more cash in the bank than Exxon. But what you're really investing in here is a brand, and just maybe one of the best brands in the history of brands.

Reasons for Caution

Apple's products, even with their "gotta-have-it" factor, are discretionary items, and the recession has cut into personal spending budgets. A company like Apple must also watch its back for competition, although not much has surfaced to take the luster off of Apple products just yet. Apple's recent release of the latest iPhone at a $99 price point may be a portent of lower top-line growth for some time.

SECTOR: **Consumer Discretionary**
BETA COEFFICIENT: **1.15**
10-YEAR COMPOUND EARNINGS PER SHARE GROWTH: **27%**
10-YEAR COMPOUND DIVIDENDS PER SHARE GROWTH: **NIL**

		2008	2007	2006	2005	2004	2003	2002	2001	2000
Revenues (Mil)		32,479	24,006	19,315	13,931	8,279	6,207	5,742	5,363	7,983
Net Income (Mil)		4,834	3,496	1,989	1,254	276	76	117	83	611
Earnings per share		5.36	3.93	2.27	1.44	0.36	0.20	0.17	0.14	0.85
Dividends per share		Nil--------								
Price	high	200.3	203.0	93.2	75.5	34.8	12.5	13.1	13.6	37.6
	low	79.1	81.9	50.2	31.3	10.6	6.4	6.7	7.2	6.8

CONSERVATIVE GROWTH

Archer Daniels Midland Co.

4666 Faries Parkway, Box 1470 ▫ Decatur, IL 62525 ▫ Phone: (217) 424–5200 ▫ Website: www.admworld.com ▫ Listed: NYSE ▫ Ticker symbol: ADM ▫ S&P rating: A ▫ Value Line financial strength rating: B++

Financial Highlights, Fiscal Year 2008

ADM's revenues jumped 57 percent last year as a combination of factors worked to drive up the price of foodstuffs to record highs. One of those factors was the cost of fuels, which was good news for ADM's ethanol business, but which played havoc with ADM's extensive transportation network. Operating margin fell 160 basis points or 1.6 percent to 4.6 percent and earnings were up only 17 percent, trailing far behind the revenue gains.

The company announced plans to continue its capital investments, approving $2.5B in capital spending over the next five years. Over the past five years, the company has spent $5.3B on new construction, expansions, and acquisitions.

Company Profile

ADM is one of the largest food processors in the world. They buy corn, wheat, cocoa, oilseeds, and other agricultural products and process them into food, food ingredients, animal feed and ingredients, and biofuels. They also resell grains on the open market.

The company owns and maintains facilities used throughout the production process. They source raw materials from sixty countries on six continents, transport them to any of their 230 processing plants via their own transportation network of 2,100 trailers, 2,200 barges, and 23,800 railcars, and then transport the finished products to the customer.

The company operates in three business segments: Oilseeds Processing, Corn Processing, and Agricultural Services.

Oilseeds Processing processes seeds such as soybeans, cottonseed, sunflower, canola, peanuts, and flaxseed into vegetable oils and protein meals for the food and feed industries. Crude vegetable oils are sold as is or are further refined into salad oils, margarine, and other food products. Partially refined oils are sold for use in paints, chemicals, and other industrial products, such as biodiesel fuel.

The solids remaining from this processing are sold into a number of applications, including edible soy protein, animal feed, pharmaceuticals, chemical, and paper.

The Corn Processing segment is engaged in wet and dry milling operations primarily in the United States. Food products from this processing are too numerous to list, but include syrup, starch, glucose, dextrose, and other sweeteners. The corn gluten and meal is sold into the animal feeds market, and the corn germ is further processed as an oilseed into vegetable oil and protein meal. Fermenting the dextrose further yields alcohol, amino acids, and other specialty food and feed products. The alcohol is processed for beverage stock or for industrial use as ethanol, the base for ethanol-blended gasolines and other fuels.

The Agricultural Services segment is the company's storage and transportation network. This operation does pretty much everything other than the actual milling and processing. They buy, store, clean, and transport grains to/from ADM facilities. They sell raw beans for use as a food ingredient and are also engaged in the resale of raw materials primarily for the animal feed and agricultural processing industries.

Reasons to Buy

The worldwide corn explosion popped ADM's share price in 2008 to an all-time high, but commodity prices have since waned and ADM is trading off 50 percent from its 2008 peak. Still, soybean prices have rebounded and are rising as soy protein demand from China continues to grow. Many farmers in the United States converted production from soy to corn last year when prices were "high as an elephant's eye," but ADM bought large quantities of soy futures from Brazil and other sources and is now reaping the benefits.

Last year's revenue surge was not a flash in the pan, as projections for 2009–2010 are for 3–4 percent annual top-line growth. As fuel prices

have moderated in the meantime, both operating and net margins are expected to improve and will drive improved earnings.

Drought conditions in Argentina have significantly curtailed its corn output, making for higher prices for ADM's main cash producer.

ADM is by far the most efficient major processor. Cargill, the industry leader, had revenues in 2008 nearly twice ADM's, but produced total earnings only 15 percent higher than ADM's.

Reasons for Caution

China has said that they will not use corn-based ethanol as a fuel adjunct. It's not clear if this decision is driven by business policy or foreign policy, but the upshot is that for now ADM and others cannot count on a piece of the burgeoning Chinese fuel market. Corn-based ethanol has also proven somewhat unpopular on the home front, but the company is well-positioned to be a leader in the bio-fuels industry whatever the preferred fuel ends up being.

SECTOR: **Consumer Staples**
BETA COEFFICIENT: **1.0**
10-YEAR COMPOUND EARNINGS PER SHARE GROWTH: **11.50%**
10-YEAR COMPOUND DIVIDENDS PER SHARE GROWTH: **11.0%**

		2008	2007	2006	2005	2004	2003	2002	2001	2000
Revenues (Mil)		69,816	44,018	36,596	35,944	36,151	30,708	23,454	20,051	12,877
Net Income (Mil)		1,834	1,561	1,312	921	744	438	458	383	300
Earnings per share		2.84	2.38	2.00	1.40	1.16	.68	.70	.58	.45
Dividends per share		.49	.43	.37	.32	.27	.24	.20	.19	.18
Price	high	48.9	47.3	46.7	25.5	22.5	15.2	14.9	15.8	14.5
	low	13.5	30.2	24.0	17.5	14.9	10.5	10.0	10.2	7.8

GROWTH AND INCOME

AT&T Inc.

175 East Houston □ San Antonio, TX 78205 □ Phone: (210) 821–4105 □ Dividend reinvestment plan available □ Website: www.att.com □ Ticker symbol: T □ Listed: NYSE □ S&P rating: B+ □ Value Line financial strength rating: A+

Financial Highlights, Fiscal Year 2008

The company reported consolidated revenues of $124B, an increase of 4 percent. Earnings per share grew 11.3 percent to $2.16, although net margins fell 25 percent to 10.4 percent. Cash flow grew 2 percent and the company's overall financial strength is good, but its debt load is significantly higher than its recent average due to the acquisitions of Cingular and the old AT&T Corp. The company has, for the moment, shelved plans to repurchase the additional shares arising from the acquisitions and will instead concentrate on reducing the debt load and improving operating margins.

Dividends increased 10 percent to $1.61, adding to the company's record of increasing quarterly dividends for twenty-five consecutive years. The total return to shareholders through dividends and share repurchase came to $15.6B.

The company added more wireless subscribers in 2008 than any other U.S. carrier. The rollout of the Apple iPhone 3G added 4.3M new subscribers, 40 percent of whom were new customers to AT&T. Overall, wireless data revenues grew 52.5 percent to $10.5B, solidifying the company's position in a rapidly growing and high-margin market.

Company Profile

By revenue, AT&T Inc. is the largest communications holding company in the United States and worldwide. Operating globally under the AT&T brand, AT&T is recognized as the leading worldwide provider of IP-based (Internet) communications services to businesses and the leading

U.S. provider of wireless, high speed Internet access; local and long distance voice; and directory publishing and advertising services. Its traditional (SBC only) wireline subsidiaries provide services in 13 states, including California, Texas, Illinois, Michigan, Ohio, Missouri, Connecticut, Indiana, Wisconsin, Oklahoma, Kansas, Arkansas, and Nevada.

They have approximately 47 million total Consumer Revenue Connections, with a sales revenue mix of 30 percent voice, 20 percent data, 4 percent directory advertising, and 46 percent wireless and other.

As part of its "three screen (television/data/voice)" integration strategy, AT&T is expanding video entertainment offerings to include such next-generation television services as AT&T U-verse TV.

Researchers and engineers at AT&T Labs have developed some of the world's major technological inventions, including the transistor, the solar cell, the cell phone, and the communications satellite. These groundbreaking technologies have enabled today's computers and electronic devices, wireless phones and VoIP.

AT&T Labs has been an industry leader in the development of DSL and other broadband Internet transport and delivery systems, wireless data networks, and new technologies and applications for networking and enterprise business needs. AT&T's predecessor companies pioneered new technologies and developed promising new products and services in a wide range of areas, including IP network management and VoIP.

Reasons to Buy

In the telecom infrastructure arena, size matters, and AT&T is the largest provider of local and long-distance voice services in the United States. They are also the largest wireless carrier in the United States and one of the largest in the world. AT&T is also the largest provider of Wi-Fi and broadband services in the United States and is one of the largest providers of IP-based communications services for businesses. They own their own global network backbone (a critical advantage in both voice and data) and are currently the only licensed wireless carrier for the iPhone and iPhone 3G.

Their aggressive roll-out of U-Verse has gone better than many had expected and is on or ahead of schedule in most geographies. This is a groundbreaking product for AT&T and will play a critical role in the future of the company's consumer presence. With it, they can gracefully transition their existing voice/DSL customers off of baseband and onto a high-speed link that delivers interactive voice, data, and television. Competitively priced, this effectively locks out cable and at the same time provides AT&T with a platform to capture additional revenues from cable and satellite television services. The next two years should yield very positive results from this initiative.

In the commercial space, they operate one of the largest VoIP (voice traffic over the Internet) networks in the world and can offer seamless integration as new/improved services appear, such as their recent introduction of high-definition video conferencing.

Reasons for Caution

AT&T's older wireline services, while critical to the U-Verse rollout, have been under pressure for the better part of a decade. The company has broad cost-cutting plans (likely including layoffs) in place and believes that synergies related to recent acquisitions will relieve the situation somewhat.

SECTOR: **Telecommunications Services**
BETA COEFFICIENT: **0.75**
10-YEAR COMPOUND EARNINGS PER SHARE GROWTH: **3%**
10-YEAR COMPOUND DIVIDENDS PER SHARE GROWTH: **4.5%**

		2008	2007	2006	2005	2004	2003	2002	2001	2000
Revenues (Mil)		124,028	118,928	63,055	43,862	40,787	40,843	51,755	54,301	53,313
Net Income (Mil)		12,867	16,950	9,014	5,803	4,884	5,051	7,219	7,972	7,746
Earnings per share		1.94	1.89	1.72	1.47	1.52	2.16	2.35	2.26	2.15
Dividends per share		1.42	1.33	1.29	1.25	1.37	1.07	1.02	1.01	0.98
Price	high	41.9	43.0	36.2	26.0	27.7	31.7	41.0	53.1	59.0
	low	20.9	32.7	24.2	21.8	23.0	18.8	19.6	36.5	34.8

Baxter International, Inc.

1 Baxter Parkway ▢ Deerfield, IL 60015 ▢ Website: www.baxter.com ▢ Listed: NYSE ▢ Ticker symbol: BAX ▢ S&P rating: A+ ▢ Value Line financial strength rating: A++

Financial Highlights, Fiscal Year 2008

Baxter had record sales and earnings in 2008, with sales up 10 percent to $12.3B and earnings up 18 percent to $2.2B. Per-share earnings jumped 21 percent to $3.16. The sales improvements were spread across product lines and geographies, but were particularly strong for the ADVATE hemophilia treatment and its GAMMAGARD treatment for auto-immune deficiencies. Earnings increases are attributed to higher sales, gross margin improvements, reduced SG&A, and a lower tax rate, even as R&D was increased 14 percent to a record $868M.

The company spent $2.0B to repurchase 32 million shares of common stock and over the last two years has increased dividends by a compounded 56 percent (20 percent in 2008).

Recently, the company purchased a 40 percent stake in Sigma International for $100M, including three-year exclusive rights for the distribution of Sigma's infusion pump. The deal also includes provisions for the possible purchase of the remaining 60 percent of the company.

Company Profile

Baxter International develops, manufactures, and markets biopharmaceuticals, drug delivery systems, and medical equipment. Their products are used to treat patients with hemophilia, immune deficiencies, infectious diseases, cancer, kidney disease, and other disorders. Based in the United States, Baxter has operations in over 100 countries and operates in three main segments: Bioscience, Medication Delivery, and Renal.

Bioscience produces pharmaceuticals derived from blood plasma. The bulk of the product line is devoted to treatments for hemophilia and its complications. Their ADVATE product is widely used for the control and prevention of bleeding episodes. The company also produces a variety of vaccines with its proprietary Vero cell technology.

Medication Delivery produces a wide range of equipment used to apply, inject, infuse, and otherwise deliver medications to the patient. If it comes in contact with the medication, Baxter probably makes it. Tubes, pumps, valves, syringes, and filters are some of the typical product lines in MD. The company also sells IV solutions and premixed drugs, as well as anesthetics.

Renal is dedicated to the treatment of patients with kidney failure who are undergoing peritoneal dialysis treatment. They supply a range of products, including home PD machines and all of the accessories and disposables associated with them, as well as equipment and supplies for clinical dialysis facilities.

Product sales are split fairly evenly between the United States and Europe (40 percent each), with the rest of world making up the balance.

Reasons to Buy

Baxter's product line, consisting mainly of treatments for chronic, life-threatening conditions, is largely immune to the vagaries of the global economy and capital markets. Its broad geographic base and high market penetrations offer further protection against smaller, local competition.

The company's ADVATE product continues to gain momentum and reached sales of $1.5B in 2008. It now holds leadership position in the United States, Europe, Japan, and several other markets.

In December 2008, the company's CELVAPAN product was given a positive opinion by the European regulatory authorities, the first cell culture–based vaccine for use against the H5N1 virus (avian flu). The advantage of a cell culture–based product over the conventional egg-based technology is that it can be produced in quantity much more quickly, which is critical when responding to a potential pandemic. Phase III trials are ongoing.

The company's solid capital structure and cash flow bode well for continued growth through selective acquisitions, and the company's recent commitments to share repurchase and dividend appreciation should be well-funded.

Reasons for Caution

The company had to recall an infusion pump product for redesign. Although the licensing agreement with Sigma provides an acceptable replacement product, it's not yet clear whether the company will have to take an impairment in 2009 on the recalled product.

SECTOR: **Health Care**
BETA COEFFICIENT: **0.6**
10-YEAR COMPOUND EARNINGS PER SHARE GROWTH: **9.0%**
10-YEAR COMPOUND DIVIDENDS PER SHARE GROWTH: **2.5%**

		2008	2007	2006	2005	2004	2003	2002	2001	2000
Revenues (Mil)		12,348	11,263	10,378	9,849	9,509	8,916	8,110	7,663	6,896
Net Income (Mil)		2,155	1,826	1,464	958	1,040	922	1,188	1,063	915
Earnings per share		2.86	3.33	3.21	2.71	2.07	2.01	1.81	1.56	1.38
Dividends per share		0.91	0.72	0.58	0.58	0.58	0.58	0.58	0.58	0.58
Price	high	71.5	61.1	48.5	41.1	34.8	31.3	59.9	55.9	45.1
	low	47.4	46.1	35.1	33.1	27.1	18.2	24.1	40.1	25.9

Becton, Dickinson and Company

1 Becton Drive □ Franklin Lakes, NJ 07417–1880 □ Phone: (201) 847–5453 □ Website: www.bd.com □
Fiscal year ends September 30 □ Listed: NYSE □ Ticker symbol: BDX □ S&P rating: A □ Value Line financial
strength rating: A++

Financial Highlights, Fiscal Year 2008

The company reported year over year growth in earnings of 32 percent (to $1.12B), far outpacing the increase in revenue of 12.5 percent (to $7.12B). Earnings per share were up 33 percent to $4.46, giving the company its fifth consecutive record year in these three categories.

Dividends were up 16.3 percent to $1.14, continuing a string of thirty-six consecutive years of dividend increases. Dividends per share have grown 180 percent in just five years.

The growth in revenues was broad-based across all the company's organizational units. Their Pharmaceutical Systems unit led with a 19 percent increase, but no single unit grew revenue less than 6 percent.

Company Profile

Becton, Dickinson is a medical technology company that serves health-care institutions, life science researchers, clinical laboratories, industry, and the general public. BD manufactures and sells a broad range of medical supplies, devices, laboratory equipment, and diagnostic products.

Becton, Dickinson focuses strategically on achieving growth in three worldwide business segments: BD Medical (formerly BD Medical Systems), BD Biosciences, and BD Diagnostics (formerly BD Clinical Laboratory Solutions).

BD products are marketed in the United States both through independent distribution channels and directly to end-users. Outside the United States, BD products are marketed through independent distribution channels and sales representatives and, in some markets, directly to end-users.

BD generates close to 50 percent of its revenues outside the United States. Worldwide demand for health-care products and services continues to be strong, despite the ongoing focus on cost containment. The health-care environment favors continued growth in medical delivery systems due in large part to the costs associated with accidents affecting both the patient and caregiver when services are provided.

BD Biosciences (17 percent of sales), one of the world's largest businesses serving the life sciences, provides research tools and reagents to study life—from normal processes to disease states—and accelerate the pace of biomedical discovery. Throughout the world, clinicians and researchers use BD Biosciences' tools to study genes, proteins, and cells to better understand disease, improve technologies for diagnosis and disease management, and facilitate the discovery and development of novel therapeutics.

BD Diagnostics (30 percent of sales) offers system solutions for collecting, identifying, and transporting specimens, as well as advanced instrumentation for quickly and accurately analyzing specimens. The business also provides services that focus on customers' process flow, supply chain management, and training and education.

BD Medical (53 percent of sales) holds leadership positions in hypodermic needles and syringes, infusion therapy devices, insulin injection systems, and pre-fillable drug-delivery systems for pharmaceutical companies. It offers the industry's broadest, deepest line of safety-engineered sharps products, as well as surgical and regional anesthesia, ophthalmology, critical care, and sharps disposal products.

Reasons to Buy

Erik A. Antonson of Value Line has given Becton, Dickinson their highest rating for timeliness and notes that, "Due to recent price momentum and favorable earnings comparisons, they ought to outperform the broader market in the year ahead. Long-term price appreciation is good relative to the stock's historic averages. The issue also receives our top Safety rank, and the dividend only sweetens the pot."

The company has recently announced an additional 10 million-share buyback program, making the total number of shares available for buyback 15.9 million. The current share base is down some 16 million (to 243M) from FY2001 levels.

The company continues to reinvest in itself, spending nearly $1B in 2008 on capital investments and R&D. This is a continuation of a long-term strategy that they have implemented well, and their dedication to maintaining it speaks to their confidence in their current position. Their five-year CAGR is 18.9 percent, compared to the S&P 500 at 5.2 percent and the S&P Health Care Equipment Index at 7.2 percent.

Operating margins have been basically flat for the most recent four years, but the company continues to do more with less, as returns on revenues, assets, and equity all show healthy gains over the same period.

SECTOR: **Health Care**
BETA COEFFICIENT: **.65**
10-YEAR COMPOUND EARNINGS PER SHARE GROWTH: **12.5%**
10-YEAR COMPOUND DIVIDENDS PER SHARE GROWTH: **14.5%**

		2008	2007	2006	2005	2004	2003	2002	2001	2000
Revenues (Mil)		7,156	6,560	5,835	5,415	4,935	4,528	4,033	3,746	3,618
Net Income (Mil)		1,128	978	841	692	582	547	480	402	393
Earnings per share		4.46	3.84	3.28	2.66	2.21	2.07	1.79	1.63	1.49
Dividends per share		1.14	0.98	0.86	0.72	0.60	0.40	0.39	0.38	0.37
Price	high	93.2	85.9	74.2	61.2	58.2	41.8	38.6	39.3	35.3
	low	58.1	69.3	58.1	49.7	40.2	28.8	24.7	30.0	21.8

The Boeing Company

100 North Riverside ▫ Chicago, IL 60606 ▫ Phone: (312) 544–2140 ▫ Website: www.boeing.com ▫ Ticker symbol: BA ▫ Listed: NYSE ▫ S&P rating: B+ ▫ Value Line financial strength rating: A+

Financial Highlights, Fiscal Year 2008

The company reported sales $60.9B, a year/year decrease of 9 percent, with an accompanying decrease in earnings of 35 percent to $2.65B. Earnings per share fell 31 percent, though the dividend increased 11 percent.

The primary cause for the falloff in sales was a labor strike that halted shipments to Boeing's commercial customers for a two-month period in late 2008. Prior to the strike the company was on pace to exceed the prior year's sales and earnings, and estimates of the financial impact of the work stoppage range from $1.5–$2.0B in FY2008/FY2009 earnings.

The company is also recovering from an $8.6B charge to share equity due to downturns in the value of its pension assets and the expected returns on those assets. Combined with a $2.9B expenditure for stock repurchase, the company's net worth went negative, leading to a downgrading of its financial strength rating from A++ to A+, but the company assures that this is a temporary situation and that it is at no risk of default on its obligations.

Worldwide, Boeing forecasts a $2.8 trillion market for new commercial airplanes during the next twenty years and projects a need for approximately 28,600 new commercial airplanes (passenger and freighter), doubling the world fleet by 2026. The vast majority of these new airplanes will be in the single-aisle (ninety seats and above) and twin-aisle (200–400 seats) categories.

Company Profile

The Boeing Company is a leading manufacturer of commercial and military aircraft. They also produce helicopters, ground transportation systems, military communications systems, missile systems, and unmanned aircraft. They also develop advanced research for various branches of the U.S. military and are the prime contractor for the Space Shuttle. Sales are split 60/40 between U.S.–based (including government) and foreign customers.

With a heritage that mirrors the first 100 years of flight, the Boeing Company provides products and services to customers in 145 countries. Boeing has been the premier manufacturer of commercial jetliners for more than forty years and is a global market leader in military aircraft, satellites, missile defense, human space flight, and launch systems and services.

Boeing is organized into four major business units: Boeing Capital Corporation, Boeing Commercial Airplanes, Connexion by BoeingSM, and Boeing Integrated Defense Systems.

Supporting these units is the Boeing Shared Services Group, which contributes common and infrastructure services that enable the company's business units to concentrate on profitable growth. In addition, Phantom Works provides advanced research and development, including advanced concepts for air traffic management.

Today, Boeing's main commercial aircraft products consist of the 717, 737, 747, 767, and 777 families of airplanes, and the Boeing Business Jet. New product development efforts are focused on the Boeing 7E7, a high-efficiency model that was expected to be in service in 2008 but has been delayed to early 2010. The company has nearly 13,000 commercial jetliners in service worldwide, which is roughly 75 percent of the world fleet.

Boeing Commercial Aviation Services provides round-the-clock technical support to help operators maintain their aircraft. Commercial Aviation Services offers a full range of engineering, modification, logistics, and information services to its global customer base, which includes the world's passenger and cargo airlines as well as maintenance, repair and overhaul facilities. Boeing also trains maintenance and flight crews in the 100-seat-and-above airliner market through Alteon, the world's largest provider of airline training.

Reasons to Buy

Boeing began 2009 with over $350B in backlog, 90 percent of which is contractual. The size of the backlog is due at least in part to a union work stoppage (since resolved) at the main production facility near Seattle, but backlog is the lifeblood of the airframe business and a four-plus-year order cushion (at current run rates) is the best possible news when facing uncertain financial markets.

Boeing's biggest customers (the commercial airlines) are in somewhat better shape after 2008's spike in fuel prices left many of them in tough financial straits. The company received orders for over 600 new commercial airliners last year and is very optimistic about the market going forward.

Boeing has taken steps to accelerate the roll-out of its newest airframe, the mid-sized, wide-body 787 Dreamliner. The schedule took a one-year delay in 2008 but major milestones have since been met and the company anticipates a release of the product in the first quarter of 2010. Over the next twenty years, they anticipate sales for this model line in excess of $600B.

The 787, Boeing's first newly designed jet since the 777 began service in 1995, will be the world's first large commercial airplane made mostly of light, durable, and less-corrosive carbon-fiber composites. Boeing says its new plane will be cheaper to maintain and will offer better fuel efficiency and more passenger comforts than planes flying today.

Reasons for Caution

Boeing ended the year having just settled a sixty-day machinists' union strike that had a significant negative impact on shipments. Boeing begins 2009 with a record backlog, but the challenge remains to execute against orders without delay. A continued weakness in the capital equity mar- kets could expose the company to more order cancellations than nor- mal. Cutbacks in U.S. defense spend- ing under the Obama administration could also prove to be a negative.

SECTOR: **Industrials**
BETA COEFFICIENT: **1.0**
10-YEAR COMPOUND EARNINGS PER SHARE GROWTH: **14.5%**
10-YEAR COMPOUND DIVIDENDS PER SHARE GROWTH: **10.0%**

		2008	2007	2006	2005	2004	2003	2002	2001	2000
Revenues (Mil)		60,909	66,387	61,530	53,621	52,457	50,485	54,069	58,198	51,321
Net Income (Mil)		2,654	4,074	3,014	2,572	1,872	809	2,275	2,316	2,511
Earnings per share		3.63	5.28	3.62	2.39	2.30	1.00	2.82	2.79	2.84
Dividends per share		1.62	1.40	1.20	1.05	0.77	0.68	0.68	0.68	0.59
Price	high	88.3	107.8	92.0	72.4	55.5	43.4	51.1	69.9	70.9
	low	36.2	84.6	65.9	49.5	38.0	24.7	28.5	27.6	32.0

Campbell Soup Company

1 Campbell Place □ Camden, NJ 08103–1799 □ Phone: (856) 342–6428 □ Website: www.campbellsoup-company.com □ Ticker symbol: CPB □ Listed: NYSE □ S&P rating: B+ □ Value Line financial strength rating: B++

Financial Highlights, Fiscal Year 2008

Campbell reported net sales of $8.0B for FY2008, an increase of 8.3 percent year to year. Gross margins fell 100 basis points to 39.6 percent due to increased cost of raw materials.

Earnings came in at $1.17B, nominally a 36.3 percent increase over the prior year, but when fully adjusted for one-time charges and credits for both years, per-share earnings from ongoing operations grew 7 percent to $2.09. Dividends grew 10 percent to $0.88 per share.

In 2008 the company completed the sale of its Godiva Chocolatier business for $462M. Also impacting earnings were the recognition of $107M in restructuring charges and related costs associated with efficiency improvements, and also $13M ($.03/share) benefit from the favorable resolution of a tax contingency.

Company Profile

Campbell Soup Company, together with its consolidated subsidiaries, is a global manufacturer and marketer of high quality, branded convenience food products. Campbell was incorporated under the laws of New Jersey on November 23, 1922; however, through predecessor organizations, it traces its heritage in the food business back to 1869.

In fiscal 2008, the company continued its focus on achieving long-term sustainable sales and earnings growth by executing against the following key strategies:

- Expanding the company's icon brands within simple meals, baked snacks, and healthy beverages;
- Trading consumers up to higher-level products centering on wellness, quality, and convenience;
- Making the company's products more broadly available in existing and new markets;
- Strengthening the company's business through outside partnerships and acquisitions;
- Increasing margins by improving price realization and company-wide productivity.

Consistent with these strategies, the company has undertaken several portfolio adjustments—namely, the sale of Godiva and certain snack food brands. These portfolio adjustments were designed to enhance the company's focus on the core simple meals, baked snacks, and healthy beverages businesses in markets with the greatest potential for growth.

Prior to the second quarter of fiscal 2008, the company's operations were organized and reported in the following segments: U.S. Soup, Sauces, and Beverages; Baking and Snacking; International Soup, Sauces, and Beverages; and Other. Beginning with the second quarter of fiscal 2008, the Away From Home business was reported as North America Foodservice.

In most of the company's markets, sales activities are conducted by the company's own sales force and through broker and distributor arrangements. In the majority of its markets, the company's products are generally resold to consumers in retail food chains, mass discounters, mass merchandisers, club stores, convenience stores, drug stores, and other retail, commercial, and noncommercial establishments.

The company's largest customer, Wal-Mart Stores, Inc., and its affiliates, accounted for approximately 16 percent of the company's consolidated net sales during fiscal 2008 and 15 percent during fiscal 2007. No other customer accounted for 10 percent or more of the company's consolidated net sales.

Reasons to Buy

Consumers are turning more and more to inexpensive prepared food alternatives. The trend showed itself by the channel through which the largest sales increases were realized: in Q3, Wal-Mart sales increased 14 percent, a sizeable increase in the food industry. With 60 percent of the overall soup market, the company is clearly the market leader and is in good position to increase volumes.

Campbell was able to respond well to markedly higher raw materials costs. Even in an inflationary cycle they were able to improve margins by 30 basis points year/year after several years of steady decline. Recent declines in raw food prices will only help the bottom line.

China and Russia together consume half the world's prepared soups. Campbell is the dominant market leader in the U.S. soup business. That would lead to bright prospects for capturing some international market share. Just a 4 percent share of those markets would constitute a unit volume increase of over 10 percent.

Reasons for Caution

It will be difficult for Campbell to organically grow market share for soups in the United States. In order for the company to achieve significant growth in its highest volume segment, sales in China and Russia markets will need to accelerate.

Campbell Soup has a modest at best record of growth for both earnings and dividends. However, new management is having a decided impact on reviving the company.

SECTOR: **Consumer Staples**
BETA COEFFICIENT: **.55**
10-YEAR COMPOUND EARNINGS PER SHARE GROWTH: **0.5%**
10-YEAR COMPOUND DIVIDENDS PER SHARE GROWTH: **1.0%**

	2008	2007	2006	2005	2004	2003	2002	2001	2000
Revenues (Mil)	7,998	7,867	7,343	7,548	7,109	6,678	6,133	6,664	6,287
Net Income (Mil)	798	771	681	707	652	626	625	649	714
Earnings per share	2.09	1.95	1.66	1.71	1.58	1.52	1.28	1.55	1.65
Dividends per share	.88	0.82	0.74	0.69	0.64	0.63	0.63	0.90	0.90
Price high	40.8	42.7	40.0	31.6	30.5	27.9	30.0	35.4	37.5
low	27.3	34.2	28.9	27.3	25.0	20.0	19.7	25.5	23.8

AGGRESSIVE GROWTH

CarMax, Inc.

12800 Tuckahoe Creek Parkway ▫ Richmond, VA 23238 ▫ Phone: (804) 747–0422 ▫ Website: www.carmax.com ▫ Listed: NYSE ▫ Ticker symbol: KMX ▫ Fiscal year ends Feb 28 (29) ▫ S&P Rating: NA ▫ Value Line financial strength rating: B+

Financial Highlights, Fiscal Year 2008

CarMax actually ends their fiscal year 2009 in February 2009, so most of the results actually cover the calendar year 2008.

FY2009 was something of a "perfect storm" against the fortunes of CarMax. The combination of severe reduction in consumer spending on durable goods, in particular, automobiles, and tight credit hurt the company in two ways. Lower consumer demand reduced revenues; tight credit markets were a further drag on consumer demand and at the same time caused profits from financing to virtually dry up.

Net revenues declined 15 percent to $6.97 billion from $8.20 billion in fiscal 2008, while net earnings decreased to $59.2 million, or $0.27 per share, from $182.0 million, or

$0.83 per share. Over 90 percent of these figures are made up by used vehicle sales; the company still retains 5 new vehicle dealer franchises. It was the first yearly decline in sales since the company was spun off from Circuit City in 2002.

During that time the average vehicle selling price declined 6 percent, and unit sales decreased 8 percent. Despite these figures, the company was able to hold the line on gross profit dollars per vehicle sold at $2,715 per unit, a drop of only $16 vs. FY2008. The company attributes its result to its proprietary management information systems, specifically, its inventory management systems. The company opened 11 used-car superstores in 2009, bringing the total to exactly 100 stores nationwide.

Profits were hurt by a decline in the financing business, which was in turn hurt by problems placing commercial paper in the financial markets. Those problems are showing signs of subsiding; in addition, first quarter 2009 sales showed a healthy uptick in volume, average selling price, and gross margins.

Despite top-line and bottom-line pressure, the company reported an increase in cash flow from operations to $264.6 million from $79.5 million in fiscal 2008, again because it was able to reduce used vehicle inventories by simply not replenishing them.

Company Profile

"The Way Car Buying Should Be": That's the slogan used by this clean-cut chain of used vehicle stores and superstores and its new big-box retail-like model for selling cars. CarMax buys, reconditions, and sells cars and light trucks at 100 retail centers in 41 metropolitan markets, mainly in the Southeast and Midwest. The company specializes in selling cars that are under six years old with less than 60,000 miles; the cars are sold below Blue Book value in a no-haggle environment. The price is the price; the emphasis is on the condition of the vehicles and on a helpful and friendly sales and transaction process. Sales representatives are compensated for cars they sell, but not in such a way that drives them to push the wrong car on a customer. The company sold some 345,465 used vehicles in FY2009 and most reports suggest they are gaining market share in the markets they serve with a high degree of customer satisfaction.

CarMax also has service operations and web-based and other tools designed to make the car selection, buying, and ownership experience easier. The offering is, at this time, anyway, unique in the industry, and most think that any potential competitor would have a long way to go to catch up.

Reasons to Buy

Quite simply, CarMax is a stock you buy if you believe the traditional dealer model is broken, and if you believe people will continue to see value in late model used vehicles.

Additionally, CarMax brings the latest in business intelligence and analytic models to the car marketing process, in procurement, merchandising, pricing, and selling the vehicles. Do green Jeep Commanders sell well in Southern California? Then let's find some, and put them on the lot there, and set a market-based price. CarMax is well ahead of the industry in making analysis-based supply and selling decisions.

In addition, a bigger picture and analytic tools allow CarMax to adjust inventories to business conditions more quickly; in the recent downturn such inventory was reduced by tens of thousands of vehicles.

Unlike most car dealers, CarMax makes money no matter who wins the domestic vs. foreign battle, or the SUV vs. economy car battle, or—well, you get the idea.

Recent announcements of dealership closings should reduce competition and bode well for CarMax. And of course, any increase in consumer confidence and post-recession car-buying activity will help. It's pretty typical that in bad times people hold off on buying cars, creating pent-up demand that will eventually return to the market. Consumer caution will make that demand more likely to re-emerge as demand for used vehicles.

The company has barely tapped lucrative markets in the Northeast, Pacific Northwest, Colorado, and many cities in the Midwest. The combination of these new markets and greater consumer acceptance of the concept should provide a strong tailwind for sales once business conditions improve.

Reasons for Caution

CarMax will always be somewhat vulnerable to economic cycles and the availability of credit, and the recent recession has proven to be no exception. CarMax is also vulnerable to competition from manufacturer's new car incentive programs. While CarMax is able to adjust quickly to changing consumer tastes, gas prices, and economic conditions, the sheer size of CarMax dealerships and inventories makes it hard to stay in front of the cost curve when things change.

SECTOR: **Retail**
BETA COEFFICIENT: 0.98
5-YEAR COMPOUND EARNINGS PER SHARE GROWTH: 16.0 PERCENT
5-YEAR COMPOUND DIVIDENDS PER SHARE GROWTH: NA

		2008	2007	2006	2005	2004	2003	2002	2001	2000
Revenues (Mil)		6,974	8,200	7,466	6,260	5,260	4,597	4,052	3,201	2,501
Net Income (Mil)		59.2	182.0	198.6	148.1	112.9	116.5	94.8	90.8	45.6
Earnings per share		0.27	0.83	0.92	0.70	0.54	0.55	0.46	0.41	0.22
Dividends per share		Nil								
Price	high	23.0	29.4	27.6	17.4	18.5	19.7	17.0	12.0	0.7
	low	5.8	18.6	13.8	12.3	9.0	6.2	6.4	1.9	0.7

Caterpillar, Inc.

100 N. E. Adams Street ▫ Peoria, Illinois 61629–5310 ▫ Phone: (309) 675–4619 ▫ Website: www.cat.com
▫ Listed: NYSE ▫ Ticker symbol: CAT ▫ S&P rating: A ▫ Value Line financial strength rating: A

Financial Highlights, Fiscal Year 2008

Caterpillar closed 2008 with $51.3B in sales, a record year, and a 14.2 percent increase over the previous year. Earnings were up only 2.2 percent, however, and were basically flat versus 2006, a year in which sales were $10B lower than 2008. Per-share earnings were actually up 7.3 percent, due to the repurchase of 7 percent of the company's shares over the last two years. Dividends also increased 17 percent year/year, continuing their run of seventy-five consecutive years of quarterly dividend payments.

The first nine months of FY2008 were good for Cat, and by the end of the year they were able to meet their 2010 financial goals two years ahead of schedule. But, as their CEO said, 2008 was a tale of two years, and the last three months saw the collapse of the credit market, the rapid decline in commodity prices, and precipitous swings in global currencies. All of these created a "perfect storm" environment for buyers and sellers of capital equipment. Caterpillar responded by rapidly switching to their "trough" business model, announcing layoffs, plant shutdowns, and other cost-saving measures.

Company Profile

Headquartered in Peoria, Illinois, Caterpillar is the world's largest manufacturer of construction and mining equipment, diesel and natural gas engines, and industrial gas turbines. It is a *Fortune* 50 industrial company with more than $31 billion in assets. Caterpillar's distinctive yellow machines are in service in nearly every country in the world—nearly half of the company's revenues are derived from outside North America.

Caterpillar's broad product line ranges from the company's line of compact construction equipment to hydraulic excavators, backhoe loaders, track-type tractors, forest products, off-highway trucks, agricultural tractors, diesel and natural gas engines, and industrial gas turbines. Cat products are used in the construction, road-building, mining, forestry, energy, transportation, and material-handling industries.

Caterpillar products are sold in more than 200 countries, and rental services are offered through more than 1,200 outlets worldwide. The company offers service through its extensive worldwide network of 220 dealers. Caterpillar products and components are manufactured in forty-one plants in the United States and forty-three more plants worldwide.

The company conducts business through three operating segment: Machinery, Engines, and Financial Products.

Machinery

Caterpillar's largest segment, the Machinery unit makes the company's well-known earthmoving equipment. Machinery's end-markets include heavy construction, general construction, mining quarry and aggregate, industrial, waste, forestry, and agriculture. End markets are very cyclical and competitive. Demand for Caterpillar's earthmoving equipment is driven by many volatile factors, including the health of global economies, commodity prices, and interest rates.

Engines

For decades, the Engine segment made diesel engines solely for the company's own earthmoving equipment. Now, Engine derives about 90 percent of sales from third-party customers, such as Paccar, Inc., the maker of well-known Kenworth and Peterbilt brand tractor/trailer trucks. Engine's major end-markets are electric power generation, on-highway truck, oil and gas, industrial/OEM, and marine.

Financial Products

The Financial Products segment, which provides 7.6 percent of revenues but 20 percent of operating profits, primarily provides financing to Caterpillar dealers and customers. Financing plans include operating and finance leases, installment sales contracts, working capital loans, and wholesale financing plans.

Reasons to Buy

Caterpillar is the world's largest supplier of heavy equipment. They make to stock, and make to order, equipment that no other company can provide. Their brand is well-known and well-regarded throughout the world. The company continues to invest in R&D, spending $1.7B in 2008 develop new products and technologies, earning over 400 patents in the process. They are the unquestioned alpha dog in the heavy equipment market, and their brand and reputation have tremendous value in a business where product reliability and support are foremost in a purchasing decision.

Prices for raw materials, which had depressed profits at Cat during the recent growth period, have stabilized recently at ten-year lows, which should allow the company to respond quickly to any uptick in demand.

Without a doubt these are the toughest times the company has faced in decades. The company expects FY2009 revenues to be down nearly 30 percent and earnings down two-thirds, to 2003 levels. As a consequence, the stock price has been punished throughout the first half of 2009, and therein lies the opportunity. The housing market is expected to remain depressed for some time, but as government funding for infrastructure-based projects begins to become available, we believe Cat and others in the sector will begin to see sales stabilize and moderate upwards.

Reasons for Caution

Caterpillar is carrying a very large debt load. At the end of FY2008, total debt was just over $35.5B, with $12.7B due in the coming year. Finances will be strained as the company builds cash reserves to meet upcoming debt maturities. The sustainability of any recovery from the recession will also be important to watch.

SECTOR: **Industrials**
BETA COEFFICIENT: **1.20**
10-YEAR COMPOUND EARNINGS PER SHARE GROWTH: **10.5%**
10-YEAR COMPOUND DIVIDENDS PER SHARE GROWTH: **11%**

	2008	2007	2006	2005	2004	2003	2002	2001	2000
Rev (Mil)	51,234	44,958	41,517	36,339	30,251	22,763	20,152	20,450	20,175
Net Income (Mil)	3,557	3,541	3,537	2,854	2,035	1,099	798	805	1,051
Earnings per share	5.71	5.37	5.17	4.04	2.88	1.57	1.15	1.16	1.51
Dividends per share	1.62	1.32	1.20	0.96	0.78	0.72	0.70	0.70	0.67
Price high	86.0	87.0	82.0	59.9	49.4	42.5	30.0	28.4	27.6
low	32.0	58.0	57.0	41.3	34.3	20.6	16.9	19.9	14.8

Chevron Corporation

6001 Bollinger Canyon Road ▫ San Ramon, CA 94583–2324 ▫ Phone: (925) 842–5690 ▫ Website: www. chevrontexaco.com ▫ Listed: NYSE ▫ Ticker symbol: CVX ▫ S&P rating: AA ▫ Value Line financial strength rating: A++

Financial Highlights, Fiscal Year 2008

Sales in 2008 for Chevron grew 23.8 percent to $265B, while net income grew 28.1 percent to $23.9B. Per-share earnings grew 33.1 percent to a heady $11.67, and return on capital employed grew 350 basis points (3.5 percent) to 26.6 percent.

The company spent $8B on share repurchase and boosted the dividend 12 percent to $2.53, for an average yield of 3 percent.

Company Profile

Chevron is the world's fourth largest publicly traded, integrated energy company based on oil-equivalent reserves and production. It is engaged in every aspect of the oil and gas industry, including exploration and production, refining, marketing and transportation, chemicals manufacturing and sales, and power generation.

Active in more than 180 countries, ChevronTexaco has reserves of 11.9 billion barrels of oil and gas equivalent and daily production of 2.6 million barrels.

In addition, it has global refining capacity of more than 2 million barrels a day and operates more than 22,000 retail outlets (including affiliates) around the world. The company also has interests in thirty power projects now operating or being developed.

Chevron's upstream success includes:

- The #1 oil and gas producer in the U.S. Gulf of Mexico Shelf and number two in the Permian Basin.
- The #1 oil producer in the San Joaquin Valley in California.
- The #1 oil and natural gas producer in Kazakhstan.
- The #1 oil producer in Indonesia and Angola.
- The #1 natural gas resource holder in Australia.
- The #1 deepwater leaseholder and number three oil and gas producer in Nigeria.
- One of the top producers and leaseholders in the deepwater Gulf of Mexico.

Its downstream business includes:

- Four refining and marketing units, which operate in North America; Europe and West Africa; Latin America; and Asia, the Middle East, and southern Africa. Downstream also has five global businesses: aviation, lubricants, trading, shipping, and fuel and marine marketing.

- The company's global refining network comprises twenty-three wholly owned and joint-venture facilities, which process more than 2 million barrels of oil per day.
- Chevron sells more than 2 million barrels of gasoline and diesel per day through more than 22,000 retail outlets under three well-known consumer brands: Chevron in North America; Texaco in Latin America, Europe, and West Africa; and Caltex in Asia, the Middle East, and southern Africa.
- CVX is the number-one jet fuel marketer in the United States and third worldwide, marketing 550,000 barrels per day in eighty countries.
- The company's industrial and consumer lubricants business operates in more than 180 countries and sells more than 3,500 products.
- Chevron's global trading business buys and sells more than six million barrels of hydrocarbons per day in some sixty-five countries.
- The company's fuel and marine marketing business is a leading global supplier and marketer of fuels, lubricants, and coolants to the marine and power markets, with about 500,000 barrels of sales per day.
- CVX's shipping company manages a fleet of thirty-one vessels and annually transports more than a billion barrels of crude oil and petroleum products.

Reasons to Buy

Obviously, the remarkable returns in 2008 owe primarily to the extraordinary spike in oil prices that occurred during that year. The numbers at the beginning of 2009, on the other hand, tell a more sobering picture: Second quarter upstream/downstream numbers from 2008 were $7.25B/($734m), but 2009 has come in at $1.5B/$530M. The return to what passes for normalcy in the oil business has nonetheless left Chevron with a mountain of cash to spend on exploration, development, acquisitions, and dividends.

The company has several new projects and project expansions slated to come on-line this year, including production facilities in Angola, Nigeria, Brazil, and the Gulf of Mexico, and processing enhancements in Kazakhstan and South Korea. With the natural gas market currently in significant oversupply, most of Chevron's focus is on petroleum development.

Chevron is one of the world's largest producers of heavy crude oil, which represents about one-third of the world's hydrocarbon reserves. Industry production of heavy oil is projected to grow by 30 percent by the end of this decade.

Reasons for Caution

The usual in the petroleum business—sharp price cycles, geopolitical risk, legal and environmental exposure. For example, Chevron is in litigation in Ecuador with regard to environmental damage that the Ecuadorian government claims is Chevron's liability. The judgment, with potential exposure of $27B, is due in 2009.

SECTOR: **Energy**
BETA COEFFICIENT: **.90**
10-YEAR COMPOUND EARNINGS PER SHARE GROWTH: **18.0%**
10-YEAR COMPOUND DIVIDENDS PER SHARE GROWTH: **7.0%**

		2008	2007	2006	2005	2004	2003	2002	2001	2000
Rev (Bil)		273.0	220.9	210.1	198.2	150.9	121.8	98.9	106.2	52.1
Net Income (Bil)		23.9	18.7	17.1	14.1	13.0	7.2	1.1	3.3	5.2
Earnings per share		11.67	8.77	7.80	6.54	6.14	3.48	0.54	1.55	3.99
Dividends per share		2.53	2.32	2.01	1.75	1.53	1.43	1.40	1.33	1.30
Price	high	104.6	95.5	76.2	66.0	56.1	43.5	45.8	49.2	47.4
	low	55.5	65.0	53.8	49.8	41.6	30.7	32.7	39.2	35.0

AGGRESSIVE GROWTH

Cintas Corporation

Post Office Box 625737 □ Cincinnati, OH 45262–5737 □ Phone: (513) 459–1200 □ Website: www
.cintas.com □ Fiscal year ends May 31 □ Listed: NASDAQ □ Ticker symbol: CTAS □ S&P rating: A
□ Value Line financial strength rating: B++

Financial Highlights, Fiscal Year 2008

Revenues grew 6.2 percent to $3.94B, while earnings were very nearly flat, growing just 0.3 percent to $335M. Dividends were up 17.9 percent.

The company supplemented internal growth with $111M in acquisitions, $67M of which was assigned to goodwill, meaning it will likely have to be written down over the coming years. The company assumed $11M in debt in the acquisitions. Although gross margins grew 6.2 percent, costs associated with these acquisitions and the dilution of net margin has pulled the bottom line down.

Company Profile

Cintas is North America's leading provider of corporate identity uniforms through rental and sales programs, as well as related business services, in-cluding entrance mats, hygiene products, cleanroom services, and first aid and safety supplies. Uniform rentals account for about 75 percent of the company's revenue and 80 percent of its earnings.

Cintas serves businesses of all sizes, from small shops to large national companies employing thousands of people. Today, more than 5 million people go to work wearing a Cintas uniform every day. That is well over 3 percent of the nonfarm, civilian work force in the United States and Canada.

Cintas provides its award-winning design capability and top quality craftsmanship to the high end of the market—hotels, airlines, cruise ships, and the like. The company delivers the proper uniform to anyone in any job classification from the doorman to the cocktail waitress in a hotel; from the mechanic to the pilot at the airlines; and even people working in the retail sector.

According to a Cintas spokesman, "Companies use Cintas uniforms to identify their employees to their customers. An employee who wears a clean, crisp, and attractive uniform is always viewed as more professional than someone in ordinary work clothes. Uniforms also complement a company's esprit de corps by building camaraderie and loyalty. Bottom line—we don't just sell uniforms—we well image, identification, teamwork, morale, pride and professionalism." Put another way, Cintas believes that when people look good, they feel good. And when they feel good, they work better. What's more, their improved attitude results in a decline in absenteeism and turnover.

Cintas reports in four operating segments: Rental Uniforms and Ancillary Products; Uniform Direct Sales; First Aid, Safety and Fire Protection Services; and Document Management Services.

Reasons to Buy

Cintas is the clear market leader in a segment with clear opportunity for grown. It's estimated that some 25 million U.S. workers purchase their own work uniforms at retail. Another 20–25 million workers have no uniform program. If the uniform industry were to penetrate these two markets, it's estimated that the total sales for the segment would rise to $11B/year.

In spite of a relatively slow year in terms of top-line growth, Cintas held market share and grew both their international business as well as their new paper management segment (on-site and off-site shredding). The latter, incidentally, is a clever initiative to leverage their customer on-site contact and delivery that could carry into other new business ideas. As employment returns to pre-2008 levels, Cintas top line and margins should return as well.

The company has very little debt and retains a strong cash flow. Should opportunities arise, they are well positioned to grow the top line or capture market share through acquisitions.

Attempts to unionize Cintas' labor pool over the last six years remain unsuccessful, and the company continues to win awards as a safe and responsible employer.

Reasons for Caution

Unemployment levels have remained in the 7–9 percent range nationwide for four consecutive quarters, and Cintas's top line has suffered as a direct result. There are fewer workers requiring uniforms, and Cintas's customers are cutting expenses wherever they can. Cintas will also need to integrate its acquired businesses quickly in order to halt a further erosion of the bottom line.

SECTOR: **Industrials**
BETA COEFFICIENT: **.95**
10-YEAR COMPOUND EARNINGS PER SHARE GROWTH: **12.5%**
10-YEAR COMPOUND DIVIDENDS PER SHARE GROWTH: **14.5%**

	2008	2007	2006	2005	2004	2003	2002	2001	2000
Revenues (Mil)	3.938	3,707	3,404	3,067	2,814	2,687	2,271	2,161	1,902
Net Income (Mil)	335	334	327	301	272	249	234	222	193
Earnings per share	2.15	2.09	1.94	1.74	1.58	1.45	1.36	1.30	1.14
Dividends per share	0.46	0.39	0.35	0.32	0.29	0.27	0.25	0.22	0.19
Price high	33.9	42.9	44.3	45.5	50.5	50.7	56.2	53.3	54.0
low	19.5	31.1	34.6	39.5	30.6	39.2	33.8	23.2	26.0

CONSERVATIVE GROWTH

The Clorox Company

1221 Broadway ▫ Oakland, CA 94612 ▫ Phone: (510) 271–2270 ▫ Website: www.clorox.com ▫ Listed: NYSE ▫ Fiscal year ends June 30 ▫ Ticker symbol: CLX ▫ S&P rating: A ▫ Value Line financial strength rating: B++

Financial Highlights, Fiscal Year 2008

Sales grew 9 percent to $5.3B, generating earnings of $461M, a decline of 7.6 percent year over year. Earnings per share remained basically flat due to share repurchase, while operating margins fell 5 percent. The decline in operating margins was largely due to the rising costs of commodities used in product manufacturing, particularly plastic resins, which account for 6 percent of production costs (cost of goods sold) companywide.

International sales grew 16 percent in 2008, now accounting for 16 percent of total sales. Earnings growth in International grew 4 percent, outpacing the flat earnings in the domestic market.

Company Profile

A leading manufacturer and marketer of consumer products, Clorox markets some of consumers' most trusted and recognized brand names, including its namesake bleach and cleaning products, Green Works natural cleaners, Armor All and STP auto-care products, Fresh Step and Scoop Away cat litter, Kingsford charcoal, Hidden Valley and K C Masterpiece dressings and sauces, Brita water-filtration systems, Glad bags, and Burt's Bees natural personal care products. With approximately 8,300 employees worldwide, the company manufactures products in more than two dozen countries and markets them in more than 100 countries.

The company's home care cleaning products primarily comprise disinfecting sprays and wipes, toilet bowl cleaners, carpet cleaners, drain openers, floor mopping systems, toilet and bath cleaning tools, and premoistened towelettes.

Clorox also provides professional products for institutional, janitorial, and food service markets, including bleaches, toilet bowl cleaners, disinfectants, food-storage bags, trash bags, barbecue sauces, mildew removers, soap scum removers, and bathroom cleaners. Its auto care products consist of protectants, cleaners, wipes, tire- and wheel-care products, washes, gel washes, waxes, and automotive fuel and oil additives.

In addition, the company offers food products, which include salad dressings and dip mixes, seasoned mini-croutons, seasonings, sauces, and marinades. Clorox sells its products to grocery stores and grocery wholesalers primarily through a network of brokers; and through a direct sales force to mass merchandisers, warehouse clubs, and military and other retail stores in the United States. It also sells its products outside the United States through subsidiaries, licensees, distributors, and joint-venture arrangements with local partners.

The company was founded in 1913 as Electro-Alkaline Company and changed its name to Clorox Chemical Corporation in 1922. It changed its name to Clorox Chemical Co. in 1928 and then to the Clorox Company in 1957.

Reasons to Buy

Even in a slowing consumer market, Clorox, due to its strong brand position (number one or two position in the market with ninety-three of its products) was able to increase prices in FY2008. Store brands have not had a significant impact on margins and as commodity prices continue to moderate, we look for improved per-share results and continued solid dividend returns (now yielding 2.8 percent).

The company remains very optimistic about its Economic Profit metric, which is profit generated over and above the cost of paying for the assets used by the business to generate profit. They anticipate that by 2013 they will be able to show year/year double-digit growth of this measure, which they refer to as "true north" as they feel it corresponds with shareholder value creation. Including the effects of the purchase of Burt's Bees, this measure was off just over 4 percent year over year.

Often held up as an example of a company with environmentally unfriendly products, Clorox has made progress in "greening up" their image, both through the acquisition of Burt's Bees and through a comprehensive educational program on the effects of its flagship product, Clorox bleach, on the environment. The company also continues to stress the "Health and Wellness" aspect of the uses of bleach in disinfecting and disease prevention.

Reasons for Caution

The company's stock price, basically flat over the last four years, has been buoyed by the company's aggressive stock repurchase activity. Earnings have declined since 2004, but the number of outstanding shares has been reduced by 35 percent. It's not clear the company will use its cash flow to continue this trend, as the buying down of debt (incurred in the acquisition of Burt's Bees in 2007) and maintenance of the dividend appear to be the goal.

SECTOR: **Consumer Staples**
BETA COEFFICIENT: **.65**
10-YEAR COMPOUND EARNINGS PER SHARE GROWTH: **10.0%**
10-YEAR COMPOUND DIVIDENDS PER SHARE GROWTH: **9.0%**

	2008	2007	2006	2005	2004	2003	2002	2001	2000
Revenues (Mil)	5,273	4,847	4,644	4,388	4,324	4,144	4,061	3,903	4,083
Net Income (Mil)	461	496	443	517	546	514	322	325	394
Earnings per share	3.24	3.23	2.89	2.88	2.43	2.33	1.37	1.63	1.75
Dividends per share	1.66	1.31	1.14	1.10	1.08	0.88	0.84	0.80	0.72
Price high	65.3	69.4	66.0	66.0	59.4	49.2	47.9	40.8	56.4
low	47.5	56.2	56.2	52.5	46.5	37.4	31.9	30.0	28.4

CONSERVATIVE GROWTH

The Coca-Cola Company

One Coca-Cola Plaza □ Atlanta, GA 30313 □ Phone: (404) 676–2121 □ Website: www.coca-cola.com □
Listed: NYSE □ Ticker symbol: KO □ S&P rating: A+ □ Value Line financial strength rating: A++

Financial Highlights, Fiscal Year 2008

Coke ended the year going just a little flat. Revenues in 2008 were up 10.7 percent on a 5 percent unit volume increase, but income was off 1.7 percent. The reduced profitability was due largely to net equity losses and unfavorable currency translations. As a result, earnings ended the year at $5.8B, which had to be something of a disappointment, given the growth in unit volume and the 11 percent increase in operating revenue.

Company Profile

The Coca-Cola Company is the world's largest beverage company, although they don't actually produce anything you'd want to drink as is. The company produces concentrates and syrups that it then sells to bottlers worldwide. These bottlers add water (still or carbonated, depending on the product), sugar, and other (often local) ingredients, then bottle and distribute the products to restaurants, retailers, and other distributors. The company owns the brand and is responsible for consumer brand marketing initiatives, while the distributors handle all downstream merchandising. The company operates in over 200 countries and markets nearly 500 brands of concentrate. These concentrates are then used to produce over 3000 different branded products, including Coca-Cola.

The total numbers are staggering: 570 billion servings per year, 1.6 billion beverages consumed per day, 18,000 servings per second, unit growth in 2008 equivalent to the entire Japanese market, processed through over 300 bottlers, and all handled through the world's largest beverage distribution system.

The company-owned bottling businesses handle 22 percent of the bottling volume, while 78 percent is done by independent, licensed bottlers in which the company has no controlling or equity interest.

Reasons to Buy

Coca-Cola has global category leadership in soft drinks, juices and juice drinks, and ready-to-drink coffees and teas. They're number two globally in sports drinks, and number three in packaged water and energy drinks. In Coca-Cola, Diet Coke, Sprite, and Fanta, they own four of the top five brands of soft drink in the world. They're everywhere, and with so many popular brands the local bottlers can "test the waters," choosing among hundreds of products for the right ones for their area.

Coke's financial stake in its bottling operations has increased in the last five years, and may increase further as its main rival, PepsiCo, has moved to consolidate more of its bottlers under company ownership. The move would be viewed as an investment by the company, with benefits paid over time in terms of improved coordination. After many requests, Coke has recently begun to allow some of its independent bottlers to begin producing non-Coke product.

Although the company has lagged behind the market in terms of non-CSD (carbonated soft drink) product offerings, the potential for growth in those markets is very encouraging. Coke has the financ-

ing and the market clout to make it rain nonfat soy lattes for a solid week, should they choose to do so. Expect them to deliver new brands and selectively acquire niche players over the next few years.

Coca-Cola is probably the most recognized brand in the world, and is almost beyond valuation. Warren Buffett once famously said, "If you gave me $100 billion and said take away the soft drink leadership in the world from Coke, I'd give it back to you and say it can't be done."

Coke has traditionally been a steady hedge stock, and to find it trading at a 35 percent discount to its recent high price with a dividend offering real value is an offer that's hard to pass up.

Reasons for Caution

If one thing stands out from a review of Coke's volumes, it's that the U.S. market requires attention. Unit volume has been flat over the last five years and actually declined in 2008. Coke may have been behind the curve with regard to the growth of sports and energy drinks, and their more traditional brands are losing popularity with younger consumers.

SECTOR: **Consumer Discretionary**
BETA COEFFICIENT: **0.55**
10-YEAR COMPOUND EARNINGS PER SHARE GROWTH: **6.0%**
10-YEAR COMPOUND DIVIDENDS PER SHARE GROWTH: **9.5%**

	2008	2007	2006	2005	2004	2003	2002	2001	2000
Revenues (Mil)	31,944	28,857	24,088	23,104	21,962	21,044	19,564	17,545	20,458
Net Income (Mil)	7,050	5,981	5,568	5,196	5,014	4,790	4,100	3,979	3,669
Earnings per share	3.02	2.57	2.37	2.17	2.06	1.95	1.65	1.60	1.48
Dividends per share	1.52	1.36	1.24	1.12	1.00	0.88	0.80	0.72	0.68
Price high	65.6	64.3	49.3	45.3	53.3	50.9	57.9	62.2	66.9
low	40.3	45.6	39.4	40.3	38.3	37.0	.42.9	42.4	42.9

CONSERVATIVE GROWTH

Colgate-Palmolive Company

300 Park Avenue ❑ New York, NY 10022–7499 ❑ Phone: (212) 310–2291 ❑ Website: www.colgate.com
❑ Listed: NYSE ❑ Ticker symbol: CL ❑ S&P rating: A+ ❑ Value Line financial strength rating: A++

Financial Highlights, Fiscal Year 2008

Colgate reported record numbers for 2008. Sales, earnings, and operating and net margins were all up year over year. Sales grew 11 percent to $15.3B, earnings increased 13 percent to $1.74B, operating margins were up 50 basis points to 19.7 percent and net margins gained 20 basis points to 12.8 percent. Given that this was all achieved on a unit volume increase of only 4 percent makes it all the more impressive and makes us wonder what (potentially) increased top-line numbers from International will do for FY2009's bottom line. It could be very good indeed.

International growth in 2008 was particularly strong, with Latin America reporting 17 percent increases in both sales and operating margin and Greater Asia/Africa reporting sales gains of 14 percent and operating margin gains of 23 percent. Latin America is now Colgate's largest market for its traditional product lines, representing 27 percent of total sales.

Pet Nutrition also did well, posting worldwide sales increases of 15.5 percent along with growth in operating margin of 11 percent.

Company Profile

Colgate-Palmolive is the second-largest domestic manufacturer of detergents, toiletries, and other household products. They are also a leader in the pet nutrition market, and their Hill's pet food brand represents 17 percent of their total sales.

Colgate is also a strong global consumer products player, marketing its products in over 200 countries and territories under such internationally recognized brand names as Colgate toothpastes and brushes, Palmolive soaps, Mennen deodorants, Ajax, Murphy Oil Soap, Fab, and Soupline/Suavitel, as well as the Hill's brands.

Reasons to Buy

Colgate is a market leader in many of the sectors in which it competes, but it is particularly strong in those areas that carry the highest margins, which includes dental care and liquid hand soaps.

The company has just finished a large global restructuring plan that they expect will generate cost savings in all areas of the company. CEO Ian Cook put it best in a lengthy statement: "The Company's four-year restructuring and business-building program (the 2004 Restructuring Program), which was finalized as of December 2008, has positioned us well to continue to generate savings throughout all areas of our business, providing funding for activities that generate growth and profitability. We are becoming ever more streamlined as we progress toward a truly global supply chain, providing us with greater flexibility and increased cost efficiencies. Since 2004, Colgate has reduced the number of manufacturing plants worldwide by over 25 percent, which includes five new state-of-the-art facilities. These new factories are environmentally friendly, making more efficient use of energy, water, materials and land."

"Our fully global approach to procurement of both direct materials and indirect goods and services is also delivering millions of dollars in savings each year, ahead of our original estimates. Our professional procurement specialists are involved in purchasing almost everything we buy. Their expert ability to obtain the best possible value by leveraging global and regional resources is helping us succeed in today's challenging cost environment. Another global initiative, Colgate Business Planning (CBP), a fully integrated commercial planning and execution discipline, from the budget process through to the store shelf, is accelerating profitable growth by contributing to higher market shares, net sales and margin growth. Supported by SAP software, CBP incorporates a strong return on investment methodology to ensure the most efficient use of promotional investments. We are making good progress in implementing CBP in phases around the world, with 87 percent of our business having implemented at least the first phase of the program as of the end of 2008."

Colgate continues to pay solid dividends, with a yield of 2.2 percent from dividends alone. The company expects to continue its trend of increasing dividends at least through 2010.

Reasons for Caution

A large contributor to Colgate's earnings growth was the impact of net selling price increases of 9.5 percent in Latin America and smaller increases in Asia/Africa. We expect these increases to moderate downward in

2009. Also, it's worth noting that this low-beta stock (0.6) is closely watched and even though the company has been buying back shares recently, it still has over half a billion common shares outstanding. Consequently it is not likely to report "surprisingly" good earnings per share.

SECTOR: **Consumer Staples**
BETA COEFFICIENT: **.6**
10-YEAR COMPOUND EARNINGS PER SHARE GROWTH: **11%**
10-YEAR COMPOUND DIVIDENDS PER SHARE GROWTH: **10.5%**

		2008	2007	2006	2005	2004	2003	2002	2001	2000
Revenues (Mil)		15,330	13,790	12,238	11,397	10,584	9,903	9,294	9,084	9,358
Net Income (Mil)		1,957	1,737	1,353	1,351	1,327	1,421	1,288	1,147	1,064
Earnings per share		3.66	3.20	2.46	2.43	2.33	2.46	2.19	1.89	1.70
Dividends per share		1.56	1.44	1.28	1.11	0.96	0.90	0.72	0.68	0.63
Price	high	82.0	81.3	67.1	57.2	59.0	61.0	58.9	64.8	66.8
	low	54.4	63.8	53.4	48.2	42.9	48.6	44.1	48.5	40.5

ConocoPhillips

600 North Dairy Ashford □ Houston, TX 77079–1175 □ Phone: (212) 207–1996 □ Website: www.
conocophillips.com □ Listed: NYSE □ Ticker symbol: COP □ S&P rating: B+ □ Value Line financial strength
rating: A+

Financial Highlights, Fiscal Year 2008

The company grew sales 28.4 percent to $241B. Reported earnings came in at a loss of $17B due to recorded impairments without which the income would have been $15.8B positive (32.8 percent growth year over year).

The company recorded noncash impairments of $34B in 2008, including $7.4B to their Lukoil investment and a $25.4B impairment to their Exploration & Production business as a function of decreased commodity prices.

Company Profile

ConocoPhillips is an integrated international energy company and is the third-largest integrated energy company in the United States, based on market capitalization and proven reserves and production of oil and gas. It is also the largest refiner in the United States Worldwide, of nongovernment controlled companies, ConocoPhillips has the eighth-largest total of proven reserves and is the fourth-largest refiner in the world. Their businesses span the hydrocarbon value chain from wellhead through refining, marketing, transportation, and chemicals.

ConocoPhillips is known worldwide for its technological expertise in deepwater exploration and production, reservoir management and exploitation, 3-D seismic technology, high-grade petroleum coke upgrading, and sulfur removal.

Headquartered in Houston, Texas, ConocoPhillips operates in more than forty countries with about 35,800 employees worldwide and assets of $86 billion.

The company has four core activities worldwide:

- *Petroleum exploration and production.* This segment primarily explores for, produces, transports, and markets crude oil, natural gas, and natural gas liquids on a worldwide basis.
- *Petroleum refining, marketing, supply, and transportation.* This segment purchases, refines, markets, and transports crude oil and petroleum products, mainly in the United States, Europe, and Asia.
- *Natural gas gathering, processing, and marketing,* including a 30.3 percent interest in Duke Energy Field Services, LLC. This segment gathers, processes, and markets natural gas produced by ConocoPhillips and others, and fractionates and markets natural gas liquids, predominantly in the United States and Trinidad.

The Midstream segment primarily consists of a 50 percent equity investment in DCP Midstream, LLC.

- Chemicals and plastics production and distribution through a 50 percent interest in Chevron Phillips Chemical Company LLC. This segment manufactures and markets petrochemicals and plastics on a worldwide basis. The Chemicals segment consists of a 50 percent equity investment in Chevron Phillips Chemical Company LLC (CPChem).

- Lukoil Investment. This segment consists of an equity investment in the ordinary shares of OAO Lukoil, an international, integrated oil and gas company headquartered in Russia. At December 31, 2008, ownership interest was 20 percent based on issued shares.

In addition, the company is investing in several emerging businesses—fuels technology, gas-to-liquids, power generation, and emerging technologies—that provide current and potential future growth opportunities.

Reasons to Buy

Buy low, sell high. Conoco's business and outlook is no worse than it was one year ago when oil was at an all-time high, and now oil is trading at less than one-third that price. Conoco's shares have tracked the rest of the big six, lagging behind some and ahead of others.

They've accounted for three significant setbacks in the last two years ($4.5B lost to Venezuelan nationalization and $35B in two noncash impairments last year) and are starting with a clean set of books and no surprises in store. If the commodity markets stabilize and Conoco executes on its cost reductions and business plans, they stand to do well in the coming recovery. Even if oil prices remain volatile, Conoco's vertical integration tends to buffer the swings in the market. Although share repurchase has been suspended, dividend growth is still in the works and current yield is over 4 percent.

Reasons for Caution

ConocoPhillips owns a 20 percent stake in Lukoil, the largest oil company in Russia and the second largest producer in the world. In 2006 the Russian government forced Shell to give up 50 percent of its share in the Sakhalin-2 gas field to Gazprom, the state-owned oil company. Given Conoco's recent $4B write-off of assets in Venezuela due to nationalization, some caution here is warranted.

SECTOR: **Energy**
BETA COEFFICIENT: **1.10**
10-YEAR COMPOUND EARNINGS PER SHARE GROWTH: **15.4%**
10-YEAR COMPOUND DIVIDENDS PER SHARE GROWTH: **9.4%**

		2008	2007	2006	2005	2004	2003	2002	2001	2000
Revenues (Bil)		240.8	187.4	183.7	179.4	135.1	104.2	56.75	26.73	20.84
Net Income (Bil)		15.86	11.89	15.55	13.64	8.11	4.59	1.51	1.71	1.92
Earnings per share		10.66	9.14	9.66	9.55	5.79	3.35	1.56	2.90	3.74
Dividends per share		1.88	1.64	1.44	1.18	0.90	0.82	0.74	0.70	0.68
Price	high	96.0	90.8	74.9	71.5	45.6	33.0	32.1	34.0	35.0
	low	41.3	61.6	54.9	41.4	32.2	22.6	22.0	25.0	18.0

AGGRESSIVE GROWTH

Costco Wholesale Corporation

999 Lake Drive ▫ Issaquah, WA 98027 ▫ Phone: (425) 313–8203 ▫ Website: www.costco.com ▫ Listed: NASDAQ ▫ Fiscal year ends Sunday nearest August 31 ▫ Ticker symbol: COST ▫ S&P rating: A ▫ Value Line financial strength rating: A

Financial Highlights, Fiscal Year 2008

Net income increased 18.5 percent to $1.28 billion, or $2.89 per diluted share, in 2008 compared to $1.08 billion, or $2.37 per diluted share, in 2007. Net sales increased 12.5 percent over 2007, driven by an 8 percent increase in comparable sales (sales in warehouses open for at least one year) and the opening of 24 new warehouses (34 opened and 10 closed due to relocations) in 2008.

Membership fees increased 14.7 percent, to $1.51 billion, primarily due to new membership signups at warehouses opened in 2008 and increased penetration of higher-fee programs. Selling, general and administrative expenses as a percentage of net sales decreased 14 basis points over the prior year.

Dividends increased 10 percent to $0.61 per share, and the company repurchased 13.8 million shares of common stock, at an average cost of $64.22 per share, totaling approximately $886.9 million.

Company Profile

Costco Wholesale Corporation operates an international chain of membership warehouses, mainly under the "Costco Wholesale" name, that carry brand name merchandise at substantially lower prices than are typically found at conventional wholesale or retail sources. The warehouses are designed to help small-to-medium-sized businesses reduce costs in purchasing for resale and for everyday business use, but as most know, the individual consumer has been their big growth driver. Costco is the largest membership warehouse club chain in the world based on sales volume and is the fifth largest general retailer in the United States.

Costco's warehouses market in a broad line of categories, including groceries, candy, appliances, television and media, automotive supplies, tires, toys, hardware, sporting goods, jewelry, watches, cameras, books, housewares, apparel, health and beauty aids, tobacco, furniture, office supplies, and office equipment.

Members can also shop for private label Kirkland Signature products, designed to be of equal or better quality than national brands, including juice, cookies, coffee, tires, housewares, luggage, appliances, clothing, and detergent. The company also operates self-service gasoline stations at a number of its U.S. and Canadian locations.

Additionally, Costco Wholesale Industries, a division of the company, operates manufacturing businesses, including special food packaging, optical laboratories, meat processing, and jewelry distribution. These businesses have a common goal of providing members with high-quality products at substantially lower prices.

Costco is open only to members and offers three types of membership: Business, Gold Star (individual), and the Executive membership. Business members qualify by owning or operating a business, and pay an annual fee ($50 in the United States) to shop for resale, business, and personal use. This fee includes a spouse card. Business members may purchase up to six additional membership cards ($40 each) for partners or associates in the business.

As of June 2009 Costco has 555 locations, 407 in the U.S. and Puerto Rico, 77 in Canada, 41 in Mexico, 21 in the United Kingdom, and 21 in Asia.

Reasons to Buy

Costco derives much of its operating income from membership fees, and the company has the best membership retention in the industry at 87 percent. Total membership at the end of FY2008 was 53.5 million.

Costco's model of drawing visits with lower prices is still valid. During a period of the lowest consumer confidence in memory (4Q2008), Costco's sales grew 13 percent, driven primarily by a 9 percent increase in comparable store sales. Because of its price leadership, the company tends to fare well in both strong and weak economies.

The company remains on solid financial ground, with negligible current debt and over $3B in cash. They are in good position to revive their earlier expansion plans at solid signs of a turnaround in consumer confidence.

Demographics are favoring the club stores. According to Mediamark Research, for the eighteen months prior to April 2008, club store membership grew 3.6 percent, while the adult population of the United States grew only 1.2 percent. Much of the growth came from high-income households, whose members may be finding bargain prices more attractive amid the lingering economic down-turn. Club stores had an 11.9 percent jump in shoppers with household incomes above $75,000, who now make up just under half of their visitors.

Reasons for Caution

Depending on how you choose to look at it, Costco may be either too dependent or not dependent enough on gasoline sales. According to the company, FY2008 same-store comps would have been 267 basis points (2.67 percent) lower if gasoline sales had been excluded.

Costco has scaled back its 2009 expansion plans due in part to concern over economic conditions, but also due to a growing concern about overexpansion and cannibalization of existing store sales. A general slow-down in U.S. suburban expansion may impact the company's future growth, but international growth opportunities may offset this concern.

SECTOR: **Retail**
BETA COEFFICIENT: **.75**
10-YEAR COMPOUND EARNINGS PER SHARE GROWTH: **12.5%**
4-YEAR COMPOUND DIVIDENDS PER SHARE GROWTH: **not meaningful**

	2008	2007	2006	2005	2004	2003	2002	2001	2000
Revenues (Mil)	72,483	64,400	60,151	52,935	48,107	41,693	37,993	34,797	32,164
Net Income (Mil)	1,283	1,083	1,103	989	882	721	700	602	631
Earnings per share	2.89	2.37	2.30	2.03	1.85	1.53	1.48	1.29	1.35
Dividends per share	0.61	0.55	0.49	0.45	0.20	Nil			
Price high	75.2	72.7	57.9	51.2	50.5	39.0	46.9	46.4	60.5
low	43.9	51.5	46.0	39.5	35.0	27.0	27.1	29.8	25.9

C.R. Bard, Inc.

730 Central Avenue □ Murray Hill, NJ 07974 □ Phone: (908) 277–8413 □ Website: www.crbard.com □
Listed: NYSE □ Ticker symbol: BCR □ S&P rating: A– □ Value Line financial strength rating: A+

Financial Highlights, Fiscal Year 2008

The company reported year over year growth in net revenue of 13 percent (to $455M) on a net sales increase of 11 percent (to $2.45B). Earnings per share were up 16 percent to $4.44 (all numbers exclude company-stated one-time adjustments). This marks the sixth consecutive year of EPS growth greater than Bard's stated target of 14 percent.

Results were positive in other major benchmarks as well: operating margin, net margin, cash flow, debt ratios. In fact, Bard showed year/year improvement in nearly every standard performance measure. Inventories and receivables were up somewhat, but they scaled to the level of sales and did not appear to affect cash flow in any significant way.

Sales were up in all four major product segments. Particularly strong were the results from the Vascular and Oncology product lines, which netted sales gains of 19 and 16 percent, respectively. The Urology products gained 8 percent, while Surgical products were nearly flat, showing only a 1 percent increase.

Overall, another excellent year in what has been a 10-year trend for Bard.

Company Profile

Founded in 1907 by Charles Russell Bard, the company markets a wide range of medical, surgical, diagnostic, and patient-care devices. It markets its products worldwide to hospitals, individual health-care professionals, extended care facilities, and alternate site facilities. Most of Bard's products fall into the category of consumables/supplies—intended to be used once and then discarded. The company operates in four core segments—Vascular, Urology, Oncology, and Surgery.

- *Urology* (30 percent of sales)—The company offers a complete line of urological diagnosis and intervention products including Foley catheters (the market leader and their largest-selling product), procedure kits and trays, urethral stents, and specialty devices for incontinence.
- *Oncology* (25 percent of sales)—Bard's products are designed for the detection and treatment of various types of cancer. Products include specialty access catheters and ports, gastroenterological products, and biopsy devices. The company's chemotherapy products serve a well-established market in which Bard holds a major market position.

- *Vascular Products* (25 percent of sales)—The company's line of vascular diagnosis and intervention products includes peripheral angioplasty stents, catheters, guide wires, introducers and accessories, vena cava filters, and implantable blood vessel replacements. They also sell electrophysiology products such as cardiac mapping and laboratory systems which support sales of the consumables.
- *Surgical Products* (17 percent of sales)—Surgical specialties products include meshes for vessel and hernia repair; irrigation devices for orthopedic and laparoscopic procedures; and topical hemostatic devices.
- *International*—Bard markets its products through twenty-two subsidiaries and a joint venture in ninety-two countries outside the United States. Principal markets are Japan, Canada, the United Kingdom, and continental Europe.

Reasons to Buy

Bard is a classic defensive play. They have a broad product line of consumables in a market that has been nearly recession-proof. Consumers will cut back on health care only as a last resort, and the majority of Bard's products fall into the area of nondiscretionary purchases.

They operate in a regulated market, but the breadth of their product line means they are not terribly exposed should one product fail early

trials or final FDA approval. They have one product line (the Foley catheter) that represents some 15 percent of revenue, but it's been in production for decades and serves as a cash cow at this point. Also, many of their products are developed and refined from previous designs, reducing R&D costs and providing manufacturing leverage.

They have the number one or number two market position across nearly 80 percent of their product line, and their product line recognizes and addresses a number of compelling trends: an aging demographic and the shift to lower-cost, patient-assisted (in-home) therapy.

The company has been successful with acquisitions recently and remains well-positioned to continue even (and particularly) during an economic slowdown. They have adequate reserves of capital and low levels of debt. If they can continue to pick the right targets, there's little reason to doubt that they can continue to grow over the next few years through acquisition.

Even after several acquisitions in the last five years, debt remains at a consistently low level, freeing up cash for (among other things) its stock buyback efforts. The company continues to buy back its stock, having reduced its outstanding shares by over 10 percent over the last ten years.

Finally, their financial results speak well of the management. Yes, the healthcare segment has been the right place at the right time for the last decade, but Bard has shown themselves capable of efficient, sustained growth with a five-year total return to share-holders over 100 percent higher than the rest of the Health Care Equipment sector.

Reasons for Caution

Bard is quite a bit smaller than its major competitors (St. Jude Medical, Boston Scientific, and Johnson & Johnson). While this does not represent risk in and of itself, it does mean they face some challenges with regard to "taking it to the next level." Bard cannot outspend their competition in R&D; the majority of their sales are domestic and their competition is better represented internationally; they are at greater risk should there be a broad and extended downturn in the industry.

SECTOR: **Consumer Health Care**
BETA COEFFICIENT: **.60**
10-YEAR COMPOUND EARNINGS PER SHARE GROWTH: **14.5%**
10-YEAR COMPOUND DIVIDENDS PER SHARE GROWTH: **5.0%**

	2008	2007	2006	2005	2004	2003	2002	2001	2000
Revenues (Mil)	2,452	2,202	1,985	1,771	1,656	1,433	1,274	1,181	1,099
Net Income (Mil)	455	406	352	327	263	204	177	143	125V
Earnings per share	4.44	3.84	3.29	3.12	2.45	1.94	1.68	1.38	1.23
Dividends per share	0.62	0.58	0.54	0.50	0.47	0.45	0.43	0.42	0.41
Price: high	101.6	95.3	85.7	72.8	65.1	40.8	32.0	32.5	27.5
low	70.0	76.6	59.9	60.8	40.1	27.0	22.0	20.4	17.5

CVS/Caremark Corporation

One CVS Drive ◻ Woonsocket, RI 02895 ◻ Phone: (914) 722–4704 ◻ Website: www.cvs.com ◻ Listed: NYSE
◻ Ticker symbol: CVS ◻ S&P rating: A ◻ Value Line financial strength rating: A

Financial Highlights, Fiscal Year 2008

CVS closed the year with $87.5B, up 14.6 percent versus FY2007. Net earnings rose 21.8 percent to $3.21B, while per-share earnings from continuing operations rose 18.5 percent to $2.27. The company added nearly 700 stores through acquisition and organic growth, and still managed to grow operating and net margins by 110 and 60 basis points (1.1 percent and 0.6 percent), respectively.

In August CVS closed on their purchase of Long's Drugs, a 521-store chain based primarily in California, but with stores in Hawaii, Nevada, and Arizona as well. Included in the deal is Long's PBM (pharmacy benefits management) business, which brought with it 8 million prescription members and 450,000 Medicare beneficiaries.

Company Profile

Stanley and Sid Goldstein were distributing health and beauty products in the early 1960s when they decided to branch out into retailing. The brothers then opened their first Consumer Value Store in Lowell, Massachusetts, in 1963. The CVS chain had grown to forty outlets by 1969, the year they sold the business to Melville Shoes. Melville underwent a restructuring in the mid-1990s, spinning off CVS and other retail units.

CVS Corporation is now the largest domestic drug store chain, based on store count. CVS operates over 6,900 retail and specialty pharmacy stores in forty states and the District of Columbia. The company holds the leading market share in thirty-two of the 100 largest U.S. drug store markets, or more than any other retail drug store chain.

Stores are situated primarily in strip shopping centers or free-standing locations, with a typical store ranging in size from 8,000 to 12,000 square feet. Most new units being built are based on either a 10,000 square foot or 12,000 square foot prototype building that typically includes a drive-thru pharmacy. The company says that about one-half of its stores were opened or remodeled over the past five years.

The Caremark acquisition in 2007 transformed CVS from a retailer into the nation's leading manager of pharmacy benefits, the middlemen between pharmaceutical companies and employees and others with drug benefit coverage.

CVS's purchase of Long's Drugs in 2008 vaulted the company into the lead position of the U.S. drug retail market, ahead of Walgreen's. Long's is only the most recent in a series of acquisitions by CVS over the past three years, including MinuteClinic, Osco

Drugs; and Sav-On Drugs in 2006; Caremark (for $26.5B) in 2007; and finally Long's (for $2.6B) in 2008. Earnings over the period have nearly tripled, although per-share earnings have grown a somewhat more modest 55 percent.

Reasons to Buy

In addition to growing revenues, CVS has added to the bottom line with both the Caremark and the Long's acquisition. Even with all the acquisition activity over the last two years, net margin has grown 40 and 60 basis points (0.4–0.6 percent, significant in the retail sector). CVS has said that they will continue to look at any acquisition that makes sense.

The company added 90 new PBM clients in 2008, which CVS says will generate an additional $7B in revenue in 2009.

At the time of the Long's purchase, CEO Thomas Ryan said CVS is "fully committed" to a planned

$2B repurchase of common shares announced in May, prior to closing the Long's deal.

Looking at the U.S. population, approximately 38 million people are 65 or older today. That number is projected to climb to 47 million by 2015, and prescription drug use is expected to rise substantially within this demographic. With leading market positions in California, Florida, and other sun-belt states, CVS feels they stand to benefit from this trend to a greater extent than most other pharmacy players.

Reasons for Caution

Drug stores face growing competition from major retailers. Wal-Mart, Target, and Costco, for instance, are among the big chains that have added pharmacies.

The Obama administration has promised to address rising health care costs by the end of 2009, but details of that plan are still being worked out.

SECTOR: Retail
BETA COEFFICIENT: 0.85
10-YEAR COMPOUND EARNINGS PER SHARE GROWTH: 14.5%
10-YEAR COMPOUND DIVIDENDS PER SHARE GROWTH: 10%

	2008	2007	2006	2005	2004	2003	2002	2001	2000
Rev (Mil)	87,472	76,330	43,814	37,006	30,594	26,588	24,182	22,241	20,088
Net Income (Mil)	3,589	2,637	1,369	1,225	959	847	719	638	734
Earnings per share	2.44	1.92	1.60	1.45	1.15	1.03	0.88	0.78	0.90
Dividends per share	0.26	0.24	0.16	0.14	0.13	0.12	0.12	0.12	0.12
Price high	44.3	42.6	36.1	31.6	23.7	18.8	17.9	31.9	30.2
low	23.2	30.5	26.1	22.0	16.9	10.9	11.5	11.5	13.9

Deere & Company

One John Deere Place ▫ Moline, IL 61265 ▫ Phone: (309) 765–4491 ▫ Website: www.deere.com ▫ Listed: NYSE ▫ Fiscal year ends October 31 ▫ Ticker symbol: DE ▫ S&P rating: A– ▫ Value Line financial strength rating: A++

Financial Highlight, Fiscal Year 2008

Deere & Company reported year/year growth in earnings of 12.6 percent (to $2.05B), trailing a 20 percent increase in revenue (to $25.8B). Earnings per share were up 17.5 percent to $4.70 on net margins of 8 percent, down 50 basis points year/year.

The company measures its internal programs and its financial health against what they refer to as Shareholder Value Add, which is, essentially, net operating margins minus the pre-tax cost of capital. Against this measure, all of Deere's operating arms were net positive contributors to shareholder value. SVA is a fairly rigorous and conservative measure that is most appropriate for longer-term projects and programs, as it tends to negate the effects of variation in the short-term cost of capital. Deere adopted this tool throughout the corporation in 2001 and feels it has been a powerful contributor to their success since then

Company Profile

Deere & Company, founded in 1837, grew from a one-man blacksmith shop into a worldwide corporation that today does business in more than 160 countries and employs more than 40,000 people around the globe.

Deere has a diverse base of operations including three equipment operations, credit operations, and four support operations:

- *Agricultural Equipment*—John Deere has been the world's premier producer of agricultural equipment since 1963. Products include tractors; combines, cotton and sugar cane harvesters; tillage, seeding and soil-preparation machinery; hay and forage equipment; materials-handling equipment; and integrated agricultural management systems technology for the global farming industry.

- *Construction and Forestry Equipment*—Deere is the world's leading manufacturer of forestry equipment, and a major manufacturer of construction equipment, including backhoes, four-wheel-drive loaders, graders, excavators, crawler dozers, log skidders, skid steer loaders, wheeled and tracked harvesters, forwarders, and log loaders.

- *Commercial and Consumer Equipment*—Deere is the world leader in premium turf-care equipment and world vehicles. The company produces a broad range of outdoor power products for both homeowners and commercial users, including tractors, mowers, utility vehicles, golf and turf equipment, and hand-held products.

- *Credit Operations*—John Deere Credit is one of the largest equipment finance companies in the United States, with more than 1.8 million accounts and a managed asset portfolio of nearly $16 billion. It provides retail, wholesale, and lease financing for agricultural, construction and forestry, and commercial and consumer equipment (including lawn and ground care),—and revolving credit for agricultural inputs and services. John Deere Credit also provides financing in Argentina, Australia, Brazil, Canada, Finland, France, Germany, Italy, Luxembourg, Spain, and the United Kingdom.

- *Support Operations*—John Deere is a major supplier of service parts for its own products as well as those of other manufacturers.

- *Power Systems*—Deere is a world leader in the production of off-highway diesel engines in the 50- to 600-horsepower range, supplying heavy-duty engines and drive train systems for OEM markets in addition to John Deere Equipment Operations.

- *Technology Services*—Includes a wide range of electronic, wireless communication, information system, and Internet-related products and services to Deere and outside customers.

- *Health Care*—John Deere Health-care subsidiaries provide health-care management services to about 4,400 employer groups and covers more than 515,000 members.

Reasons to Buy

Most think of Deere as simply a manufacturer of capital equipment—large tractors, combines, bulldozers, etc. But Deere has leveraged its close relationship with its customers, farmers for example, to create business opportunities for which they are uniquely positioned. Their financing arm, for instance, sells crop insurance to many of the same people who buy their farm equipment. These same farmers also rent land to Deere for Deere's joint ventures in wind farms.

Deere's products are competitive worldwide. The company sells over 50 percent of its units outside the United States and Canada and has recently entered into a joint venture in China to produce construction equipment for the Chinese market.

The real story on Deere at this time is not the numbers they put up exiting 2008 (which were good), nor is it the numbers they've put up since (disappointing, but not alarming), but the buying opportunity created by the market's desertion of this excellent stock. Deere's products are the gold standard in most of their markets and the company's finances are in great shape. They have solid management, well-regarded products, and a loyal customer base. Deere is in a good position to capitalize on a return to normalcy in both the commodity and credit markets. As agriculture remains indispensable as "the world's work," the long-term future of this business is sound.

Reasons for Caution

Deere exited 2008 with high inventories and cash at its lowest point in several years. Working capital is at its lowest point since the 2001 recession.

SECTOR: **Industrials**
BETA COEFFICIENT: **1.40**
10-YEAR COMPOUND EARNINGS PER SHARE GROWTH: **8.0%**
10-YEAR COMPOUND DIVIDENDS PER SHARE GROWTH: **8.5%**

		2008	2007	2006	2005	2004	2003	2002	2001	2000
Revenues (Mil)		25,804	21,489	19,884	19,401	17,673	13,349	11,703	11,077	11,169
Net Income (Mil)		2,053	1,822	1,453	1,447	1,406	643	319	153	486
Earnings per share		4.70	4.01	3.08	2.94	2.78	1.32	0.67	0.32	1.03
Dividends per share		1.06	0.91	0.78	0.61	0.53	0.44	0.44	0.44	0.44
Price	high	94.9	93.7	50.7	37.4	37.5	33.7	25.8	23.1	24.8
	low	28.5	45.1	33.5	28.5	28.4	18.8	18.8	16.8	15.2

Dentsply International, Inc.

P.O. Box 872 ▫ 221 West Philadelphia Street ▫ York, PA 17405–0872 ▫ Phone: (717) 849–4243 ▫ Website: www.dentsply.com ▫ Listed: NASDAQ ▫ Ticker symbol: XRAY ▫ S&P rating: A– ▫ Value Line financial strength rating: B++

Financial Highlights, Fiscal Year 2008

Dentsply returned a solid 2008, with revenues up 9.2 percent to $2.2B and per-share earnings up 13.3 percent to $1.88. Net income was up 11.3 percent to $286M. Recent acquisitions contributed nearly 35 percent of total growth.

The company made several acquisitions in 2008 mainly on the international front, including a 60 percent ownership in Zhermack S.p.A., a dental consumable products manufacturer and distributor; E.S. Holding N.V., a manufacturer and sales and marketing organization of dental laboratory products; Dental Depot Lomberg B.V., a sales and marketing organization of orthodontic products; and Apollonia & Fama Implant S.r.l., a sales and marketing organization of dental implant products. The company also purchased an additional interest in Materialise Dental in 2008.

Company Profile

Dentsply designs, develops, manufactures, and markets a broad range of products for the dental market. The company believes that it is the world's leading manufacturer and distributor of dental prosthetics, precious metal dental alloys, dental ceramics, endodontic instruments and materials, prophylaxis paste, dental sealants, ultrasonic scalers, and crown and bridge materials; the leading United States manufacturer and distributor of dental x-ray equipment, dental handpieces, intraoral cameras, dental x-ray film holders, film mounts, and bone substitute/grafting materials; and a leading worldwide manufacturer or distributor of dental injectable anesthetics, impression materials, orthodontic appliances, dental cutting instruments, and dental implants. In all, the company produces or resells over 120,000 items, or SKUs, protected by more than 2,000 patents.

Dentsply has a presence in more than 120 countries, though its main operations take place in the United States, Canada, Germany, Switzerland, Italy, the United Kingdom, Japan, and Italy. The company has an extensive sales network of over 2,100 sales representatives, distributors, and importers. Many of Dentsply's products are bestsellers in the domestic dental market. Its products are manufactured both domestically and internationally and have some of the most well-established brand names in dental circles, such as Caulk, Cavitron, Ceramco, Dentsply, Detrey, Midwest, R&R Rinn, and Trubyte.

Reasons to Buy

Demographics, at least in the domestic market, are working in the company's favor. Older people tend to spend more on dental care, and every office visit, whether it be for a simple cleaning or full endodontic repair, uses Dentsply consumables.

Trends in the global economy also favor Dentsply. Dental care in the developing world, particularly India and China, is growing far faster than in the mature domestic market. International sales represent over 60 percent of Dentsply's total sales, and they have very good presence in global markets.

The company has a good track record of dependable earnings and share growth. Despite the recent economic downturn, they have grown both top and bottom lines with negligible declines in margins. They are nearly debt-free and have cash to support both share repurchase and acquisitions, should opportunities arise. They continue to invest heavily in R&D and maintain their record of introducing an average of 25 new products per year.

Reasons for Caution

Until economic conditions improve, Dentsply's top line will likely moderate as people defer elective dental procedures.

SECTOR: **Health Care**
BETA COEFFICIENT: **.85**
10-YEAR COMPOUND EARNINGS PER SHARE GROWTH: **14%**
10-YEAR COMPOUND DIVIDENDS PER SHARE GROWTH: **9.5%**

	2008	2007	2006	2005	2004	2003	2002	2001	2000
Revenues (Mil)	2,194	2,010	1,810	1,715	1,694	1,571	1,514	1,129	890
Net Income (Mil)	286	260	224	216	196	173	146	110	101
Earnings per share	1.88	1.68	1.41	1.34	1.20	1.07	0.92	0.70	0.65
Dividends per share	.19	0.16	0.14	0.12	0.11	0.10	0.09	0.09	0.09
Price high	47.1	47.8	33.8	29.2	28.4	23.7	21.8	17.4	14.5
low	22.8	29.4	26.1	25.4	20.9	16.1	15.7	10.9	7.7

Diebold, Inc.

5995 Mayfair Road ▫ North Canton, OH 44720-8077 ▫ Phone: (330) 490–4000 ▫ Website: www.diebold. com ▫ Listed: NYSE ▫ Ticker symbol: DBD ▫ S&P Rating: NA ▫ Value Line financial strength rating: A

Financial Highlights, Fiscal Year 2008

Sales in 2008 totaled $3.17B, up 7.3 percent from 2007. That figure exceeds the normal growth run rate primarily because of a surge of Chinese deliveries in advance of the 2008 Olympics, and that plus the 2009 recession will make year-to-year comparisons difficult. Operating margins also enjoyed a revival closer to 11 percent after a few years below the 10 percent mark. With these figures in mind, it's not surprising that total net profit grew some 62 percent to $173M in 2008; however, again, 2009 will almost certainly be weaker due to the global slowdown and especially the slowdown in the financial sector, where most of its largest customers reside.

With the recent downturn the company focused on several cost reduction initiatives, including the consolidation of distribution centers and the offshoring of some manufacturing, including a reported 85-percent shift of ATM machine manufacturing to "low cost geographies." These initiatives accounted for a good portion of the revival to 11 percent operating margins. During Q1 2009, the company reported weaker demand particularly from U.S. regional banks and Russia and Eastern Europe, but that orders "remained solid" in Asia Pacific, Latin America, and with U.S. *large* banks. Despite a weaker top line, the company reported a 5 percent increase in operating cash flow in the quarter.

Company Profile

Diebold is a "safe" company and has been from the beginning. Founded in 1859 in Cincinnati, Ohio, as a manufacturer of safes, the company has evolved to provide a complete assortment of banking hardware and technology, the most obvious and prominent of which you'll see on the outside of a bank are its ubiquitous ATM machines.

Diebold, Inc., engages in the development, manufacture, sale, installation, and service of banking and financial services systems, including automated self-service transaction systems (ATMs), and electronic and physical security systems including safes, vaults, depositories, card and biometric security systems, and other systems designed to handle processing and physical flow of currency and other materials for banks. It also sells and services electronic voting and election systems and software worldwide. The company also offers an assortment of consulting, monitoring, and outsourcing solutions to the banking industry.

Reasons to Buy

Although banks and financial services companies have fallen on tough times and may cut back spending in the short run, Diebold is well positioned strategically to capture new business in a different way. As banks and financial services companies downsize and "rightsize" they will be looking for consulting services and outsourced solutions, and Diebold is aligning itself to provide such a set of solutions and services. In fact, Diebold was listed in June 2009 among the International Association of Outsourcing Professionals (IAOP) 10 best outsourcing providers within the services industry, its third consecutive year on the list.

As banks and financial services companies rethink themselves, there will be a greater need not only for services but for new infrastructure and technology. This plus growth in international markets as more overseas banks automate in emerging markets like China and India should help drive future demand.

Diebold also continues to make gains on the technology front, with ATM-based tools to accept large cash deposits, a big drain on inside teller bank resources servicing retailers and other large cash customers. What could be an eventual mainstream acceptance of biometric security systems—fingerprint or eye pattern recognition—could also result in a future growth spurt.

In March 2008 United Technologies made an unsolicited $40 per-share bid for the company, which was rejected as insufficient. The company appears to be in a good position to receive such takeover bids in the future.

Finally, the company continues to focus on cash flow and shareholder returns, with a 3.9 percent yield (July 2009). Moreover, the company has increased its dividend some *fifty-six consecutive years*. As of July 2009, the company was selling at prices not seen since the late 1990s; at that time, net revenues per share were about $17, compared to almost $48 in 2008.

Reasons for Caution

The global downturn in banking and financial institution performance is a nagging negative, but as pointed out, could bring new greater business opportunity as that industry's consolidation and reinvention progress. Some of Diebold's products are tied to legacy check processing, and as checks and even cash become less widely circulated as, say, people become enabled to buy and sell with their cell phones, Diebold will have to make the appropriate adjustments. Despite the recent upturns in margins due to process improvements, industry margins have been on a long, slow downtrend.

The company was also involved in an action with the SEC over revenue recognition policy, which caused a restatement of earnings 2003–2006, but that matter has since been resolved.

SECTOR: **Industrials**
BETA COEFFICIENT: **0.97**
10-YEAR COMPOUND EARNINGS PER SHARE GROWTH: **2.0%**
10-YEAR COMPOUND DIVIDENDS PER SHARE GROWTH: **6.5%**

	2008	2007	2006	2005	2004	2003	2002	2001	2000
Revenues (Mil)	3,170	2,964	2,906	2,587	2,381	2,110	1,940	1,760	1,744
Net Income (Mil)	173.5	108.0	121.7	136.3	184.0	174.8	158.1	140.5	136.5
Earnings per share	2.61	1.62	1.82	1.92	2.54	2.40	2.19	1.96	1.92
Dividends per share	1.00	0.94	0.86	0.82	0.74	0.68	0.66	0.64	0.62
Price high	40.4	54.5	47.1	57.8	56.4	57.4	43.6	41.5	34.8
low	22.5	28.3	36.4	33.1	43.9	33.5	30.3	25.8	21.5

GROWTH AND INCOME

Dominion Resources, Inc.

P.O. Box 26532 ▫ Richmond, VA 23261–6532 ▫ Phone: (804) 819–2156 ▫ Website: www.dom.com ▫
Listed: NYSE ▫ Ticker symbol: D ▫ S&P rating: B+ ▫ Value Line financial strength rating: B++

Financial Highlights, Fiscal Year 2008

Dominion's revenues increased marginally to $27.9B, up 2.7 percent. Earnings from ongoing operations rose to $1.78B, an increase of 26.2 percent. Dividends rose 5 percent to $1.58/share.

The company added nearly 37, 000 new customer accounts to its Dominion Virginia Power (DVP) business, began construction on a 585 megawatt coal facility in southwestern Virginia, and brought on-line nearly 800 megawatts of new generation capacity, which includes nuclear, gas, and wind sources. Dominion also completed the farm-out of drilling rights to more than 100,000 acres of Marcellus Shale in the Appalachian Basin.

Company Profile

Dominion is one of the nation's largest producers of energy, with a portfolio of more than 26,500 megawatts of generation and 7,800 miles of natural gas transmission pipeline. Dominion also owns and operates the nation's largest underground natural gas storage system with about 960 billion cubic feet of storage capacity serving retail energy customers in eleven states. Dominion's strategy is to be a leading provider of electricity, natural gas, and related services to customers in the energy-intensive Midwest, Mid-Atlantic and Northeast regions of the United States, a potential market of fifty million homes and businesses where 40 percent of the nation's energy is consumed.

As of August 2007, Dominion has three reporting business segments:

Dominion Virginia Power is responsible for all regulated electric distribution and electric transmission operations in Virginia and North

Carolina. It is also responsible for Dominion Retail and all customer service, as well as our nonregulated retail energy marketing operations. DVP's electric transmission and distribution operations serve residential, commercial, industrial, and governmental customers in Virginia and northeastern North Carolina.

Dominion Generation includes the generation operations of Dominion's merchant fleet and regulated electric utility, as well as energy marketing and price risk management activities for our generation assets. Their utility generation operations primarily serve the supply requirements for the DVP segment's utility customers. Their generation mix is diversified and includes coal, nuclear, gas, oil, and renewables.

Dominion Energy includes Dominion's Ohio regulated natural gas distribution company, regulated gas transmission pipeline and storage operations, regulated LNG operations, and Appalachian natural gas E&P business. Dominion Energy also includes producer services, which aggregates natural gas supply, engages in natural gas trading and marketing activities and natural gas supply management, and provides price risk management services to Dominion affiliates.

The gas transmission pipeline and storage business serves gas distribution businesses and other customers in the Northeast, Mid-Atlantic, and Midwest.

Reasons to Buy

Dominion has filed for a rate increase with the Virginia commission that would raise $288M with a one percent premium for effective performance. This rate increase would be based on a 13.5 percent ROE. As part of their longer-term plan to complete the build-out of an additional 3,900 megawatts of generation capacity for Virginia customers, the company is also filing two additional requests for $176M based on a 14.5 percent ROE.

Free cash flow covered the costs of all operations, maintenance, and dividends. The company plans to divest itself of certain assets to pay down debt, and plans to access the equity markets only to fund further expansion.

The company will continue to lease out the remainder of its 800,000 acres of Marcellus Shale. The 100,000 acres already leased generated $347M in pretax income, in addition to a 7.5 percent royalty on future gas generation from the assigned leases.

The company's current dividend of $1.58 represents a 3.8 percent dividend yield at mid-2009 share prices.

Recent changes in Virginia law will now allow utilities to recover from customers on a dollar-for-dollar basis the under-recovered costs for natural gas, coal, uranium, and other fuels. Prior to this change, the shareholders absorbed the loss. In the period from 2004–2007, this amounted to over $2B in pre-tax earnings.

Reasons for Caution

The company plans to add $900M in common shares over the next two years, diluting existing shareholders, and expanding dividend payments somewhat.

SECTOR: **Utilities**
BETA COEFFICIENT: **.70**
10-YEAR COMPOUND EARNINGS PER SHARE GROWTH: **7.5%**
10-YEAR COMPOUND DIVIDENDS PER SHARE GROWTH: **1.5%**

		2008	2007	2006	2005	2004	2003	2002	2001	2000
Revenues (Mil)		16,290	15,674	16,482	17,971	13,972	12,078	10,218	10,558	9,260
Net Income (Mil)		1,781	1,414	1,704	1,033	1,425	1,261	1,378	775	624
Earnings per share		3.04	2.13	2.40	1.50	2.13	1.96	2.41	1.49	1.25
Dividends per share		1.58	1.46	1.38	1.34	1.30	2.58	1.29	1.29	1.29
Price	high	48.5	49.4	42.2	43.5	34.5	33.0	33.6	35.0	34.0
	low	31.3	39.8	34.4	33.3	30.4	25.9	17.7	27.6	17.4

AGGRESSIVE GROWTH

Dover Corporation

280 Park Avenue □ New York, NY 10017–1292 □ Phone: (212) 922–1640 □ Website:
www.dovercorporation.com □ Listed: NYSE □ Ticker symbol: DOV □ S&P rating: A □ Value Line
financial strength rating: A

Financial Highlights, Fiscal Year 2008

2008 was a record year for Dover in terms of revenue (up 4.7 percent to $7.57B), earnings (up 6.3 percent to $695M), and earnings per share (up 14 percent to $3.67). Net margin was a healthy 9.2 percent and cash flow per share was a record $5.14, up 11 percent year/year. Dividends were up 17 percent.

Unfortunately, the fourth quarter slowdown experienced by most of the industrials did not miss Dover, and many of Dover's traditional customers are still having liquidity concerns. Margins will likely be thin through most of 2009 until spending in the capital goods sector picks up.

Company Profile

Dover Corporation is a diversified industrial manufacturer comprised of over forty operating companies that manufacture specialized industrial products and manufacturing equipment.

Dover's overall strategy is to acquire and develop platform businesses, marked by growth, innovation, and higher-than-average profits margins. Traditionally, the company has focused on purchasing entities that could operate independently. However, over the past ten years, Dover has put increased emphasis on also acquiring businesses that can be added to existing operations. Dover operates as a decentralized corporation, but provides resources as necessary and implements best practices company-wide, as appropriate.

The company measures all of its businesses against a set of metrics it refers to as "PerformanceCounts." These are:

- Eight or more inventory turns
- 10 percent or greater annual earnings growth
- 15 percent or greater operating margins
- 20 percent or less working capital as a percent of assets
- 25 percent or greater after-tax return on investment

The companies are organized into four reporting segments by their addressed markets: Electronic Technologies, Engineered Systems, Fluid Management, and Industrial Products. The corporation grows by acquisition and targets 8–10 percent of revenue annually for acquisition capital. Its operating companies are expected to show organic growth at 5–7 percent of revenue.

Their acquisition criteria are fairly specific. They seek high value-added, engineered industrial products whose performance is critical to the customer, have defensible differentiation, and whose markets have high barriers to entry. They focus on industrial components and products sold to a broad customer base of industrial and/or commercial users and prefer longer product life cycles with low or moderate market revenue and market volatility.

In other words, dot.coms need not apply.

They also look for companies with existing regional or national distribution systems and with potential for global distribution. They strongly prefer to keep existing management in place whenever possible, as they are

buying for the long term. They buy business both as additions to current business operations (looking for synergy) and as more or less independent "stand-alone" businesses, although the stand-alone business should still fit into one of the company's four operating segments.

Reasons to Buy

Dover is a company the likes of which you don't see very often anymore. Many of the mid-sized conglomerates were busted up and sold for parts back in the glory (gory) days of hostile takeovers. Dover has survived and done well by growing carefully and profitably, while focusing on a few key markets where they have core competencies and which work best with their style of management. This is a conservatively run operation that just happens to generate over 10 percent free cash flow, year in and year out.

The company is in the midst of a number of initiatives to reduce costs and leverage their existing assets. The cost reductions have already begun to pay off, adding $.15/share in 2008 with additional improvement expected in 2009. They are also consolidating facilities across their businesses in order to eliminate redundancy with no impact to the top line. Finally, they are projecting a $75–$100M cost savings as a result of their new global procurement strategy, to take effect in the 2010–2011 timeframe.

Reasons for Caution

As we mentioned, Dover serves the industrial sector exclusively. As industrials were significantly challenged in late 2008 and continue to be so throughout 2009, expect some of Dover's businesses to perform better than others. In particular, they expect their automotive and infrastructure businesses will experience meaningful slowdowns with an uncertain recovery.

SECTOR: **Industrials**
BETA COEFFICIENT: **1.15**
10-YEAR COMPOUND EARNINGS PER SHARE GROWTH: **6.5%**
10-YEAR COMPOUND DIVIDENDS PER SHARE GROWTH: **8.5%**

	2008	2007	2006	2005	2004	2003	2002	2001	2000
Revenues (Mil)	7,569	7,226	6,512	6,078	5,488	4,413	4,184	4,460	5,401
Net Income (Mil)	695	661	562	510	413	285	211	167	525
Earnings per share	3.67	3.26	2.73	2.50	2.00	1.40	1.04	0.82	2.57
Dividends per share	.90	0.80	0.71	0.65	0.62	0.57	0.54	0.52	0.48
Price high	54.6	54.6	51.9	42.2	44.1	40.4	43.6	43.6	54.4
low	23.4	44.3	40.3	34.1	35.1	22.8	23.5	26.4	34.1

GROWTH AND INCOME

E. I. DuPont De Nemours

1007 Market Street □ Wilmington, DE 19898 □ Phone: (800) 441–7515 □ Website: www.dupont.com □
Ticker symbol: DD □ Listed: NYSE □ S&P rating: A- □ Value Line financial strength rating: A++

Financial Highlights, Fiscal Year 2008

Revenues grew only 4 percent (to $30.5B) in 2008, while earnings fell 18 percent (to $2.48B) versus 2007. The biggest declines were in Coating and Color Technologies and Performance Materials, both of which are closely tied to domestic and international auto production.

Cost of goods sold (COGS) was up 11 percent (7 percent over sales) due to the high costs of petroleum, which is one of DuPont's major raw materials as well as a cost driver for the high- energy content of its products. Operating margin was down over 360 basis points (3.6 percent) to 11 percent, which is quite low for DuPont. Net margin was down over 220 basis points, or 2.2 percent.

Company Profile

DuPont was founded in 1802 and was incorporated in Delaware in 1915. DuPont is a world leader in science and technology in a range of disciplines, including biotechnology, electronics materials and science, safety and security, and synthetic fibers.

Recently, the company strategically realigned its businesses into five market- and technology-focused growth platforms:

- Agriculture and Nutrition
- Coatings and Color Technologies
- Electronic and Communication Technologies
- Performance Materials
- Safety and Protection

The company has operations in about seventy-five countries worldwide and about 55 percent of consolidated net sales are made to customers outside the United States. Subsidiaries and affiliates of DuPont conduct manufacturing, seed production, or selling activities, and some are distributors of products manufactured by the company.

DuPont has one of the largest R&D budgets of any company in the world. In 2008, DuPont spent $1.4 billion on research and development, representing a spending level that has been fixed at 5 percent of net sales from 2006–2008, enabling the company to bring more than a thousand new products to market per year. In 2007, the company was ranked No. 1 in the Patent Board 500 ranking of patent portfolios of companies across the globe, with about 2000 new patent filings and over 20,000 patents in force worldwide. DuPont operates more than fifty R&D centers around the world, aiming to attract the best available scientific talent and take advantage of the regional knowledge necessary to create products that cater to the varying needs of customers in every market. DuPont's research is concentrated at its Wilmington, Delaware, facilities.

DuPont's modern research is focused on renewable bio-based materials, advanced biofuels, energy-efficient technologies, enhanced safety products, and alternative energy technologies.

Reasons to Buy

DuPont is a raw material supplier for many of the industries that are currently "in disfavor," to employ the more genteel language popular among some stock analysts. Basically, their customers aren't buying DuPont products. So why should one consider buying DuPont stock? Well, at the beginning of 2008 the company's prospects were great. The share price had been basically flat since 2002, but the company had been growing the top and bottom line at a steady pace and, by the way, had been throwing off regular dividend yields in the 3-4 percent range year after year.

So what's changed? Some customers, notably those attached to the U.S. auto industry (and the auto industry itself) have experienced major downturns, and DuPont's share price has been beaten down as a result. The company is going through a restructuring and is eliminating $1B in fixed costs, the charges for which will record in 2009. The rest of the company, the agricultural, electronics, and safety segments (which constitute 65 percent of operating income) are growing throughout the recession.

So if the stock price is a bet on future earnings, and 2010 earnings are projected at above 2005 levels, and you could pick up this stock for half of what it cost in 2005, would you? If the stock is still trading in the mid-20s and the yield is still in the 4 percent range at the start of 2010, it would seem to make sense.

Reasons for Caution

The company is carrying nearly $10B in debt ($2B current). With its reduced cash flow the company will be hard-pressed to buy significant top-line growth and will need to be successful with its cost structure improvements.

It should be noted that revenue from a pharmaceutical licensing agreement with Merck is for ingredients in products which come off patent protection in 2010, and all royalties are scheduled to end in 2013. These changes, however, have been baked into the prices discussed above.

SECTOR: **Materials**
BETA COEFFICIENT: **1.05**
10-YEAR COMPOUND EARNINGS PER SHARE GROWTH: **−0.5%**
10-YEAR COMPOUND DIVIDENDS PER SHARE GROWTH: **2.5%**

		2008	2007	2006	2005	2004	2003	2002	2001	2000
Revenues (Mil)		30,529	30,653	28,982	26,639	27,340	26,996	24,006	24,726	28,268
Net Income (Mil)		2,477	2,988	3,148	2,100	2,390	1,607	2,012	1,236	2,884
Earnings per share		2.73	3.22	2.88	2.32	2.38	1.65	2.01	1.19	2.73
Dividends per share		1.64	1.52	1.48	1.46	1.40	1.40	1.40	1.40	1.40
Price	high	52.5	53.9	49.7	54.9	49.4	46.0	49.8	49.9	74.0
	Low	21.3	42.3	38.5	37.6	39.9	34.7	35.0	32.6	38.2

eBay, Inc.

2145 Hamilton Avenue ▢ San Jose, CA 95125 ▢ Phone: (408) 376–7400 ▢ Website: www.ebay.com ▢
Listed: NASDAQ ▢ Ticker symbol: EBAY ▢ S&P rating: A- ▢ Value Line financial strength rating: A+

Financial Highlights, Fiscal Year 2008

Despite slowdowns in the global e-commerce market, revenues were up 11 percent in 2008, led by a $500M increase from the payments segment (up 26 percent). The larger Marketplaces segment, eBay's most visible business, was up only 1 percent. Skype was a pleasant surprise, reporting in with a 44 percent increase to $526M. The number of registered users jumped 47 percent to over 400 million.

Income was up 8.7 percent to $1.78B, and operating margin grew 610 basis points or 6.1 percent to 40.1 percent.

2008 marked the first time that PayPal's transactions from outside eBay Marketplace were greater than the level of transactions from within eBay, marking the service's growing acceptance in the broader market.

Acquisitions made during the year included Bill Me Later, a credit issuer that enhances eBay's payments business, and Fraud Sciences, a risk management provider. The company also acquired the two leading classified ad sites in Denmark.

Company Profile

eBay provides an Internet-based auction and retailing space that enables buyers and sellers worldwide to engage in commerce. Everything imaginable (not including regulated or prohibited items) has been sold on eBay, or probably will be soon. It's been called "the world's garage sale," but in addition to its consumer-to-consumer segment, eBay also provides a global storefront to businesses and retailers worldwide that would otherwise never have the sort of reach that eBay gives them. In fact, eBay's business model is more that of an integrated e-commerce site than a classifieds/auction house.

eBay operates in three segments: Marketplaces, Payments, and Communications. The Marketplace segment provides the infrastructure for global commerce on a variety of eBay's businesses, including the traditional eBay platform, StubHub, Shopping.com, Rent.com, and Half.com. The Payments segment includes online payments providers PayPal and Bill Me Later. The Communications segment was formed for Skype, which is a VoIP (internet phone) service that provides free calls worldwide to other Skype users and low-cost calls to traditional phones.

Unlike their major e-commerce competitor, Amazon, eBay holds no inventory. All of their retailing revenues are based on listing, transaction, and marketing fees. Other revenue sources include interest earned on deposits in PayPal accounts and interest and fees earned on the Bill Me Later loan portfolio.

Reasons to Buy

eBay has been one of the major pioneers of e-commerce and one of the few companies to actually make money at it. They've learned that it's easier to sell something that people already want, as opposed to developing a product and then trying to convince people that they need it.

eBay is a top business in all three of its operating segments. Marketplaces had over $100B in transactions last year on preowned items alone. PayPal handled over $60B in payment volume in 2008, and processes the transactions for over 9 percent of all e-commerce worldwide. Skype was one of the first to market with voice-over-IP service and has grown its leading market share dramatically.

The Skype business, however, despite its gains in the marketplace, will be spun off in 2010 to allow eBay to focus on its core business of e-commerce. This is wise, as the entry of competing products from traditional providers such as AT&T, Verizon, and others to the communications marketplace leaves eBay with too many fronts to defend in a highly competitive marketplace.

Reasons for Caution

eBay has a 25 percent stake in Craigslist, an Internet-based classified ad service. In 2008 the two companies have engaged in legal proceedings over Craigslist's issuance of shares and its creation of a poison pill agreement that would have made it impossible for eBay to sell its stake to anyone other than Craigslist's cofounders. Craigslist has countersued, alleging a series of legally actionable business practices on the part of eBay. Perhaps a tempest in a teapot, but it bears watching, as eBay and Craigslist are in competition for many of the same customers.

SECTOR: **Consumer Discretionary**
BETA COEFFICIENT: **1.15**
5-YEAR COMPOUND EARNINGS PER SHARE GROWTH: **63.4%**
10-YEAR COMPOUND DIVIDENDS PER SHARE GROWTH: **Nil**

	2008	2007	2006	2005	2004	2003	2002	2001	2000
Revenues (Mil)	8,541	7,672	5,969	4,552	3,271	2,165	1,214	749	431
Net Income (Mil)	1,780	1,638	1,126	1,082	778	447	250	90	48.3
Earnings per share	1.36	1.19	0.79	.78	.57	.34	.21	.08	.04
Dividends per share	Nil								
Price high	33.5	40.7	47.9	58.9	59.2	32.4	17.7	18.2	31.9
low	10.9	28.6	22.8	30.8	31.3	16.9	12.2	7.1	6.7

Ecolab, Inc.

370 Wabasha Street North ❑ St. Paul, MN 55102–1390 ❑ Phone: (651) 293–2809 ❑ Website: www.ecolab.com ❑ Listed: NYSE ❑ Ticker symbol: ECL ❑ S&P rating: A ❑ Value Line financial strength rating: A

Financial Highlights, Fiscal Year 2008

Ecolab posted another solid year of revenue, earnings, and dividend growth. Earnings were up 12 percent to a record $6.1B, while earnings grew a more modest 5 percent to $448M. Dividends grew 12 percent to $0.53/share, marking the 17th consecutive annual dividend rate increase and the 72nd consecutive year of dividend payments. Dividend yield remains at its 10-year average of 1.2 percent, due to steady increases in share price.

Return on shareholder's equity was 23 percent, making 2008 the 17th consecutive year that Ecolab has met its internal goal for ROE of 20 percent or greater.

Henkel AG completed its sale of approximately 73M shares of Ecolab stock to private and institutional investors. Henkel had held this stock as part of a joint venture which has since been fully acquired by Ecolab. Henkel announced its intention to sell the stock in early 2008 and the sale was completed in November. In a tough market, Ecolab and Henkel found private investors for the bulk of these shares, with Ecolab buying 11M shares itself at a discount. Ecolab also bought additional shares on the open market, bringing its total repurchase on the year to 12.1M shares.

Company Profile

Ecolab is the global leader in cleaning, sanitizing, and food safety and infection prevention products and services. Founded in 1923 and headquartered in St. Paul, Minnesota, Ecolab serves customers in more than 160 countries across North America, Europe, Asia Pacific, Latin America, the Middle East, and Africa, and employs more than 26,000 associates. The company delivers comprehensive programs and services to the food-service, food and beverage processing, hospitality, health-care, government and education, retail, textile care, commercial facilities, and vehicle wash industries.

The company conducts its domestic business under these segments:

- *Institutional Division* is the leading provider of cleaners and sanitizers for utensils, laundry, kitchen cleaning, and general housecleaning; product-dispensing equipment and dishwashing racks; and related kitchen sundries to the food-service, lodging, and health-care industries. It also provides products and services for pool and spa treatment.
- *Food & Beverage Division* offers cleaning and sanitizing products and services to farms,

dairy plants, food and beverage processors, and pharmaceutical plants.

- *Kay Division* is the largest supplier of cleaning and sanitizing products for the quick-service restaurant, convenience store, and food retail markets.

Ecolab also sells janitorial and health-care products (detergents, floor care, disinfectants, odor control, and hand care under the Airkem and Huntington brand names); textile care products for large institutional and commercial laundries; vehicle care products for rental, fleet, and retail car washes; and water-treatment products for commercial, institutional, and industrial markets.

Other domestic services include institutional and commercial pest elimination and prevention; and the commercial kitchen equipment repair services.

Around the world, the company operates directly in nearly seventy countries. In addition, the company reaches customers in more than 100 countries through distributors, licensees and export operations, with more than fifty state-of-the-art manufacturing and distribution facilities worldwide.

Reasons to Buy

In light of several well-publicized food contamination incidents over the past two years, Ecolab's customers have a renewed focus on cleanliness and sanitation in food preparation and serving, which is the heart of Ecolab's Institutional business. Ecolab is leveraging this positive attention by growing their presence in mainland China, where they have found a receptive customer base and huge opportunity.

Ecolab's opportunistic acquisitions have paid off handsomely, with Microtek and Evocation in particular returning solid top- and bottom-line growth. The company enters 2009 in well-positioned financially for further acquisitions.

Ecolab is the clear market leader in its two largest businesses: Institutional and Food/Beverage. It maintains a well-trained service force for these two industries, giving it strong presence in its smaller, growing segments.

Sales in 2008 were split nearly evenly between U.S. and international sales, and the company sources its raw materials in local markets, moderating the influence of fluctuations in recent currency values.

Reasons for Caution

A large portion of Ecolab's customer base is in the hard-hit restaurant and hospitality industry, so near-term results might be hurt by weakness in these customer segments. Ecolab is also vulnerable to swings in raw materials prices, and some cleaning products may run afoul of "green" initiatives.

SECTOR: **Materials**
BETA COEFFICIENT: **0.85**
10-YEAR COMPOUND EARNINGS PER SHARE GROWTH: **12.50%**
10-YEAR COMPOUND DIVIDENDS PER SHARE GROWTH: **11.0%**

	2008	2007	2006	2005	2004	2003	2002	2001	2000
Revenues (Mil)	6,138	5,470	4,896	4,535	4,185	3,762	3,404	2,321	2,264
Net Income (Mil)	464	427	369	320	310	277	210	188	209
Earnings per share	1.86	1.70	1.43	1.23	1.19	1.06	0.80	0.73	0.79
Dividends per share	.52	0.52	0.40	0.35	0.33	0.29	0.27	0.26	0.24
Price high	52.3	52.8	46.4	37.2	35.6	27.9	25.2	22.1	22.8
low	29.6	37.0	33.6	30.7	26.1	23.1	18.3	14.3	14.0

`AGGRESSIVE GROWTH`

EnCana Corporation

P.O. Box 2850 ▫ Calgary, Alberta ▫ Canada T2P 2S5 ▫ Phone: (403) 645–4737 ▫ Website: www.encana.com
▫ Ticker symbol: ECA ▫ Listed: NYSE ▫ S&P rating: B+ ▫ Value Line financial strength rating: B++

Financial Highlights, Fiscal Year 2008

Encana's revenue (net of royalties) grew 39 percent to just over $30B, by far their best year. Net earnings were up 50 percent to $5.94B, with per-share earnings up 53 percent to $7.91. Again, record results for the company. Dividends increased 100 percent to $1.60/share.

Total production of oil and natural gas was up just 6 percent over 2007, but an average 35 percent increase in natural gas prices drove the significant revenue growth.

On May 15, 2008 the board of directors of EnCana Corp. unanimously approved a proposal to split EnCana into two "highly focused" energy companies, one focused on petroleum and services, and the other a pure natural gas play. Due largely to the rapid decline in the price of oil on the world market that occurred in Q3 2008, and due partly to the dismal credit market, the company announced in October 2008 that the proposed split would be delayed indefinitely. As of May 2009 the company remains intact.

Company Profile

EnCana is one of North America's leading independent crude oil and natural gas exploration and production companies. EnCana pursues growth from its portfolio of unconventional long-life resource plays situated in Canada and the United States. The company defines resource plays as large contiguous accumulations of hydrocarbons, located in thick and extensive deposits, which typically have low geological and commercial development risk and low average decline rates.

EnCana's disciplined pursuit of these unconventional assets enabled it to become North America's largest natural gas producer and a leading developer of oil sands through its unique in-situ recovery methods.

Barron's Andrew Bary writes, "Producing crude from oil sands is dirty: The bitumen typically is strip-mined, then separated from the surrounding sands in a process that produces waste water that sits in giant pools. Once separated, bitumen needs to be heated, usually with natural gas, to produce crude oil. Environmental critics decry the strip-mining, its ugly aftereffects and the energy-intensive upgrading process, which produces greenhouse gases and other emissions."

The company is also engaged in exploration and production activities internationally and has interests in mid-stream operations and assets, including natural gas storage facilities, natural gas processing facilities, power plants, and pipelines.

EnCana operates under two main divisions: Upstream and Midstream and Marketing.

The Upstream division manages EnCana's exploration for, and development of, natural gas, crude oil and natural gas liquids, and other related activities. Following the merger in 2002, the majority of EnCana's Upstream operations are situated in Canada, the United States, Ecuador, and the United Kingdom's central North Sea. From the time of the merger through early 2004, EnCana focused on the development and expansion of its highest growth, highest return assets in those key areas. In 2004, the company sharpened its strategic focus to concentrate on its inventory of North American resource play assets. In focusing its portfolio of assets, EnCana completed a number of significant acquisitions during the past three years.

EnCana's Midstream and Marketing activities are comprised of natural gas storage operations, natural gas liquids processing and storage, power generation operations, and pipelines. The company's marketing groups are focused on enhancing the sale of Upstream proprietary production. Correspondingly, the marketing groups undertake market optimization activities, including third-party purchases and sales of product, which provides operational flexibility for transportation commitments, product type, delivery points, and customer diversification.

Reasons to Buy

Encana is the largest producer of natural gas in North America, a position it gained through both well-though-out acquisitions and through internally developed drilling and extraction techniques.

In 2008 they produced 3.8 billion cubic feet per day (bcfd) of natural gas, an eight percent increase over 2007's output. Gas and oil production combined grew 6 percent over the same period.

Encana has nearly twenty trillion cubic feet equivalent of proven reserves, or just over twelve years of production at current rates. In 2008 the company added reserves equivalent to 150 percent of production at very competitive costs.

The company generated $2.3B in free cash flow in 2008 and enters

2009 with less than $300M due debt. The strong cash position is encouraging, given Encana's commitment to dividend growth—the dividend was doubled in 2008 to $1.60, resulting in a yield of 2.3 percent.

Reasons for Caution

Lower demand will result in reduced production in 2009, and revenues are expected to fall by as much as 35 percent, with per-share earnings declining by a similar percentage. There are signs of a natural gas glut as new production comes on-line and liquefied natural gas distribution accelerates. The shares might be a timely play if you believe in the long-term strength of energy prices.

SECTOR: **Energy**
BETA COEFFICIENT: **1.20**
10-YEAR COMPOUND EARNINGS PER SHARE GROWTH: **26.0%**
10-YEAR COMPOUND DIVIDENDS PER SHARE GROWTH: **13%**

	2008	2007	2006	2005	2004	2003	2002	2001	2000
Revenues (Mil)	27,345	21,446	16,399	14,573	11,810	10,216	7,064	6,333	4,835
Net Income (Mil)	4,405	3,959	3,270	3,241	1,976	1,375	794	822	696
Earnings per share	5.86	5.18	3.91	3.64	2.11	1.44	0.82	1.58	1.37
Dividends per share	1.60	.80	.38	0.28	0.20	0.16	0.13	0.13	0.13
Price high	99.4	75.9	55.9	59.8	28.7	20.0	16.2	14.8*	
low	34.0	42.4	39.5	26.4	19.0	15.0	11.4	11.3*	

*EnCana was formed from a merger between PanCanadian Energy Corporation and Alberta Energy Company on April 5, 2002.

Energen Corporation

605 Richard Arrington Jr. Boulevard North □ Birmingham, AL 35203–2707 □ Phone: (205) 326–8421 □ Website: www.energen.com □ Listed: NYSE □ Ticker symbol: EGN □ S&P rating: BBB □ Value Line financial strength rating: A

Financial Highlights, Fiscal Year 2008

Energen's net income rose 4.1 percent in 2008 to $322M, while revenues grew 9.3 percent to $1.57B. Net margin fell 140 basis points (1.4 percent) to 20.1 percent (and expect more dramatic declines in 2009), though cash flow improved 7.5 percent to $7.03. With the end-of-year plunge in the stock price, the usual Total Return ratios applicable to capital-heavy companies are not particularly illustrative, but all fell dramatically and will continue to do so through 2009.

Company Profile

Energen is a holding company for its two subsidiaries: Energen Resources and Alagasco. Energen Resources is engaged primarily in the exploration and production of natural gas, natural gas liquids and petroleum in the continental United States. Alagasco is the largest natural gas distribution utility in the state of Alabama. It purchases natural gas from other distributors and suppliers and delivers it to its residential, industrial, and commercial customers throughout the state. It also transports natural gas, on a fee basis, for other suppliers and users located along its transportation network.

Energen's oil and gas operations are focused primarily on increas-ing production and adding proved reserves through the acquisition and development of oil and gas properties. Energen also explores for and develops new reservoirs, primarily in areas in which it already has an operating presence. Energen does no refining, and substantially all gas, oil and natural gas liquids are sold to third parties. The company's production is located in the San Juan Basin in New Mexico, the Permian Basin in western Texas, the Black Warrior Basin in Alabama, and the north Louisiana/east Texas region. Nearly two-thirds of Energen's proved reserves are natural gas, with petroleum and natural gas liquids making up the rest.

Alagasco's service territory covers central/north Alabama and includes some 185 cities and communities in twenty-eight counties with a total population of 2.4 million, including Birmingham and Montgomery. The Alagasco distribution system includes about 9,810 miles of main and more than 11,494 miles of service lines, distribution facilities, and customer meters. The system is connected to the Southern Natural Gas Company and the Transcontinental Gas Pipe Line Company, as well as to several intrastate natural gas pipeline systems and to Alagasco's two liquefied natural gas facilities.

Reasons to Buy

Energen has weathered the deterioration of oil and gas prices better than most due to their nearly 65 percent hedged volumes and its steady income from the Alagasco business. Energen reduces its risks in the Resources business by acquiring proven, producing reserves rather than relying heavily on exploration. Once in production, Energen further reduces risks by selling through fixed-price contracts of up to three-year duration. In the past, Energen has hedged up to 80 percent of its production in this way. So, unlike many oil and gas plays, liquidity is not an issue, and they have more than sufficient cash flow to support future development and exploratory operations, as well as opportunistic acquisitions.

Energen has been engaged in the exploration of gas shales in northern Alabama for just over a year, with mixed results. The shales are the same age and type as other producing deposits in Texas, and so hold a great deal of promise. The company has experience with the unique extraction methods required for this type of deposit, and if the wells do bring the expected returns, the benefits would

"change the company," according to the CEO.

Energen has completed the purchase of Range Resource Corporation's interests in the Permian Basin, in the middle of ERC's current operations in that area. The acquisition includes 13,000 acres, 445 active producing wells, and 54 active injector wells in an area with over seventy years of production history. The price was right for ERC, as 90 percent of the price was based on proven, producing reserves and the other 10 percent on proven, undeveloped reserves. Also, its location offers easy and seamless integration into ERC existing pipelines.

Reasons for Caution

Although the company is sometimes lumped in with public utilities, 85 percent of its income and nearly all of its growth potential is from oil and gas. As such, it is a riskier play than any utility, though perhaps less risky than other energy issues. This edition's change of Energen from a Conservative Growth to an Aggressive Growth stock reflects this position.

SECTOR: Energy
BETA COEFFICIENT: 1.15
10-YEAR COMPOUND EARNINGS PER SHARE GROWTH: 21.5%
10-YEAR COMPOUND DIVIDENDS PER SHARE GROWTH: 4.50%

		2008	2007	2006	2005	2004	2003	2002	2001	2000
Revenues (Mil)		1,569	1,435	1,394	1,128	937	842	677	785	556
Net Income (Mil)		316	309	274	173	127	110	70.6	67.9	53.0
Earnings per share		4.38	4.28	3.73	2.37	1.74	1.55	1.05	1.09	0.88
Dividends per share		0.48	0.46	0.44	0.40	0.38	0.37	0.36	0.35	0.34
Price	high	79.6	70.4	47.6	44.3	30.1	21.0	16.0	20.1	16.8
	low	23.0	43.8	32.2	27.0	20.0	14.1	10.8	10.8	7.4

Entergy Corporation

639 Loyola Avenue □ New Orleans, LA 70113 □ Phone: (504) 529–5262 □ Website: www.entergy.com □
Ticker symbol: ETR □ Listed: NYSE □ S&P rating: BBB □ Value Line financial strength rating: A

Financial Highlights, Fiscal Year 2008

Entergy's operating revenues grew 14 percent to $13.1B in 2008, and net income grew 7.6 percent to $1.22B. Per-share earnings grew 10.7 percent to $6.20, the company repurchased approximately 4 million shares, and the dividend was increased 16 percent to $3.00 per share.

Company Profile

Entergy Corporation is an integrated energy utility engaged primarily in electric power production and retail electric distribution operations. Entergy owns and operates power plants with approximately 30,000 megawatts (MW) of electric generating capacity and provides electricity to 2.7 million utility customers in Arkansas, Louisiana, Mississippi, and Texas.

The company operates primarily through two business segments: U.S. Utility and Non-Utility Nuclear.

U.S. Utility generates, transmits, distributes, and sells electric power in a four-state service territory that includes portions of Arkansas, Mississippi, Texas, and Louisiana, including the City of New Orleans. It also operates a small natural gas distribution business.

Non-Utility Nuclear owns and operates five nuclear power plants located in the northeastern United States and sells this electric power primarily to wholesale customers. This business also provides maintenance services to other nuclear power plant operators. These five plants make Entergy the second largest nuclear electric generator in the United States, behind Excelon.

In mid-2007, Entergy filed notice of its plans to spin off its nonregulated nuclear generation business. In mid-2008, the NRC gave its approval for the proposed plan, but Entergy later put the plan on hold, citing "complete disarray" in the credit markets, which would have made the sale too expensive. Now, in early 2009, Entergy, pending approval from the states of New York and Vermont, seems prepared to proceed with the plan, which calls for the nuclear facilities to be re-formed as Enexus Energy. Entergy shareholders would be granted Enexus shares on a 1:1 basis. Entergy and Enexus would then form a joint venture, EquaGen, which would manage each company's nuclear units.

Reasons to Buy

Carbon caps and a federal cap-and-trade plan seem very likely in the Obama administration's energy plan at this point. This will benefit noncarbon emitters like nuclear plants.

Entergy's planned spin-off of its nuclear assets has been well-received by the markets and could clear the path for an eventual sale, although this is speculative at best. At a minimum it will provide for an optimal capital structure and simplified participation in the capital markets. Plus you get a free share of stock. Woo-hoo!

The company is authorized to buy back an additional 8 million shares of stock (about 4.5 percent of outstanding shares) in 2009, further enhancing the already welcome 3 percent dividend yield.

Entergy's operational excellence has been recognized throughout the industry. In 2008, amid turmoil in the capital markets, Entergy received a perfect 10 rating from *GovernanceMetrics International*, one of fewer than 50 companies to receive such a score of the 4,200 companies reviewed. Similarly, *Institutional Shareholder Services Corporate Services* awarded Entergy a perfect 100 percent rating for corporate governance in its utility ranking. Finally, for the seventh year in a row, Entergy was named to the *Dow Jones Sustainability Index*, placing Entergy in the top

10 percent of the largest 2,500 companies in the world, based on "long-term economic, environmental, and social criteria." 2008 was the third consecutive year that Entergy was the only U.S. utility listed on the index.

And, any company brave enough to quote Jeff Spicoli from *Fast Times at Ridgemont High* in their annual report deserves a look-see.

Reasons for Caution

Entergy's public utility operations are located in hurricane territory, along the Gulf Coast of the United States. In 2008, Hurricanes Gustav and Ike and major ice storms reduced cash flow by $314 million due to costs from downtime and system repairs. As a result, Entergy carries higher reserves and pays higher insurance premiums than other similar operators.

Recently, the Obama administration passed over Entergy in its granting of loan guarantees for new nuclear plant starts, but Entergy had already requested the NRC to hold its pending approvals, so this action was somewhat expected.

SECTOR: **Public Utility**
BETA COEFFICIENT: **.70**
10-YEAR COMPOUND EARNINGS PER SHARE GROWTH: **9.5%**
10-YEAR COMPOUND DIVIDENDS PER SHARE GROWTH: **4.5%**

	2008	2007	2006	2005	2004	2003	2002	2001	2000
Revenues (Mil)	13,094	11,484	10,932	10,106	10,124	9,195	8,305	9,621	10,016
Net Income (Mil)	1241	1,135	1,133	943	933	874	878	717	711
Earnings per share	6.20	5.60	5.36	4.40	3.93	3.69	3.68	3.08	2.97
Dividends per share	3.00	2.58	2.16	2.16	1.89	1.60	1.34	1.28	1.22
Price high	127.5	125.0	94.0	79.2	68.7	57.2	46.8	44.7	43.9
low	61.9	89.6	66.8	64.5	50.6	42.3	32.1	15.9	23.7

GROWTH AND INCOME

ExxonMobil Corporation

5959 Las Colinas Boulevard □ Irving, TX 75039–2298 □ Phone: (972) 444–1538 □ Website: www. exxonmobil.com □ Listed: NYSE □ Ticker symbol: XOM □ S&P rating: A+ □ Value Line financial strength rating: A++

Financial Highlights, Fiscal Year 2008

ExxonMobil's 2008 was a record year in terms of revenue ($459B), income ($45.2B), earnings per share ($8.69), cash flow ($11.58 per share), dividends ($1.55), and return on capital (38 percent). Although these results in large part reflect the effects of the recent run-up in the price of petroleum, which peaked in July 2008 at nearly $150 per barrel, the company had strong performance across all its operations, including upstream petroleum exploration and development.

The company initiated eight major upstream projects and acquired equity in two others.

The company replaced 103 percent of production with proved oil and gas reserve additions of 1.5 billion oil-equivalent barrels.

Exxon announced that they will exit the U.S. retail gasoline business and will sell off their portfolio of company-owned gas stations (approximately 2300 units). The announcement came not long after vagaries in oil and gasoline inventories caused the spot and futures prices of gasoline to drop below fair-market value, and briefly caused refining profits to go negative.

Company Profile

ExxonMobil is the world's largest publicly traded oil company. They are engaged in the exploration, production, manufacture, transportation, and sale of crude oil, natural gas, and petroleum products. It also has a stake in the manufacture of petrochemicals, packaging films, and specialty chemicals.

Divisions and affiliated companies of ExxonMobil operate or market products in the United States and some 200 other countries and territories. Their principal business is energy, involving exploration for, and production of crude oil and natural gas, manufacture of petroleum products and transportation and sale of crude oil, natural gas and petroleum products.

The company is a major manufacturer and marketer of basic petrochemicals, including olefins, aromatics, polyethylene, and polypropylene plastics and a wide variety of specialty products. It also has interests in electric power generation facilities.

Here, in a nutshell, is ExxonMobil:

- The company conducts oil and gas exploration, development, and production in every major accessible producing region in the world.

- ExxonMobil has the largest energy resource base of any nongovernment company, and it is the world's largest nongovernment natural gas marketer and reserves holder.
- ExxonMobil is the world's largest fuels refiner and manufacture of lube base stocks used for making motor oils.
- The company has refining operations in twenty-six countries, 42,000 retail service stations in more than 100 countries and lubricants marketing in almost 200 countries and territories.
- ExxonMobil markets petrochemical products in more than 150 countries. Ninety percent of the company's petrochemical assets are in businesses that are ranked number one or number two in market position.

Reasons to Buy

Exxon is the largest publicly traded oil company in the world, and in the oil business there are strategic advantages that accrue to size. Having the resources to bring to bear on an opportunity can mean the difference between winning and losing an exploration or development award.

The world will continue to need oil for quite some time, and Exxon has the largest reserve base in the industry. At 2007 levels, they have over thirty years of production in current reserves and have replaced over 100 percent of production every year for the last fifteen years.

Exxon's return on upstream capital employed is nearly 70 percent higher than the industry average. They get far more revenue in return for each exploration/development/production dollar spent than their competitors. And since upstream represents over 75 percent of earnings, they have significant cost advantages over their competition.

Robert Mikowski, Jr. states the case very clearly and succinctly: "Exxon's real strength is its productivity. Corporate projects are accomplished with a level of efficiency that makes them among the industry's most profitable. What it comes down to is that a company this big can always find ways do things better, given a well-trained and motivated workforce. Moreover, dedication to a business model that tightly weaves the oil producing, refining, and chemicals lines together has paid off handsomely. There's reason to think the future will hold more of the same."

Reasons for Caution

ExxonMobil's revenues will be significantly lower in the coming year. Lowered demand for oil and weakened price realizations will depress earnings at least until there are clear signs of a sustainable economic recovery. The sheer size of the company and its reported profits make it a target for the general public and legislators oriented toward populist causes; this could also create a negative climate for the stock particularly if energy prices escalate again.

SECTOR: **Energy**
BETA COEFFICIENT: **.75**
10-YEAR COMPOUND EARNINGS PER SHARE GROWTH: **16.0%**
10-YEAR COMPOUND DIVIDENDS PER SHARE GROWTH: **5.0%**

		2008	2007	2006	2005	2004	2003	2002	2001	2000
Rev (Mil)		404,552	377,640	370,998	291,252	246,738	204,506	187,510	206,083	210,392
Net Income (Mil)		45,220	40,610	39,090	36,100	25,330	17,030	11,011	15,105	16,910
Earnings per share		8.69	7.28	6.62	5.71	3.89	2.56	1.69	2.18	2.41
Dividends per share		1.55	1.37	1.28	1.14	1.06	0.98	0.92	0.91	0.88
Price	high	96.1	95.3	79.0	66.0	52.0	41.1	44.6	45.8	47.7
	low	56.5	69.0	56.4	49.2	39.9	31.6	29.8	35.0	34.9

AGGRESSIVE GROWTH

Fair Isaac Corporation

901 Marquette Avenue Suite 3200 □ Minneapolis, MN 55402–3232 □ Phone: (612) 758–5200 □ Website: www.fairisaac.com □ Listed: NYSE □ Ticker symbol: FIC □ Fiscal year ends September 30 □ S&P Rating: NA □ Value Line financial strength rating: B++

Financial Highlights, Fiscal Year 2008

Customers for the company's analytics and scoring solutions are still concentrated in the lending and financial services industry, and as a result it is no surprise that FY2008 and the early part of 2009 have seen soft business conditions. The Strategy Machines Solutions segment (discussed further below) reported 2008 revenues of $388M, down 4.1 percent from 2007, and the smaller Scoring Solutions segment reported a drop of 13.1 percent to $156M. The other two divisions were flat.

Net profits suffered a bigger hit as a percentage, declining some 22 percent to $81.2M for the year. However, the company embarked on an aggressive cost-cutting program, and has actually eked out a gain in profits for the early part of 2009 despite declining revenues.

Company Profile

Fair Isaac Corporation provides decision support analytics and solutions to help businesses improve and automate decision making. The most well known of these solutions is the "FICO score"—an analytic single-figure estimate of a consumer's creditworthiness used in the credit industry and for other purposes such as employment and insurance.

The company operates through four segments: Strategy Machine Solutions, Scoring Solutions, Professional Services, and Analytic Software Tools. The Strategy Machine Solutions segment (52 percent of revenue) offers preconfigured decision management applications for marketing, customer management, fraud prevention, and insurance claims management. The Scoring Solutions segment (21 percent) engineers and manages the FICO scoring model and offers it to loan originators and other financial institutions. The Professional Services segment (20 percent) provides consulting services to help customers develop their own analytics and applications of those analytics, while the Analytic Software Tools segment (7 percent) offers end-user software products that businesses use to build their own tailored decision management applications.

About 73 percent of the company's revenues are derived from transaction and unit-priced products, such as the access and sale of a FICO score. About 71 percent of revenues are derived from the consumer credit, financial services, and insurance industries. Overseas revenue has grown from 29 percent to 33 percent of total revenues in the past three fiscal years.

Reasons to Buy

The world is moving toward where FIC is: with an increasing acceptance of analytics-based decision-making tools in a variety of industries; the need for speed and accuracy for credit, insurance, and other kinds of transactions. The scope of application is growing beyond the financial space into insurance, health care, government, and a broad range of other commercial applications. Imagine the eventual use of scoring models to predict health-care risks and outcomes, for instance.

Not only are FIC solutions likely to penetrate further into U.S. business, but acceptance (and base data required to run the models) are increasing overseas. The growth in international revenues and earnings should continue.

It appears that the mid-2009 share price of $15 reflects the worst of the recession. That price has declined some two-thirds from the 2005–2006 peak, yet per-share cash flows are down less than 20 percent to about $2.50 a share, suggesting a price-to-cash-flow ratio of about 6.

The company has a fairly strong balance sheet, with cash per share in mid 2009 of $5.33 against the $15 share price, although that cash amount is exceeded by the company's debt.

Reasons for Caution

The global downturn in the financial services industry has clearly hit Fair Isaac. Declining loan applications simply mean fewer transactions involving their scores. However, as the lending economy recovers, greater credit diligence is likely to mean even greater use of analytics as offered by FIC, and the greater use of such analytics in other businesses should offset this softness in the long run.

SECTOR: **Business Services**
BETA COEFFICIENT: **1.73**
10-YEAR COMPOUND EARNINGS PER SHARE GROWTH: **17.0%**
10-YEAR COMPOUND DIVIDENDS PER SHARE GROWTH: **14.0%**

		2008	2007	2006	2005	2004	2003	2002	2001	2000
Revenues (Mil)		744.8	822.2	825.4	798.7	706.2	629.3	392.4	256.0	298.0
Net Income (Mil)		81.2	104.7	103.5	134.5	108.9	107.2	61.3	46.1	20.5
Earnings per share		1.64	1.82	1.50	1.86	1.49	1.41	1.00	0.89	0.60
Dividends per share		0.08	0.08	0.08	0.08	0.08	0.05	0.04	0.02	0.02
Price	high	32.2	41.8	47.8	48.5	41.5	43.1	29.6	31.1	15.4
	low	10.4	32.1	32.5	32.3	23.7	28.0	19.4	13.4	10.8

AGGRESSIVE GROWTH

FedEx Corporation

942 South Shady Grove Road ◻ Memphis, TN 38120 ◻ Phone: (901) 818–7200 ◻ Website: www.fedex.com ◻ Fiscal year ends May 31 ◻ Listed: NYSE ◻ Ticker symbol: FDX ◻ S&P rating: A- ◻ Value Line financial strength rating: B++

Financial Highlights, Fiscal Year 2008

FedEx revenue grew 8 percent to $38B, while earnings fell significantly, dropping by 44 percent to $1.13B year/year. Per-share earnings fell by a similar percentage to $3.60 from $6.48 the prior year.

Operating margins fell from 9.3 percent in FY2007 to 5.5 percent, primarily due to a 30 percent increase in overall fuel costs. Yield (the revenue generated per package) actually increased 4.4 percent in 2008.

The company's overall financial position improved somewhat, with a 24 percent reduction in long-term debt to $2B, but the big story for 2008 is the simply the decline in volumes due to the worldwide economic downturn and fluctuating fuel prices.

Company Profile

FedEx Corporation is the world's leading provider of guaranteed express delivery services. Using a $4 million inheritance as seed money, Frederick W. Smith founded FedEx in 1971 when he was only twenty-seven. The company now operates 1.4 million ground vehicles and 677 aircraft, and employs nearly 300,000 people. The company offers a wide range of express delivery services for the time-definite transportation of documents, packages, and freight. Commercial and military charter services are also offered by FedEx.

The company's operations are as follows:

- *FedEx Express* is the world's largest express transportation company, providing fast, reliable delivery to 214 countries, including every address in the United States.

- *FedEx Ground* is North America's second-largest ground carrier for small-package business shipments, including business-to-residential service through FedEx Home Delivery.
- *FedEx Freight* is the largest U.S. regional less-than-truckload freight company, providing next-day and second-day delivery of heavyweight freight within the United States and from key international markets.
- *FedEx Custom Critical* is the "24/7" option for urgent shipments, proving nonstop, door-to-door delivery in the contiguous United States, Canada, and Europe.
- *FedEx Trade Networks* facilitates international trade as the largest-volume customs filer in the United States, and a one-stop source for freight forwarding, advisory services, and trade technology.

From the 2008 Annual Report: "FedEx express has built, by far, the largest intercontinental air express network. It connects, door-to-door, more than 90 percent of the world's economic activity in one to three business days. It augments the highest service levels in the industry with a broad array of complementary services, including FedEx Trade Networks and new domestic express networks within the United Kingdom, China and India. Through the FedEx express network, we give customers around the world more choices, more flexibility and more access than ever before. The FedEx ground network now offers the fastest origin-to-destination lanes in the ground parcel business nationally, in both the commercial and home delivery sectors. In fact, in the last five years, FedEx ground has reduced its transit times by at least a day in more than half of its lanes. And FedEx Smart-Post is now the industry leader for low-weight packages delivered by the U.S. Postal service."

Reasons to Buy

FedEx's FY2009 results will be dismal. Most estimates put earnings near $3.50/share on the low end (with a wide range of uncertainty regarding any upside), down 40 percent from 2008's numbers. We like their rebound prospects for 2010, however, for a number of reasons: cost/capacity reductions, acquisitions, and growth in international business.

The company has initiated over $1B in cost-reduction programs to take effect in 2009 and 2010, and have asked individual business segments to investigate further cost-cutting measures should business conditions remain depressed.

The company has traditionally done well with its acquisitions, returning improved earnings with rapid integration into the company's systems. The addition of Watkins Freight adds a significant and needed link to the company's freight services. FedEx can now offer long-haul less-than-truckload (LTL) services in the domestic U.S. market.

FedEx has grown its International priority service at a compound annual growth rate (CAGR) of over 14 percent over the last eight years. In the process, the business has grown its revenue contribution from 17 percent to 26 percent of the company's overall sales. The company has invested heavily in China and is now number two in market share, with 22 percent (DHL leads with 32 percent). Their European operations have shown similarly strong results.

Finally, the departure of DHL from the domestic U.S. market (good timing on their part, actually) has reduced margin pressures on FedEx ground and express businesses, which should ameliorate somewhat the softening of FedEx's top line.

Reasons for Caution

The FedEx Office (formerly FedEx Kinko's) business continues to drag down margins. In 2008 the company wrote off $891M in goodwill ($2.22 per/share book value) and reduced expansion plans dramatically. Early press notices in 2009 hint at a possible divestiture should results and forecasts not improve, but the operation still represents a significant storefront opportunity for small business and some larger business customers. The trick will be to "rightsize" the operations and overcome some of the customer service negatives built into the Kinko's brand.

SECTOR: **Transportation**
BETA COEFFICIENT: **1.00**
10-YEAR COMPOUND EARNINGS PER SHARE GROWTH: **14.50%**
10-YEAR COMPOUND DIVIDENDS PER SHARE GROWTH: **No dividend prior to 2002.**

		2008	2007	2006	2005	2004	2003	2002	2001	2000
Revenues (Mil)		37,953	35,214	32,294	29,363	24,710	22,487	20,607	19,629	18,257
Net Income (Mil)		1,821	2,073	1,855	1,449	838	830	710	663	688
Earnings per share		5.83	6.67	5.98	4.82	2.76	2.74	2.39	2.26	2.32
Dividends per share		0.40	0.37	0.33	0.29	0.24	0.20	Nil		
Price	high	99.5	121.4	120.0	105.8	100.9	78.0	61.4	53.5	49.8
	low	53.9	89.5	96.5	76.8	64.8	47.7	42.8	33.2	30.6

Fluor Corporation

6700 Las Colinas Blvd. ▫ Irving, TX 75039 ▫ Phone: (469) 398–7000 ▫ Website: www.fluor.com ▫ Listed: NYSE ▫ Ticker symbol: FLR ▫ S&P rating: A- ▫ Value Line financial strength rating: A++

Financial Highlights, Fiscal Year 2008

The company reported year/year growth in earnings of 35 percent (to $720M), which tracked in increase in total revenue of 34 percent (to $22.3B). Earnings per share were also up 34 percent to $3.93, giving the company its third consecutive record year in these three categories.

The company also reported increased levels of new awards and backlog. While there is no guarantee that these revenues will be realized, these numbers are standard benchmarks in industries where a single project can span several years. New award in 2008 totaled $25.1B, leading to a net Consolidated Backlog for the company of $33.2B, up 10 percent over the previous year. The company claims their backlog is "outpacing the competition" (Bechtel, among others).

Fluor ended 2008 with approximately $2.1B in cash and securities, with negligible long-term debt. They posted a record return on total capital of 23.2 percent.

Company Profile

Fluor is one of the world's largest publicly owned engineering, procurement, construction, maintenance, and project management companies.

Their business addresses five main industry segments:

- *Oil & Gas*, where they serve "all facets" of the upstream, downstream, and petrochemical markets, including oilfields, refineries, and pipelines. Oil & Gas operations account for 58 percent of the company's overall revenue
- *Industrial and Infrastructure*, their most diverse organization, including transportation, mining, life sciences, telecom, manufacturing, and commercial and institutional projects. I & I accounts for 15 percent of the company's revenue.
- *Government*, including programs for the U.S. Departments of Energy, Defense, and Homeland Security. Government contracts account for 6 percent of Fluor's revenue.
- *Global Services*, providing operations and maintenance, supply chain, equipment services, and contract staffing, generates 12 percent of the company's revenue.
- *Power, design, build, commission, and retrofit* of electric generation facilities based on coal, natural

gas, and nuclear fuels (9 percent of revenue).

Reasons to Buy

Obviously, these are not great times for the capital project market. Fluor's main customer base (oil and petrochemical) have seen sharp price declines following the recent commodity boom. The capital market decline has had perhaps its greatest impact on just the sort of projects that Fluor specializes in. Nonetheless, Fluor has managed to retain its $30B backlog and remains optimistic for an accelerated recovery in the global financial markets. If they can exit 2009 with a similarly healthy backlog, they will be in very good position to capitalize on what almost has to be a more robust world economy.

Fluor's backlog is split evenly between the United States and rest-of-world. Whether the U.S. economy leads or follows a worldwide financial recovery, Fluor will be well positioned to take advantage. For example, Fluor recently completed the world's largest polysilicon production facility in mainland China and has contracts for wind farms in the United Kingdom.

Fluor is more diversified than many of its competitors and is spread across more highly profitable businesses. While the bulk of Fluor's backlog (80 percent) is in Oil & Gas, the rest of their operations actually contributed over 40 percent of the operating profit in 2008.

Fluor has the highest credit rating of any company in the sector. While this won't guarantee access to capital, it keeps them at the front of the line and ahead of their competition.

Finally, although we're not necessarily bargain hunters, it doesn't hurt that Fluor's stock is trading at nearly half its year-ago price, when its business (on paper) was no stronger than it is today.

Reasons for Caution

There's no overestimating the effect of the current dismal financial markets on the capital-intensive industries that account for the bulk of Fluor's revenues. While Fluor is positioned well to ride out the coming year and recover quickly, there's no getting around the possibility that a protracted recovery will require many of the operators in this segment to take hard measures.

Also, Fluor does a fair amount of business in parts of the world which have the potential for political and social instability. This is nothing new for companies in the oil business, but it bears repeating.

Finally, this is a stock that needs to be closely monitored. One significant contract delay or cancellation, or a couple of disputed claims or cost overruns can have a measurable impact on Fluor's stock price even in the best of times. Fluor is an excellent company but this may not be a stock for the faint of heart.

SECTOR: **Heavy Construction**
BETA COEFFICIENT: **1.35**
10-YEAR COMPOUND EARNINGS PER SHARE GROWTH: **14.5%**
10-YEAR COMPOUND DIVIDENDS PER SHARE GROWTH: **5.0%**

	2008	2007	2006	2005	2004	2003	2002	2001	2000
Revenues (Mil)	2,452	2,202	1,985	1,771	1,656	1,433	1,274	1,181	1,099
Net Income (Mil)	455	406	352	327	263	204	177	143	125
Earnings per share	3.37	2.25	1.48	1.31	1.08	1.12	1.07	0.81	0.66
Dividends per share	0.50	0.40	0.32	0.32	0.32	0.32	0.32	0.32	0.50
Price: high	101.4	86.1	51.9	39.6	27.6	20.4	22.5	31.6	24.3
low	28.6	37.6	36.8	25.1	18.0	13.3	10.0	15.6	10.5

AGGRESSIVE GROWTH

FMC Corporation

1735 Market Street □ Philadelphia, PA 19103 □ Phone: (215) 299–6000 □ Website: www.fmc.com □
Ticker symbol: FMC □ Listed: NYSE □ S&P rating: B– □ Value Line financial strength rating: A

Financial Highlights, Fiscal Year 2008

FMC's revenue of $3.12B was up 18 percent from the prior year, while income was up 26.5 percent. Per-share earnings were up 36.2 percent to $4.63. Margins grew significantly, with operating margins up 120 basis points or 1.2 percent to 21 percent, and net margin up 150 basis points to 11.3 percent. Over the last three years the company has repurchased approximately 6 percent of its outstanding shares and plans to spend another $200M on share repurchase through 2011.

Agricultural Products and Industrial Chemicals led revenue growth with 19 percent each, and Industrial Chemicals led earnings growth with a 118 percent gain over the prior year, due primarily to sharply higher prices obtained for phosphate rock owing to increased agricultural demand and reduced worldwide supplies.

Company Profile

FMC Corporation is a diversified chemical company serving agricultural, industrial and consumer markets globally for more than a century with innovative solutions and applications. The company employs some 5,000 people throughout the world. FMC operates its businesses in three segments: Agricultural Products, Specialty Chemicals, and Industrial Chemicals.

FMC Agricultural Products provides crop protection and pest control products for worldwide markets. The global business offers a strong portfolio of insecticides and herbicides. FMC is also a leader in innovative packaging for the industry.

In the Specialty Chemicals Group, FMC BioPolymer is the world's leading producer of alginate, carrageenan, and microcrystalline cellulose. FMC Lithium is one of the world's leading producers of lithium-based products and is recognized as the technology leader in specialty organolithium chemicals and related technologies.

In the Industrial Chemicals Group, FMC Alkali Chemicals is the world's largest producer of natural soda ash and the market leader in North America. Downstream products include sodium bicarbonate, sodium cyanide, sodium sesquicarbonate, and caustic soda. FMC Hydrogen Peroxide is the market leader in North America with manufacturing sites in the United States, Canada, and Mexico. FMC Active Oxidants is the world's leading supplier of persulfate products and a major producer of peracetic acid and other specialty oxidants. Based in Barcelona, Spain, FMC Foret is a major chemical producer supplying customers throughout Europe, the Middle East, and Africa with a diverse range of products including hydrogen peroxide, peroxygens, phosphates, silicates, zeolites, and sulfur derivatives.

Reasons to Buy

FMC serves geographically diverse markets in a variety of (typically) resilient, recession-tolerant industries. Pesticides, herbicides, basic raw materials for which there are no practical substitutes . . . all are in demand virtually around the clock and around the world. FMC is the number one or number two supplier in nearly every business in which they participate,

and have developed manufacturing strategies that allow them to be the lowest-cost producer in each of their businesses.

FMC is well positioned as the leading supplier of lithium-based compounds used in the lithium-ion battery industry. Lithium batteries are used extensively in technology products such as laptops, music players, and soon, electric cars. Every current hybrid car currently in production uses nickel metal hydride (NiMH) battery chemistry, but lithium batteries appropriate for automobile usage are not far off. Lithium's unparalleled power-to-weight ratio and rapid recharge cycle time make cars lighter and more amenable to typical usage patterns.

The first carmaker to release a product using lithium-ion battery chemistry was Tesla Motors, but Toyota, Honda, and others are working aggressively on making the technology ready for prime time. The future is still a bit cloudy, but ". . . we'll get there. Lithium ion has too many advantages," said John German, manager of Environmental and Energy Analyses for American Honda.

Since the sell-off of its military vehicles business in 2002, FMC seems to be flying under the radar of most investors. Even with its outstanding growth and quality earnings since 2003 the company is trading at price-earnings multiples under ten.

Reasons for Caution

Companies involved in the production of pesticides and herbicides are under heightened scrutiny with regard to environmental degradation and industrial safety. There is some public-relations risk. Product misuse or industrial accidents can lead to expensive litigation and loss of business.

SECTOR: **Materials**
BETA COEFFICIENT: **1.35**
10-YEAR COMPOUND EARNINGS PER SHARE GROWTH: **0.50%**
10-YEAR COMPOUND DIVIDENDS PER SHARE GROWTH: **NM**

	2008	2007	2006	2005	2004	2003	2002	2001	2000
Revenues (Mil)	3,115	2,633	2,347	2,150	2,051	1,921	1,853	1,943	3,926
Net Income (Mil)	351	132.4	216.4	171.9	135.2	67.5	87.5	99.6	212.3
Earnings per share	4.63	3.40	2.74	2.20	1.60	.95	1.28	1.60	3.36
Dividends per share	0.48	0.42	0.36						
Price high	80.2	59.0	39.0	31.9	25.3	17.4	21.2	42.0	38.6
low	28.5	35.6	25.9	21.6	16.5	7.1	11.5	22.8	23.0

FPL Group, Inc.

700 Universe Boulevard □ Juno Beach, FL 33408 □ Phone: (561) 694–4697 □ Website: www.investor.fplgroup
.com □ Listed: NYSE □ Ticker symbol: FPL □ S&P rating: A □ Value Line financial strength rating: A+

Financial Highlights, Fiscal Year 2008

Earnings for FY2008 grew 24.9 percent to $1.64B on revenues of $16.4B, which grew 7.5 percent. Adjusted earnings per share grew 10 percent, the third straight year of double-digit growth at FPL Group.

Of the company's two reporting segments, Next Era Energy was the only contributor to the growth in earnings. The renewable energy segment turned in $915M, or $2.27 per share, versus $540M and $1.35 per share in 2007. By contrast, FPL contributed $789M in earnings in 2008 ($1.96/share) versus $896M ($2.09/share) in 2007. Next Era's earnings growth year/year was 68 percent, versus a decline of 6 percent from FPL.

Company Profile

FPL Group is a leading clean energy company with 2008 revenues of more than $16 billion, approximately 39,000 megawatts of generating capacity, and more than 15,000 employees in 27 states and Canada. Headquartered in Juno Beach, Florida, FPL Group's principal subsidiaries are NextEra Energy Resources, LLC, the largest generator in North America of renewable energy from the wind and sun; and Florida Power & Light Company, which serves 4.5 million customer accounts in Florida and is one of the largest rate-regulated electric utilities in the country. Through its subsidiaries, FPL Group collectively operates the third largest U.S. nuclear power generation fleet.

Next Era Energy, LLC (formerly FPL Energy, LLC), FPL Group's competitive energy subsidiary, is a leader in producing electricity from clean and renewable fuels. Together, FPL's and FPL Energy's generating assets represent nearly 33,000 megawatts of capacity. FLP FiberNet, LLC, provides fiber-optic services to FPL and other customers, primarily telecommunications companies in Florida.

FPL is recognized as one of the "cleaner" producers in the United States, with just over half of its generation coming from natural gas, and less than 15 percent coming from coal and oil. By contrast, coal makes up 50 percent of the fuel mix for electricity generation nationwide. Next Era Energy is the largest owner and operator of the wind generating facilities in the United States.

Reasons to Buy

FPL is the largest provider in a growing energy market, and has been one of the best-performing stocks in the utility market over the past several years. Since 2002, measured by total shareholder return, FPL has outperformed 84 percent of the companies in the S&P Utility Index and 85 percent of the companies in the S&P 500 Index. During the period, total return was 127 percent, compared with 32 percent for the total utility index and negative 10 percent for the S&P 500 Index.

In spite of a slightly declining customer base in 2008 and reduced kilowatt-hour sales, the company was able to produce impressive earnings growth. The primary driver for this growth is favorable tax treatments of FPL's renewable energy production. Given the continued interest in these resources, it is expected that the government's incentives will continue for some time, and at least through 2011. FPL is well-positioned to take advantage of this opportunity—they have a total pipeline of 30,000 megawatts of wind projects and a plan to add 1,100 megawatts of new wind projects in 2009. Their total current investment in wind resources is over $8B.

The company has requested tariff increases of $1.25B through 2011 with a planned ROE of 12.5 percent. Their strong balance sheet has enabled the company to raise significant levels of capital even in unsteady markets, raising $1.3B at competitive rates in the 4Q2008 alone.

Reasons for Caution

FPL's stock (in mid-2009) trades at a premium to the market, based largely on the appeal of the company's unique wind power play. As a result, the dividend yield is not as attractive as other plays in the utility sector.

SECTOR: **Utilities**
BETA COEFFICIENT: **.75**
10-YEAR COMPOUND EARNINGS PER SHARE GROWTH: **7.0%**
10-YEAR COMPOUND DIVIDENDS PER SHARE GROWTH: **5.5%**

	2008	2007	2006	2005	2004	2003	2002	2001	2000
Revenues (Mil)	16,410	15,263	15,710	11,846	10,522	9,630	8,311	8,475	7,082
Net Income (Mil)	1,639	1,312	1,261	885	887	883	710	796	719
Earnings per share	4.07	3.27	3.23	2.32	2.46	2.45	2.01	2.31	2.07
Dividends per share	1.78	1.64	1.50	1.42	1.30	1.20	1.16	1.12	1.08
Price high	73.8	72.8	55.6	48.1	38.1	34.0	32.7	35.8	36.5
low	33.8	53.7	37.8	35.9	30.1	26.8	22.5	25.6	18.2

General Dynamics Corporation

2941 Fairview Park Drive ❑ Suite 100 ❑ Falls Church, VA 22042–4513 ❑ Phone: (703) 876–3195 ❑ Dividend reinvestment plan not available ❑ Website: www.generaldynamics.com ❑ Listed: NYSE ❑ Ticker symbol: GD ❑ S&P rating: A ❑ Value Line financial strength rating: A++

Financial Highlights, Fiscal Year 2008

General Dynamics' revenue grew to $29.3B, an increase of 7.6 percent over 2007. Income grew 17.3 percent to $2.44B, with net margins increasing 70 basis points to 8.3 percent and operating margins improving by 110 basis points.

Per-share earnings grew 20.2 percent to $6.13. Per-share earnings have more than doubled since 2004, and dividends have risen 86 percent to $1.34 over the same period. Dividends may well increase again in 2009, as free cash flow continues to increase, reaching $2.6B or 106 percent of earnings from continuing operations in 2008.

Disregarding the very good earnings results for a moment, the big news for GD in 2008/2009 was the significant increase in orders, resulting in a 58.3 percent growth in the backlog to $74.1B from FY2007's ending backlog of $46.8B. The biggest part of this increase came from Marine Systems, which booked orders for several classes of support ships, including $13.8B for eight additional Virginia-class submarines. These submarines will be delivered through 2019, doubling GD's currently scheduled deliveries of this class of ships beginning in 2011.

Company Profile

General Dynamics was officially established February 21, 1952, although it has organizational roots dating back to the late 1800s. The company was formed after its predecessor and current operating division, Electric Boat, acquired the aircraft company Canadair Ltd. and began building the first nuclear-powered submarine, the USS *Nautilus*.

General Dynamics has four main business segments. Aerospace designs, manufactures, and provides services for mid-size, large cabin, and ultralong-range business aircraft under the Gulfstream brand. Combat Systems supplies land and amphibious combat machines and systems, including armored vehicles, power trains, turrets, munitions and gun systems, and is currently the only provider of U.S. military tanks. Information Systems and Technology's expertise lies in specialized data acquisition and processing, in advanced electronics, and in battlespace information networks and management systems. Marine Systems designs and builds submarines, surface combatants, auxiliary ships, and large commercial vessels.

Reasons to Buy

Just over half of GD's contracts are fixed-price contracts, which put the contractor at risk for cost overruns or schedule delays. Contracts which are paid on a Cost Reimbursement basis are generally less risky, but provide less of an incentive for timely completion. GD's ability to deliver large projects like the submarine *New Hampshire* ahead of schedule and under budget has paid off in a big way for the Marine Division, which returned operating earnings growth at double the rate of sales growth for the year. The group's significant order intake during 2008, the resulting backlog and the continued strength of execution position Marine Systems to lead the company in sales and earnings growth over the next several years.

The company's record backlog does not include an additional estimated $10B backlog of contract

value associated with an indefinite-delivery, indefinite-quantity contract for the development and deployment of secure wireless networks for U.S. domestic law-enforcement agencies. Including the value of this contract would put the Information Systems' business book-to-bill ratio at approximately 2.2 for the year.

Reasons for Caution

The company's Gulfstream aircraft line, which had closed the year with a backlog of $22.5B, has seen some softening in demand. Customer cancellations and defaults have caused the company to trim production, particularly in the mid-sized aircraft. Total production starts will number 97 aircraft, down from 156 in 2008.

SECTOR: **Industrials**
BETA COEFFICIENT: **0.95**
10-YEAR COMPOUND EARNINGS PER SHARE GROWTH: **15.0%**
10-YEAR COMPOUND DIVIDENDS PER SHARE GROWTH: **10.5%**

	2008	2007	2006	2005	2004	2003	2002	2001	2000
Revenues (Mil)	29,300	27,240	24,063	20,975	19,178	16,617	13,829	12,163	10,356
Net Income (Mil)	2,443	2,072	1,856	1,448	1,203	998	1,051	943	901
Earnings per share	6.13	5.10	4.20	3.58	2.99	2.50	2.54	2.33	2.24
Dividends per share	1.34	1.16	0.89	0.78	0.70	0.63	0.60	0.55	0.51
Price high	95.1	94.6	78.0	61.2	55.0	45.4	55.6	48.0	39.5
low	47.8	70.6	56.7	48.8	42.5	25.0	36.7	30.3	18.2

General Mills, Inc.

Post Office Box 1113 ▫ Minneapolis, MN 55440–1113 ▫ Phone: (763) 764–3202 ▫ Website: www
.generalmills.com ▫ Listed: NYSE ▫ Fiscal year ends last Sunday in May ▫ Ticker symbol: GIS ▫ S&P rating:
A– ▫ Value Line financial strength rating: A+

Financial Highlights, Fiscal Year 2008

For the fiscal year ended May 27, 2008, General Mills net sales grew 10 percent to $13.7 billion, while year-to-year earnings growth was up 13 percent. Diluted earnings per share (EPS) totaled $3.52, up 10.7 percent from $3.18 in 2007.

Growth in sales was fairly broad-based, with all nine of the major operating divisions reporting at least 5 percent dollar growth. Products introduced within the last year represented approximately 6 percent of overall sales.

Segment operating profit margin fell off slightly, from an average of 18 percent over the last three years to 17.6 percent this year. This was due to increases in raw material costs (up 7 percent) and marketing expenses (up 13 percent).

Company Profile

General Mills is the second-largest domestic producer of ready-to-eat breakfast cereals. It is also a leading producer of other well-known packaged consumer foods. Their sales are broken out into three major segments: U.S. Retail ($9.1B), International ($2.6B), and Bakery and Foodstuffs ($2.0B). They also have unconsolidated net sales in the Joint Venture segment ($1.2B)

Major cereal brands, most of which bear the Big G label, include Cheerios, Wheaties, Lucky Charms, Total, and Chex cereals. Other consumer packaged food products include baking mixes (Betty Crocker and Bisquick); meals (Betty Crocker dry packaged dinner mixes); Progresso soups; Green Giant (canned and frozen vegetables); snacks (Pop Secret microwave popcorn, Bugles snacks, grain and fruit snack products); Pillsbury refrigerated and frozen dough products; frozen breakfast products and frozen pizza and snack products; organic foods and other products, including Yoplait and Colombo yogurt. The company's holdings include many other brand names, such as Häagen-Dazs ice cream and a host of joint ventures.

The company's international businesses consist of operations and sales in Canada, Europe, Latin America, and the Asia/Pacific region. In those regions, General Foods sells numerous local brands, in addition to internationally recognized brands, such as Häagen-Dazs ice cream, Old El Paso Mexican foods, and Green Giant vegetables. Those international businesses have sales and marketing organizations in thirty-three countries.

Reasons to Buy

The company has recognized the international market's growing demand for packaged foods and has responded with a 21 percent year over year growth in international sales with higher profitability than the overall product line. This is notable for a company that has a stated sales growth goal of "low single digits" overall, and significant in light of the overall growth of overseas retail channels. International sales are expected to be a key driver for profit growth in the coming years. The company is well-positioned for economic recovery and for changing buying patterns in international markets.

General Mills' emphasis on financial health and stability over sales and market share growth is reassuring. They plan for slow, measured growth over the next several years while continuing to provide a solid total return to shareholders. Over the last three years the company has provided a total return of over 10 percent, compared with the segment average of 4.4 percent.

The company has continued its policy of share repurchase, further reducing the number of outstanding shares by 10 percent following the 28 percent increase resulting from the purchase of Pillsbury.

General Mills is most attractive as a stable, steady growth component to your overall portfolio.

The company has increased its presence in select retail channels such as Club Stores, Drug/Discount/Dollar stores, and Superstores, and the results have paid off with "double-digit" gains in sales through these growing channels.

Reasons for Caution

The company carries a significant debt load (over 40 percent long-term debt/capital). In part a legacy of the purchase of Pillsbury in 2002 and in part due to other more recent acquisitions, their debt is the highest in the industry. Even though working capital for the last decade has been financed through debt, the only material effect seems to have been depression of dividends.

Profitability in the food sector is driven to large degree by commodity pricing. The company's purchasing strategies of late have been defensive and may depress earnings somewhat, at least until the recent volatility in the commodity markets moderates somewhat.

SECTOR: **Consumer Staples**
BETA COEFFICIENT: **.50**
10-YEAR COMPOUND EARNINGS PER SHARE GROWTH: **7.5%**
10-YEAR COMPOUND DIVIDENDS PER SHARE GROWTH: **3.5%**

	2008	2007	2006	2005	2004	2003	2002	2001	2000
Revenues (Mil)	13,652	12,442	11,640	11,244	11,070	10,506	7,949	7,078	6,700
Net Income (Mil)	1,288	1,144	1,090	1,100	1,055	917	581	643	614
Earnings per share	3.52	3.18	2.90	2.74	2.85	2.43	1.70	2.20	2.00
Dividends per share	1.57	1.44	1.34	1.24	1.10	1.10	1.10	1.10	1.10
Price: high	72.0	61.5	59.2	53.9	50.0	49.7	51.7	52.9	45.3
low	51.0	54.2	47.0	44.7	43.0	41.4	37.4	37.3	29.4

AGGRESSIVE GROWTH

Goodrich Corporation

Four Coliseum Center ▫ 2730 West Tyvola Road ▫ Charlotte, NC 28217 ▫ Phone: (704) 423–5517 ▫
Website: www.goodrich.com ▫ Ticker symbol: GR ▫ Listed: NYSE ▫ S&P rating: B ▫ Value Line financial
strength rating: B+

Financial Highlights, Fiscal Year 2008

Goodrich's sales grew 10 percent to $7.06B versus FY2007. Net income grew an impressive 41 percent, to $681M. The increase in income was driven by strong performance across all three operating segments and reduced SG&A expenses.

Operating margins rose 110 basis points (1.1 percent) to 17.2 percent, and per-share earnings grew 43 percent to $5.39. The company raised dividends 12 percent to raise the recent yield to 1.8 percent.

In February 2009 Airbus selected Goodrich to provide the wheels, brakes, air data, and ice protection systems for the new A350 XWB aircraft.

In December 2008 Goodrich formed Rolls-Royce Goodrich Engine Control Systems Limited, a joint venture with Rolls-Royce Group plc (R-R), operating as Aero Engine Controls (JV). The JV was formed to design, develop, and manufacture engine control systems with improved performance for R-R engines. The JV combines Goodrich's commercial original-equipment engine controls design and manufacturing business with R-R's expertise in the integration of such controls into the engine. Goodrich will retain the aftermarket products and services associated with the JV's current and future products.

In April 2008 Pratt and Whitney selected Goodrich to provide the engine nacelles for its new PW1000G engine.

Company Profile

One might have thought its principal business was tires, but in fact Goodrich Corporation, a *Fortune*

500 company, is a global supplier of systems and services to the aerospace, defense, and homeland security markets. With annual revenues of $5.9 billion, Goodrich is headquartered in Charlotte, North Carolina, and employs more than 23,000 people worldwide in over ninety facilities across sixteen countries.

Goodrich offers an extensive range of products, systems, and services for aircraft and engine manufacturers, airlines, and defense forces around the world. Goodrich products, including aerostructures, actuation systems, landing gear, engine control systems, sensors, and safety systems, are on almost every aircraft in the world. The company's transformation into one of the globe's largest aerospace companies has been driven by a combination of strategic acquisitions and internal growth.

Goodrich is organized into three business units. The Actuation and Landing Systems segment provides systems, components, and related services pertaining to aircraft taxi, takeoff, flight control, landing, and stopping, and engine components. The Nacelles and Interior Systems segment produces products and provides maintenance, repair, and overhaul services associated with aircraft engines, and aircraft interior products, including slides, seats, cargo, and lighting systems. The Electronic Systems segment produces a broad array of systems and components that provide flight performance measurements, flight management information, engine controls, fuel controls,

electrical power systems, safety data, and reconnaissance and surveillance systems.

The company's sales are nearly evenly spread across three markets: commercial aircraft manufacturers, commercial aircraft aftermarket, and military and space market.

Reasons to Buy

Goodrich is positioned well in its markets, with substantial backlogs in both the commercial and military segments. Total backlog on Jan 1, 2009 was $15.5B, with $4.2B of that amount firm and $2.9B of the total to be filled in 2009.

As airlines take older, less efficient aircraft off-line (either temporarily or permanently), newer aircraft with higher levels of Goodrich content will be brought on-line, increasing Goodrich's maintenance revenues.

The company is in good financial shape, with little current debt and substantial cash reserves. This, along with strong cash flow and healthy net margins, should provide more than adequate funding levels for increased levels of R&D and independent program development.

The joint venture with Pratt could simply be a business arrangement to better accommodate existing programs, or (best case) it could turn into a bed of new product development. In any case it's a positive step for Goodrich as they should gain expertise in one of their core businesses and strengthen their ties with a major customer.

Reasons for Caution

As air travel has tapered off recently, Goodrich's revenue stream has tipped toward the less-profitable OEM business and away from maintenance. This trend is not expected to last, but until it does Goodrich's margins may moderate downward.

SECTOR: **INDUSTRIALS**
BETA COEFFICIENT: **1.10**
10-YEAR COMPOUND EARNINGS PER SHARE GROWTH: **3%**
10-YEAR COMPOUND DIVIDENDS PER SHARE GROWTH: **- 3%**

		2008	2007	2006	2005	2004	2003	2002	2001	2000
Revenues (Mil)		7062	6,392	5,878	5,396	4,724	4,383	3,910	4,184	4,364
Net Income (Mil)		674	484	336	244	172	38	244	306	318
Earnings per share		5.33	3.79	2.66	1.97	1.43	0.33	2.31	2.87	2.97
Dividends per share		0.90	0.80	0.80	0.80	0.80	0.80	0.88	1.10	1.10
Price	high	71.1	75.7	47.4	45.8	33.9	30.3	34.4	44.5	43.1
	low	25.1	45.0	37.2	30.1	26.6	12.2	14.2	15.9	21.6

W. W. Grainger, Inc.

100 Grainger Parkway ▫ Lake Forest, IL 60045 ▫ Phone: (847) 535–0881 ▫ Website: www.grainger.com
▫ Ticker symbol: GWW ▫ Listed: NYSE ▫ S&P rating: AA+ ▫ Value Line financial strength rating: A++

Financial Highlights, Fiscal Year 2008

Grainger's FY2008 sales increased 6.7 percent year/year (to $6.85B), while earnings over the same period increased a healthy 14.1 percent (to $475M). Earnings per share were up a remarkable 22 percent year/year.

The company took on $500M in debt, ostensibly to finance further expansion/acquisitions. It has no other significant long-term debt.

Grainger's Lab Safety Supply (LSS), a leading business-to-business direct marketer of safety and other industrial products in the United States and Canada, was folded into the Grainger Industrial Supply brand, and its products will be carried alongside Grainger's main lines at Grainger distribution centers.

Company Profile

Grainger is North America's leading broad-line supplier of facilities maintenance products, providing quick and easy access to products through a network of over 600 branches, eighteen distribution centers, and several websites. Grainger offers repair parts, specialized product sourcing, and inventory management. Grainger sells principally to industrial and commercial maintenance departments, contractors, and government customers. The company has nearly 2 million customers.

Acklands-Grainger, Inc., is Canada's leading broad-line distributor of industrial, fleet, and safety products. It serves a wide variety of customers through 166 branches and five distribution centers across Canada. It also offers bilingual websites and catalogs. Grainger, S.A. de C.V. is Mexico's leading facilities maintenance supplier, offering customers more than 40,000 products. Local businesses have access through a Spanish-language catalog, online at *www.grainger .com.mx* or over the counter at one of six branches.

Grainger serves customers in eight categories:

- Government, including government offices, schools, and correctional institutions on the state and local levels, many military installations, and the U.S. Postal Service on the federal level.
- Heavy manufacturing customers are usually involved in textile, lumber, metals, and rubber industries.
- Light manufacturing, including food, pharmaceutical, and electronic customers.
- Transportation customers involved in the shipbuilding, aerospace, and automotive industries.

- Retail, including grocery stores, restaurants, and local gas stations.
- Contractor sales for firms involved in maintaining and repairing existing facilities.
- Commercial customers including hospitals, hotels, and theaters.
- Reseller and distributors selling Grainger products to customers in many different end markets.

Many of Grainger's customers are corporate account customers, primarily *Fortune* 1000 companies that spend more than $5 million annually on facilities maintenance products. Corporate account customers represent about 25 percent of Grainger's total U.S. sales. Both government and corporate account customer groups typically sign multiyear contracts for facilities maintenance products or a specific category of products, such as lighting or safety equipment.

Reasons to Buy

Grainger is far and away the biggest presence in the MRO (Maintenance, Repair, and Operational) world. Their only broad-line competitor is one-quarter their size, and the rest of the market is highly fragmented (Grainger has 4–5 percent market share). They also have the deepest catalog, with over 180,000 different items available at any given time. It's estimated that 40 percent of purchases in the MRO market are unplanned, so having the broadest inventory and having it in stock is a big advantage for Grainger.

Over the last five years Grainger has repurchased 21.7 percent of its outstanding shares, and they plan to continue the practice in the coming years. They ended 2008 with nearly $400M in cash, and have over the last five years averaged free cash flow of 15 percent of earnings.

The company earned $6.09/ share in 2008, giving it a trailing P/E ratio of 11.5 which, for a company whose earnings have increased 16 percent CAGR over the last five years, is remarkably cheap. We don't emphasize ratios for ratios' sake here, but this one just screams for attention.

The 2008 dividend increase has pushed the dividend yield to 2 percent—again, for a company that's growing earnings as quickly as Grainger and which is retiring stock at the rate of 4 percent per year, that's like getting 6 percent for free.

Reasons for Caution

Grainger is growing outside the United States, but at the moment they are still closely tied to the domestic industrial sector, and as such they are exposed to reduced levels of discretionary purchasing. However, since a fair amount of Grainger's business is emergency/nondiscretionary, only a portion of their sales are actually at risk.

SECTOR: **Industrials**
BETA COEFFICIENT: **1.0**
10-YEAR COMPOUND EARNINGS PER SHARE GROWTH: **8.5%**
10-YEAR COMPOUND DIVIDENDS PER SHARE GROWTH: **9.5%**

	2008	2007	2006	2005	2004	2003	2002	2001	2000
Revenues (Mil)	6,850	6,418	5,884	5,527	5,050	4,667	4,644	4,754	4,977
Net Income (Mil)	479	420	383	346	277	227	236	211	175
Earnings per share	6.09	4.94	4.25	3.78	3.02	2.46	2.50	2.23	1.86
Dividends per share	1.55	1.40	1.16	0.92	0.79	0.74	0.72	0.70	0.67
Price high	94.0	98.6	80.0	72.4	67.0	53.3	59.4	49.0	56.9
low	58.9	68.8	60.6	51.6	45.0	41.4	39.2	29.5	24.3

AGGRESSIVE GROWTH

Harris Corporation

1025 West NASA Boulevard ◻ Melbourne, FL 32919 ◻ Phone: (321) 727–9383 ◻ Website: www.harris.com ◻ Ticker symbol: HRS ◻ Fiscal year ends Fridays closest to June 30 ◻ Listed: NYSE ◻ S&P rating: B+ ◻ Value Line financial strength rating: A

Financial Highlights, Fiscal Year 2008

In 2008 Harris's revenue grew 25 percent to $5.3B, of which 13 percent was organic growth. Net income grew 18 percent to $462M, or $3.26 per share, also up 18 percent. In early 2009 Harris announced their intention to sell Harris Stratex Networks and will no longer list revenues from the segment under continuing operations.

In April 2009 the company was awarded a $600M, 10-year contract to modernize the U.S. military's satellite communication terminals. In another announcement, Harris had signed an agreement to acquire Tyco Electronic Wireless Systems business for $675M in cash. Net of allowable tax expenses, the deal will cost $615 in FY2009. Wireless System's revenue in FY2007 was $463M, with earnings of $86M.

Company Profile

Harris is an international communications and information technology company serving government and commercial markets in more than 150 countries. Headquartered in Melbourne, Florida, the company has annual revenue of about $4 billion and more than 16,500 employees, including more than 7,000 engineers and scientists. Harris is dedicated to developing communications products, systems, and services for global markets, including government communications, RF communications, broadcast communications, and wireless transmission network solutions.

Major Product Areas (excluding Stratex, to be sold):

- *Government Communications.* Harris conducts advanced research studies, develops prototypes, and produces and supports state-of-the-art communications and information systems for mission-critical communications challenges of military and government customers. These activities also provide a research base for commercial products and services.
- *RF Communications.* Harris is a leading worldwide supplier of tactical radio communication products, systems, and networks to military and government organizations, and a provider of high-grade encryption solutions. These solutions address the demanding requirements of U.S., NATO, and Partnership for Peace Forces, as well as government agencies and embassies around the world.
- *Broadcast Communications.* Digital technology dominates today's world of television and radio broadcasting. Harris has solidified its leadership position in this industry with total content delivery solutions, including advanced digital transmission, automation, asset management, digital media, network management, and video infrastructure solutions.

Reasons to Buy

The software certification in August of the Falcon III Manpack Radio design is a significant event, and Harris is really just at the beginning of what is likely to be a very healthy revenue stream. Follow-on business will likely include additional platform integrations, sales to allies and support branches, and the inevitable and very profitable spares contracts.

The acquisition of Wireless Systems will add slightly to earnings in FY2010 and be a significant contributor in 2011–2012. Wireless brings with it a large installed customer base and well-developed sales channels serving federal, state, and local public safety channels. The sale of Stratex will allow the company to focus on its core businesses.

The company has great cash flow and a sound capital structure. They're well-positioned for selective acquisitions and will continue to repurchase shares and boost dividends. In June 2009 the company turned down preliminary buyout offers in the neighborhood of $10B, saying that it was under an expected offer of $75–$85/share. So two things to consider: Some people feel the company is worth at least $75/share, and Harris's CEO feels it's worth more.

Reasons for Caution

The sale of Stratex will generate impairment charges of $183M and loss of revenue going forward, and military budgets are under tighter review, which will delay fulfillment on some existing contracts and could impact future awards.

SECTOR: **Information Technology**
BETA COEFFICIENT: **1.10**
10-YEAR COMPOUND EARNINGS PER SHARE GROWTH: **8.0%**
10-YEAR COMPOUND DIVIDENDS PER SHARE GROWTH: **1.5%**

		2008	2007	2006	2005	2004	2003	2002	2001	2000
Revenues (Mil)		5,311	4,243	3,475	3,001	2,519	2,093	1,876	1,955	1,807
Net Income (Mil)		462	391	310	202	126	90	83	101	70
Earnings per share		3.39	2.80	2.22	1.46	0.94	0.68	0.63	0.75	0.48
Dividends per share		.60	0.44	0.32	0.24	0.20	0.16	0.10	0.10	0.20
Price	high	66.7	66.9	49.8	45.8	34.6	19.7	19.3	18.5	19.7
	low	27.6	45.9	37.7	26.9	18.9	12.7	12.0	10.4	10.4

GROWTH AND INCOME

H.J. Heinz Company

One PPG Place ◻ Pittsburgh, PA 15222 ◻ Phone: (412) 456–5700 ◻ Website: www.heinz.com ◻ Listed: NYSE ◻ Ticker symbol: HNZ ◻ S&P rating: BBB ◻ Value Line financial strength rating: A+

Financial Highlights, Fiscal Year 2008

Heinz closed out their 2008 fiscal year in April 2009 with gains in revenues (up 12 percent to $10.1B), earnings (up 9.2 percent to $923M), operating income (up 8.5 percent to $1.6B), and earnings per share (up 10.5 percent to $2.63). Of the company's four product categories, three (Ketchup and Sauces, Infant/Nutrition, and Other) showed organic sales growth, while Meals and Snacks fell 3.5 percent.

Overall, unfavorable currency translation had a significant influence on revenues, reducing net sales overall by 6.6 percent. Approximately 60 percent of the company's revenue and the majority of its net income is generated outside of the United States.

Company Profile

H.J. Heinz Company manufactures and markets food products such as condiments and sauces, frozen food, soups, desserts, entrees, snacks, frozen potatoes, appetizers, and other processed food products for consumers and commercial customers. The company's best known product, its ketchup, has a 60 percent market share in the United States, 70 percent in Canada, and nearly 80 percent in the United Kingdom. Condiments and sauces (including ketchup) accounts for approximately 42 percent of the company's revenue, with Meals and Snacks producing 45 percent, and Infant/Nutrition making up the remainder.

The Heinz portfolio includes 150 brands that hold either the number one or number two market share positions in their categories, with presence on five continents and in over 50 countries. The company sells its products through its own direct sales organizations, through independent brokers and agents, and to distributors to retailers and commercial users. The company has operations in North America, Africa, Latin America, Europe, the Asia Pacific, and the Middle East.

Heinz's laboratories develop the company's recipes, which are then duplicated at one of the 79 company-owned factories or one of several leased factories. Most of the bulk raw products are sourced locally when possible, and are purchased against futures contracts in order to stabilize pricing, while other ingredients are purchased on the spot market.

Heinz operates in five segments—four defined by territory of service, and one by customer base. The North American Consumer Products includes all operations for all consumer product lines in the United States and Canada. Europe, Asia/Pacific, and Rest of World run operations parallel to NACP, but targeting only their geographies. U.S. Foodservice also serves the United States, but only the commercial and institutional customers.

Reasons to Buy

Heinz shed a number of brands to Del Monte back in 2003 and benefited through generally improved margins and per-share earnings. It looks like Heinz is preparing to do another round of "re-focusing," as management has committed to dedicating a larger share of resources to its top brands, 15 of which produce 70 percent of the company's revenue.

Conversely, Heinz is also focused on new brand introductions,

leveraging its relatively new Global Innovation and Quality Center. Part of the company's product development goals is to derive 15 percent of revenues from products introduced within the previous 36 months. Out with the old, in with the new.

Heinz is having success in emerging markets ($1.3B in sales in FY2008) and plans to make growth there an area of emphasis, anticipating fully a third of their sales growth to come from those markets over the next several years. Heinz's ABC soy sauce brand is already Indonesia's top consumer brand and one of the leading brands worldwide.

Heinz continues to emphasize its dividend and will likely increase it over the next few years. At mid-2009 share prices it yields 3.9 percent.

Reasons for Caution

Processed foods in general are starting to get some push-back from segments of the U.S. consumer population as people are beginning to broadly associate a reliance on convenience foods with obesity and other nutritional problems. The company is also vulnerable to the ever-present threat of generic products.

SECTOR: **Consumer Staples**
BETA COEFFICIENT: **0.65**
10-YEAR COMPOUND EARNINGS PER SHARE GROWTH: **2.5%**
10-YEAR COMPOUND DIVIDENDS PER SHARE GROWTH: **2.0%**

	2008	2007	2006	2005	2004	2003	2002	2001	2000
Revenues (Mil)	10,148	10,070	9,002	8,643	8,913	8,414	8,236	9,431	9,430
Net Income (Mil)	923	845	792	750	823	779	713	847	904
Earnings per share	2.90	2.63	2.38	2.18	2.34	2.20	2.03	2.39	2.55
Dividends per share	1.66	1.52	1.40	1.20	1.14	1.08	1.49	1.60	1.55
Price high	53.0	48.8	46.8	39.1	40.6	36.8	43.5	47.9	48.0
low	35.3	41.8	33.4	33.6	34.5	28.9	29.6	36.9	30.8

AGGRESSIVE GROWTH

Hewlett-Packard Compan

3000 Hanover Street ◻ Palo Alto, CA 94304 ◻ Phone: (866) 438–4771 ◻ Website: www.hp.com ◻ Listed: NYSE ◻ Ticker symbol: HPQ ◻ S&P rating: A ◻ Value Line financial strength rating: A++

Financial Highlights, Fiscal Year 2008

HP continued to grow the top line at a steady pace, posting a 13.5 percent increase (to $118.4B) in revenues against a 14.7 percent increase in earnings (to $8.33B). Operating margins, an area of focus for HP recently, grew 9 percent to 13.1 percent, but the net margin remained flat year over year at 7 percent.

In August 2008 HP acquired EDS, a large computer services company. The purchase had an immediate impact to HP's bottom line, contributing operating income to the tune of $2.5B, more than HP PC operations and nearly as much as their Storage and Servers. In just five months of contribution from EDS, HP's Services segment grew revenue 35 percent year/year.

The news from HP's cash cow, the Imaging and Printing segment, was less encouraging. Revenue growth in this segment was only 3.2 percent year/year. Even though this business is still by far the biggest contributor to operating income and margins, the company depends on this revenue to fund growth. Imaging's revenue growth was the lowest in the company.

Company Profile

Hewlett-Packard is a global technology solutions provider to consumers, businesses, and institutions. The company's offerings span IT infrastructure, services, business and home computing, and imaging and printing.

The company is organized around six reporting segments:

* Personal Systems Group is the leading provider of personal computers in the world based on unit volume shipped and annual

revenue. PSG provides commercial PCs, consumer PCs, workstations, handheld computing devices, calculators and other related accessories, software, and services for the commercial and consumer markets.

- The Imaging and Printing Group is the leading imaging and printing systems provider in the world for consumer and commercial printer hardware, printing supplies, printing media, and scanning devices. IPG is also focused on imaging solutions in the commercial markets, from managed print services solutions to addressing new growth opportunities in commercial printing and capturing high-value pages in areas such as industrial applications, outdoor signage, and the graphic arts business.

- Enterprise Storage and Servers provides a broad portfolio of storage and server solutions. ESS aims to optimize the combined product solutions required by different customers and provide solutions for a wide range of operating environments, spanning both the enterprise and the SMB markets. ESS provides storage and server products in a number of categories, including the entry-level and mid-range ProLiant servers, and the business-critical systems, which include the high-end Superdome and fault-tolerant Integrity servers.

- HP Services provides a portfolio of multivendor IT services, including technology services, consulting and integration, and outsourcing services. HPS also offers a variety of services tailored to particular industries such as communications, media and entertainment, manufacturing and distribution, financial services, health and life sciences, and the public sector, including government services. HPS collaborates with the Enterprise Storage and Servers and HP Software groups, as well as with third-party system integrators and software and networking companies to bring solutions to HP customers.

- HP Software is a leading provider of enterprise and service provider software and services. Their portfolio consists of enterprise IT management software, business reporting solutions, and integrated voice/data development platforms.

- HP Financial Services supports and enhances HP's global product and service solutions, providing a broad range of value-added financial life-cycle management services. HPFS enables HP's worldwide customers to acquire complete IT solutions, including hardware, software, and services. The group offers leasing, financing, utility programs and asset recovery services, as well as financial asset management services for large global and enterprise customers.

Reasons to Buy

CEO Mark Hurd is starting to look like a turnaround specialist. Not that HP was a "troubled" business, but in 2005 operating expenses accounted for nearly 96 percent of total revenue. Hurd was appointed CEO in Q2 2005, and since then net margins are up 25 percent, operating margins are up 45 percent, and per-share earnings have more than doubled. He's running the company with a renewed focus on the numbers and has been more effective at communicating an overall strategy than was his predecessor. HP plans to continue its cost-cutting over the next year to further increase operating margins.

HP's acquisition of EDS, which has so far worked out very well in terms of both top- and bottom-line contribution, could be the start of a longer-term strategy to make HP look just a bit more like their far-more-profitable competitor, IBM. HP generated $15B more in revenue in 2008 than did IBM, but IBM generated over $6B more in operating income than did HP, due largely to its very profitable services business. If HP can successfully emulate IBM's model, it could be good news going forward for HP.

HP has emerged a winner in head-to-head competition with Dell after years of lagging; it is also coming out on top vs. Lexmark and other names in the printing and imaging business, although this "switch" is less profound. HP is better positioned for international growth than many of its rivals, and HP has once again assumed the role as the lead IT brand worldwide.

Reasons for Caution

The Printing and Imaging business has shown signs of weakness and has been underperforming the rest of the company for a year. The company is still vulnerable to the ups and downs of the PC business, which are in turn sensitive to the economy and consumer preferences. The enterprise hardware operations are likewise sensitive to the economy, and the company still needs to prove that it can make the most of the EDS acquisition.

SECTOR: **Information Technology**
BETA COEFFICIENT: **1.0**
10-YEAR COMPOUND EARNINGS PER SHARE GROWTH: **6.5%**
10-YEAR COMPOUND DIVIDENDS PER SHARE GROWTH: **2.0%**

	2008	2007	2006	2005	2004	2003	2002	2001	2000
Revenues (Bil)	118.4	104.3	91.66	86.67	79.91	73.06	72.35	45.23	48.78
Net Income (Mil)	8,329	7,264	6,198	4,708	4,067	3,557	2,409	1,739	3,561
Earnings per share	3.25	2.68	2.18	1.62	1.33	1.16	0.79	0.89	1.73
Dividends per share	0.32	0.32	0.32	0.32	0.32	0.32	0.32	0.32	0.32
Price high	51.0	53.5	41.7	30.3	26.3	23.9	24.1	37.9	77.8
low	28.2	38.2	28.4	18.9	16.1	14.2	10.8	12.5	29.1

Honeywell International, Inc.

101 Columbia Road ❑ P.O. Box 2245 ❑ Morristown, NJ 07962–2245 ❑ Phone: (973) 455–2222 ❑ Website: www.honeywell.com ❑ Ticker symbol: HON ❑ Listed: NYSE ❑ S&P rating: B ❑ Value Line financial strength rating: A+

Financial Highlights, Fiscal Year 2008

Honeywell's sales growth eased a bit in 2008 to 5.8 percent, driving net sales to $36.6B. Earnings grew 14.3 percent to $2.8B, while operating margin fell 110 basis points. Net margin increased 50 basis points, largely on the sale of operating assets. Dividends increased 10 percent to $1.10, and the company repurchased 1.8 percent of its outstanding shares.

In June 2008 the company agreed to terms on the purchase of Intelligent Automation Corp., a leading supplier of helicopter on-board diagnostic systems used in military and commercial aircraft. Terms were not disclosed.

Also in June 2008 Honeywell sold its Consumable Solutions business to B/E Aerospace for $1.05B ($800M in cash, the balance in B/E common stock) in order to focus more on its core business. The Consumables Solutions unit distributes aerospace fasteners and hardware, among other services, and generated 2007 revenue of $524M.

Company Profile

Honeywell is a diversified technology and manufacturing leader, serving customers worldwide with aerospace products and services (40 percent of sales); control technologies for buildings, homes, and industry (31 percent); automotive products (15 percent); and specialty materials (14 percent).

Honeywell globally manages its business operations through four segments: Aerospace, Automation and Control Solutions, Specialty Materials, and Transportation Systems.

The Aerospace segment primarily makes cockpit controls, power generation equipment, and wheels and brakes for commercial and military aircraft. It is also a leading maker of jet engines for regional and business jet manufacturers. Demand for the company's aircraft equipment is driven primarily by expansion in the global jetliner fleet, particularly jets with one hundred or more seats. Since 1993, the global airliner fleet has grown at a 3 percent annual pace. The Aerospace segment is also a major player in the $35-billion global aircraft maintenance, repair, and overhaul industry, which is growing at a 2.2 percent annual rate.

Honeywell's Automation and Control Solutions segment is best known as a global maker of home and office climate controls equipment. It also makes home automation systems, energy-efficient lighting controls, as well as security and fire alarms.

The Specialty Materials operation makes specialty chemicals and fibers, which are sold primarily to the food, pharmaceutical, and electronic packaging industries.

The Transportation System segment consists of a portfolio of brand name car-care products, such as Fram filters, Prestone antifreeze, Autolite spark plugs, and Simoniz car waxes. The unit is also a major large truck brake manufacturer.

Reasons to Buy

In April 2008, Honeywell announced that it had been chosen to supply the latest generation of its HTF7000 turbofan propulsion system family for Embraer's new MSJ and MLJ business aircraft. The contract is valued at more than $23 billion including aftermarket sales and services over the life of the agreement.

Nine months after the official start of the recession and assuming better times ahead we're probably at the bottom of Honeywell's business cycle. All of the customers who could have cancelled or delayed orders have done so by now, and what's left is for Honeywell to ship firm orders and look closely at operations for cost-cutting opportunities, which they have committed to do.

The company is in good financial condition. With adequate cash on hand and solid cash flow, it's likely that dividend growth, share repurchases, and debt reduction will continue. In the current environment of slow top-line growth this is a good formula for increasing shareholder value.

Reasons for Caution

The company needs to improve its operating margin. Granted, 2008 was a tough year for commodities and specialty materials (Honeywell uses aluminum, titanium, etc.), so look for gains here in 2009 and 2010.

SECTOR: **Industrials**
BETA COEFFICIENT: **1.15**
10-YEAR COMPOUND EARNINGS PER SHARE GROWTH: **4.5%**
10-YEAR COMPOUND DIVIDENDS PER SHARE GROWTH: **6.5%**

		2008	2007	2006	2005	2004	2003	2002	2001	2000
Revenues (Mil)		36,556	34,589	31,367	27,653	25,601	23,103	22,274	23,652	25,023
Net Income (Mil)		2,792	2,444	2,083	1,736	1,281	1,344	1,644	1,672	2,293
Earnings per share		3.75	3.16	2.52	1.92	1.49	1.56	2.00	2.05	2.83
Dividends per share		1.10	1.00	0.91	0.83	0.75	0.75	0.75	0.75	0.75
Price	high	63.0	62.3	45.8	39.5	38.5	33.5	40.9	53.9	60.5
	low	23.2	43.1	35.2	32.7	31.2	20.2	18.8	22.2	32.1

Hormel Foods Corporation

1 Hormel Place ◻ Austin, MN 55912–3680 ◻ Phone: (507) 437–5007 ◻ Listed: NYSE ◻ Website: www
.hormel.com ◻ Ticker symbol: HRL ◻ S&P rating: A+ ◻ Value Line financial strength rating: A

Financial Highlights, Fiscal Year 2008

Hormel ended the year on a poor quarter (down 30 percent year/year), but still managed a 9.1 percent increase in revenues over FY2007. Earnings, however, fell 5.4 percent versus the prior year, primarily due to losses in an investment trust established "to fund supplemental executive retirement and deferred income plans," according to the very second paragraph in the annual report.

So what Hormel is saying is this: Had the value of the trust remained flat for the year, the Company would have been able to post an earnings increase (we calculate the company would have posted an earnings increase of 4 percent year over year). Or, another way of looking at it is this—had Hormel's operating margin in 2008 not fallen .21 percent, earnings would have been essentially flat year to year.

The fund's assets are valued and reported on a mark-to-market basis (a practice we endorse and respect), but we feel the company has a responsibility to emphasize and report on shortfalls over which it has control, rather than those it does not. No one's buying Hormel stock because of the company's investment savvy. We prefer the cheese to be where it belongs: in our bratwurst.

Fully diluted per-share earnings came in at $2.08, down 4 percent from FY2007, and the company bought back 1.5 percent of its outstanding shares. Dividends increased 23 percent, raising the yield to 2.0 percent.

The company purchased Boca Grande Foods, a manufacturer of liquid portion products, which added approximately $10M in net sales to the Specialty Group in 2008.

Company Profile

Founded by George A. Hormel in 1891 in Austin, Minnesota, Hormel Corporation is a multinational manufacturer of consumer-branded meat and food products, many of which are among the best-known and trusted in the food industry. The company, according to management, "enjoys a strong reputation among consumers, retail grocers, and foodservice, and industrial customer for products highly regarded for quality, taste, nutrition, convenience and value."

The company's business is reported in five segments: Refrigerated Foods, Grocery Products, Jennie-O Turkey Store, Specialty Foods, and All Other. The company's products include hams, bacon, sausages, franks, canned luncheon meats, stews, chiles, hash, meat spreads, shelf-stable microwaveable entrees, salsas, and frozen processed meats.

These products are sold in all fifty states by a Hormel Foods sales force assigned to offices in major cities throughout the United States. Their efforts are supplemented by sales brokers and distributors.

The headquarters for Hormel Foods is in Austin, Minnesota, along with its Research and Development division and flagship plant. Company facilities that manufacture meat and food products are situated in Iowa, Georgia, Illinois, Wisconsin, Nebraska, Oklahoma, California, and Kansas. In addition, custom manufacturing of selected Hormel Foods products is performed by various companies according to corporate guidelines and quality standards.

Hormel has thirty-four brands in the number one or two market positions and continues to develop new products every quarter. Nearly 25 percent of their revenues come from products introduced in the last eight years. Their goal is to, by 2012, reach $2B in annual sales from products introduced since 2000.

Reasons to Buy

Hormel had a great year in the grocery products segment. Operating profits of 15.7 percent in the most "convenience" oriented of Hormel's lines offers proof that people are still willing to pay for ease-of-use in spite of a tight economy. If Hormel can find the right product mix (and it looks like they can) in the rest of their prepared food lines, then 2010 should be a strong year for them.

Hormel is similar to many of the companies in this book in that they've experienced solid growth over the last five years, only to get knocked back a bit by the problems that came to a head in Q4 2008. And like other companies in this book, Hormel is using the time to re-assess the market, their product offerings, and their internal processes in order to improve efficiency and exit the downturn a stronger company.

Reasons for Caution

Continued uncertainty around raw material costs (grain, live hogs) have forced the company to remain hedged at higher than normal levels and prices. Until these markets stabilize and these higher-cost materials work their way through the system, margins will be depressed.

SECTOR: **Consumer Staples**
BETA COEFFICIENT: **.70**
10-YEAR COMPOUND EARNINGS PER SHARE GROWTH: **11.5%**
10-YEAR COMPOUND DIVIDENDS PER SHARE GROWTH: **7.5%**

	2008	2007	2006	2005	2004	2003	2002	2001	2000
Revenues (Mil)	6,755	6,193	5,745	5,414	4,780	4,200	3,910	4,124	3,675
Net Income (Mil)	286	302	286	254	232	186	189	182	170
Earnings per share	2.08	2.17	2.05	1.82	1.65	1.33	1.35	1.30	1.20
Dividends per share	0.74	0.60	0.56	0.52	0.45	0.42	0.39	0.37	0.35
Price high	42.8	41.8	39.1	35.4	32.1	27.5	28.2	27.3	21.0
low	24.8	30.0	31.9	29.2	24.9	19.9	20.0	17.0	13.6

CONSERVATIVE GROWTH

International Business Machines Corporation

New Orchard Road □ Armonk, New York 10504 □ Phone: (800) 426–4968 □ Website: www.ibm.com □
Listed: NYSE □ Ticker symbol: IBM □ S&P rating: A □ Value Line financial strength rating: A++

Financial Highlights, Fiscal Year 2008

The company reported year/year growth in net revenue of 15 percent (to $16.7B) on a net sales increase of just 5 percent (to $103.65B). Earnings per share were up a whopping 24 percent to $8.93 (all numbers are indicative of continuing operations only). This makes six consecutive years of double-digit EPS growth at IBM.

IBM has traditionally had strong cash flow, and 2008 was no exception. Free cash flow was up $1.9B to $14.3B (an increase of 15.3 percent). The 2008 free cash flow is up nearly 80 percent over the last five years. Over the last nine years, Big Blue has generated over $84B in free cash flow and exited 2008 with nearly $13B in cash and liquid securities, even after spending $10.6B in share repurchase and distributing $2.6B in dividends.

Margins grew to their highest level in more than a decade. Gross margins grew for the fifth consecutive year to 44.1 percent, while net margins grew 1.4 percent to 11.9 percent. Income rose to 16.1 percent. This growth is due in large part to IBM's continuing emphasis on exiting the low-margin hardware businesses and concentrating on the higher-margin software and services.

Sales were up in four of the five major product segments. The biggest gains were in Software (8.2 percent), Technology Services (8.8 percent), and Business Services (5.1 percent). Sales of hardware (Systems and Technology) were down 10.8 percent, primarily due to selected divestitures.

Company Profile

Big Blue is the world's leading provider of computer hardware and services. IBM makes a broad range of computers, notebooks, mainframes, and network servers. The company also develops software (it is number two, behind Microsoft) and peripherals. The company continues to innovate and invent, and has for the last sixteen years led the world in the number of U.S. patents issued. In 2008, over 70 percent of the more than 4,000 patents issued were for software and services.

In 2008, IBM derived over 75 percent of its revenue and 82 percent of its income from the Software and Services businesses. The company continues to design and produce mainframes and has its label on five of the top ten supercomputers in the world. They also produce high-margin commercial servers and Enterprise-level installations, but they have exited the lower-margin hardware businesses, such as consumer PCs and hard drives.

Reasons to Buy

Once viewed as a teetering giant of the computer industry, with a massive IP portfolio but with an uncertain product strategy, IBM has over the last decade successfully re-invented itself as a powerhouse in the Software and Services sector. While their gross margins in hardware remain healthy (but shrinking) at 38 percent, their margins in the much larger Services arms are at 30 percent and growing, and Software generates 14 percent more revenue than hardware at margins of over 85 percent.

Not long ago, many companies felt they had to have in-house Information Technology departments to service their IT needs. Now, most have found that it's far more efficient to contract those services out to someone who can provide data warehousing, website development and maintenance, regional/national/global IT infrastructure, etc., without requiring a commitment in fixed assets. This is where IBM has leveraged their expertise, and as this trend continues and as businesses grow their reliance on these services, IBM benefits.

They've successfully implemented a global focus to their growth. Revenue growth outside of United States, Europe, and Japan was double the growth of IBM's "major markets" and now represents 18 percent of their total revenue. Their focus is on high-margin, long-term global infrastructure and services, model that has proven to be very successful over the last decade.

They continue to innovate and are in a great position to acquire whatever technology they choose not to develop internally. They have world-class semiconductor design and production facilities and license design, manufacturing, and packaging services and products.

Their services income is largely based on long-term contracts which are not as subject to the vagaries of the world economy as would be sales of hardware.

Reasons for Caution

IBM has carved out a very large chunk of the outsourced IT business. Innovation in this area can be rapid and disruptive, and margins can shrink precipitously as a result. IBM will have to stay ahead of the curve with innovative and compelling products and defensive product strategies in order to maintain revenue growth.

Competition in the services area is heating up, with Hewlett-Packard's purchase of EDS and Oracle's pending acquisition of Sun Microsystems. These two moves could create competitors with strong synergies and a compelling sales pitch to new customers.

SECTOR: **Information Technology**
BETA COEFFICIENT: **0.95**
10-YEAR COMPOUND EARNINGS PER SHARE GROWTH: **9.5%**
10-YEAR COMPOUND DIVIDENDS PER SHARE GROWTH: **14.5%**

		2008	2007	2006	2005	2004	2003	2002	2001	2000
Revenues (Mil)		103,630	98,786	91,424	91,134	96,503	89,131	81,186	83,067	88,396
Net Income (Mil)		12,334	10,418	9,492	7,934	8,448	7,583	3,579	7,495	8,093
Earnings per share		8.93	7.18	6.06	4.91	4.39	4.34	3.07	4.69	4.44
Dividends per share		1.90	1.50	1.10	.078	0.70	0.66	0.60	0.55	0.51
Price	high	130.9	121.5	97.4	99.1	100.4	94.5	124.0	124.7	134.9
	low	69.5	88.8	72.7	71.8	81.9	73.2	54.0	83.8	80.1

Illinois Tool Works, Inc.

3600 West Lake Ave. □ Glenview, IL 60025–5811 □ Phone: (847) 657–4104 □ Website: www.itw.com □
Listed: NYSE □ Ticker symbol: ITW □ S&P rating: A+ □ Value Line financial strength rating: A++

Financial Highlights, Fiscal Year 2008

Revenues increased 6.7 percent in 2008 over 2007, primarily due to revenues from acquisitions and the favorable effect of currency translation. Organic growth actually declined 2.5 percent year over year. Income fell 13.3 percent to $1.58B due to declines in base revenues and the lower margins of acquired companies, including acquisition-related expenses, which reduced overall margins.

Operating income in 2008 declined 4.5 percent (to $2.34B) over 2007 due to the decline in base business revenues and increased restructuring expenses, partially offset by the positive effect of currency translation and income from acquisitions.

During 2008, 50 businesses were acquired worldwide with international businesses representing approximately 39 percent of the annualized acquired revenue.

Company Profile

ITW is a diversified manufacturing company with 875 decentralized business units in fifty-four countries, employing approximately 65,000. The businesses are organized into six major segments, each contributing fairly equally to revenue:

- Industrial Packaging includes steel, plastic, and paper products used for bundling, shipping, and protecting goods in transit. Primary brands include Acme, Signode, Pabco, and Strapex. Major end markets served are primary metals, general industrial, construction, and food/beverage.

- Power Systems and Electronics produces equipment and consumables associated with specialty power conversion, metallurgy, and electronics. Their primary products include arc-welding equipment and consumables, solder materials and equipment and services for electronics assembly. Primary brands include AXA Power, Hobart, Kester, and Weldcraft.

- Transportation includes transportation-related components, fasteners, fluids, and polymers, as well as truck remanufacturing and related parts and service. Their major end markets are automotive OEM and automotive aftermarket.

- Food Equipment produces commercial food equipment and related service. Their major brands include Hobart, Traulsen, Vulcan, and Wolf.

- Construction Products concentrates on tools, fasteners, and other products for construction applications. Their major end markets are residential, commercial, and renovation construction.

- Polymers and Fluids businesses produce adhesives, sealants, lubrication and cutting fluids, and hygiene products. Their primary brands include Futura, Kraft, Devcon, and Rocol.

Finally, the remaining ITW brands include a cornucopia of businesses addressing a dozen or more markets. Brands well-known to industrial users (and probably not many others) include Chemtronics, DeVilbiss, Magnaflux, and Texwipe.

Reasons to Buy

If ITW had simply played the cards it had at the beginning of the year, revenues would have fallen versus 2007. Instead, ITW's FY2008 acquisitions put the top line into the black, for a total swing of plus 9.2 percent. This is ITW's business model. But during a weakening economy it cuts into operating margins.

ITW has a rigorous policy (their "80/20" rule) of focusing the bulk of their resources on those businesses and products that generate the bulk of their revenue which, they claim, is only 20 percent of any portfolio. ITW feels strongly that this is a major factor in their record of efficient, conservative growth and that adherence to this and other core principles will serve them well in thriving during an economic downturn.

They entered 2009 expecting another year of declining growth, but with a very strong cash position.

They are prepared to ride out this current downturn and plan to make value-based acquisitions as signs of a recovery appear. They anticipate that the combination of reduced valuations throughout the economy and the eventual freeing up of the credit markets will create numerous opportunities for growth.

Illinois Tool's record of sustained quality earnings is the result of a very practical view of the world. The company relies on market penetration—rather than price increases—to fuel operating income growth. These results then generate the cash needed to fund ITW's growth through both investing in core businesses and acquisitions.

ITW will be going through several weak quarters, perhaps as long as all the way through 2009. Earnings should rebound in 2010 in part due to macro conditions, and in part due to ITW's acquisitions and restructuring efforts.

Reasons for Caution

ITW's end markets are precisely those that have been affected most by the recession, particularly the automotive and construction sectors. The company expects that turnarounds in those sectors will lag the recovery of the rest of their portfolio.

On an industry-wide average, growth by acquisition fails in nearly 50 percent of cases. ITW's track record of picking winners is impressive, but a tough economy can stress even well-run businesses. ITW must maintain their batting average here or risk further declines in operating margin.

SECTOR: **Industrials**
BETA COEFFICIENT: **0.95**
10-YEAR COMPOUND EARNINGS PER SHARE GROWTH: **11.5%**
10-YEAR COMPOUND DIVIDENDS PER SHARE GROWTH: **14.5%**

		2008	2007	2006	2005	2004	2003	2002	2001	2000
Revenues (Mil)		15,869	16,171	14,055	12,922	11,731	10,036	9,468	9,293	9,984
Net Income (Mil)		1,583	1,870	1,718	1,495	1,340	1,040	932	806	958
Earnings per share		3.04	3.36	3.01	2.60	2.20	1.69	1.51	1.32	1.58
Dividends per share		1.15	1.12	0.71	0.59	0.52	0.47	0.45	0.41	0.38
Price	high	55.6	60.0	53.4	47.3	48.4	42.4	38.9	36.0	34.5
	low	28.5	45.6	41.5	39.3	36.5	27.3	27.5	24.6	24.8

CONSERVATIVE GROWTH

International Paper Company

400 Atlantic Street ▫ Stamford, CT 06921 ▫ Phone: (901) 419–4957 ▫ Dividend reinvestment plan available ▫ Website: www.internationalpaper.com ▫ Ticker symbol: IP ▫ Listed: NYSE ▫ S&P rating: B+ ▫ Value Line financial strength rating: B+

Financial Highlights, Fiscal Year 2008

FY2008 was a rather tumultuous year for International Paper. The company reported net sales of $24.8B, an increase of 13.4 percent over FY2007. Earnings from ongoing operations, on the other hand, fell 14 percent to $829M, even though operating margins grew to a record high 22.1 percent.

It's less than enlightening to compare IP's year-over-year results in FY2008. The company sold off assets, closed a number of facilities, bought a $6B business, and in the process took several significant one-time charges, including nearly $1.5B in impaired goodwill, all in FY2008. The company, after having sold off the vast majority of its forestry holding in 2007 and re-aligning to focus on just a few core businesses, appar-

ently decided that this was the right time to clear the books of as much old business as it possibly could and begin measuring the performance of the "new" company with a clean baseline.

The company's ongoing operations in 2008 were healthy, generating record positive cash flows while allowing the company to retire over 12 percent of its stock and returning its second-best EPS since FY2000.

Company Profile

International Paper Company (International Paper), incorporated in 1941, is a global paper and packaging company that is complemented by a North American merchant distribution system, with primary markets and manufacturing operations in North America, Europe, Latin America, Russia, Asia, and North

Africa. During the year ended December 31, 2008, the company operated 23 pulp, paper, and packaging mills; 157 converting and packaging plants; 19 recycling plants; and three bag facilities. During 2008, the production facilities in Europe, Asia, Latin America, and South America included eight pulp, paper and packaging mills; 53 converting and packaging plants; and two recycling plants. The company operates in six segments: Printing Papers, Industrial Packaging, Consumer Packaging, Distribution, Forest Products, and Specialty Businesses and Other. On August 4, 2008, International Paper completed the acquisition of the assets of Weyerhaeuser Company's Containerboard, Packaging, and Recycling (CBPR) business.

International Paper produces uncoated printing and writing papers. The uncoated papers business produces papers for use in copiers, desktop and laser printers, and digital imaging. Market pulp is used in the manufacture of printing, writing, and specialty papers; towel and tissue products; and filtration products. Pulp is also converted into nonpaper products such as diapers and sanitary napkins.

International Paper is the largest manufacturer of containerboard in the United States. Its products include linerboard, medium, whitetop, recycled linerboard, recycled medium, and saturating kraft. About 80 percent of its production is converted domestically into corrugated boxes and other packaging by the 137 United States container plants. The company's coated paperboard business produces coated paperboard for a variety of packaging and commercial printing end uses.

Through xpedx, the company's North American merchant distribution business, IP provides distribution services and products to a number of customer markets, supplying commercial printers with printing papers and graphic prepress, printing presses, and postpress equipment; building services and away-from-home markets with facility supplies; and manufacturers with packaging supplies and equipment.

Reasons to Buy

Investors backed away from IP in 2008 when the company moved to refocus its business. There were questions about where the changes would take the company and whether the changes, right or wrong, were too late in coming.

Now that the picture going forward is a bit more clear, the stock price has recovered somewhat (though still 60 percent below its 2007 peak). Earnings in the first part of 2009 have begun to recover and the purchase of Weyerhaeuser's CBPR business has helped the top line.

We feel most of IP's bad news from 2008 is behind it or has already been baked into the current price and forecasts. Even so, the story here is of a longer-term recovery than is the case with most of the stocks in this book. The potential for a more substantial recovery over the next few years is very good.

Reasons for Caution

IP's customers have significantly cut back on purchases during the current downturn, particularly in IP's core cut paper lines. Spending on these business staples will recover as the general business environment recov-ers, but this will lag other indicators, perhaps by two or more calendar quarters. The gradual evolution to digital media is also a long term drag, although new customized printing technologies should offset this trend somewhat.

SECTOR: **Materials**
BETA COEFFICIENT: **1.20**
10-YEAR COMPOUND EARNINGS PER SHARE GROWTH: **4.5%**
10-YEAR COMPOUND DIVIDENDS PER SHARE GROWTH: **0%**

		2008	2007	2006	2005	2004	2003	2002	2001	2000
Revenues (Mil)		24,829	21,890	21,995	24,097	25,548	25,179	24,976	26,363	28,180
Net Income (Mil)		829	1,168	635	513	634	382	540	214	969
Earnings per share		1.96	2.70	2.18	1.06	1.30	0.80	1.12	0.44	2.16
Dividends per share		1.00	1.00	1.00	1.00	1.00	1.00	1.00	1.00	1.00
Price	high	33.8	41.6	38.0	42.6	45.0	43.3	46.2	43.3	46.2
	low	10.2	31.0	30.7	27.0	37.1	33.1	31.3	30.7	26.3

Iron Mountain Incorporated

745 Atlantic Avenue □ Boston, MA 02111 □ Website: www.ironmountain.com □ Listed: NYSE □ Ticker symbol: IRM □ S&P rating: BB □ Value Line financial strength rating: B

Financial Highlights, Fiscal Year 2008

IRM's revenues increased 11.9 percent over 2007, of which about 75 percent was organic growth driven by strong performance across all segments, but data protection and secure shredding were standouts. Of the 11.9 percent gain, about 3 percent was due to the effects of positive currency translation.

Growth rates in the storage business have been very steady over the last eight quarters, but service revenue growth has moderated significantly, down some 700 basis points (7 percent) in the worst-case fourth quarter of 2008. Service revenues are far more discretionary and client-spending levels are impacted to a greater extent by economic downturns.

Company Profile

Iron Mountain is the world's leading provider of record, document, and information-management services. Businesses that require or desire off-site, secure storage, and/or archiving of data in physical or electronic form contract with IRM for whatever level of service meets their needs.

In general, IRM provides three major types of service: records management, data protection and recovery, and information destruction (with apologies to Stephen Hawking).

All three services include both physical and electronic media.

Revenues accrue to the company through two streams—storage and services. Storage revenues consist of recurring per-unit charges related to the storage of material or data. The storage periods are typically many years, and the revenues from this service account for just over half of IRM's total revenue over the last five years. Service revenue comes from charges for any number of services, including those related to the core storage service and others such as temporary access, courier operations, secure destruction, data recovery, media conversion, and the like.

IRM's client base is deep and diverse. They have over 90,000 clients, including 93 percent of the *Fortune* 1000 and over 90 percent of the *FTSE* 100. They have over 900 facilities in 165 markets worldwide, and they are six times the size of their nearest competitor.

Reasons to Buy

Mr. Buffett said, "Never invest in a business you cannot understand." I don't believe that's ever going to be a problem for IRM's investor relations team. The business model here is about as straightforward as it gets, which may be part of the appeal as a stock.

A common observation of IRM's critics is that paper records are dying off and most data is now generated and stored electronically, creating opportunity for competitors like IBM and EMC. This is true, but it ignores a couple of facts: Existing paper still needs to be stored for a long time, and there's a lot of it.

It also ignores a number of other important points. For one, IRM's current customers would need a very good reason to split their data storage business between two vendors, one doing only electronic storage and the other doing electronic storage *plus everything else as well*. Second, if competitors for the electronic storage business become a problem, IRM can price their electronic storage below market and still be quite profitable. And last, for the customer base that IRM serves, this is not a burdensome expense. Changing vendors could likely cost them more than they might ever hope to save.

Yes, brand-new companies that have few paper records and no data center (cloud model) would have little need for IRM's services, but they wouldn't need someone like EMC, either. For now, IRM has a pretty good moat.

Regulatory initiatives, such as Sarbanes-Oxley and recent requirements for e-mail storage have been a boon to IRM's business. Revenues have more than doubled since the passage of "SOX" in late 2002.

Reasons for Caution

The company has made over 150 acquisitions since going public in 1996. The resulting debt load is one problem and is reflected in the company's relatively weak financial strength ratings. Another is the difficulty and risk in integrating that many businesses into an organization that needs to operate with a minimum of process variation.

SECTOR: **Information Technology**
BETA COEFFICIENT: **1.05**
10-YEAR COMPOUND EARNINGS PER SHARE GROWTH: **55.4%**
10-YEAR COMPOUND DIVIDENDS PER SHARE GROWTH: **Nil**

		2008	2007	2006	2005	2004	2003	2002	2001	2000
Revenues (Mil)		3055	2730	2350	2078	1817	1501	1318	1171	986
Net Income (Mil)		152	153	129	114	94.2	84.6	67.0	(32.2)	(5.9)
Earnings per share		.78	.76	.64	.57	.48	.44	.35	(0.17)	(0.03)
Dividends per share		Nil								
Price	high	37.1	38.8	29.9	30.1	23.4	18.1	15.2	13.5	11.6
	low	16.7	25.0	22.6	17.8	17.2	13.4	9.0	9.4	8.2

Johnson & Johnson

One Johnson & Johnson Plaza ▫ New Brunswick, NJ 08933 ▫ Phone: (800) 950–5089 ▫ Website: www.jnj.com
▫ Listed: NYSE ▫ Ticker symbol: JNJ ▫ S&P rating: A+ ▫ Value Line financial strength rating: A++

Financial Highlights, Fiscal Year 2008

Johnson & Johnson posted sales gains year over year of 4.3 percent to $63.7B. Earnings grew 6.8 percent and adjusted earnings per share grew 9.6 percent. Dividends grew 11 percent to $1.80 and the company spent $8.1B on share repurchases.

The company grew revenues in two of its three main operating segments, with only Pharmaceuticals reporting a year over year decline in sales. This was primarily due to the introduction of generic competition for both Risperdal and Procrit, two of their top four selling drugs, although the total decline for the segment was just 1.2 percent. Consumer Health Care, on the other hand, grew sales 10.8 percent to $16B, while Medical Devices and Diagnostics grew 6.4 percent to $23.1B.

The company made several acquisitions throughout the year, including Mentor Corporation (breast implants and other cosmetic/reconstructive devices), Omrix Biopharmaceuticals, SurgRx (ultrasonic devices), and Amic AB (in vitro diagnostics).

Company Profile

Johnson & Johnson is the largest and most comprehensive health-care company in the world, with 2008 sales of more than $63 billion. J&J offers a broad line of consumer products and over-the-counter drugs, as well as various other medical devices and diagnostic equipment.

The company has three reporting segments: Consumer Health Care, Medical Devices and Diagnostics, and Pharmaceuticals. In those segments, Johnson & Johnson has more than 200 operating companies in fifty-four countries, selling some 50,000 products in more than 175 countries. One of Johnson & Johnson's premier assets is its well-entrenched brand names, which are widely known in the United States as well as abroad. And as a marketer, J&J's reputation for quality has enabled it to build strong ties to health-care providers.

Its international presence includes not only marketing, but also production and broad distribution capability in regions outside the United States. Strategically, these rest-of-world markets in places like China, Latin America, and Africa offer growth potential for mature product lines.

The company has a stake in a wide variety of health segments: anti-infectives, biotechnology, cardiology and circulatory diseases, the central nervous system, diagnostics, gastrointestinals, minimally invasive therapies, nutraceuticals, orthopedics, pain management, skin care, vision care, women's health, and wound care.

The company's well-known trade names include Band-Aid adhesive bandages, Tylenol; Stayfree, Carefree, and Sure & Natural feminine hygiene products; Mylanta; Pepcid AC; Neutrogena; Johnson's baby powder, shampoo, and oil; and Reach toothbrushes.

The company's professional items include ligatures and sutures, mechanical wound closure products, diagnostic products, medical equipment and devices, surgical dressings, surgical apparel and accessories, and disposable contact lenses.

Reasons to Buy

J&J's pharmaceuticals took it on the chin last year when patent protections expired on two of its top drugs. Still, it had nine separate billion-dollar drugs, and the near-term pipeline looks promising with four new submittals for approval and several new applications and indications for existing products under review.

The company's five-year Compound Annual Growth Rate (CAGR) for international sales is 13.6 percent, and J&J's International sales now make up over 50 percent of the total. As standards of medical care rise internationally and as the potential for health care funding reform in the United States increases, J&J's growth outside the United States is particularly appealing.

The company exited 2008 with nearly $14B in cash and exceptional free cash flow, so more acquisitions, further dividend increases, and continued share repurchase look to be more than fully funded.

To update last year's numbers and illustrate J&J's track record:

- Their seventy-sixth consecutive year of sales increases.
- Their twenty-fifth consecutive year of earnings increases, adjusted for special items.
- Their forty-sixth consecutive year of dividend increases.

Reasons for Caution

As noted in last year's edition, Johnson & Johnson is a very conservative company and a very conservative stock with nearly three billion shares outstanding. As a consequence, the upside will be somewhat limited, but then so will be the downside.

SECTOR: **Health Care**
BETA COEFFICIENT: **.60**
10-YEAR COMPOUND EARNINGS PER SHARE GROWTH: **13%**
10-YEAR COMPOUND DIVIDENDS PER SHARE GROWTH: **14.5%**

		2008	2007	2006	2005	2004	2003	2002	2001	2000
Revenues (Mil)		63,747	61,095	53,324	50,514	47,348	41,862	36,298	32,317	29,139
Net Income (Mil)		12,949	10,576	11,053	10,411	8,509	7,197	6,651	5,668	4,800
Earnings per share		4.57	4.15	3.73	3.35	2.84	2.40	2.18	1.84	1.63
Dividends per share		1.80	1.62	1.46	1.28	1.10	0.93	0.82	0.70	0.62
Price	high	72.8	68.8	69.4	70.0	64.2	59.1	65.9	61.0	53.0
	low	52.1	59.7	56.6	59.8	49.2	48.0	41.4	40.3	33.1

Johnson Controls, Inc.

P.O. Box 591 ◻ Milwaukee, WI 53201–0591 ◻ Phone: (414) 524–2375 ◻ Fiscal year ends September 30 ◻ Website: www.johnsoncontrols.com ◻ Listed: NYSE ◻ Ticker symbol: JCI ◻ S&P rating: A+ ◻ Value Line financial strength rating: A

Financial Highlights, Fiscal Year 2008

Sales grew 10 percent to $38.1B while earnings grew 7.8 percent to $1.4B over FY2007. Margins held up nicely in spite of major changes in the market for many of Johnson's raw materials, to say nothing of their energy costs. Dividends rose 17 percent to $0.52/share.

In July 2008 a joint venture formed by Johnson and other creditors of Plastech Engineered Products acquired Plastech's interior products assets. Plastech had been a major supplier to Johnson and had been granted financial considerations by Johnson in the past in order to maintain assurance of supply. In February 2008, Plastech entered into Chapter 11 bankruptcy proceedings, but Johnson and other Plastech creditors protested, asserting that Plastech was not eligible for such protection. Johnson contributed $135M in cash and various production assets and retains a 70 percent share in the joint venture.

Company Profile

Johnson Controls is a large manufacturer of automotive and building heating, ventilation, and air conditioning controls (HVAC), and energy controls and products. Their products are found in over 200 million vehi-

cles, 12 million homes and one million commercial buildings.

Their automotive business is one of the world's largest automotive suppliers, providing interior products and systems to more than 30 million vehicles annually. Their technologies include seating and overhead systems, door systems, floor consoles, instrument panels, cockpits, and integrated electronics. Customers include virtually every major automaker in the world. The business produces automotive interior systems for original equipment manufacturers (OEMs) and operates approximately 185 wholly and majority-owned manufacturing or assembly plants in 29 countries worldwide. Additionally, the business has partially owned affiliates in Asia, Europe, North America, and South America. In fiscal 2008, the automotive business accounted for 48 percent of the company's consolidated net sales.

Building efficiency is a global leader in delivering integrated control systems, mechanical equipment, services, and solutions designed to improve the comfort, safety, and energy efficiency of nonresidential buildings and residential properties with operations in more than 125 countries. Revenues come from facilities management, technical services, and the replacement and upgrade of controls/HVAC mechanical equipment in the existing buildings market, where the company's large base of current customers leads to repeat business, as well as with installing controls and equipment during the construction of new buildings. Customer relationships often span entire building lifecycles. In fiscal 2008, building efficiency accounted for 37 percent of the company's consolidated net sales.

The power solutions business is a leading global producer of lead-acid automotive batteries, serving both automotive original equipment manufacturers and the general vehicle battery aftermarket. They produce more than 120 million lead-acid batteries annually. They also offer Absorbent Glass Mat (AGM), nickel-metal-hydride and lithium-ion battery technologies to power hybrid vehicles. Approximately 75 percent of automotive battery sales worldwide in fiscal 2008 were to the automotive replacement market, with the remaining sales to the OEM market.

Sales of automotive batteries generated 15 percent of the company's fiscal 2008 consolidated net sales.

Reasons to Buy

In September 2008 the company's backlog was approximately $9.2B, an increase of $1.1B over the prior year. And though revenues for 2009 will be down significantly due to the rapid decline in the demand for automobiles and unfavorable currency swings (over 60 percent of JCI's revenue comes from outside of the United States), the prospects for 2010 are much brighter.

The Obama administration has announced programs and incentives that affect JCI's business favorably, chief among them the renewed emphasis on energy efficiency in homes and buildings, and the incentives provided for research in vehicles powered by alternative energy.

Johnson's joint venture with Saft Advanced Power Solutions (JCS) is providing lithium-ion batteries to the Dodge Sprinter development program and has recently signed on with Ford to provide batteries for their upcoming (2012) plug-in hybrid. The Ford automobile is projected to deliver the cost-per-mile equivalent of a 120-mpg gasoline-powered car. JCI's subsidiary Varta has set up a JCS development center in Hanover, Germany, to support the European market.

JCI's traditional businesses will continue to provide top-end growth (adjusted for recovery conditions) and their backlog should see them through several rough quarters.

Reasons for Caution

The company's current high multiple seems to be a bet on the plug-in hybrid business. This segment needs to be assessed with current information before making a large commitment.

SECTOR: **Industrials**
BETA COEFFICIENT: **1.25**
10-YEAR COMPOUND EARNINGS PER SHARE GROWTH: **16%**
10-YEAR COMPOUND DIVIDENDS PER SHARE GROWTH: **12%**

		2008	2007	2006	2005	2004	2003	2002	2001	2000
Revenues (Mil)		38,062	34,624	32,235	27,883	25,363	22,646	20,103	18,427	17,155
Net Income (Mil)		1,400	1,252	1,028	909	818	683	601	542	472
Earnings per share		2.33	2.09	1.75	1.50	1.41	1.20	1.09	0.85	0.85
Dividends per share		0.52	0.44	0.37	0.33	0.28	0.24	0.22	0.21	0.19
Price	high	36.5	44.5	30.0	25.1	21.1	19.4	15.5	13.8	10.9
	low	13.6	28.1	22.1	17.5	16.5	12.0	11.5	8.0	7.6

GROWTH AND INCOME

Kellogg Company

One Kellogg Square □ P.O. Box 3599 □ Battle Creek, MI 49016–3599 □ Phone: (269) 961–6636 □ Website: www.kelloggcompany.com □ Ticker symbol: K □ Listed: NYSE □ S&P rating: A– □ Value Line financial strength rating: A

Financial Highlights, Fiscal Year 2008

Net sales grew 9 percent over 2007 to $12.8B, while net earnings rose 4 percent to $1.15B. Earnings per share and dividends both grew 8 percent to $2.99 and $1.30, respectively. Gross profit fell 21 basis points, or 0.21 percent, to 41.9 percent, largely due to increased costs of raw materials and energy.

The company acquired a number of brands and tangible assets throughout the year, including Mother's Cookies (full disclosure—we love 'em), Bear Naked Granolas and Trail Mixes, a Chinese cookie maker called Navigable Foods, and United Bakers, the leading producer of crackers, biscuits, and cereals in Russia.

Company Profile

Founded in 1906, Kellogg is the world's leading producer of cereal and a leading producer of convenience foods, including cookies, crackers, toaster pastries, cereal bars, frozen waffles, meat alternatives, pie crusts, and cones.

The company's brands include Kellogg's, Keebler, Pop-Tarts, Eggo, Cheez-It, Nutri-Grain, Rice Krispies, Special K, Murray, Austin, Morningstar Farms, Famous Amos, Carr's, Plantation, and Kashi.

The company operates in two segments: Kellogg North America (NA) and Kellogg International, with NA generating two-thirds of the company's revenue. NA is further divided into Cereals, Snacks, and Frozen/Specialty categories. International operates as three regional entities: Europe, Latin America, and Asia Pacific. The company produces more than 1500 different products, manufactured in nineteen countries and marketed in more than 180 countries around the world.

Kellogg's is a conservatively run company, emphasizing long term thinking and leveraging existing brand strengths while keeping a sharp focus on costs savings.

Reasons to Buy

Kellogg's owns just over a third of the U.S. market for ready-to-eat cereals, which makes them the market leader in probably the most mature food category in the world. But, having invented it over a hundred years ago, they have not been idle with regard to growing it beyond what most could imagine. Last year, for instance, they released Special K Chocolatey Delight, Fruit Loops Smoothie, and Corn Pops Peanut Butter. Maybe not everyone's cup of tea, but this is how you stay on top.

Kellogg's began full-scale implementation of a cost-cutting program that piloted very well. They project the program will reduce cost of goods sold some 4 percent in 2009, and up to $1B through 2010.

Kellogg's strategy since 2001 has been to "win in cereal and expand snacks," meaning "hold onto market share in the mature segment and grow the newer segment with product innovation." This has worked well for them, as 25 percent of their revenues are from cereals and snacks have grown (organically and through acquisition) to 30 percent of overall revenue. If they continue to succeed with this strategy we can expect to see continued steady growth in both top and bottom lines.

We like Kellogg's growth in international markets. As discretionary income rises, so does consumption of prepared foods, and the international markets will reward companies who have the right products.

The company has a compelling history of slow but steady growth. Year after year they target low single digit growth and year after year, with very few exceptions, they hit the target. They're also committed to dividend growth and year after year they deliver (current yield is about 3 percent). This is a stock that will let you sleep at night, and in the morning you can reward your good judgment with an Eggo waffle.

Reasons for Caution

Kellogg's is tied closely to the ups and downs of the grain market. Rising energy costs, disastrous weather, disruptive farm policies . . . any number of things can materially affect the cost of all of Kellogg's raw materials, and if the 2010 commodity markets are as tumultuous as the 2008 markets were, then Kellogg's will be playing defense and returns will likely suffer. Particularly in a soft economy, Kellogg's also faces threats from generic and store branded products, especially on the cereal aisle.

SECTOR: **Consumer Staples**
BETA COEFFICIENT: **.60**
10-YEAR COMPOUND EARNINGS PER SHARE GROWTH: **5%**
10-YEAR COMPOUND DIVIDENDS PER SHARE GROWTH: **3.6%**

	2008	2007	2006	2005	2004	2003	2002	2001	2000
Revenues (Mil)	12,822	11,776	10,907	10,177	9,614	8,812	8,304	8,853	6,955
Net Income (Mil)	1,148	1,103	1,004	980	891	787	711	533	652
Earnings per share	2.99	2.76	2.51	2.26	2.14	1.92	1.73	1.31	1.61
Dividends per share	1.30	1.24	1.14	1.06	1.01	1.01	1.01	1.01	1.00
Price high	58.5	56.9	51.0	47.0	45.3	38.6	37.0	34.0	32.0
low	35.6	48.7	42.4	42.4	37.0	27.8	29.0	24.3	20.8

GROWTH AND INCOME

Kraft Foods Inc.

Three Lakes Drive □ Northfield, IL 60093 □ Phone: (847) 646–2000 □ Website: www.kraft.com □ Listed: NYSE □ Ticker symbol: KFT □ S&P rating: A- □ Value Line financial strength rating: A+

Financial Highlights, Fiscal Year 2008

Kraft's revenues grew 14.9 percent to $42.8B, driven largely by a 40 percent increase in snack revenues as a result of last year's acquisition of Groupe Danone, who are one of the top biscuit (cookie) makers in Europe. Cheeses also did well, growing revenues 7.7 percent to $7.5B.

Earnings fell 2.1 percent on a 90 basis point (0.9 percent) decline in operating margin, due in main to increased prices for commodity ingredients. Net margin fell 120 basis points or 1.2 percent to 6.6 percent, the lowest since the formation of the company in 2001. Dividends increased 8 percent and the company repurchased 65 million shares of common stock.

The company issued approximately $7B in senior unsecured notes, the proceeds to be used primarily for refinancing of the debt issued to purchase Groupe Danone in 2007 and other short-term debt.

In August the company completed its split off of the Post cereals brands and the company recorded a gain of discontinued operations of $937M.

Company Profile

Kraft is the second largest food and beverage company in the world and the largest in the United States. Their products are manufactured in 168 different facilities in seventy countries and distributed in over 150 countries. Many of their brands are recognizable around the world, including their nine "billion-dollar" brands: Kraft, Jacobs, LU, Maxwell House, Milka, Nabisco, Oreo, Philadelphia, and Oscar Mayer.

The company operates eight segments, with Europe and Developing

Markets constituting 40 percent of revenue, and U.S. Beverages, U.S. Cheese, U.S. Convenient Meals, U.S. Grocery, U.S Snacks, and Canada & North America Foodservice evenly dividing the remaining 60 percent.

Reasons to Buy

Kraft's top position with its many brands (more than fifty with over $100M in sales) makes it a solid defensive stock for uncertain times. Kraft claims there's a Kraft brand in over 99 percent of American homes, a fact that would be hard to dispute. There's security and comfort in the familiarity of a recognized brand, and familiarity would seem to be Kraft's best defense against the price-eroding effects of store brands.

The company has completed a five-year restructuring program designed to reduce costs and to locate the resources involved in product-line decisions closer to the markets served. First quarter 2009 net profits were up 10 percent over the year ago quarter, due primarily to reduced SG&A, so things seem to be working. Net

margins should continue to recover through 2010.

Through the first half of 2009, there have been no signs of the spiky pricing that characterized the 2008 commodities markets. Kraft will benefit from lower prices overall and reduced hedging requirements. Currency values seem to have stabilized as well, reducing their exposure to loss of revenue in international markets.

At mid-2009 share prices, the current dividend yield is 3.9 percent and is expected to grow over the next eighteen months.

Reasons for Caution

In a down economy consumers are looking to save money wherever they can, and for many the most obvious place to do so is when comparing adjacent products on a grocery shelf. Kraft's brands are always under pricing pressure from store brands, but especially so as long as consumer confidence is flagging. Kraft's top-line organic growth will slow until they can get some pricing flexibility.

SECTOR: **Consumer Staples**
BETA COEFFICIENT: **0.65**
7-YEAR COMPOUND EARNINGS PER SHARE GROWTH: **7.0%**
7-YEAR COMPOUND DIVIDENDS PER SHARE GROWTH: **23.0%**

		2008	2007	2006	2005	2004	2003	2002	2001	2000
Revenues (Mil)		42,777	37,241	34,356	34,113	32,168	31,010	29,709	33,875	-----
Net Income (Mil)		2,844	2,906	3,203	3,183	3,205	3,452	3,505	1,882	-----
Earnings per share		1.88	1.82	1.94	1.88	1.87	2.00	2.02	1.17	-----
Dividends per share		1.10	1.02	0.94	0.85	0.75	0.63	0.54	0.26	-----
Price	high	35.0	37.2	36.7	35.7	36.1	39.4	43.9	35.6	-----
	low	24.8	30.0	27.4	27.9	29.5	26.3	32.5	29.5	-----

Lowe's Companies, Inc.

1000 Lowe's Boulevard ❑ Mooresville, NC 28117 ❑ Phone: (704) 758–3579 ❑ Website: www.lowes.com
❑ Listed: NYSE ❑ Ticker symbol: LOW ❑ S&P rating: A+ ❑ Value Line financial strength rating: A+

Financial Highlights, Fiscal Year 2008

The continued downturn in the housing market took its toll on Lowe's again this year, as sales were basically flat versus FY2007 and below even its reduced forecast of 3 percent growth. Revenues for the year were $48.2B with earnings of $2.2B, down a full 28 percent year/year.

Earnings per share were $1.49, a 20 percent decrease versus FY2007, but just a penny under the guidance Lowe's gave to start the year.

Company Profile

Lowe's Companies, Inc., is the second-largest domestic retailer of home-improvement products serving the do-it-yourself and commercial business customers. (Home Depot is number one.) Capitalizing on a growing number of U.S. households (about 100 million) the company has expanded from fifteen stores in 1962 and now has nearly 1650 stores in the United States and Canada. The company sells more than 40,000 home-improvement products, including plumbing and electrical products, tools, building materials, hardware, outdoor hard lines, appliances, lumber, nursery and gardening products, millwork, paint, sundries, cabinets, and furniture.

The company obtains its products from about 6,500 merchandise vendors from around the globe, in most instances dealing directly with foreign manufacturers, rather than third-party importers.

In order to maintain appropriate inventory levels in stores and to enhance efficiency and distribution, Lowe's operates fourteen highly automated, efficient, state-of-the-art regional distribution centers strategically situated near store clusters and rail/truck lines.

Lowe's serves both retail and commercial business customers. Retail customers are primarily do-it-yourself homeowners and others buying for personal and family use. Commercial business customers include building contractors, repair and remodeling contractors, electricians, landscapers, painters, plumbers, and commercial building maintenance professionals.

During 1999, Lowe's acquired Eagle Hardware & Garden, a thirty-six-store chain of home-improvement and garden centers in the West. The acquisition accelerated the company's West Coast expansion and provided a stepping-stone for Lowe's into ten new states and a number of key metropolitan markets.

The company has largely transformed its store base from a chain of small stores into a chain of home-improvement warehouses. Their largest prototype store (the largest in the industry) has 150,000 square feet of sales floor and another 35,000 dedicated to lawn and garden products. The company's core stores are built on three smaller platforms between 94,000 and 117,000 square feet, and they recently opened their first 66,000 square foot format store in order to penetrate smaller, underserved markets.

Reasons to Buy

Other than flat sales, falling profits and no clear end in sight for the decline in the housing market, it wasn't that bad of a year for Lowe's. Seriously, they were able to ride out one of the very worst years for the segment in memory while managing to claim a few trophies: they actually gained 110 basis points (1.1 percent) of market share versus the competition; the fact that they were able to hold down expenses in a steadily worsening climate during the year and exit the year with earnings very close to their guidance speaks well of their business controls; and finally, although their income was off 28 percent on the year, Home Depot over the same period saw a decline in income of 43 percent.

A bright spot for Lowe's has been the growth of its DIFM sales (Do It For Me, a contractor or installer-assisted sales model, as opposed to DIY), which have grown approximately 20 percent year/year since 2004, significantly faster than total sales. They have responded by expanding the program from just flooring to include roofing, fencing, windows, and siding installa-

tions. Lowe's estimates this market as a $150B opportunity.

Despite reduced volumes, their gross margins (reflective of the prices paid to suppliers) fell only 45 basis points year-over-year.

Lowe's is scaling back its store openings even as organic growth is shrinking year over year. Over-served markets (California, Florida) will see minimal growth this year, whereas profitable markets (Texas) will remain in the growth plans. Also, Lowe's major competitor has seen healthier margins (albeit lower volumes) in its Canadian stores, and Lowe's is increasing its store openings in Canada.

Reasons for Caution

Even though over half of its regions had positive comps in 2008, total same-store sales were off 7.2 percent overall and nearly 10 percent in the fourth quarter. It was all part of a larger macroeconomic shift: in 2008 consumer spending contracted at the fastest rate in over twenty-five years. If confidence does not return to the consumer sector by Q1 2010, Lowe's recovery may be delayed even further.

SECTOR: **Retail**
BETA COEFFICIENT: **1.00**
10-YEAR COMPOUND EARNINGS PER SHARE GROWTH: **24.0%**
10-YEAR COMPOUND DIVIDENDS PER SHARE GROWTH: **22.0%**

	2008	2007	2006	2005	2004	2003	2002	2001	2000
Revenues (Mil)	48,230	48,283	46,926	43,243	36,464	30,838	26,491	22,111	18,779
Net Income (Mil)	2,195	2,809	3,105	2,770	2,176	1,844	1,471	1,023	810
Earnings per share	1.49	1.86	1.99	1.73	1.36	1.18	0.95	0.65	0.53
Dividends per share	0.33	0.32	0.18	0.11	0.08	0.06	0.04	0.04	0.04
Price: high	28.5	35.7	34.8	34.9	60.5	30.3	25.0	24.5	16.8
low	15.8	21.8	26.2	25.4	23.0	16.7	16.3	11.0	8.6

GROWTH AND INCOME

Lubrizol Corporation

29400 Lakeland Boulevard □ Wickliffe, OH 44092–2298 □ Phone: (440) 347–1206 □ Website: www
.lubrizol.com □ Listed: NYSE □ Ticker symbol: LZ □ S&P rating: BB □ Value Line financial strength rating: B+

Financial Highlights, Fiscal Year 2008

The company reported top-line growth of 12 percent to $5.03B and earnings growth of 16 percent $3.9B, due primarily to an improvement in the combination of price and product mix and a smaller favorable currency impact, offset somewhat by a 2 percent decrease in volume.

Gross margins declined 13.5 percent primarily due to a 22 percent increase in the cost of raw materials and a 7 percent per-unit increase in manufacturing costs. Included in these are the costs associated with the shutdown of the Houston facilities due to Hurricane Ike and temporary shutdowns of various production lines in response to fourth-quarter market conditions.

The company took a $331M noncash goodwill impairment in 2008, primarily related to its Per-formance Coatings and Engineered Polymer product lines. The impairment is not expected to have an impact on Lubrizol's ratings or future business outlook given the fact that it is noncash in nature. As a result of this writedown and other restructuring charges, the company reported negative earnings of ($66.1M); this does not, however, reflect the health of ongoing operations.

Company Profile

Lubrizol is an innovative specialty chemical company that produces and supplies technologies that improve the quality and performance of its customers' products in the global transportation, industrial, and consumer markets. Typical applications include additives for engine oils, machine lubricants, additives for gasoline and diesel fuel, and additives for pharmaceuticals and specialty materials.

From the company's 10-K: "We are geographically diverse, with an extensive global manufacturing, supply chain, technical, and commercial infrastructure. We operate facilities in twenty-seven countries, including production facilities in twenty-one countries and laboratories in nine countries, in key regions around the world through the efforts of about 7,800 employees. Including the 2004 acquisition of Noveon International for the period ended December 31, 2004, we derived about 48 percent of our consolidated total revenues from North America, 28 percent from Europe, 18 percent from the Asia/ Pacific and the Middle East regions, and 6 percent from Latin America. We sell our products in more than 100 countries."

The company reports results from two segments—Lubrizol Additive and Lubrizol Advanced Materials. For 2008, the revenue split between the two was 70/30, respectively. Operating income, however, was split 83/17. Versus FY 2007, revenue growth from Additives was 17 percent against only one percent growth from Advanced Materials.

The company's key strategic focus to achieve top-line and earnings growth includes driving organic growth and product innovation, new products and new applications. The company will also focus on selective acquisitions either in specialty chemicals or industrial fluids, complementing Lubrizol's existing business lines.

Reasons to Buy

The company has taken positive steps to set the Advanced Materials segment on firmer ground while continuing to grow both the top and bottom line results from its larger Additive segment. Unprofitable product lines have been shed, and growth in manufacturing capacity in China and India should drive down per-unit costs. Reduction and greater stability in raw materials pricing should also improve operating margins.

The company announced a number of new products in 2008, two of which have the potential to be disruptive in their respective markets. One is a new diesel fuel additive that Lubrizol claims is three times more effective in controlling injector deposits than anything currently available. Fuel additives of this type are very important to the transportation and industrial applications, and if the product can be manufactured at a competitive price then the company could see real returns this year.

The second is a new acrylic viscosity modifier platform that provides significant advantages in terms of formulation flexibility as well as final performance of the end product.

Given the challenges of 2008 and Lubrizol's response, we're confident that they are well-positioned for improved profitability over the next three to four years. In addition, the company has traditionally generated dividend yields in the low 3 percent range—although 2008's yield was only 2.5 percent, that should increase.

Reasons for Caution

The Advanced Materials segment will continue to suffer through the slow-down in the automotive and housing segments (primarily the Temp-Rite plumbing line of plumbing products). Given its current low contribution to revenue, however, even a further 20 percent decline would not be catastrophic.

SECTOR: **Materials**
BETA COEFFICIENT: **1.20**
10-YEAR COMPOUND EARNINGS PER SHARE GROWTH: **5.5%**
10-YEAR COMPOUND DIVIDENDS PER SHARE GROWTH: **1.5%**

	2008	**2007**	**2006**	**2005**	**2004**	**2003**	**2002**	**2001**	**2000**
Revenues (Mil)	5,027	4,499	4,041	3,622	3,156	2,049	1,980	1,839	1,771
Net Income (Mil)	281	283	106	189	139	91	126	94	103
Earnings per share	4.09	4.05	2.62	2.36	2.48	2.04	2.45	1.84	1.94
Dividends per share	1.23	1.16	1.04	1.04	1.04	1.04	1.04	1.04	1.04
Price high	61.4	70.0	50.8	44.5	37.4	34.4	36.4	37.7	33.9
low	26.7	48.8	38.0	35.2	29.4	26.5	26.2	24.1	18.3

3M Company

3M Center, Building 225-01-S-15 ⸆ St. Paul, MN 55144–1000 ⸆ Phone: (651) 733–8206 ⸆ Website:
www.MMM.com ⸆ Listed: NYSE ⸆ Dividend reinvestment plan available ⸆ Ticker symbol: MMM ⸆
S&P rating: A+ ⸆ Value Line financial strength rating: A++

Financial Highlights, Fiscal Year 2008

3M's sales grew just 3.2 percent in 2008, to $25.27B, while earnings fell 15.5 percent to $3.46B. Reflecting the spike in the costs of many of 3M's raw materials in 2008, operating margin fell 430 basis points (4.3 percent) to 25.2 percent, and net margin fell 300 basis points (3 percent) to 13.7 percent. Per-share earnings fell 12.7 percent to $4.89. Not a good year for the numbers all the way around.

In April 2008, 3M acquired Aearo Holding Corp. Aearo manufactures and sells personal protection and energy absorbing products, which expands 3M's platform by adding hearing protection as well as eyewear and fall protection product lines to 3M's existing line of safety products.

Company Profile

The 3M Company, originally known as the Minnesota Mining and Manufacturing Co., is a $24 billion diversified manufacturing technology company with leading positions in industrial, consumer and office, health care, safety, electronics, telecommunications, and other markets. The company has operations in more than sixty countries and serves customers in nearly 200 countries.

3M's operations are divided up among six segments:

- The Industrial and Transportation segment serves a broad range of markets, such as appliance, paper and packaging, food and beverage, electronics, automotive (OEM), and automotive aftermarket. Industrial and Transportation products include industrial tapes, a wide variety of abrasives, adhesives, specialty materials, filtration products, and products for the separation of fluids and gases.
- The Health Care segment serves markets that include medical clinics and hospitals, pharmaceuticals, dental and orthodontic practitioners, and health information systems. Products and services provided to these and other markets include medical and surgical supplies, skin health and infection prevention products, drug delivery systems, dental and orthodontic products, health information systems, and anti-microbial solutions.
- The Safety, Security, and Protection Services segment serves a broad range of markets that increase the safety, security, and productivity of workers, facilities,

and systems. Major product offerings include personal protection, safety and security products, energy control products, building cleaning and protection products, track and trace solutions, and roofing granules for asphalt shingles.

- The Consumer and Office segment serves markets that include retail, home improvement, building maintenance, and other markets. Products in this segment include office supply products including the familiar tapes and Post-It notes, stationery products, construction and home improvement products, home care products, protective material products, and consumer health care products.
- The Display and Graphics segment serves markets that include electronic display, traffic safety, and commercial graphics. This segment includes optical film solutions for electronic displays; computer screen filters; reflective sheeting for transportation safety; commercial graphics systems; and projection systems, including mobile display technology and visual systems products.
- The Electro and Communications segment serves the electrical, electronics, and communications industries, including electrical utilities. Products include electronic and interconnect solutions, microinterconnect systems, high-performance fluids, high-temperature and

display tapes, telecommunications products, electrical products, and touch screens and touch monitors.

Reasons to Buy

3M's leading position as a supplier of specialty materials and consumables to industry make it the canary in the coal mine. And while it's often the first to feel the effects of a recession, fortunately it can also be among the first to recover. FY2009 will be the second down year in a row for 3M, but a turnaround is likely in early 2010; whether the company is a bargain will depend on what's happened with the share price by then.

Jeremy J. Butler of Value Line Investment Survey said it well on May 15, 2009: "For the more conservative long-term investor, this is a wonderful buying opportunity. This is a rare chance to acquire part of a top-quality company at a bargain-basement price. The shares are selling at a little over half their peak of $97 in 2007. We have ample reason to believe that by 2012–2014, 3M will be earning over $6.00 a share. Even with a conservative market P/E of 15, the equity should be selling at around $90 by then. (We continue to use a multiple of 16.) And the smooth ride there (Stock Price Stability rating is 100) should be sweetened by the well-funded dividend. Meanwhile, we look for the company to start its earnings recovery in 2010, when we think it can earn about $4.40 a share. By then, global demand from both the public and private sectors should be improving as economies recover."

Reasons for Caution

3M is a valued stock and a respected company, and even after a bad 2008 and what will surely be a bad 2009, it may be hard to pick these shares up on the cheap. Anything close to a 15 multiple could be a bargain. A protracted or even accelerated downturn in world and especially U.S. manufacturing would also hurt results.

SECTOR: **Industrials**
BETA COEFFICIENT: **.75**
10-YEAR COMPOUND EARNINGS PER SHARE GROWTH: **10.5%**
10-YEAR COMPOUND DIVIDENDS PER SHARE GROWTH: **6.5%**

		2008	2007	2006	2005	2004	2003	2002	2001	2000
Revenues (Mil)		25,269	24,462	22,923	21,167	20,011	18,232	16,332	16,079	16,724
Net Income (Mil)		3,460	4,096	3,851	3,111	2,990	2,403	1,974	1,430	1,782
Earnings per share		4.89	5.60	5.06	3.98	3.75	3.09	2.50	1.79	2.32
Dividends per share		2.00	1.92	1.84	1.68	1.44	1.32	1.24	1.20	1.16
Price	high	84.8	97.0	88.4	87.4	90.3	85.4	65.8	63.5	61.5
	low	50.0	72.9	67.0	69.7	73.3	59.7	50.0	42.9	39.1

Marathon Oil Corporation

5555 San Felipe Road □ Houston, TX 77056 □ Phone: (713) 629–6600 □ Website: www.marathon.com □
Listed: NYSE □ Ticker symbol: MRO □ S&P rating: BBB+ □ Value Line financial strength rating: A+

Financial Highlights, Fiscal Year 2008

Marathon's revenues grew 19 percent versus FY2007, driven by higher realizations in the Exploration and Production Segment and higher refined product and selling prices in the Refining, Marketing, and Transportation segment.

Earnings fell 10 percent versus FY2007, driven by a decline in the refining and wholesale gross margin per gallon in the RM&T segment, and also by a noncash impairment in the Oil Sands Mining segment of $1.4B, as certain profitability assumptions around those assets became suspect. The rest of the reporting operations turned in year/year gains in earnings.

The company sold its interest in Pilot Travel Centers LLC for $700M and also sold noncore assets and acreage in offshore Norway for $301M.

Company Profile

Marathon Oil is a vertically integrated producer, refiner, and marketer of petroleum and natural gas products. It sells crude to other refiners, but its primary revenue stream is through the sale of its refined petroleum products to resellers and to end consumers via company-owned retail locations.

Marathon operates in four segments: Exploration and Production, Oil Sands Mining, Refining, Marketing, and Transportation, and Integrated Gas. E&P is a worldwide producer and marketer of liquid hydrocarbons and natural gas. OSM mines, extracts, and transports bitumen from deposits in Alberta, Canada, and upgrades it to produce synthetic crude. RM&T refines, markets, and transports petroleum products throughout the Midwest and southeastern regions of the United States. Finally, IG transports liquefied natural gas and methanol worldwide.

The company has exploration rights/interests in the United States, Angola, Norway, Indonesia, Equatorial Guinea, Libya, Canada, and the United Kingdom. The bulk of their activities are in the Gulf Coast of the United States.

Marathon, via acquisition, holds a 20 percent outside-operated interest in an oil sands mining joint venture in Alberta, Canada. Oil sands mining bears no resemblance to any of Marathon's other oil production processes, and operates more closely to a coal surface mine. Output from these operations is on the order of 30,000 barrels of synthetic crude per day, with significantly higher than normal refining costs.

In July 2008, the company announced that it was evaluating a split of Marathon into two separate, publicly traded companies. In February 2009, the board concluded that it was in the best interest of the shareholders to remain a single company.

Reasons to Buy

Marathon is on schedule to bring its Garyville, Louisiana, refinery on-line in early 2010, adding an expected 180,000 barrels per day refining capacity, making Garyville the fourth-largest refinery in the country. Other refiners have put plant expansions on the back burner recently, but only after they realized that they couldn't get their new equipment on-line prior to Garyville. Being first, Marathon was also able to utilize post-Katrina tax-exempt recovery bonds and financed $1B of the project with low-interest, thirty-year fixed loans.

Marathon did a commendable job navigating the 2008 minefield of oil price spikes and declines. Their vertical integration is a double-edged sword, but they managed to get through the ups and downs without cutting off both hands.

The company has been very successful with its recent Exploration and Production activities. They have a success rate of over 60 percent on major exploratory wells since 2002, and of the segment's estimated 2012 production, 85 percent is already on stream.

The company has good fuels flexibility at the retail level, with the ability to blend e10 ethanol-blended fuels throughout its network. Should oil prices spike again, Marathon can reformulate quickly and take advantage of what may well be a glut of ethanol on the market.

In the last four years, the company's combined retail gasoline and merchandise sales have grown from $5.14B to $6.54B, or a CAGR of 6.2 percent, which are healthy retail comps.

Reasons for Caution

Cap-and-trade legislation could become costly for refiners, depending on the details of the implementation (still unknown as of mid-2009). Also, the OSM business will likely be on hiatus until crude prices rise enough to provide profitable operations here.

SECTOR: **Energy**
BETA COEFFICIENT: **1.30**
10-YEAR COMPOUND EARNINGS PER SHARE GROWTH: **20.5%**
10-YEAR COMPOUND DIVIDENDS PER SHARE GROWTH: **8.50%**

		2008	2007	2006	2005	2004	2003	2002	2001	2000
Revenues (Mil)		72,128	59,389	59,917	58,596	45,135	36,678	27,470	28,340	29,861
Net Income (Mil)		3,528	3,755	4,636	3,051	1,314	1,012	563	1,318	1,308
Earnings per share		4.95	5.43	6.42	4.22	1.94	1.63	0.91	2.13	2.10
Dividends per share		0.96	0.92	0.77	0.61	0.52	0.48	0.46	0.46	0.44
Price	high	63.2	67.0	49.4	36.3	21.3	16.8	15.1	16.9	15.2
	low	19.3	41.5	30.2	17.8	15.	9.9	9.4	12.5	10.3

McCormick & Company, Inc.

18 Loveton Circle □ P.O. Box 6000 □ Sparks, MD 21152–6000 □ Phone: (410) 771–7244 □ Website: www.mc-cormick.com □ Listed: NYSE □ Ticker symbol: MKC □ S&P rating: A- □ Value Line financial strength rating: A

Financial Highlights, Fiscal Year 2008

In 2008 revenues rose 8.9 percent to $3.2 billion, driven by price increases taken to offset higher costs, as well as increased volume and product mix, and favorable foreign currency exchange rates. Earnings per share were $1.94 in 2008 compared to $1.73 in 2007, an increase of 12.1 percent. Dividends rose 10 percent to $0.88/share.

The company achieved $31 million of incremental cost reductions, including $11 million of savings from the restructuring initiated in 2005.

In July 2008, McCormick acquired the assets of the Lawry's business from a subsidiary of Unilever for $604 million in cash. This is McCormick's largest acquisition to date.

Company Profile

McCormick is a global leader in the manufacture, marketing, and distribution of spices, herbs, seasonings, specialty foods and flavors to the entire food industry. Customers range from retail outlets and food manufacturers to food service businesses. The company was founded in 1889 and has approximately 7,500 full-time employees in facilities located around the world. Major sales, distribution, and production facilities are located in North America and Europe. Addi-tional facilities are based in Mexico, Central America, Australia, China, Singapore, Thailand, and South Africa. In 2008, 41.9 percent of sales were outside the United States.

Industrial customers include food-service and food-processing businesses, as well as retail outlets. This industrial segment was responsible for 42 percent of sales and 19 percent of operating profits. A majority of the top 100 food companies are MKC's customers.

McCormick's U.S. consumer business (58 percent of sales and 81 percent of operating profits), its oldest and largest, is dedicated to the manufacture and sale of consumer spices, herbs, extracts, proprietary seasoning blends, sauces, and marinades. They are sold under such brand names as McCormick, Schilling, Produce Partners, Golden Dipt, Old Bay, and Mojave.

Many of the spices and herbs purchased by the company are of foreign origin; significant quantities of some materials, such as paprika, dehydrated vegetables, onion and garlic, and food ingredients other than spices and herbs originate in the United States.

McCormick is a direct importer of certain raw materials, mainly black pepper, vanilla beans, cinnamon, herbs, and seeds from the countries of origin. The raw materials most important to the company are onion, garlic, and capsicums (paprika and chili peppers), which are produced in the United States; black pepper, most of which originates in India, Indonesia, Malaysia, and Brazil; and vanilla beans, a large portion of which the company obtains from the Malagasy Republic and Indonesia.

Reasons to Buy

In addition to being the largest branded producer of spices in North America, McCormick is also the largest private-label producer of spices in North America. This would be a bit like playing chess against yourself, except that at any point in the game you can decide to pool both white and black pieces and attack the players at the next table. In the end, the company's strength in the private label market ensures at least some measure of price protection for its branded products. As an example, this year saw McCormick acquire Lawry's, its last major branded competitor in the consumer space.

The company expects to see growth of 4–6 percent for the foreseeable future. Of that, 2–3 percent is organic growth, 1–2 percent is from new products, and 1–3 percent is from acquisitions. The company generates sufficient cash flow to fund all new product initiatives and has easy access to the capital markets for acquisitions.

McCormick has paid a dividend every year since 1925, and this year raised dividends for the twenty-third consecutive year.

Reasons for Caution

There are no real reasons for caution, except that MCK does not have the engines that some companies do to drive growth; performance in an economic recovery is not likely to be stellar. That said, the company is a solid performer and a solid defensive play.

SECTOR: **Consumer Staples**
BETA COEFFICIENT: **.60**
10-YEAR COMPOUND EARNINGS PER SHARE GROWTH: **12%**
10-YEAR COMPOUND DIVIDENDS PER SHARE GROWTH: **10.5%**

		2008	2007	2006	2005	2004	2003	2002	2001	2000
Revenues (Mil)		3,177	2,916	2,716	2,592	2,526	2,270	2,045	2,372	2,124
Net Income (Mil)		282	230	202	215	214	199	180	147	138
Earnings per share		2.14	1.92	1.72	1.56	1.52	1.40	1.29	1.05	1.00
Dividends per share		0.88	0.80	0.72	0.64	0.56	0.46	0.42	0.40	0.38
Price	high	42.1	39.7	39.8	39.1	38.9	30.2	27.3	23.3	18.9
	low	28.2	33.9	30.1	29.0	28.6	21.7	20.7	17.0	11.9

McDonald's Corporation

One McDonald's Plaza □ Oak Brook, IL 60523 □ Phone: (630) 623-3000 □ Website: www.mcdonalds.com □
Listed: NYSE □ Ticker symbol: MCD □ S&P rating: A □ Value Line financial strength rating: A++

Financial Highlights, Fiscal Year 2008

McDonald's posted increased revenues of $23.5B in 2007, a 3.2 percent increase over 2007. Earnings rose 19.3 percent to $4.2B, with a net margin increase of 240 basis points, or 2.4 percent, to 17.9 percent. Operating margin was up a super-sized 1020 basis points or 10.2 percent to 32.5 percent (2007 operating margin was depressed due to impairment charges related to the sale of its businesses in Latin America). Per-share earnings were up 15 percent to $3.67, and global comps were up 6.9 percent year/year.

The company generated $5.9B in cash in 2008, up 20 percent from 2007. Correspondingly, the company repurchased 50 million shares of stock and increased the dividend 8.5 percent to $1.63/share.

In Q22008 the company sold its minority interest in the U.K.-based Pret A Manger for $229M.

Company Profile

The company franchises and operates McDonald's restaurants. At 2008 year-end there were approximately 32,000 restaurants in 118 countries, over 25,000 of which were operated by franchisees and 6,500 were operated by the company. Franchisees pay for and own the equipment, signs, and interior of the businesses, and are required to reinvest in same from time to time. The company owns the land and building or secures leases for both company-operated and franchised restaurant sites.

Revenues to the company come in the form of sales from company-owned stores and rents, fees, royalties, and other revenue streams from the franchisees. The company is primarily a franchisor and has recently begun to sell off more of its company-owned stores, in the process realizing benefits to cash flow, reduced operational costs, and reduced exposure to commodities prices.

McDonald's completely dominates the Fast Food Hamburger Restaurant market segment with a 35 percent market share. Burger King and Wendy's are the next largest competitors at 4 percent market share each. In the overall Fast Food segment, McDonald's is still the single biggest player with a 19 percent market share by revenue, followed by Doctor's Associates, Inc. (Subway) with a 10 percent share.

The company expects capital expenditures for 2009 to be approximately $2 billion. About half will be reinvested in existing restaurants and the rest will be used primarily to open about 1,000 restaurants (950 traditional and 50 satellites). The company expects net additions of about 650 restaurants (750 net traditional additions and 100 net satellite closings).

The company generates about 64 percent of its revenue outside the United States. Revenue growth in 2008 was strongest in APMEA (Asia Pacific, Middle East, and Asia), with growth of 18 percent year/year. Europe (where a Big Mac is called a Royale with Cheese) was next with 11 percent growth, and finally the United States, with just a 2 percent growth year/year.

Reasons to Buy

In the early part of the decade, McDonald's had been adding mainly company-owned stores in an effort to boost revenues, but profitability suffered. In 2003, McDonald's initiated a new strategy that called for increasing sales at its existing stores by expanding menu options, expanding store hours, and renovating stores. They also began franchising a higher percentage of its stores, driving revenue with reduced capital expense. The strategy has paid off handsomely—revenues have grown by 37 percent, which would be impressive on its own, but net margin is up 720 basis points or 7.2 percent, and net income is up nearly 130 per-

cent over the same period. As a result, share price is up over 500 percent from its 2003 lows.

McDonald's is growing rapidly in China, where in 2008 they opened their 1,000th store. Local menus continue to evolve, and the convenience that fast food provides is highly valued.

Menu additions are proving very popular, and consumers are welcoming the novelty of the newer menu items like McCafe, brewed teas, and expanded salad selections.

As the economic downturn continues, consumers continue to trade down in their dining habits, and McDonald's is reaping the benefits. Their recent profitability is expected to continue through 2011, boosting cash flow and likely share repurchases and dividend increases.

Reasons for Caution

Not a lot of trouble to be seen. An economic turnaround might change consumer preferences in the United States, but a rising global economy is not bad news for McDonald's, where greater disposable income in developing economies would only benefit the company.

SECTOR: **Restaurants**
BETA COEFFICIENT: **0.70**
10-YEAR COMPOUND EARNINGS PER SHARE GROWTH: **9.5%**
10-YEAR COMPOUND DIVIDENDS PER SHARE GROWTH: **24.0%**

		2008	2007	2006	2005	2004	2003	2002	2001	2000
Revenues (Mil)		23,522	22,787	21,586	20,460	19,065	17,141	15,406	14,870	14,243
Net Income (Mil)		4,201	3,522	2,873	2,509	2,358	1,831	1,692	1,772	1,977
Earnings per share		3.67	2.91	2.30	1.97	1.93	1.43	1.32	1.36	1.32
Dividends per share		1.63	1.50	1.00	0.67	0.55	0.40	0.24	0.23	0.22
Price	high	67.0	63.7	44.7	35.7	33.0	27.	30.7	35.1	43.6
	low	45.8	42.3	31.7	27.4	24.5	12.1	125.	24.8	26.4

AGGRESSIVE GROWTH

Medtronic, Inc.

710 Medtronic Parkway N. E. □ Minneapolis, MN 55432–5604 □ Listed: NYSE □ Phone: (763) 505–2692 □ Website: www.medtronic.com □ Ticker symbol: MDT □ S&P rating: AA- □ Value Line financial strength rating: A++

Financial Highlights, Fiscal Year 2008

Medtronic's revenues grew 8 percent year/year to $14.6B, while income rose 10 percent to $3.28B. Per-share earnings grew 12 percent, and operating margins grew slightly even in the face of some significant acquisition activity. Dividends increased 17 percent to $.63/share, and the company bought back five million shares of stock.

The company spent approximately $1.75B during the year to acquire five companies (Core Valve, Ablation Frontiers, CryoCath, Ventor Technologies, and Restore Medical) whose products supplement Medtronic's existing product lines. Still, the company exited the year in a stronger cash position than they began, and is well-positioned for further acquisitions in 2010.

Company Profile

Medtronic is the world's leading medical technology company, providing lifelong solutions for people with chronic disease. Key businesses include:

- Medtronic Cardiac Rhythm Management develops products that restore and regulate a patient's heart rhythm, as well as improve the heart's pumping function. The business markets implantable pacemakers, defibrillators, cardiac ablation catheters, monitoring and diagnostic devices, and cardiac resynchronization devices, including the first implantable device for the treatment of heart failure.
- Medtronic Cardiac Surgery develops products that are used in both arrested and beating

heart bypass surgery. The business also markets the industry's broadest line of heart valve products for both replacement and repair, plus autotransfusion equipment and disposable devices for handling and monitoring blood during major surgery, as well as cardiac ablation devices to treat a variety of heart conditions.

- Medtronic Vascular develops products and therapies that treat a wide range of vascular diseases and conditions. These products include coronary, peripheral, and neurovascular stents; stent graph systems for diseases and conditions throughout the aorta; and distal protection systems.

- Medtronic Neurological and Diabetes offers therapies for movement disorders, chronic pain, and diabetes. It also offers diagnostics and therapeutics for urological and gastrointestinal conditions, including incontinence, benign prostatic hyperplasia (BPH), enlarged prostate and gastroesophageal reflux disease (GERD).

- Medtronic Spinal, ENT, and SNT develops and manufactures products that treat a variety of disorders of the cranium and spine, including traumatically induced conditions, deformities, and tumors.

Reasons to Buy

Medtronic has a dominant market share in three of its seven core lines (ICD, Diabetes, and Neurological), and all of its core businesses grew last year. Five of the seven turned in double-digit growth. The economic downturn will affect some parts of Medtronic's business, but the top line is largely unaffected as most of their products are nondiscretionary purchases.

Medtronic is a pioneer in the emerging field of medicine that promises to restore normal brain function and chemistry to millions of patients with central nervous system disorders. The company's DBS (Deep Brain Stimulation) systems treat disorders by modulating the nervous system with electrical stimulation, chemicals, and biological agents delivered in precise amounts to specific sites in the brain and spinal cord. This system has been used successfully to treat the most severe symptoms of conditions such as Parkinson's disease.

This year, Medtronic's DBS system began trials for a psychiatric application—treatment of severe depression. This is the first time a Medtronic product has been used to address a psychiatric condition. The DBS system was also approved this year (on a humanitarian basis, limited to 4000 units) for the treatment of debilitating Obsessive-Compulsive Disorder.

Medtronic's stock performance has been relatively flat from 2003 through most of 2008, the recent downturn in its price appears to not reflect the fundamentals. This is an opportunity to pick up a solid stock at a discount.

Reasons for Caution

Medtronic's highest revenue-producing product, its ICD (pacemaker) line, has been followed closely over the last few years for signs of market saturation. Although growth in the United States has decreased, the international market has kept pace (no pun intended) and the company feels comfortable with projecting a growth rate in the mid-single digits over the next few years.

ICD growth had been in the low double digits as recently as 2003.

The company is also managing a potential recall of a small number of its older ICD devices. There will likely be some litigation involved, but at this time the company's exposure is felt to be quite low.

Finally, the company may be vulnerable to federal and other initiatives to cut health-care costs.

SECTOR: **Health Care**
BETA COEFFICIENT: **.75**
10-YEAR COMPOUND EARNINGS PER SHARE GROWTH: **16.0%**
10-YEAR COMPOUND DIVIDENDS PER SHARE GROWTH: **16.5%**

	2008	2007	2006	2005	2004	2003	2002	2001	2000
Revenues (Mil)	14,599	13,515	12,299	11,292	10,055	9,087	7,665	6,411	5,552
Net Income (Mil)	3,282	2,984	2,798	2,687	2,270	1,959	1,600	984	1,282
Earnings per share	2.92	2.61	2.41	2.21	1.86	1.63	1.30	0.80	0.85
Dividends per share	0.63	0.47	0.41	0.36	0.31	0.28	0.25	0.20	0.12
Price: high	57.0	58.0	59.9	58.9	53.7	52.9	49.7	62.0	62.0
low	28.3	44.9	42.4	48.7	44.0	42.2	32.5	36.6	32.8

Monsanto Company

800 North Lindbergh Boulevard □ St Louis, MO 63167 □ Phone: (314) 694–1000 □ Website: www.monsanto.com □ Listed: NYSE □ Ticker symbol: MON □ S&P Rating: A+ □ Value Line financial strength rating: A

Financial Highlights, Fiscal Year 2008

Helped along by a boom in crop prices and farming, 2008 was a banner year for Monsanto, a business already on a roll from strength in its product niches and technology leadership in agriculture. Net sales in 2008 increased some $3 billion over 2007, with strong contributions from both its herbicides and seed operations. Net income rocketed to $3.62 per share from $1.79 in the same period. Operating margins, already exceeding 20 percent through the last decade, improved to a stellar 29 percent in 2008.

Cash flow generation is also very strong. Net cash provided by operating activities in 2008 was $2.8B compared to $1.85B in 2007, and free cash flow was some $772 million compared to $57 million in 2007. The company deployed some $1B for acquisitions during the year.

Company Profile

Monsanto was once a major chemical company with a broad pedigree ranging from saccharin to sulfuric acid to Agent Orange and DDT, Monsanto was absorbed into Pharmacia Upjohn in 2000, which kept its pharmaceutical products and spun off the agricultural products business into a "new" Monsanto in 2002. Today's Monsanto provides a set of leading-edge, technology-based agricultural products for use in farming in the United States and overseas. The company has two primary business segments: Seeds and Genomics and Agricultural Productivity.

The Seeds and Genomics segment produces seeds for a host of crops, most importantly corn and soybeans but also canola, cotton, and a variety of vegetable and fruit seeds. Many of the seed products are bioengineered for "traits" to provide greater yields and to be more resistant to insects and weeds. Familiar to many consumers, especially those who travel in the Midwest, might be the DeKalb seed brand, but there are many others.

The Agricultural Productivity segment offers glyphosate-based herbicides, popularly known and sold under the Roundup brand, for agricultural, industrial, and residential lawn and garden applications. Beyond this market-leading product, the division also offers other selective herbicides for control of pre-emergent annual grass and small seeded broadleaf weeds in corn and other crops. The company owns many of the major brands in both seed and herbicide markets.

The company also partners with other agricultural and chemical companies to develop other high-tech "ag" and food processing solutions, including Cargill, BASF, and Biotechnology, Inc.

Reasons to Buy

The company has been in a leadership position in all of its markets for a decade. As efficiency in agriculture has more important, the company's technology solutions should continue to carry the day.

As Value Line puts it, Monsanto ". . . appears to have engineered a 'recession-resistant' model." The company will not only fare well as bioengineered seed becomes more mainstream, but will also prosper from international expansion in these markets.

Financial performance, especially in the past three years, is rock solid; the company generates significant margins, profits, and free cash flow. At press time, the company's stock was off

almost 50 percent from its 2008 high, making it a good apparent fit for the "growth at a reasonable price" model.

Reasons for Caution

The company has leadership and a strong lock on key markets, providing among other things substantial pricing power and profit margin performance. But even the best-engineered companies can't grow forever.

Patents have expired and competition is starting to hit the market for Roundup; the company is adjusting well by offering new packaging and delivery methods for the products and by strengthening its offerings in the biotech and seed businesses. Still, the company's success alone may draw competition, which could cause performance to deteriorate. Excellent management and technological leadership are the best antidotes for these negatives.

SECTOR: **Industrials**
BETA COEFFICIENT: **0.6**
5-YEAR COMPOUND EARNINGS PER SHARE GROWTH: **30.0%**
5-YEAR COMPOUND DIVIDENDS PER SHARE GROWTH: **19%**

		2008	2007	2006	2005	2004	2003	2002	2001	2000
Revenues (Mil)		11,365	8,563	7,344	6,294	5,457	4,936	4,673	5,462	5,493
Net Income (Mil)		1,895	1,027	722.1	565.7	434.0	334.0	313.0	297.0	175.0
Earnings per share		3.39	1.98	1.31	1.05	0.61	0.64	0.60	0.57	0.34
Dividends per share		0.83	0.55	0.34	0.34	0.28	0.24	0.24	0.24	0.05
Price:	high	145.8	116.3	53.5	39.9	28.2	14.5	17.0	19.4	13.7
	low	63.5	49.1	37.9	25.0	14.0	6.8	6.6	13.4	9.9

NIKE, Inc.

One Bowerman Drive ▫ Beaverton, OR 97005 ▫ Phone: (503) 671–6453 ▫ Website: www.nikebiz.com ▫
Listed: NYSE ▫ Ticker symbol: NKE ▫ Value Line financial strength rating: A+

Financial Highlights, Fiscal Year 2008

NIKE's sales grew 14.1 percent to $18.62B in FY2008, while income rose 18.9 percent to $1.73B versus 2007. Operating margins were flat, while net margin rose 40 basis points (0.4 percent) to 9.3 percent. Per-share earnings rose 19.6 percent to $3.44, and dividends rose 24 percent to $0.88 per share.

On February 22, the company sold the Bauer brand of hockey skates and equipment for $200M in cash. On March 3, the company acquired the Umbro brand of sports apparel for $582 million. Earlier in the year, the company sold the Starter brand of athletic apparel for $60M in cash.

Company Profile

NIKE's principal business activity is the design, development, and worldwide marketing of footwear, apparel, equipment, and accessory products. NIKE is the largest seller of athletic footwear and athletic apparel in the world. Their products are sold to retail accounts, through NIKE-owned retail outlets, and through a mix of independent distributors and licensees in over 180 countries around the world.

NIKE does not manufacture; virtually all of their products are manufactured by independent contractors. Virtually all of their footwear and apparel products are produced outside the United States, while equipment products are produced both in the United States and abroad.

NIKE's footwear products are designed primarily for athletic use, although a large percentage of the products are designed and worn for casual or leisure purposes. Their leading athletic shoes are designed for men, women and children for running, training, basketball, and soccer use, although they also carry brands for casual wear.

They also sell apparel and accessories for most of the sports addressed by their shoe lines, as well as athletic bags and accessory items. NIKE apparel and accessories are designed to complement their athletic footwear products, feature the same trademarks and are sold through the same marketing and distribution channels. They also market apparel with licensed college and professional team and league logos.

They also have a number of wholly owned subsidiaries, including Cole Haan, Converse, Hurley, and Umbro who variously design, distribute, and license dress, athletic, and casual footwear; sports apparel; and accessories. In FY 2008, these subsidiary brands, together with NIKE Golf accounted for approximately 43 percent of total revenues.

The company has more than 25,000 retail accounts in the United

States, including footwear stores, sporting goods stores, athletic specialty stores, department stores, skate, tennis and golf shops, and other retail accounts.

The company makes substantial use of a "futures" ordering program, which allows retailers to order five to six months in advance of delivery with the commitment that their orders will be delivered within a set time period at a fixed price. In FY2008, 86 percent of their U.S. wholesale footwear shipments of NIKE-branded products were made under the futures program.

Reasons to Buy

NIKE continues to grow its base of company-owned stores, which now number over 550. Gross margins at these stores can be significantly higher—over 2500 basis points or 25 percent higher at full retail prices, less at the outlet stores.

NIKE's highest growth region was Asia Pacific, turning in 26 percent year/year revenue gain, versus 21 percent in the Americas, 19 percent in EMEA, and 4 percent in the United States. Asia Pacific's income growth was even better, at 36 percent year over year. Asia Pacific now accounts for 15.5 percent of NIKE's total revenue, versus 34.2 percent from the United States. The AP increases were driven primarily by demand in China, where revenues increased over 50 percent. Continued sales growth in a market the size of mainland China would be very good for NIKE shares.

In 2008, NIKE spent 12.5 percent of revenue on advertising. As their presence grows in new markets, however, product familiarity and the ubiquity of the brand allows them to spend less for advertising to generate incremental sales.

Reasons for Caution

The NIKE brand is a discretionary purchase for most of its market. Some will continue to buy upscale, branded athletic footwear and apparel regardless of the state of the economy, but most can and will defer the purchase of those latest and greatest $120 speed demons. Expect sales to moderate until economic conditions improve.

SECTOR: **Consumer Discretionary**
BETA COEFFICIENT: **0.90**
10-YEAR COMPOUND EARNINGS PER SHARE GROWTH: **11%**
10-YEAR COMPOUND DIVIDENDS PER SHARE GROWTH: **15%**

		2008	2007	2006	2005	2004	2003	2002	2001	2000
Revenues (Mil)		18,627	16,326	14,955	13,740	12,253	10,697	9,893	9,488	8,995
Net Income (Mil)		1,734	1,458	1,392	1,212	945	749	668	590	580
Earnings per share		3.44	2.86	2.63	2.25	1.76	1.39	1.23	1.08	1.05
Dividends per share		0.88	0.71	0.59	0.48	0.37	0.27	0.24	0.24	0.24
Price	high	70.6	67.9	50.6	45.8	46.2	34.3	32.1	30.0	28.5
	low	42.7	47.5	37.8	37.6	32.9	21.2	19.3	17.8	12.9

Norfolk Southern

Three Commercial Place ❑ Norfolk, VA 23510-2191 ❑ Phone: (757) 629–2680 ❑ Website: www.nscorp. com ❑ Listed: NYSE ❑ Ticker Symbol: NSC ❑ S&P Rating: BBB+ ❑ Value Line financial strength rating: B+

Financial Highlights, Fiscal Year 2008

While traffic volumes fell in 2008 and fuel prices were up, increasing costs, NSC's 2008 net income highballed 17 percent overall and 19 percent in railway operations because of fuel surcharges the company was able to pass on. Revenues increased some 13 percent, and the operating ratio, a key measure of operating costs to revenues, declined to an industry-leading 71.1 percent compared to 72.6 percent in 2007. This means that some 28.9 cents of every dollar collected can go to cover fixed costs, a very healthy sum by industry standards.

Diluted per-share earnings were up 23 percent due to stronger income and share purchases. The company purchased and retired some 19.4 million shares at a total cost of $1.1 billion. This gives an average price of $57 a share—not great considering a share price range of $26 to $75 during the 12 months ending July 2009. The company generated some $2.7B in cash flow from operations on $10.6B in revenues—a healthy return. The company also reported record net profit margins of 16.1 percent, very high for the industry and well above the 5 to 10 percent reported in the 2000–2005 period.

NSC has announced a projected decline in 2009 revenues due to the weak economy and decreased fuel surcharges. What remains to be seen are how long this will last and whether costs can be controlled; lower fuel prices put at least some wind behind their back.

Company Profile

Norfolk Southern Corp. was formed in 1982 as a holding company in 1982 when the Norfolk & Western Railway merged with the Southern Railway. Including lines received in split takeover (with CSX) of Conrail, the current railroad operates 21,000 route-miles of track in 22 eastern and southern states.

Company business is about 29 percent coal, 19 percent intermodal, 12 percent agricultural and consumer products, 12 percent metals and construction, and 38 percent other. Within those categories, the railroad transports the usual mix of raw materials, intermediate products like parts, and manufactured goods. The company has been an innovator in the intermodal business, that is, combining trucking and rail services—the "Roadrailer," a train of coupled-together highway vans on special wheelsets is an example; at the terminal, a cab simply backs up to the van and drives it off.

The company provides a number of logistics services and has substantial traffic to and from ports and overseas destinations.

Reasons to Buy

A combination of factors makes the long-term future of U.S. railroads look bright, not the least of which is the increasing cost of energy used for transportation. The figure often cited by rival CSX of being able to move a ton of freight 473 miles on a gallon of fuel is telling, especially when that figure is more than three times the equivalent figure for long-haul trucking, never mind the extra labor involved for the truck as well.

True, the railroad industry has been anything but glamorous for the past fifty years; it is an old technology, although recent improvements have modernized railroading considerably, including hybrid diesel electric locomotives and GPS tracking for shipments among others.

It's hard not to like NSC's operating ratio of 71.3 percent, one of the leaders in the industry and more than 8 points better than our second favorite rival Union Pacific. This railroad has done an excellent job containing costs and sizing its physical plant for its demand.

NSC has proven over the last 30 years that they can compete effectively for long-haul truck business with their intermodal offerings, and have some of the most competitive service and terminal structures in the business. They have gained market share from trucks. Additionally, NSC serves some of the more dynamic and up-and-coming manufacturing markets in the United States, namely, Asian and other foreign-owned manufacturing facilities found particularly in the Southeast; this bodes well for increases in high-value traffic.

The dividend yield of 3.6 percent is also attractive, and it appears that the current stock price (mid-2009) fully reflects the effects of the recession. If the company can generate this kind of operating performance and cash flow in a recession, the future is certainly bright in a fully performing economy.

Reasons for Caution

NSC is a railroad, and railroads are transportation businesses, and they suffer when there isn't much to transport. Norfolk Southern, because of its geography servicing many coal producers and coal consumers, not to mention export coal, is vulnerable to economic cycles and moreover, vulnerable to factors that might diminish coal usage. Today we're seeing two of those factors come into play—environmental regulation and the relatively low price of coal's major competitor, natural gas. At almost 30 percent of traffic, NSC is vulnerable to swings in the coal market, but that said, traffic gains generated in other areas have helped offset this exposure.

Also, while rail transportation is inherently more energy efficient and higher energy prices can move more traffic into the business, higher oil prices also increase the company's cost structure. So a "stagflation" environment of higher costs without corresponding higher traffic could hurt the company.

SECTOR: **Transportation**
BETA COEFFICIENT: **0.99**
10-YEAR COMPOUND EARNINGS PER SHARE GROWTH: **7.5%**
10-YEAR COMPOUND DIVIDENDS PER SHARE GROWTH: **2.0%**

	2008	2007	2006	2005	2004	2003	2002	2001	2000
Revenues (Mil)	10,661	9,432	9,407	8,527	7.312	6,468	6,270	6,170	6,159
Net Income (Mil)	1,716	1,464	1,481	1,161	870	529	460	362	1,306
Earnings per share	4.52	3.68	3.58	2.82	2.18	1.35	1.18	0.94	0.55
Dividends per share	1.22	0.96	0.68	0.48	0.36	0.30	0.26	0.24	0.80
Price　　high	75.5	59.6	57.7	45.8	36.7	24.6	27.0	24.1	22.8
low	26.7	41.4	45.4	39.1	29.6	20.4	17.3	17.2	13.4

CONSERVATIVE GROWTH

Northern Trust Corporation

50 South La Salle Street □ Chicago, IL 60675 □ Phone: (312) 444–4281 □ Website: www.northerntrust. com □ Ticker symbol: NTRS □ Listed: NASDAQ □ S&P rating: AA– □ Value Line financial strength rating: B++

Financial Highlights, Fiscal Year 2008

In FY2008, Northern Trust grew revenues 21 percent to $4.33B. Net income grew 9 percent $795M, with diluted per-share earnings growing 7 percent to $3.47. Assets grew 21 percent to $73B, and deposits grew 21 percent as well, to $55.3B.

On June 26, 2008, the company announced that it had acquired Lakepoint Investment Partners LLC of Cleveland, Ohio, an investment management firm with $586M under management.

In April, the company also announced the opening of a new office in Abu Dhabi in the United Arab Emirates.

Company Profile

Northern Trust Corporation, founded in 1889, is a multibank holding company headquartered in Chicago that provides personal wealth management and financial services and corporate and institutional services through the Corporation's principal subsidiary, the Northern Trust Company, and other bank subsidiaries located in eighteen states.

Global offices are situated in Amsterdam, Bangalore, Beijing, Dublin, Hong Kong, Limerick, London, Singapore, Tokyo, and Toronto. The Corporation also owns two investment management subsidiaries, Northern Trust Investments, N.A., and Northern Trust Global Advisors, Inc. As of March 31, 2009, Northern Trust Corporation had approximately $79 billion in banking assets, more than $522 billion in assets under management, and $2.8 trillion in assets under custody.

Northern Trust Corporation organizes client services around two principal business units: Personal Financial Services (PFS) and Corporate and Institutional Services (C&IS). Northern Trust Global Investments (NTGI) provides investment products and services to clients of both PFS and C&IS.

Personal Financial Services offers personal trust, estate administration, private banking, residential real estate mortgage lending, securities brokerage, and investment management services to individuals, families, and small businesses. PFS operates through a network of 84 offices in the eighteen states where Northern Trust operates. Approximately 25 percent of the *Forbes* 400 list of the wealthiest American families employ NTRS for asset management or administration.

Corporate and Institutional Services is a leading provider of trust, global custody, investment, retirement, commercial banking, and treasury management services worldwide. They provide asset management services to large corporations and institutions such as foundations, public retirement funds, insurance companies, and endowments. Other services include benefit payments, portfolio analysis, and electronic funds transfer.

Northern Trust's institutional clients reside in over forty countries and include corporations, public retirement funds, foundations, endowments, governmental entities, and financial institutions.

Reasons to Buy

Northern Trust generates the majority of its revenues from fee-based services to its clients. Most fees are based on asset value, so as deposits go up, or as asset valuations increase, NTRS's revenue increases. NTRS is thus motivated to grow conservatively and protect capital investment at all costs.

NTRS's clients concerns, and thus NTRS asset management strategy, is focused on capital preservation. NTRS's investment strategy is very conservative and their leverage is the lowest among all their competitors.

This is a private bank and the size of the individual accounts means that much of their value is not secured or guaranteed by any agency of any government. NTRS's clients pay significant fees, and in return they expect the bank to survive a downturn in the global economy, a plague of locusts, and a direct nuclear strike and remain standing with assets intact. Consequently, NTRS does not underwrite mortgage loans to subprime borrowers, nor do they lend directly to hedge funds. They are not in the investment banking or credit card business. This conservative approach to asset management has allowed them to ride out the housing crisis, credit crunch, and general economic downturn relatively unscathed. This is a safe, secure growth company because many of the wealthiest organizations and people in the world pay it to be so.

Reasons for Caution

NTRS is issuing shares and debt to redeem its TARP preferred stock, which will dilute its common share earnings.

SECTOR: **Financials**
BETA COEFFICIENT: **1.15**
10-YEAR COMPOUND EARNINGS PER SHARE GROWTH: **9.5%**
10-YEAR COMPOUND DIVIDENDS PER SHARE GROWTH: **10.5%**

		2008	2007	2006	2005	2004	2003	2002	2001	2000
Total Assets (Mil)		82,054	67,611	60,712	53,414	45,277	41,450	39,478	39,665	36,022
Net Income (Mil)		782	727	665	584	506	418	447	488	485
Earnings per share		3.47	3.24	3.00	2.64	2.33	1.95	1.97	2.11	2.08
Dividends per share		1.12	1.03	0.94	0.84	0.76	0.68	0.68	0.68	0.62
Price	high	88.9	83.2	61.4	55.0	51.3	48.8	62.7	82.3	92.1
	low	33.9	56.5	49.1	41.6	38.4	27.6	30.4	41.4	46.8

AGGRESSIVE GROWTH

Patterson Companies, Inc.

1031 Mendota Heights Road ◻ St. Paul, MN 55120–1419 ◻ Phone: (651) 686–1775 ◻ Website: www
.pattersondental.com ◻ Listed: NASDAQ ◻ Ticker symbol: PDCO ◻ S&P rating: B+ ◻ Value Line financial
strength rating: A

Financial Highlights, Fiscal Year 2008

Patterson's top-line grew 7 percent to $3B, moderating their 5-year sales CAGR of 13 percent. Earnings grew 8 percent to $225M, while per-share earnings increased 12 percent due to the repurchase of 18 million shares of stock (debt financed).

The company continues to grow through acquisition. They added major distributors in both their dental and veterinary businesses and opened branch offices both through acquisition and internal growth. And while debt grew substantially (to $655M), they have managed to reduce their overall cost of capital by 100 basis points, or 1 percent.

Sales in the smaller of the company's operations, Veterinary and Medical, outpaced the larger segment by a fair margin. While Dental grew at only 6 percent, Medical and Veterinary grew at 11 and 12 percent, respectively.

The company also committed to a cost reduction program, recognizing the opportunities presented by several recent acquisitions.

Company Profile

Patterson Companies is a value-added distributor operating in three segments. Dental Supply (75 percent of sales) provides a virtually complete range of consumable dental products, equipment, and software; turnkey digital solutions; and value-added services to dentists and dental laboratories throughout North America. Veterinary Supply is the nation's second-largest distributor of consumable veterinary supplies, equipment, diagnostic products, vaccines, and pharmaceuticals to companion-pet veterinary clinics. Rehabilitative Supply distributes medical supplies and assistive products globally. The unit's global customer base includes hospitals, long-term-care facilities, clinics, and dealers.

Patterson Dental is also a leader in bringing new products to market. They are the exclusive North American distributor of the CEREC 3D dental restorative system. The CEREC 3D product allows the practitioner to complete a crown procedure in just one office visit, where a traditional procedure requires two or more visits. By strengthening office productivity and enabling the dentist to perform more restorative procedures, CEREC technology is generating new revenue opportunities for dental practices. CEREC procedures also result in improved clinical outcomes with numerous advantages for the patient. It is a conservative treatment that requires no impressions or temporary caps, and the ceramic, metal-free crown is tooth-colored, highly durable, and biocompatible.

Patterson Dental also is the leading provider of digital radiography systems, which rank high on the wish list of most dentists. Unlike traditional film-based x-rays, digital systems create instant images. The resulting increase in office productivity enables dentists to treat more patients. The benefits of digital radiography are increased when it is integrated with the appropriate software, including Patterson's proprietary EagleSoft line. This integration creates an electronic database that combines the patient's dental record with digital information from the x-ray, intra-oral camera, CEREC, and other digital equipment. With a current market penetration of only about 20 percent, it is believed that digital radiography eventually will be installed in most dental offices.

Reasons to Buy

The company has found opportunity in the largely fragmented and undeveloped dental distribution market, and is capitalizing through consolidation and the offering of a greater level of value-add than their competitors. This value takes the form of financing, local service and support, and software services. In their Dental business, they also have exclusive licenses for the distribution of widely used equipment—the most popular dental chair in the industry, and the aforementioned CEREC 3D system.

The CEREC is an imaging and milling system that allows the dentist to take an image of the area to be restored and in less than thirty minutes have a crown, inlay, or other device which is custom-fitted to the patient's existing dental structure. It's a compelling proposition for high-volume offices where patient throughput is at a premium and the equipment can be fully utilized. Patterson's exclusive license to this product is a powerful foot in the door for new accounts.

We like the company's moves into the companion-pet veterinary and rehabilitative markets, both of which are driven by a growing and profitable demographic.

Lastly, the company remains in a strong financial position to continue its successful strategy of acquisition and consolidation.

Reasons for Caution

The company's top-line success is driven in large part by the sale of big-ticket items, some of which are discretionary and where volumes have diminished in the recent quarters. As the economy turns around we expect those sales to improve, but it may take several quarters of sustained growth before Patterson's customers are persuaded to commit to new investments.

SECTOR: **Health Care**

BETA COEFFICIENT: **.90**

10-YEAR COMPOUND EARNINGS PER SHARE GROWTH: **19.5%**

10-YEAR COMPOUND DIVIDENDS PER SHARE GROWTH: **No dividend**

		2008	2007	2006	2005	2004	2003	2002	2001	2000
Revenues (Mil)		2,998	2,798	2,615	2,421	1,969	1,657	1,416	1,156	1,040
Net Income (Mil)		225	208	198	184	150	116	95	76	64
Earnings per share		1.69	1.51	1.43	1.32	1.09	0.85	0.70	0.57	0.48
Dividends per share		Nil								
Price	high	37.8	40.1	38.3	53.8	43.7	35.8	27.6	21.1	17.3
	low	15.8	28.3	29.6	33.4	29.7	17.7	19.1	13.8	8.2

Paychex, Inc.

911 Panorama Trail South □ Rochester, NY 14625–0397 □ Phone: (585) 383–3406 □ Website: www.paychex.com □ Listed: NASDAQ □ Ticker symbol: PAYX □ S&P rating: A+ □ Value Line financial strength rating: A

Financial Highlights, Fiscal Year 2008

Paychex's top line grew 10 percent in 2008 to $2.07B while earnings grew 12 percent to $576M. Net income was 28 percent of total revenue. Before you take that check to the bank, there's more.

Diluted earnings per share grew 16 percent to $1.56, while dividends grew 52 percent to $1.20/share. Return on stockholder's equity for the year was 39 percent. The company repurchased $1B worth of stock (5.8 percent of outstanding shares), has no debt, and finished the year with over $400M in cash and liquid securities.

Is there a catch? Sort of. Paychex's fiscal year ends May 31, so all of 2008's financial data misses the start of the third calendar quarter, when the full force of the financial crisis really began to be felt. Since then, the picture has become decidedly less rosy, but this is still a very attractive issue.

Company Profile

Paychex, Inc., is a leading provider of payroll, human resource, and benefits outsourcing solutions for small- to medium-sized businesses. Paychex was founded in 1971. The company has more than 100 offices and serves more than 572,000 payroll clients in the United States and an additional 1,200 clients in Germany.

Paychex offers a comprehensive portfolio of services and products that allow its clients to meet their diverse payroll and human resource needs. These include:

- payroll processing
- payroll tax administration services
- employee payment services
- regulatory compliance services (new-hire reporting and garnishment processing)
- comprehensive human resource outsourcing services
- retirement services administration
- workers' compensation insurance services
- health and benefits services
- time and attendance solutions
- medical deduction, state unemployment, and other HR services and products

The company's products are marketed primarily through their direct sales force, the bulk of which is focused on payroll products. The remainder specialize in Human Resource Services. In addition to the direct sales force, the company utilizes their relationships with existing clients, CPAs, and banks for new client referrals. Approximately two-thirds of their new clients come via these referral sources.

The company also sells a Major Market Services product for its larger clients. The MMS product is a license that allows the client to run the Paychex software on the client's own servers and administer the payroll function with its own personnel.

In addition, Advantage Payroll Services Inc. ("Advantage"), a wholly owned subsidiary of Paychex, Inc., has license agreements with independently owned associate offices ("Associates"), which are responsible for selling and marketing Advantage payroll services and performing certain operational functions, while Paychex, Inc. and Advantage provide all centralized back-office payroll processing and payroll tax administration services. The marketing and selling by the associates is conducted under their own brands and logos.

Reasons to Buy

Paychex's primary market is firms with fewer than 100 employees. Of the more than 7 million businesses in that market, fewer than 20 percent use a payroll processing service. Consequently, there is tremendous growth potential for Paychex, particularly since their biggest competitor, ADP, concentrates its efforts on larger firms.

Fragmentation in the market and Paychex's extremely strong financial position would allow the company to grow market share through acquisition should they decide to do so.

Outsourcing of nonvalue-added functions is a trend that makes a great deal of sense for the majority of businesses in the United States, and Paychex is aggressively exploring the boundaries of the concept. They administer 10 percent of the 401(k) plans in the country, and they now offer health insurance and experienced 93 percent growth in that segment year/year.

Reasons for Caution

Unemployment in the United States is as high as it's been since the recession of the early 1980s. With fewer employees, Paychex fees are reduced as well. Also, some clients keep funds on deposit with Paychex to expedite payroll processing and payment. In 2007 Paychex earned 7.1 percent of its total revenue on the float from these funds, but with interest rates at their recent low levels, that revenue is also reduced. In 2008 that float returned only 6.3 percent of total revenue.

SECTOR: **Information Technology**
BETA COEFFICIENT: **.95**
10-YEAR COMPOUND EARNINGS PER SHARE GROWTH: **20.4%**
10-YEAR COMPOUND DIVIDENDS PER SHARE GROWTH: **27.4%**

		2008	2007	2006	2005	2004	2003	2002	2001	2000
Revenues (Mil)		2,066	1,887	1,675	1,445	1,294	1,099	955	870	728
Net Income (Mil)		576	515	465	369	303	294	274	255	190
Earnings per share		1.56	1.35	1.22	0.97	0.80	0.78	0.73	0.68	0.51
Dividends per share		1.20	0.79	0.61	0.51	0.47	0.44	0.42	0.33	0.22
Price	high	37.1	47.1	42.4	43.4	39.1	40.5	42.2	51.0	61.3
	low	24.5	36.1	33.0	28.8	28.8	23.8	20.4	28.3	24.2

AGGRESSIVE GROWTH

Peet's Coffee and Tea

1400 Park Avenue □ Emeryville, CA 94608-3520 □ Phone: (510) 594–2100 □ Website: www.peets.com □
Listed: NASDAQ □ Ticker symbol: PEET □ S&P rating: BBB □ Value Line financial strength rating: B+

Financial Highlights, Fiscal Year 2008

For 2008, Peet's reported sales of $285M, a 14 percent increase of FY2007. Income rose 21.7 percent to 11.2M, propelled by a 100 basis point (1 percent) increase in operating margins (to 11.3 percent) and a 20 basis point (0.2 percent) increase in net margins (to 3.9 percent).

Earnings per share rose 23 percent to $0.80. They exited the year with $35 per share in working capital, and they carry no debt.

Company Profile

Peet's Coffee & Tea is a specialty coffee roaster and marketer of fresh roasted whole bean coffee and tea. They sell coffee under strict freshness standards through multiple channels of distribution including grocery stores, home delivery, office, restaurant and foodservice accounts, and company-owned and operated stores in six states.

The company was founded in 1966 and is widely considered to be the first ultrapremium coffee retailer in the United States, and an inspiration for Starbucks and others. The company was purchased by two of the founders of Starbucks after they sold that firm in 1987 to Howard Schultz and other investors.

The business is operated through two reportable segments: retail and specialty sales.

As of December 28, 2008 they operated 188 retail stores in six states through which they sell whole bean coffee, beverages and pastries, tea, and other related items. The stores are designed to facilitate the sale of fresh whole bean coffee and to encourage customer trial of coffee through coffee beverages. Like Starbucks, Peet's stores have attractive environments and are effective gathering places for all walks of urban and suburban life. Freshness standards are in place to not serve brewed coffee more than thirty minutes old; higher priced drinks are made to order.

In addition to sales through retail stores, the company sells products through a network of nearly 8,500 grocery stores, including Safeway, Albertson's, Ralph's, Kroger, Publix, and Whole Foods Market. To support these sales, they have developed an extensive sales and distribution system. Route sales reps deliver directly to their stores anywhere between one to three times per week, properly shelve the product, rotate to ensure freshness, sell and erect free-standing displays, and forge store-level selling relationships.

Unlike Starbucks, Peet's products are available for home delivery through a dedicated website.

In the foodservice and office business, they sell directly and audit quality through their own staff of sales and account managers. Additionally, they have developed relationships with foodservice and office distributors to expand the account base in select markets and channels.

Reasons to Buy

As size provides a measure of safety, there aren't too many small-cap companies profiled in this book. However, Peet's is a company that delivers a sought-after product, a quality customer experience, and a sound, conservative business plan that offers significant long-term growth poten-

tial. "Small cap value" is a good place to be with at least a portion of your portfolio.

Will they grow as quickly as Starbucks? That's not their plan. Peet's is scheduled to add only twenty-five to thirty more stores in 2009, but in the last 18 months have added 3,800 new grocery outlets. No surprise; Peet's generates two-thirds of its revenue at its retail stores, but generates two-thirds of its earnings from its grocery and direct-to-consumer business. The most profitable part of their business is also the most scalable part of their business. Peet's has so far wisely avoided the temptation to "go wide" with thousands of stores like Starbucks; the brand isn't quite as strong or ubiquitous as Starbucks but delivers a strong value promise to customers. Also, while Starbucks has already built out across the 50 states, Peet's is still a fresh idea and brand in many markets.

Warren Thorpe of Value Line notes: "On balance, we estimate a top-line advance of nearly 11 percent, to $315 million, this year. And we are initiating our 2010 revenue forecast at $355 million. We look for good margin expansion beginning next year. The company has made a number of investments in the past several quarters that promise to increase profitability. A new, more efficient roasting facility ought to add 40–50 [0.4–0.5 percent] basis points a year to the gross margin. Moreover, technology investments, such as inventory and labor management systems, stand to yield margin benefits in the coming years. Also, the more efficient use of capital that should result stands to obviate the need to borrow in order to fund future expansion."

Reasons for Caution

Peet's maintains its own fleet of delivery trucks and other direct selling ex-

penses; it also incurs significant costs in acquiring its raw materials from geographically remote locations. Also, this stock is not a secret—expect to find it trading for high multiples.

SECTOR: **Restaurant**
BETA COEFFICIENT: **0.85**
10-YEAR COMPOUND EARNINGS PER SHARE GROWTH: **n/a**
10-YEAR COMPOUND DIVIDENDS PER SHARE GROWTH: ***

		2008	2007	2006	2005	2004	2003	2002	2001	2000
Revenues (Mil)		285	250	211	175	146	120	104	94.4	84.3
Net Income (Mil)		11.2	9.2	8.9	10.7	8.8	5.2	4.7	1.2	d2.3
Earnings per share		0.80	0.65	0.63	0.74	0.63	0.39	0.40	0.14	0.50
Dividends per share										
Price	high	29.8	30.4	32.8	37.3	27.4	23.5	19.1	17.8	—
	low	17.8	23.0	24.3	23.0	16.1	12.6	10.6	5.8	

PepsiCo, Inc.

700 Anderson Hill Road □ Purchase, NY 10577–1444 □ Phone: (914) 253–3055 □ Website: www.pepsico. com □ Listed: NYSE □ Ticker symbol: PEP □ S&P rating: A+ □ Value Line financial strength rating: A++

Financial Highlights, Fiscal Year 2008

Sales grew 10 percent year/year to $43.2B, while reported earnings fell 7.2 percent to $5.14B. These reported earnings carry a number of restructuring, impairment, and other charges—PepsiCo's non-GAAP earnings are shown in their Annual Report as $5.89B, an increase of 5 percent over FY2007. Reported earnings per share fell 4 percent to $3.21 ($3.68 undiluted, an increase of 9 percent). Dividends rose 12 percent to $1.60/ share.

Company Profile

PepsiCo is a leading global beverage, snack, and food company. They manufacture or use contract manufacturers, market and sell a variety of salty, convenient, sweet and grain-based snacks; carbonated and noncarbonated beverages; and foods in approximately 200 countries, with their largest operations in North America (United States and Canada), Mexico, and the United Kingdom.

They are organized into three business units and six reportable segments (in parentheses), as follows:

- PepsiCo Americas Foods (PAF), which includes Frito-Lay North America (FLNA), Quaker Foods North America (QFNA), and all

of the Latin American food and snack businesses (LAF), including the Sabritas and Gamesa businesses in Mexico;

- PepsiCo Americas Beverages (PAB), which includes PepsiCo Beverages North America and all of the Latin American beverage businesses; and
- PepsiCo International (PI), which includes all PepsiCo businesses in the United Kingdom, Europe, Asia, Middle East and Africa.

The remaining two segments are United Kingdom & Europe (UKEU), and Middle East, Africa & Asia (MEAA).

Many of PepsiCo's brand names are over 100 years old, but the corporation is relatively young. PepsiCo was founded in 1965 through the merger of Pepsi-Cola and Frito-Lay. Pepsico now has at least eighteen brands that generate over $1B in retail sales. The top two brands are Pepsi-Cola and Mountain Dew, but beverages constitute less than half of Pepsi's sales. They are primarily a snack company, and beverages come in second. Frito-Lay brands alone account for more than half of the U.S. snack chip industry.

PepsiCo began its international snack food operations in 1966. Today, with operations in more than forty countries, it is the leading multinational snack chip company, accounting for more than one quarter of international retail snack chip sales. Brand Pepsi and other Pepsi-Cola products—including Diet Pepsi, Pepsi-One, Mountain Dew, Slice, Sierra Mist, and Mug brands—account for nearly one-third of total soft drink sales in the United States, a consumer market totaling about $60 billion. Pepsi-Cola also offers a variety of noncarbonated beverages, including Aquafina bottled water, Lipton ready-to-drink tea, and Frappuccino ready-to-drink coffee through a partnership with Starbucks.

PepsiCo acquired Tropicana, including the Dole juice business, in August 1998 and now markets these products in sixty-three countries. Tropicana Pure Premium is the third largest brand of all food products sold in grocery stores in the United States.

Gatorade was acquired by the Quaker Oats Company in 1983 and became a part of PepsiCo as part of the Quaker merger in 2001. Created in 1965, Gatorade is now the world's leading sports drink.

Reasons to Buy

Most people (quite rightly) associate PepsiCo with the Pepsi-Cola branded products, but the fact is that Pepsi-branded products constitute less than half of the company's beverage revenue, and beverage products constitute less than half of revenue overall. This bodes well, as carbonated sweetened beverages are slowly losing regard with target markets in favor of fruit drinks, juices, and sport drinks. PepsiCo is well-positioned with a broad array of brands and products to serve its prime demographics.

PepsiCo owns 33 percent and 43 percent of its two largest independent bottlers and is in negotiations to acquire the remaining interest in each in a cash/stock deal worth $6B. Doing so would eliminate a number of manufacturing redundancies and give PepsiCo control of nearly 80 percent of its North American distribution. Short-term expenses would rise, but reduced costs and improved efficiencies would soon improve the bottom line.

Reasons for Caution

As a large-scale processor and reseller, PepsiCo is exposed to swings in the prices of raw materials, and 2008 was a wild year in commodities. Obviously, the company hedges its largest-use materials, but their hedging program in FY2008 netted a $346M mark-to-market debit against earnings. Certainly, there will be good years and bad years in any hedging strategy, but $346M is a lot of exposure. It will be worth seeing how their strategy works going forward.

SECTOR: **Consumer Staples**
BETA COEFFICIENT: **.60**
10-YEAR COMPOUND EARNINGS PER SHARE GROWTH: **10%**
10-YEAR COMPOUND DIVIDENDS PER SHARE GROWTH: **10.5%**

		2008	2007	2006	2005	2004	2003	2002	2001	2000
Revenues (Mil)		43,251	39,474	35,137	32,562	29,261	26,971	25,112	23,512	25,480
Net Income (Mil)		5,142	5,543	5,065	4,078	4,174	3,494	3,313	2,660	2,540
Earnings per share		3.21	3.34	3.00	2.39	2.44	2.01	1.85	1.47	1.42
Dividends per share		1.60	1.43	1.16	1.01	0.85	0.63	0.60	0.58	0.56
Price	high	79.8	79.0	66.0	60.3	55.7	48.9	53.5	50.5	49.9
	low	49.7	61.9	56.0	51.3	45.3	36.2	34.0	40.3	29.7

AGGRESSIVE GROWTH

Perrigo Company

515 Eastern Avenue ▫ Allegan, MI 49010 ▫ Phone: (269) 673–8451 ▫ Website: www.perrigo.com ▫
Listed: NASDAQ ▫ Ticker symbol: PRGO ▫ S&P rating: NA ▫ Value Line financial strength rating: B++

Financial Highlights, Fiscal Year 2008

For 2008, Perrigo's net sales increased 25.9 percent to $1.82B, while adjusted net income rose 80.6 percent to $150M. Diluted earnings per share rose only (!) 77.5 percent to $1.58, as outstanding shares rose 1.5 percent.

Perrigo's operating margin rose 380 basis points, or 3.8 percent, to 15.6 percent, and net margin rose 280 basis points, or 2.8 percent, to 8.2 percent. Dividends grew 16 percent to a token $0.21/share.

The company had a number of significant approvals in 2008, including Omeprazole 20mg, Clobetasol foam, and other generics with a total retail branded equivalent sales volume of $930M. In January 2008, the company acquired Galpharm Healthcare, a U.K.-based distributor of store brand OTC products. The acquisition should add $55M/year to Perrigo's top line.

Company Profile

Perrigo is the world's largest manufacturer of over-the-counter (OTC) pharmaceutical products for the store brand market. They also manufacture generic prescription (Rx) pharmaceuticals, nutritional products, and active pharmaceutical ingredients (API). The company operates in three segments: Consumer Healthcare, Rx, and API. Consumer Healthcare makes private-label OTC drugs and nutritional products. Rx produces generic prescription drugs, and API makes chemicals and pharmaceutical products under contract. The company has other miscellaneous businesses that together constitute about 10 percent of revenues. Consumer Healthcare is by far the largest segment, generating about 75 percent of Perrigo's revenue in 2008.

The company's success depends upon its ability to manufacture and quickly market generic equivalents to branded products. They employ internal R&D resources to develop product formulations, and also manufacture in quantity for their customers. They also develop retail packaging specific to the customer's needs. The company produces and market over 1,100 store brand products to approximately 100 customers, including Wal-Mart, CVS, Walgreens, Kroger, Safeway, Costco, and other national and regional drugstores, supermarkets, and mass merchandisers. Wal-Mart is their single largest customer and accounts for 20 percent of Perrigo's net sales in 2008. The retail market size for the branded equivalents of Perrigo's most widely used products is over $12 billion.

The company's products are manufactured in nine separate facilities around the world. Its major markets are in North America, Mexico, the United Kingdom, and China. Their main Consumer Healthcare customers include food, drug, and mass merchandise retailers; club stores; dollar stores; and wholesalers. Their main Pharmaceuticals customers include wholesalers, food, drug and mass merchandise retailers; drug distributors; governments; and group purchasers.

Reasons to Buy

Perrigo expects that over the next five years, prescription drugs worth $10B in sales will be approved for OTC use. Rx-to-OTC switches is one of Perrigo's main revenue drivers, so these products will be in Perrigo's crosshairs.

Similarly, Perrigo sees an addition $3B in sales of branded Rx products with potential for generic equivalent product introductions.

Just one year after Dexcel Pharma received FDA approval for its 20mg Omeprazole tablets, Dexcel signed an agreement granting Perrigo exclusive rights to market and distribute the heartburn treatment. Annualized revenues to Perrigo are expected to be in the neighborhood of $150M to $200M. Nice neighborhood.

It's still too early to say what the Obama Administration will bring to the Healthcare Reform party, but we'd be very much surprised if the upshot was not good for generic drug manufacturers. Players like Perrigo and Teva reduce the cost of pharmaceuticals to providers and end users alike, and have learned (over time) to play nice with Big Pharma through exclusive licensing agreements. An expansion of that role would be politically expedient and uncomplicated to implement.

Reasons for Caution

Should Wal-Mart make significant changes to their OTC pharmaceutical sourcing, Perrigo's revenues could be materially impacted. Perrigo is slowly reducing their reliance on this large customer.

SECTOR: **Healthcare**
BETA COEFFICIENT: **0.65**
10-YEAR COMPOUND EARNINGS PER SHARE GROWTH: **7.50%**
10-YEAR COMPOUND DIVIDENDS PER SHARE GROWTH: -----

		2008	2007	2006	2005	2004	2003	2002	2001	2000
Revenues (Mil)		1,822	1,447	1,366	1,024	898	826	826	753	738
Net Income (Mil)		150	78.6	74.1	37.9	67.5	51.9	44.5	41.2	19.3
Earnings per share		1.58	0.84	0.79	0.49	0.93	0.73	0.59	0.55	0.26
Dividends per share		.21	.18	.17	.16	.13	.05			
Price	high	43.1	36.9	18.7	19.9	25.0	16.7	14.8	18.3	9.4
	low	27.7	16.1	14.4	12.8	15.6	10.5	9.3	7.4	5.0

GROWTH AND INCOME

Piedmont Natural Gas Company, Inc.

P.O. Box 33068 ▫ Charlotte, NC 28233 ▫ Phone: (704) 731–4226 ▫ Dividend reinvestment program is available ▫ Fiscal year ends October 31 ▫ Listed: NYSE ▫ Website: www.piedmontng.com ▫ Ticker symbol: PNY ▫ S&P rating: A– ▫ Value Line financial strength rating: B++

Financial Highlights, Fiscal Year 2008

Revenues for 2008 grew to $2.09B, a 22.1 percent increase over FY2007. Net income increased 5.4 percent to $110M, while diluted earnings per share increased 6.4 percent to $1.49. Margin for the year was up 5.5 percent to $553M.

Residential per-customer revenues were up 7 percent over 2007, while residential per-Dekatherm revenues were up 6 percent. Degree-days were up 7.3 percent over the prior year.

System throughput for fiscal year 2008 totaled 210 million Dekatherms, an increase of 2.1 percent over the previous year. Of that total, 121 million Dekatherms were delivered to large-volume customers, and another 89 million Dekatherms were delivered to temperature-sensitive residential and commercial customers.

Company Profile

Incorporated in 1950, Piedmont Natural Gas is an energy services company primarily engaged in the transportation, distribution, and sale of natural gas and propane to residential, commercial, and industrial customers in North Carolina, South Carolina, and Tennessee.

The company is the second-largest natural gas utility in the Southeast, serving 950,000 natural gas customers. Piedmont Natural Gas and its nonutility subsidiaries and divisions are also engaged in acquiring, marketing, transporting, and storing natural gas for large-volume customers, and in retailing residential and commercial gas appliances.

Other business interests in which the company is engaged that are not subject to state utility regulation include the sale of propane and investments in a natural gas pipeline and an interstate LNG (liquefied natural gas) storage facility and marketing natural gas and other energy products and services to deregulated markets.

PNY's joint ventures include:

- SouthStar Energy Services LLC is an equity participant (or part owner) in Georgia's largest retail natural gas marketer.
- Pine Needle LNG Company, LLC, is an equity participant in a liquefied natural gas facility that's among the nation's largest.
- Cardinal Pipeline Company, LLC, is an equity participant in a 102-mile intrastate pipeline serving portions of North Carolina.
- EasternNC Natural Gas is an equity participant in a venture that is expanding natural gas distribution into fourteen counties in eastern North Carolina.

Reasons to Buy

Piedmont added 20,500 customers in 2008 (a 2 percent increase), making them one of the fastest-growing gas distributors in the country. Although new residential installations were significantly lower this year due to the dismal housing market, Piedmont experienced a 17 percent increase in their rate of conversion (customers switching to gas from electricity or propane).

Dividends were increased again in 2008 to an annualized $1.04 per share, creating a dividend yield of 3.8 percent. Piedmont's total shareholder return for FY2006 through FY2008 is 56 percent, which puts them in the 96th percentile for their industry.

In March 2009, analyst Eldon Turner wrote: "A major concern for investors of mid to large cap nongrowth companies is their current and future pension obligations. When PNY reported 2008 full year, it indicated that its O & M expense (operation and maintenance) in FY08 decreased primarily because of lower pension expense accruals. Per its 10k, it looks like the company will have manageable and conservative growth in its 2009 and 2010 pension obligations.

One of the factors in picking a defensive stock is a solid and sustainable dividend. 2007 dividend rate was $.99, 2008 was $1.03 and there is no indication from the full year reports that the dividend will change in 2009. The dividend yield in '07 was 3.6 percent; '08, 3.7 percent; and my contention is that it won't change in '09."

At the time of this writing (June '09), Piedmont is trading over 30 percent off of its fifty-two-week high, creating a buying opportunity for this quality issue.

Reasons for Caution

It should be noted for this stock (and for any of the other income-biased stocks in this book) that the current 15 percent maximum federal tax rate on corporate dividends is due to expire in 2010. Depending on one's individual tax situation, a significantly higher rate may affect the owners of companies like Piedmont.

SECTOR: **Utilities**
BETA COEFFICIENT: **.65**
10-YEAR COMPOUND EARNINGS PER SHARE GROWTH: **4.5%**
10-YEAR COMPOUND DIVIDENDS PER SHARE GROWTH: **5.0%**

		2008	2007	2006	2005	2004	2003	2002	2001	2000
Revenues (Mil)		2.089	1,711	1,925	1,761	1,530	1,221	832	1,108	830
Net Income (Mil)		110	104	97	101	95	74	62	65	64
Earnings per share		1.49	1.40	1.28	1.32	1.27	1.11	0.04	1.01	1.00
Dividends per share		1.03	1.00	0.96	0.92	0.86	0.82	0.79	0.76	0.72
Price	high	35.3	28.9	28.4	25.8	24.4	22.0	19.0	19.0	19.7
	low	21.7	22.0	23.2	21.3	19.2	16.6	13.7	14.6	14.3

Praxair, Inc.

39 Old Ridgebury Road ▫ Danbury, CT 06810–5113 ▫ Phone: (203) 837–2354 ▫ Website: www.praxair
.com ▫ Listed: NYSE ▫ Ticker symbol: PX ▫ S&P rating: A ▫ Value Line financial strength rating: A

Financial Highlights, Fiscal Year 2008

Praxair had another strong year in 2008, with sales up 15 percent to $10.8B, and earnings up 13.4 percent to $1.34B. Adjusted per-share earnings were up 16 percent, and the company achieved a record operating cash flow of over $2B. The company repurchased 3 percent of its shares and raised dividends 25 percent to $1.50.

Company Profile

Praxair, Inc., is a global *Fortune* 500 company that supplies atmospheric, process, and specialty gases; high-performance coatings; and related services and technologies. The company, which was spun off to Union Carbide shareholders in June 1992, is the largest producer of industrial gases in North and South America and the second-largest supplier of industrial gases in the world.

Praxair's primary products are atmospheric gases—oxygen, nitrogen, argon, and rare gases (produced when atmospheric air is purified, compressed, cooled, distilled, and condensed), and process and specialty gases—carbon dioxide, helium, hydrogen, semiconductor process gases, and acetylene (produced as by-products of chemical production or recovered from natural gas).

The company also designs, engineers, and constructs cryogenic and noncryogenic gas supply systems for

companies who choose to produce their own atmospherics on site. This is obviously a more capital-intensive solution for Praxair, but results in lower delivered cost to the customer and higher returns for Praxair, as energy costs (the only expense involved, as raw materials are free) are paid by the customer. Contracts for these installations can run to twenty years.

Praxair Surface Technologies is a subsidiary that applies metallic and ceramic coatings and powders to metal surfaces in order to resist wear, high temperatures, and corrosion. Aircraft engines are its primary market, but it serves others, including the printing, textile, chemical, and primary metals markets, and provides aircraft engine and airframe component overhaul services.

Praxair adopted its name in 1992, from the Greek word "praxis," or practical application, and "air," the company's primary raw material. PX was originally founded in 1907 when it was the first company to commercialize cryogenically separated oxygen. Over the century of its existence, Praxair has remained a leader in the development of processes and technologies that have revolutionized the industrial gases industry. The company introduced the first distribution system for liquid gas in 1917, and developed on-site gas supply by the end of World War II. In the 1960s, Praxair introduced a noncryogenic means of air separation, and since then has continued to introduce innovative applications technologies for various industries. PX holds almost 3,000 patents. Praxair serves a wide range of industries: food and beverages, health care, semiconductors, chemicals, refining, primary metals and metal fabrication, as well as other areas of general industry.

Reasons to Buy

A quarter of the company's revenue and over half of the company's earnings come from a business model that generates a contracted return (with some variability) for five to twenty years, depending on the product. Praxair builds a cryogenic plant at the customer's site and customers pay (either directly or indirectly) for all the costs associated with running the plant, getting in return assurance of supply for their industrial gases while paying only for what they need with no initial capital cost outlay. It's a great model for both parties and is, at times, the only solution possible if the customer's site is fairly remote. Praxair's standard contracts include energy surcharge pass-through and take-or-pay provisions.

Praxair is signing up subsidiaries in China to serve its customers' needs. Praxair China now has fifteen wholly owned subsidiaries and at least ten joint ventures. Asian markets account for 8 percent of Praxair's sales.

The petroleum industry is recovering heavier and heavier crude oil sources, such as the tar sands in Alberta. To refine these sources at existing facilities requires the input of greater and greater volumes of hydrogen. The largest of Praxair's 42 current major projects are hydrogen production facilities in North America serving refineries, and hydrogen for refining is now Praxair's largest growth market.

Finally, Praxair is moving quickly on a solution for carbon sequestration at coal fired facilities (primarily power plants) that may be funded soon by the DOE and, if successful, could generate revenues on the order of $150M per installation.

Reasons for Caution

There appear to be no major downsides short of continued deep recession and weakness in global industrial production.

SECTOR: **Materials**
BETA COEFFICIENT: **1.0**
10-YEAR COMPOUND EARNINGS PER SHARE GROWTH: **11.5%**
10-YEAR COMPOUND DIVIDENDS PER SHARE GROWTH: **19.0%**

		2008	2007	2006	2005	2004	2003	2002	2001	2000
Revenues (Mil)		10,796	9,402	8,324	7,656	6,594	5,613	5,128	5,158	5,043
Net Income (Mil)		1,335	1,177	988	726	697	585	548	432	432
Earnings per share		4.19	3.62	3.00	2.20	2.10	1.77	1.66	1.50	1.49
Dividends per share		1.50	1.20	1.00	0.72	0.60	0.46	0.38	0.34	0.31
Price	high	77.6	92.1	63.7	54.3	46.2	38.3	30.6	28.0	27.5
	low	53.3	58.0	50.4	41.1	34.5	25.0	22.4	18.3	15.2

CONSERVATIVE GROWTH

The Procter & Gamble Company

Post Office Box 599 ▫ Cincinnati, Ohio 45201–0599 ▫ Phone: (800) 742–6253 ▫ Website: www.pg.com
▫ Listed: NYSE ▫ Fiscal year ends June 30 ▫ Ticker symbol: PG ▫ S&P rating: A+ ▫ Value Line financial
strength rating: A++

Financial Highlights, Fiscal Year 2008

Net sales in fiscal 2008 increased 9.3 percent to $83.5 billion on a 4 percent unit sales increase. The 2008 fiscal year presents the first full year's results after accounting for the Gillette acquisition costs, and the integration appears to be going well with only positive impact to the bottom line. Per-share measures of earnings and cash flow grew ahead of sales, as did net margins. The sale of the Folgers brand (announced four days after the close of FY08) had no impact to the top line. The company plans to use the sale to kick off a restructuring (with an estimated cost of $400M) which will impact FY09 but is expected to lead to productivity improvements and margin expansion.

Organic sales were up 5 percent, with major contributions from Baby and Family Care (up 8 percent, driven by paper products Charmin, Pampers, and Bounty) and Fabric and Home Care (up 6 percent, driven by the innovation of "compacted" liquid laundry detergents). All of the six major reporting sectors in which P&G operates (including the above, Beauty, Grooming, Health Care, and Snacks/Coffee/Pet Care), saw increases in organic sales ranging from 4 to 9 percent.

Net earnings grew 17 percent during the fiscal year to $12.1 billion. Net earnings increased behind sales growth and a 100-basis point (1 percent) improvement in net earnings margin, primarily due to lower SG&A and a lower tax rate. Diluted net earnings per share increased 20 percent to $3.64, exceeding net earnings growth due to $10B in share repurchase activity. The dilution effect of the Gillette purchase has been eliminated, with the effect being a 4 percent increase in earnings per share growth.

Gross margin was down 70 basis points to 51.3 percent of net sales, largely due to commodity and energy cost increases, offset somewhat by improvements in manufacturing efficiency and product reformulations. SG&A increased 6 percent to $25.7B but fell as a percentage of net sales by 100 basis points due to higher product volumes.

The company's operating cash flow for the fiscal year was $15.8 billion, an increase of 18 percent over the prior year. Operating cash increased primarily due to higher net earnings and noncash charges, and was well ahead of target. Since the beginning of the decade, PG has been a cash-generation machine, producing $60B in free cash flow since FY2000. PG's product markets demand innovation to sustain growth, and PG has been able to maintain a healthy level of R&D spending, even in the recent downturn. This is a significant advantage that contributes greatly to the maintenance of margins and competitiveness in the market.

Company Profile

Procter & Gamble dates back to 1837, when William Procter and James Gamble began making soap and candles in Cincinnati, Ohio. The company's first major product introduction took place in 1879 when it launched Ivory soap. Since then, P&G has continually created a host of blockbuster products and currently has twenty-four billion-dollar brands.

P&G is a uniquely diversified consumer—a products company with a strong global presence. P&G today markets its broad line of products to nearly 5 billion consumers in more than 180 countries.

The company is a recognized leader in the development, manufacturing, and marketing of superior quality laundry, cleaning, paper, personal care, food, beverage, and healthcare products, including prescription pharmaceuticals.

Among the company's nearly 300 brands are Gillette, Tide, Always, Whisper, Pro-V, Oil of Olay, Pringles, Duracell, Ariel, Crest, Pampers, Pantene, Vicks, Bold, Dawn, Head & Shoulders, Cascade, Iams, Zest, Bounty, Braun, Comet, Scope, Old Spice, Charmin, Tampax, Downy, Cheer, and Prell.

Total 2008 sales exceeded $83 billion and the company has nearly 110,000 employees working in more than eighty countries.

Reasons to Buy

Regardless of developments in the world economy, people will continue to shave, bathe, do laundry, and care for their babies. And P&G is the global leader in Baby Care, Feminine Care, Fabric Care, and Shaving Products. Pampers alone generates over $8B in revenue. Everyone should consider at least one defensive play in their portfolio, and P&G deserves to be at the top of the list.

Procter & Gamble has more than doubled sales in faster-growing, higher-margin categories, such as beauty, health care, and home care. According to a company spokesman, "More than 70 percent of the company's growth, or roughly $20 billion in net sales, has come from organic growth and strategic acquisitions in these businesses. Well over half of P&G sales now comes from these faster-growing higher-margin businesses."

P&G regard innovation as one of their key differentiators and aggressively pursues new market opportunities, both in the U.S. market and globally. The company is among the top ten patent-producing companies in the world. And rather than rely solely on their in-house R&D, they actively partner with smaller firms who may have a better view of local markets. In the past six years they've more than tripled the number of product ideas generated outside their own labs. Today, over half their innovation is generated by their innovation partners, which puts them in position to take advantage of local consumer trends in the growing and increasingly brand-conscious world economy.

In April 2009, company CEO A. G. Lafley said: "Back in 2000 we set a goal of having partners for half of all new products. We hit that goal in 2007–2008. That obviously saves us a lot of money. We can take a P&G dollar and turn it into a dollar and a half to two dollars. Virtually all the work you don't see—taking an order from a retailer or wholesaler, processing orders, scientists working in research centers—is all run collaboratively in back rooms with partners. So our operating margin increases, even though we're still spending on R&D and branding and capital to support innovation."

Writing in January 2009 for *Value Line Investment Survey*, Orly Seidman wrote: "P&G's exposure to emerging markets and recent currency fluctuations may also lead to some near-term pressure. Nevertheless, P&G's ongoing stock-buyback program ought to bolster per-share figures. This, coupled with the company's other strengths, including a well-diversified and price-tiered portfolio, product innovation, and ongoing restructuring efforts, ought to help it post a 10 percent share-net advance in fiscal 2009." And in April 2009: ". . . investors should note that these top-quality shares retain our Highest marks

for Safety (1) and Financial Strength (A++)."

The March 2009 issue of *Fortune* magazine ranks Procter & Gamble sixth in its list of most admired companies. In its list of nine key attributes, P&G was ranked first in its industries in Innovation, People Management, Quality of Management, Financial Soundness, Long-term Investment, and Global Competitiveness.

Reasons for Caution

In a slow economy, consumers will be motivated to save wherever possible. Among Procter & Gamble's chief competitors for shelf space are low-cost store brands and generics. A change in consumer preference may dilute market share for P&G, but since they have either the number one or number two retail position in the vast majority of their key global categories, P&G feels that any shift in purchasing patterns will damage their traditional competitors more than it will themselves.

P&G has seen its raw materials costs rise in recent months due in part to currency fluctuations and rising expenses. This does not necessarily create a competitive disadvantage for P&G (as many of these commodities are used by their competitors as well), but this will put pressure on margins in a period of retail pricing inflexibility. Exchange rate volatility was called out as a risk area in CFO J. Moeller's message to analysts in February 2009.

SECTOR: **Consumer Staples**
BETA COEFFICIENT: **.55**
10-YEAR COMPOUND EARNINGS PER SHARE GROWTH: **10.5%**
10-YEAR COMPOUND DIVIDENDS PER SHARE GROWTH: **11%**

		2008	2007	2006	2005	2004	2003	2002	2001	2000
Revenues (Mil)		83,503	76,476	68,222	56,741	51,407	43,377	40,238	39,244	39,951
Net Income (Mil)		12,075	10,340	8,684	7,257	6,481	5,186	4,352	2,922	4,230
Earnings per share		3.64	3.04	2.64	2.53	2.32	1.85	1.54	1.04	1.24
Dividends per share		1.45	1.28	1.15	1.03	0.93	0.82	0.76	0.70	0.64
Price	high	73.8	75.2	64.2	59.7	57.4	50.0	47.4	40.9	59.2
	low	54.9	60.4	52.8	51.2	48.9	39.8	37.1	28.0	26.4

AGGRESSIVE GROWTH

Raytheon Company

870 Winter Street ▫ Waltham, MA 02451 ▫ Phone: (781) 522–3000 ▫ Website: www.raytheon.com
▫ Ticker symbol: RTN ▫ Listed: NYSE ▫ S&P rating: A- ▫ Value Line financial strength rating: A+

Financial Highlights, Fiscal Year 2008

Raytheon's top line grew 8.8 percent year/year to $23.2B while earnings grew 13.6 percent to $1.67B. Earnings per share rose 19.3 percent to $3.95 as the company bought back 6.1 percent of its outstanding shares. Dividend yield grew to 1.9 percent on a 10 percent increase in declared dividends.

Funded backlog grew 6.7 percent to $22B, while total backlog grew 6.2 percent to $38.9B.

The U.S. government accounted for 87 percent of Raytheon's sales in FY2008, including foreign military sales. International customers constituted 20 percent of total sales in 2008.

Company Profile

Raytheon is a global leader in technology-driven solutions that pro-
vide integrated mission systems for the critical defense and nondefense needs of its customers. Raytheon's integrated businesses assure mission success with a broad range of products and services in government electronics, space, information technology, technical services, business, aviation, and special mission aircraft. Raytheon's businesses include:

- Integrated Defense Systems is Raytheon's leader in Joint Battlespace Integration, providing affordable, integrated solutions to a strong international and domestic customer base, including the U.S. Missile Defense Agency, the U.S. Armed Forces, and the Department of Homeland Security.

- Network Centric Systems Headquartered in McKinney, Texas, develops and produces mission solutions for networking, command and control, battlespace awareness, and air traffic management. Programs include civilian applications, command and control systems, integrated communications systems, and netted sensor systems. NCS serves all branches of the United States military, the National Guard, the Department of Homeland Security, the Federal Aviation Administration, and other U.S. national security agencies, as well as international customers.

- Intelligence and Information Systems (IIS) is a leading provider of intelligence and information solutions that provide the right knowledge at the right time, enabling our customers to make timely and accurate decisions to achieve mission goals of national significance.

- Raytheon Technical Services Company LLC (RTSC) provides technical, scientific, and professional services for defense, federal, and commercial customers worldwide. It specializes in Mission Support, counter-proliferation and counter-terrorism, base and range operations, and customized engineering services.

- Missile Systems designs, develops, and produces missile systems for critical requirements, including air-to-air, strike, surface Navy air defense, land combat missiles, guided projectiles, exo-atmospheric kill vehicles, and directed energy weapons.

- Space and Airborne Systems (SAS) is a leader in designing and developing integrated systems for crucial missions. For decades, Raytheon has supported military and civil customers with focused, forward-looking technology.

Reasons to Buy

The Department of Defense base budget has a compound annual growth rate (CAGR) of 7 percent from 2001 through 2009, where it totals $512B. Emergency funding for operations in Iraq and Afghanistan has risen from $63B in 2003 to $183B in FY2008, and Congress is expected to approve two more rounds of funding for FY2009. This represents a CAGR (through FY2008) of 24 percent.

The company sees significant growth opportunities from international markets. In 2008, growth in orders booked from international customers exceeded 13.4 percent.

Funding for the U.S. Department of Homeland Security has risen from $23B in FY2003 to $40B in FY2008, a CAGR of 9 percent.

The company has made free cash flow a focus of its strategy for financial health. The company will enter 2010 in a strong financial position with very good cash flow and a solid backlog. The company also has $1.3B remaining in authorized funds for stock repurchase which, if utilized, should reward investors for several years to come.

Reasons for Caution

The U.S. government's level of spending on economic reconstruction and a new political agenda under President Barack Obama may force cuts in defense spending in future years.

SECTOR: **Industrials**
BETA COEFFICIENT: **.70**
10-YEAR COMPOUND EARNINGS PER SHARE GROWTH: **1.0%**
10-YEAR COMPOUND DIVIDENDS PER SHARE GROWTH: **2.5%**

	2008	2007	2006	2005	2004	2003	2002	2001	2000
Revenues (Mil)	23,174	21,301	20,291	21,894	20,245	18,109	16,760	16,867	16,895
Net Income (Mil)	1,674	1,474	1,155	942	661	535	861	489	498
Earnings per share	3.95	3.80	2.56	2.08	1.49	1.29	2.15	1.35	1.46
Dividends per share	1.12	1.02	0.96	0.88	0.80	0.80	0.80	0.80	0.80
Price high	67.5	65.9	54.2	40.6	41.9	34.0	45.7	37.4	33.3
low	41.8	1.03	9.43	6.02	9.32	4.32	6.32	4.01	7.9

Ross Stores, Inc.

4440 Rosewood Drive ❏ Pleasanton, CA 94588-3050 ❏ Phone: (925) 965–4400 ❏ Website: www.rossstores.com ❏ Ticker symbol: ROST ❏ Listed: NASDAQ ❏ S&P rating: BBB ❏ Value Line financial strength rating: A

Financial Highlights, Fiscal Year 2008

Ross closed out FY2008 with record sales and earnings, improved comps, increased operating margins, reduced COGS (percentage basis), and a nice bump to the dividend. Not bad for a retailer operating in the midst of the lowest consumer confidence levels in decades.

Revenues grew 8.6 percent to $6.49B, with earnings advancing 17 percent to $261M. Gross margins rose 110 basis points (1.1 percent) to 25.8 percent, the net margin rose 30 basis points to 4.7 percent, and the dividend rose 25 percent to $0.40/ share. The company continued its 12-year trend of stock buyback, reducing outstanding shares by 6.9 million last year.

Company Profile

Ross Stores and its subsidiaries operate two chains of off-price retail apparel and home accessories stores. They ended FY2008 with a total of 956 stores, of which 904 were Ross Dress for Less locations in 27 states and Guam and 52 were dd's DISCOUNTS stores in four states. Just over half the company's stores are located in three states—California, Florida, and Texas.

Both chains target value-conscious women and men between the ages of 18 and 54. Ross's target customers are primarily from middle income households, while the dd's DISCOUNTS target customer is typically from more moderate income households. Merchandising, purchasing and pricing, and the locations of the stores, are all aimed at these customer bases. Ross offers first-quality, in-season, name-brand and designer apparel, accessories, footwear, and home fashions for the entire family at savings of 20 percent to 60 percent off department and specialty store regular prices. dd's DISCOUNTS features more moderately priced assortments of first-quality, in-season, name-brand fashion apparel, accessories, footwear, and home fashions for the entire family at everyday savings of 20 percent to 70 percent off moderate department and discount store regular prices.

Ross believes they derive a competitive advantage by offering a wide assortment of products within each of their merchandise categories in organized and easy-to-shop store environments.

Reasons to Buy

Traditionally, discount stores do well during a recession. Ross is no exception, having added a hundred stores and running 30 percent gross margins during the 2001 downturn. They've also done well during the most recent downturn, with another increase in gross margins and record profits in 2008. People have less money in their pockets and discount merchandisers have more products available at deeper discounts.

During the recovery after the worst of an economic downturn, though, it's not clear that all of these customers are returning to full-price stores for all of their shopping. Ross, TJX, and (to a lesser extent) Dollar Stores all posted solid growth for a full two years following the end of 2001. The discount stores may well be earning some permanent market share during these slowdowns, which would bode well for a good 2010–2011 for Ross.

Ross is improving their infrastructure, implementing information system enhancements and process changes to improve merchandising capabilities ("micro-merchandising"). The new tools are designed to strengthen their ability to plan, buy, and allocate at a more local versus regional level. They expect to complete the chain-wide rollout to all merchandise categories in fiscal 2010. The long-term objective of these investments is to fine tune merchandise offerings to address more localized customer preferences and thereby gradually increase sales productivity and gross profit margins in both newer and existing regions and markets.

Reasons for Caution

Ross has a high concentration of stores in two of the states hit worst by the recession: California and Florida. If the recession lasts well into 2010, consumers in these states may not be just switching to off-price stores, but may cut back purchases across the board. Additionally, as traditional retailers cut back on buying and fine tune inventories, less merchandise will be available for off-price retailers.

SECTOR: **Retail**
BETA COEFFICIENT: **.90**
10-YEAR COMPOUND EARNINGS PER SHARE GROWTH: **13.5%**
10-YEAR COMPOUND DIVIDENDS PER SHARE GROWTH: **21%**

		2008	2007	2006	2005	2004	2003	2002	2001	2000
Revenues (Mil)		6,486	5,975	5,570	4,944	4,240	3,920	3,351	2,987	2,709
Net Income (Mil)		305	261	242	200	180	228	201	155	152
Earnings per share		2.33	1.90	1.70	1.36	1.19	1.47	1.26	0.96	0.91
Dividends per share		0.40	0.32	0.26	0.22	0.18	0.13	0.10	0.09	0.08
Price	high	41.6	35.2	31.8	31.4	32.9	28.1	23.6	17.1	12.2
	low	21.2	24.4	22.1	22.3	21.0	16.3	15.9	8.3	6.0

Schlumberger Limited

5599 San Felipe, 17th Floor ❑ Houston, TX 77056 ❑ Phone: (713) 375–3535 ❑ Website: www.slb.com ❑
Ticker symbol: SLB ❑ Listed: NYSE ❑ S&P rating: A+ ❑ Value Line financial strength rating: A+

Financial Highlights, Fiscal Year 2008

Leading into one of the toughest business environments in the company's history, Schlumberger posted positive results for the year, growing revenues 17 percent to $27.2B. Earnings grew as well, up 5 percent to $7.01B, but earnings growth tapered off dramatically from 2007 and 2006, which saw increases of 31 and 77 percent, respectively.

All oilfield business segments grew by double-digits in 2008, and in particular Schlumberger's well services, drilling, and measurements operations grew substantially. Revenue from operations in Latin America increased 28 percent due to higher sales of Integrated Project Management products in its Central America and Peru/Colombia/Ecuador markets as well as higher offshore well services sales in its Brazil operations. Higher demand for oilfield services in Russia led to a 24 percent increase in 2008 revenue in Schlumberger's Europe/CIS/Africa market.

Company Profile

Schlumberger Limited is the world's leading oilfield services company supplying technology, information solutions, and integrated project management that optimize reservoir performance for customers in the oil and gas industry. Founded in 1926, today the company employs more than 76,000 people in eighty countries.

The company operates in two business segments:

Schlumberger Oilfield Services supplies a wide range of products and services from formation evaluation through directional drilling, well cementing and stimulation, well completions and productivity to consulting, software, information management, and IT infrastructure services that support core industry operational processes. WesternGeco, which accounted for 10 percent of the company's revenue, provides reservoir imaging, monitoring, and development services to land, marine, and shallow-water well projects.

Schlumberger manages its business through twenty-eight "GeoMarket" regions, which are grouped into five geographic areas: North America, Latin America, Europe, Commonwealth of Independent States and Africa, and Middle East and Asia. The GeoMarket structure offers customers a single point of contact at the local level for field operations and brings together geographically focused teams to meet local needs and deliver customized solutions.

The company was founded by the two Schlumberger brothers who invented wireline logging as a technique for obtaining downhole data in oil and gas wells. Today, it continues to build on its track record of providing leading-edge exploration and production technology. Schlumberger invests more each year in R&D than all other oilfield services companies combined.

Reasons to Buy

As the oil economy goes, so goes Schlumberger, and the oil economy in Q3'08 . . . well, you know the story by now. If not, one look at the stock's trading range for 2008 tells all. But let's not dwell on the past—you can't buy stocks there.

The big question with regard to Schlumberger, obviously, is—can they rebound? There's no question that they're a well-run company at the top of their game, but the problem is that they (and their customers) have been whipsawed by swings in oil and natural gas prices in the last twelve months. Oil has gone from over $145/bbl to under $35/bbl and now to $70; the rapid development that took place when prices were high has led to a glut of natural gas in the marketplace and similarly collapsing prices.

Fortunately, Schlumberger has seen boom/bust cycles before. This is not, as they say in Texas, their first rodeo. Schlumberger has thrived by diversifying their business both geographically and over the lifecycle of a producing resource, giving them the ability to provide services throughout a worldwide expansion/contraction cycle.

Also, unlike a lot of players in the oil business, they've been prudent with their money. Income from the boom years has been used to fund selected acquisitions of companies that operate only in their core business segment. They've also plowed money back into the company in the form of increased spending on R&D, returned it to the shareholders in increased dividends (up over 110 percent since 2004), set it aside for share repurchase ($8B approved through 2011), and retained it as cash (Schlumberger exited 2008 with $3.7B on-hand).

Most analysts expect the oil economy to resume growth in mid-2010. Schlumberger will see the effects of that rebound first, so 2010 should be a good year overall for them. International presence is also a strength.

Reasons for Caution

This is the oil business. Rapid changes in the world economy, geopolitical trends, the global environment . . . all have major effects on the supply and demand for petroleum and natural gas. Pure oil plays have always been high-risk and high-return, and Schlumberger's customers are all part of that world.

SECTOR: **Energy**
BETA COEFFICIENT: **1.20**
10-YEAR COMPOUND EARNINGS PER SHARE GROWTH: **13%**
10-YEAR COMPOUND DIVIDENDS PER SHARE GROWTH: **6%**

	2008	2007	2006	2005	2004	2003	2002	2001	2000
Revenues (Mil)	27,163	23,277	19,230	14,309	11,480	13,893	13,474	13,746	9,611
Net Income (Mil)	5,397	5,177	3,747	2,022	1,236	911	694	809	735
Earnings per share	4.42	4.18	3.04	1.67	1.03	0.78	0.60	0.71	0.64
Dividends per share	0.81	0.70	0.48	0.41	0.38	0.38	0.38	0.38	0.38
Price high	112.0	114.8	74.8	51.5	34.9	28.1	31.2	41.4	44.4
low	37.1	56.3	47.9	31.6	26.3	17.8	16.7	20.4	26.8

AGGRESSIVE GROWTH

Sigma–Aldrich Corporation

3050 Spruce Street ▫ St. Louis, MO 63103 ▫ Phone: (314) 771–5765 ▫ Website: www.Sigma-Aldrich.com
▫ Ticker symbol: SIAL ▫ Listed: NASDAQ ▫ S&P rating: A ▫ Value Line financial strength rating: A

Financial Highlights, Fiscal Year 2008

Sales for FY2008 grew 9 percent to $2.2B, with earnings tracking at just under 10 percent growth to 342M. Operating margins fell slightly, 60 basis, or 0.6 percent, points to 27.4 percent, dividends increased 13 percent to $.52 per share, and the company repurchased 10 million shares of stock, but the company ended the year with good liquidity ($227M in cash).

The company announced a number of new partnerships during the year that will expand its portfolio of antibodies available for cell research. In June it entered into a five-year collaboration to develop optimal cell lines for the production of monoclonal antibodies. Scientists at the University of California, San Francisco will lead the research into antibodies for a variety of cancer targets, autoimmune diseases, stem cell characteristics, and commonly neglected disease targets. The company also announced a partnership to distribute the highly validated Prestige antibodies powered by Atlas Antibodies, the commercial arm of the Human Proteome Resource. Sigma-Aldrich is also collaborating with AbD Serotec, a Division of MorphoSys, to design, produce, and distribute unique recombinant research antibodies using MorphoSys's proprietary HuCAL GOLD technology.

Company Profile

Sigma-Aldrich is a manufacturer and reseller of chemicals used in research and large-scale manufacturing activities. The company sells over 100,000 chemicals, about half of which it manufactures internally. They also stock over 30,000 laboratory equipment items. Most of the company's 88,000 customer accounts are research institutions that use basic laboratory essentials like solvents, reagents, and other supplies. The company also sells chemicals in large quantities to pharmaceutical companies, but no single account provided more than 2 percent of Sigma-Aldrich's total sales in 2008. Sigma-Aldrich's business model is to provide their generic and specialized products with expedited (in most cases, next day) delivery.

Sigma-Aldrich operates four business units, each catering to a separate class of customer and product. Research Essentials sells common lab chemicals and supplies such as biological buffers, cell culture reagents, biochemicals, solvents, reagents, and other lab kits to customers in all sectors. Research Specialties sells organic chemicals, biochemicals, analytical reagents, chromatography consumables, reference materials, and high-purity products. Research Biochemicals provides "first to market products" to high end biotech labs, selling immunochemical, molecular biology, cell signaling, and neuroscience biochemicals. Fine Chemicals fills large-scale orders of organic chemicals and biochemicals used for production in the pharmaceutical, biotechnology, and the high-tech electronics industry.

The company's biochemical and organic chemical products and kits are used in scientific and genomic research, biotechnology, pharmaceutical development, the diagnosis of disease, and as key components in pharmaceutical and other high technology manufacturing. Sigma–Aldrich has customers in life science companies, university and government institutions, hospitals, and industry. The company operates in thirty-six countries and has over 7,900 employees providing service in 165 countries worldwide. Nearly half their sales were to U.S. customers; one third to Canada, Asia Pacific, and Latin America; and the rest to Europe.

Reasons to Buy

Sigma-Aldrich turned in another solid year of growth in revenues and earnings, despite the financial uncertainties that plagued most industries in the last half of 2008. No company is recession-proof, but S-A's customer base is heavily research-oriented, and many are on firm multiyear budgets. As a consequence, their revenues are less exposed to the vagaries of the purely commercial markets. Federal outlays for research should increase under the Obama administration on top of a 16 percent increase in the National Science Foundation budget in 2009.

Sigma-Aldrich's performance in 2008 extended its record to thirty-four consecutive years of continuous growth in sales and earnings per share for the chemical business. All business units and geographic regions contributed to sales growth. Their return on equity of 22.8 percent exceeded their long-term goal of 20 percent for the sixth consecutive year. The company's financial position remained strong, with a debt to capital ratio of 34.6 percent at December 31, 2008. Operating cash flow again exceeded $400 million.

Reasons for Caution

In mid-2009, the company's shares have rebounded well, to nearly $50/ share and are trading at multiples in the high-teens. Earnings in 2009 should not disappoint, but it may be hard to call this stock "a bargain waiting for a recovery."

SECTOR: **Industrials**
BETA COEFFICIENT: **.95**
10-YEAR COMPOUND EARNINGS PER SHARE GROWTH: **11.5%**
10-YEAR COMPOUND DIVIDENDS PER SHARE GROWTH: **14%**

	2008	2007	2006	2005	2004	2003	2002	2001	2000
Revenues (Mil)	2,201	2,039	1,798	1,667	1,409	1,298	1,207	1,179	1,096
Net Income (Mil)	342	311	276	258	233	193	131	141	139
Earnings per share	2.65	2.34	2.05	1.88	1.67	1.34	0.89	0.94	0.83
Dividends per share	0.52	0.46	0.42	0.38	0.26	0.21	0.17	0.17	0.16
Price high	63.0	56.6	39.7	33.6	30.8	29.0	26.4	25.7	20.4
low	34.3	37.4	31.3	27.7	26.6	20.5	19.1	18.1	10.1

Southern Company

30 Ivan Allen Jr. Boulevard NW ◻ Atlanta, GA 30308 ◻ Phone: (404) 506–5000 ◻ Website: www
.southernco.com ◻ Listed: NYSE ◻ Ticker Symbol: SO ◻ S&P Rating: BBB+ ◻ Value Line financial strength
rating: A

Financial Highlights, Fiscal Year 2008

"Southern Company Reports Solid Earnings for 2008 Despite Weak Economy, Mild Weather": Now, as we emerge from the 2008–2009 stock market disaster, isn't that a headline we'd all like to hear about a company we own? That's the appeal of a company like SO.

For 2008, the company really reported essentially flat results, but in a year like this, flat can be pretty solid. The company earned $1.74B or $2.26 a share, compared to 41.73B or $2.29 a share the year before, that despite the spike in energy prices that occurred during 2008. If you were to exclude some special items, the company actually earned $2.37 a share in 2008. Revenues increased some 11.6 percent to $17.1B during the year.

Part of the reason for the steady performance, other than the typically steady performance generic to all utilities, is that SO does most of its business in the U.S. Southeast, an area overall less vulnerable to the economic downturn. That said, a noticeable downturn in electric usage started late in the year. The company's own residential and commercial base saw a decrease in kilowatt-hour usage on the order of 2.0 percent, but wholesale energy sales limited the total kilowatt-hour sales to a decrease 0.8 percent from 2007. The company is adjusting to it by managing costs closely; a recent layoff reduced fixed costs by some $40M.

Company Profile

Through its four primary operating subsidiaries Georgia Power, Alabama Power, Mississippi Power, and Gulf Power, Southern Company serves some 4.4 million customers in a large area of Georgia, Alabama, Mississippi, northern Florida, and parts of the Carolinas. The company also wholesales power to other utilities in a wider area.

The revenue mix is balanced: 33 percent residential, 31 percent commercial, 21 percent industrial, 13 percent other. The service area includes the Atlanta metropolitan area and a large base of modern manufacturing facilities like the many Asian-owned manufacturing facilities in the region. The fuel mix is more diverse and less vulnerable to price fluctuations than some, with 64 percent coal, 16 percent oil and gas, 14 percent nuclear, and 1 percent hydroelectric. That said, with the amount of coal-fired plants SO must work to stay up with environmental regulations and pay close attention to transportation costs.

The company also has engaged in telecommunications services, operating as a regional wireless carrier in Alabama, Georgia, southeastern Mississippi, and northwest Florida and operating some fiber optic networks collocated on company rights of way. The company also provides consulting services to other utilities.

Reasons to Buy

Southern serves a growing, diverse, and somewhat recession-resistant customer base. There is no dominant industry in the region, the ups and downs of which have to be contended with.

The company has been a very steady earner and dividend payer for years. Dividends increased every year since 2001; however, payout ratio remains at a relatively high 70 percent of total earnings. That said, the 5.6 percent yield (mid-2009) is attractive in today's environment.

For those who like steady rocks to cling to in a stock market storm, SO stock is resistant to market moves with a beta of only 0.37. Stated differently, the stock was only off 12 percent from its comparable 2008 level, and the year's trading range, for a $31 stock, was between $26.50 and $40.

Reasons for Caution

Electric utilities are always subject to rate and other forms of regulation, and one never knows what will happen in that arena. Additionally, utilities are always vulnerable to capital costs and the attractiveness of alternative fixed income investments, and are sensitive to rising interest rates, especially if they rise quickly. Finally, all electric utilities are exposed to new environmental regulations and the need to replace aging infrastructure.

SECTOR: **Utilities**
BETA COEFFICIENT: **0.37**
10-YEAR COMPOUND EARNINGS PER SHARE GROWTH: **3.0%**
10-YEAR COMPOUND DIVIDENDS PER SHARE GROWTH: **2.0%**

		2008	2007	2006	2005	2004	2003	2002	2001	2000
Revenues (Mil)		17,127	15,353	14,356	13,554	11,902	11,251	10,549	10,155	10,066
Net Income (Mil)		1,807	1,782	1,608	1,621	1,589	1,602	1,510	1,306	1,501
Earnings per share		2.25	2.28	2.10	2.13	2.06	1.97	1.85	1.61	2.10
Dividends per share		1.66	1.60	1.54	1.48	1.42	1.39	1.36	1.34	1.34
Price	high	40.6	39.3	37.4	36.5	34.0	32.0	31.1	35.7	35.0
	low	29.8	33.2	30.5	31.1	27.4	27.0	23.2	20.9	20.4

St. Jude Medical, Inc.

One Lillehei Plaza □ St. Paul, MN 55117 □ Phone: (651) 766–3029 □ Website: www.sjm.com □ Listed: NYSE □ Ticker symbol: STJ □ S&P rating: B+ □ Value Line financial strength rating: A

Financial Highlights, Fiscal Year 2008

In 2008, St. Jude saw sales grow 15.4 percent to $4.36B, while unadjusted earnings grew 23.6 percent to $807M. Earnings adjusted primarily for the In-Process R&D associated with the MediGuide acquisition and various other items netted earnings to $384M, or a decline of 31.3 percent.

Operating margin grew 90 basis points to 29.5 percent, and (unadjusted) net margin grew 120 basis points to 18.5 percent. Not uncommon for a growth-oriented, research-driven company, no dividend was paid. All in all though, it was another very strong year financially for St. Jude.

The company made two acquisitions to augment their Atrial Fibrillation segment: EP MedSystems, which provides them an entry into two new market segments, and MediGuide, which has produced technology that provides for improved intra-body navigation during invasive procedures.

Another acquisition, Radi Medical Systems AB, expands the company's reach into two areas of the cardiovascular procedures market.

Company Profile

St. Jude Medical, Inc., is dedicated to the design, manufacture, and distribution of cardiovascular medical devices including pacemakers, implantable cardioverter defibrillators (ICDs), vascular closure devices, catheters, and heart valves.

Their Cardiac Rhythm Management therapy portfolio (62 percent of SJM 2008 revenue) includes products for treating heart rhythm disorders—including atrial fibrillation—as well as heart failure. Its products include ICDs, pacemaker systems, and a variety of diagnostic and therapeutic electrophysiology catheters.

Atrial Fibrillation (AF) is the world's most common cardiac arrhythmia, affecting more than 5 million people worldwide. It reduces the normal output of the heart, is a known risk factor for stroke, is often associated with heart failure, and can greatly impair a person's quality of life. AF is encountered by all of the company's physician customers and remains one of the most difficult conditions for the medical profession to treat.

In addition to its electrophysiology catheters, the company develops catheter technologies for the Cardiology/Vascular Access therapy area. Those products include hemostasis introducers, catheters, and a leading vascular closure device.

In Cardiac Surgery therapy, the company has been the global leader in mechanical heart valve technology for more than twenty-five years. St. Jude

Medical also develops a line of tissue valves and valve-repair products. In 2003, the company expanded its presence in cardiac surgery with a minority investment in Epicor Medical, Inc., which is developing a surgical approach for atrial fibrillation.

Finally, the company's Neuromodulation segment produces neurostimulation products, which are implantable devices for use primarily in chronic pain management.

St. Jude Medical products are sold in more than 120 countries. The company has twenty principal operations and manufacturing facilities around the world.

Reasons to Buy

Most project St. Jude to grow both top and bottom lines, as much as 9 percent/year in revenue and 12 percent/year in earnings through the end of 2010.

Since Medicare's approval of the use of neurostimulation devices for pain management, St. Jude's Neurostimulation segment has grown rapidly, last year turning in over 21 percent growth year to year. The company's atrial fibrillation line has been extremely well received, with sales growing nearly 69 percent over the period 2006–2008.

Few of St. Jude's products are likely to come under the restrictions of any new federal health-care guidelines,

as their products target or are used to target life-threatening conditions, none of which involve discretionary procedures. The only non-life-threatening condition addressed by St. Jude is chronic pain, and their neuromodulation products have proven to be cost effective and otherwise preferable to alternative treatments.

On April 9, 2008, Standard & Poor's Stock Reports awarded St. Jude a BUY rating. Robert M. Gold said, "We are concerned about the sluggishness that we see throughout ICD markets. However, we think the global ICD market can grow by about 7 percent in 2008, and we expect faster growth from St. Jude as it continues to gain market share."

On May 29, 2009, Erik A. Antonson of Value Line Investment Survey wrote: "We like this issue. It is ranked favorably for timeliness and offers above-average three- to five-year capital gains potential. . . . Double-digit annual growth over the long haul appears attainable."

Reasons for Caution

The MediGuide acquisition may have been a bit of a reach. St. Jude essentially took an impairment in the current year of over $300M due to the fact that the technology acquired was not ready for market and may not be for another two to three years, if ever.

SECTOR: **Health Care**
BETA COEFFICIENT: **.80**
10-YEAR COMPOUND EARNINGS PER SHARE GROWTH: **18.0%**
10-YEAR COMPOUND DIVIDENDS PER SHARE GROWTH: **no dividend**

		2008	2007	2006	2005	2004	2003	2002	2001	2000
Revenues (Mil)		4,363	3,779	3,302	2,915	2,294	1,932	1,590	1,347	1,179
Net Income (Mil)		807	652	548	394	410	339	276	203	156
Earnings per share		2.31	1.85	1.47	1.04	1.10	0.92	0.76	0.57	0.46
Dividends per share		Nil								
Price	high	48.5	48.1	54.8	52.8	42.9	32.0	21.6	19.5	15.6
	low	25.0	34.9	31.2	34.5	29.9	19.4	15.3	11.1	5.9

AGGRESSIVE GROWTH

Staples, Inc.

500 Staples Drive □ Framingham, MA 01702 □ Phone: (800) 468–7751 □ Website: www.staples.com
□ Listed: NASDAQ □ Ticker symbol: SPLS □ S&P rating: B+ □ Value Line financial strength rating: A+

Financial Highlights, Fiscal Year 2008

Staples had two stories to tell for 2008. One, the full-year organic business results, and the other, inclusive of the results following the $4.8B purchase of Corporate Express, concluded on July 2, 2008.

The results from ongoing operations showed declines in net sales of 2.7 percent, driven mainly by a decline in North American comps (comparable same store sales) of 9 percent. Also down were North American Delivery (down 0.3 percent) and International Operations (down 0.1 percent in local currency).

Including the contribution of Corporate Express, things look significantly better. Sales growth jumps to 19.2 percent (to a record $23.1B). North American Delivery grew sales 35 percent, and International Operations grew 70.4 percent.

Looking at the consolidated numbers, earnings fell 7.1 percent to $923M, earnings per share fell 10 percent to $1.29, and net margins fell 22 percent to 4.0 percent. Some of this can be attributed to acquisition costs, but the bulk of the decline is due to the drop in organic sales.

Company Profile

Staples, Inc., launched the office supplies superstore industry with the opening of its first store in Brighton (near Boston), Massachusetts, in May 1986. Its goal was to provide small business owners the same low prices on office supplies previously enjoyed only by large corporations.

Staples is now a $16 billion retailer of office supplies, business services, furniture, and technology to consumers and businesses from home-based businesses to *Fortune* 500 companies in 27 countries throughout North and South America, Europe, Asia and Australia.

Staples is the largest operator of office stores in the world, with 2,218 stores of all types. It also supplies through mail order catalogs, e-commerce and a contract business.

The company operates three business segments: North American Retail, North American Delivery, and European operations. The company's North American Retail segment consists of the company's U.S. and Canadian business units that sell office products, supplies, and services.

Staples North American Delivery segment consists of the company's U.S. and Canadian contract, catalog, and Internet business units that sell and deliver office products, supplies, and services directly to customers.

Staples European Operations segment consists of the company's business units, which operate 383 retail stores in the United Kingdom, Germany, the Netherlands, Portugal, and Belgium. The company also sells and delivers office products and supplies directly to businesses throughout the rest of Europe. The company's delivery operations comprise the catalog business (Staples Direct and Quill Corporation), the contract stationer business (Staples National Advantage and Staples Business Advantage), and the Internet e-commerce business (Staples.com). Quill, acquired in 1998, is a direct mail catalog business, serving more than one million medium-sized businesses in the United States.

At the retail level, stores operate under the names "Staples–The Office Superstore" and "Staples Express." The prototype store had, up until recently, about 24,000 square feet of sales space, which the company reduced to 20,000 in fiscal 2003. Stores carry about 8,500 stock items.

Express stores are much smaller, with between 6,000 and 10,000 square feet of sales space. They also handle fewer items, generally about 6,000, and are situated in downtown business sectors. By contrast, the larger units tend to be situated in the suburbs.

Sales by product are: North American Retail, 41 percent; North American Delivery, 38 percent; and International, 21 percent. Sales by product line are: office supplies and services, 47 percent; business machines and telecommunications services, 28 percent; computers and related products, 18 percent; and office furniture, 7 percent.

Reasons to Buy

The Corporate Express deal, at first contentious, turned friendly as the offers increased to the eventual selling price. As a result, most of the CE management remained in place and the transition went smoothly. A full year of CE revenue contribution should add another $4B to Staples's top line, and Gary Balter at Credit Suisse Global expects the deal to save the combined companies $250M in costs over the next three years.

In terms of revenue, Staples is now roughly twice the size of its nearest competitor, Office Depot, and nearly three times the size of the next largest player, OfficeMax. Additionally, Staples is far more profitable than either of its competitors.

Reasons for Caution

Consumer (and corporate) spending has been soft for the better part of a year and looks to remains so throughout 2009. Saturation in

North America is also a risk, as many existing cities and suburbs have all the office supply superstore coverage they need. Growth in international segments and in smaller-format stores is key. This stock may be better viewed as one with longer-term potential, but is none-the-less the dominant player in its market.

SECTOR: **Retail**
BETA COEFFICIENT: **1.15**
10-YEAR COMPOUND EARNINGS PER SHARE GROWTH: **17.5%**
10-YEAR COMPOUND DIVIDENDS PER SHARE GROWTH: *

	2008	2007	2006	2005	2004	2003	2002	2001	2000
Revenues (Mil)	23,084	19,373	18,161	16,079	14,448	13,181	11,596	10,744	10,674
Net Income (Mil)	924	996	974	834	708	552	417	307	264
Earnings per share	1.29	1.38	1.32	1.04	0.93	0.75	0.63	0.44	0.39
Dividends per share	.33	0.29	0.17	0.13	Nil				
Price: high	26.6	27.7	28.0	24.1	22.5	18.6	15.0	13.0	19.2
low	13.6	19.7	21.1	18.6	15.8	10.5	7.8	7.3	6.9

*Dividends paid only since 2004.

Starbucks Corporation

2401 Utah Avenue South ◻ Seattle, WA 98134 ◻ Phone: (206) 447–1575 ◻ Website: www.starbucks.com
◻ Listed: NASDAQ ◻ Ticker symbol: SBUX ◻ S&P rating: BBB ◻ Value Line financial strength rating: A

Financial Highlights, Fiscal Year 2008

For 2008, Starbucks posted a revenue increase of 10 percent to $10.4B and earnings of $315M, a 53.2 percent drop from the previous year. The earnings include a one-time pre-tax adjustment of $267M for restructuring (store closings)—without that accounting, earnings would have netted to $582M, a 13.5 percent decrease year over year.

Gross margins (16.3 percent), operating margins (11.9 percent), and net margins (5.1 percent) are all at 10-year lows, although cash flow remains strong at $1.46/share, off just 3 percent from the previous year.

Same-store sales (those open more than 13 months) were off 3 percent, the first year-to-year drop in the company's history. The company responded with plans to close 600 stores in the U.S. through 2009, and later added 300 more for a total of 900 closings.

Company Profile

Starbucks Corporation, formed in 1985, today is the leading retailer, roaster, and brand of specialty coffee in the world. The company sells whole bean coffees through its specialty sales group, mail-order business, supermarkets, and online. The company has 7,138 company-owned stores in the United States and 2,048 in international markets, in addition to 7,689 licensed stores worldwide. Retail sales constitute the bulk of its revenue. They also have joint ventures with Pepsi-Cola and Dreyer's to develop bottled coffee drinks and ice creams, and a partnership with Kraft Foods to distribute coffee in grocery stores. All channels outside the company-operated retail stores are collectively known as specialty operations.

The company's retail goal is to become the leading retailer and brand of coffee in each of its target markets through product quality and by providing a unique Starbucks experience, which the company defines as a third place beyond home and work. The "experience" is built upon superior customer service and a clean, well-maintained retail store that reflects the personality of the community in which it operates, thereby building a high degree of customer loyalty.

Starbucks's strategy for expanding its retail business is to increase its market share by selectively opening additional stores in existing markets and opening stores in new markets to support its long-term strategic objectives.

Starbucks retail stores are typically located in high-traffic, high-visibility locations. Because the company can vary the size and format, its stores are located in or near a variety of settings, including downtown and suburban retail centers, office buildings, and university campuses.

The company's specialty operations strive to develop the Starbucks brand outside the company-operated retail store environment through a number of channels, with a strategy to reach customers where they work, travel, shop, and dine. The strategy employs various models, including licensing arrangements, foodservice accounts and other initiatives related to the company's core businesses.

In its licensed retail store operations, the company leverages the expertise of its local partners and shares Starbucks operating and store development experience. Most licensees are prominent retailers with in-depth market knowledge and access. As part of these arrangements, Starbucks receives license fees and royalties and sells coffee, tea, and related products for resale in licensed locations.

During fiscal 2008, 438 Starbucks licensed retail stores were opened in the United States and, as of September 28, 2008, the company's U.S. licensees operated 4,329 stores. During fiscal 2008, 550 International licensed stores were opened. At September 28, 2008, the company's International operating segment had a total of 3,134 licensed retail stores. Product sales to and royalty and license fee revenues from U.S. and International licensed retail stores accounted for nearly half of Starbucks's specialty revenues in 2008.

Reasons to Buy

The company recognizes that its diminishing returns on capital are due largely to its over-expansion at a time of declining consumer confidence. The steps they have taken (closing of underperforming stores, job elimination, and other infrastructure-based cost cutting) seem necessary and appropriate. The one thing they should not do, and which they have not done, is to diminish the brand in any way at all. Existing retail stores will provide the same (and even enhanced) experience and will serve the same quality products; licensees will continue to receive Starbucks training and will operate under the same guidelines as before; new stores will continue to open in prime locations as appropriate.

When the company announced that they would be closing hundreds of stores, angry customers organized to protest the action. This is the sort of brand loyalty that most companies can only dream about. Will Starbucks's stock return to the days when it was able to maintain P/E ratios in the mid-40s for years on end? That's not clear, but the company is far and away the leader in its market, with a loyal customer base in the United States and a steadily growing presence in Europe and Asia. For all intents and purposes, Starbucks has replaced the corner lounge and restaurant forever for a number of population segments, from young people to businesspeople to mommies caring for their children during the day. The stock appears to be a solid long-term candidate with very good near-term turnaround potential. The current negative investor sentiment appears to underestimate the long-term value of this brand and franchise.

Reasons for Caution

During this recession, discretionary spending has taken a hit. And even though folks still have to get their jolt of coffee, many are getting by with less. Same store sales have continued to decline in early 2009 even as Starbucks is closing the lower-performing stores. There could be more closings ahead, with associated charges and reductions in revenue. Let's hope it's not a double shot this time around.

SECTOR: **Restaurant**
BETA COEFFICIENT: **1.10**
10-YEAR COMPOUND EARNINGS PER SHARE GROWTH: **24.5%**
10-YEAR COMPOUND DIVIDENDS PER SHARE GROWTH: *****

		2008	2007	2006	2005	2004	2003	2002	2001	2000
Revenues (Mil)		10,383	9,412	7,787	6,369	5,294	4,076	3,289	2,649	2,169
Net Income (Mil)		525	673	519	495	392	268	218	181	137
Earnings per share		0.71	0.87	0.73	0.61	0.48	0.34	0.28	0.23	0.18
Dividends per share										
Price	high	21.0	36.6	40.0	32.5	32.1	16.7	12.9	12.8	12.7
	low	7.1	19.9	28.7	22.3	16.5	9.8	9.2	6.7	5.8

Stryker Corporation

P.O. Box 4085 ❑ Kalamazoo, MI 49003–4085 ❑ Phone: (616) 385–2600 ❑ Website: www.strykercorp.com ❑ Listed: NYSE ❑ Ticker symbol: SYK ❑ S&P rating: A+ ❑ Value Line financial strength rating: A++

Financial Highlights, Fiscal Year 2008

The company reported sales of $6.72B, a 12 percent increase over the prior year. Fully diluted net earnings were $1.15B, a 16.3 percent increase over FY2007, and representing a net margin of 17.1 percent. International sales grew at a slightly higher rate than did domestic sales.

Earnings per share rose 17.3 percent to $2.78, and dividends rose 21.2 percent to $0.40 per share.

Six of the company's eight core businesses achieved industry-leading growth rates, their best-ever company performance.

During the year the company repurchased 17.4 million shares of common stock at a cost of $1.0B in the open market.

Company Profile

Stryker Corporation was founded in 1941 by Dr. Homer H. Stryker, a leading orthopedic surgeon and the inventor of several orthopedic products. The company now ranks as a dominant player in a $12 billion global orthopedics industry. SYK has a significant market share in such sectors as artificial hips, prosthetic knees, and trauma products.

Stryker develops, manufactures, and markets specialty surgical and medical products worldwide. These products include orthopedic implants, trauma systems, powered surgical instruments, endoscopic systems, and patient care and handling equipment.

In addition to replacement parts sales, Stryker's Physiotherapy Associates division provides physical, occupational, and speech therapy to orthopedic and neurology patients in over 400 clinics worldwide. The physical therapy business represents a solid complementary business for Stryker, in view of the high number of its surgeon customers who prescribe physical therapy following orthopedic surgery.

Stryker's revenue is split roughly 60/40 among Implants and Equipment and 64/36 domestic and international. In terms of Medical Technology sales alone, Stryker is the tenth largest supplier in the world and are number one in sales in the $35.6B orthopedic market. They are also number one (by a 3/1 margin) in the $3.3B worldwide operating room equipment market, and a strong number two in the $1.9B patient handling market.

A major component of Stryker's success is the optimal use of resources in manufacturing and distribution. Taking advantage of information technology and leading-edge work-flow management practices, the company monitors quality and service levels at its sixteen plants throughout North America and Europe for continuous improvement. This attention to operations has resulted in the inclusion of Stryker facilities in the elite *Industry Week* "Best Plants" list twice in the last three years. The Stryker Instruments plant in Kalamazoo, Michigan, was named one of the best plants in 2000, and the Howmedica Osteonics facility in Allendale, New Jersey, was honored in 1998.

Reasons to Buy

The company just can't seem to stop turning in double-digit gains in revenue. FY2008 was the eighth year in a row for this accomplishment, a number matched by only a few companies in the *Fortune* 500. Over the same period, the company's CAGR in earnings is close to 24 percent, so it isn't just growth at the expense of profitability.

The company's projection for FY2009 reads as follows: "The Company continues to face depressed demand for certain MedSurg Equipment products due to the general economic slowdown. In addition, the Company anticipates that a slowdown in elective procedures for certain of its Orthopaedic Implants products may occur. The Company projects that diluted net earnings per share for 2009 will be in the range of $3.12 to $3.22, an increase of 10 percent to 14 percent over adjusted diluted net earnings per share from

continuing operations of $2.83 in 2008. The financial forecast for 2009 anticipates a constant currency net sales increase in the range of 6 percent to 9 percent. If foreign currency exchange rates hold near January 31, 2009, levels, the Company anticipates an unfavorable impact on net sales of approximately 4.0 percent to 4.5 percent in the first quarter of 2009 and an unfavorable impact on net sales of approximately 3.5 percent to 4.5 percent for the full year of 2009."

So there you have it. If the current economic slowdown continues and sales are impacted as much as 4.5 percent over the full year, per-share earnings will only increase 10 to 14 percent year over year. This may be the best worst-case scenario in this book.

Reasons for Caution

If the new administration's healthcare initiatives impact the overall rate of medical spending, reimbursements for the types of procedures that use Stryker products may be reduced. It's too soon to say, however, what those initiatives are likely to be, nor can we predict with any certainty the likelihood of their passage through Congress.

SECTOR: **Health Care**
BETA COEFFICIENT: **.80**
10-YEAR COMPOUND EARNINGS PER SHARE GROWTH: **22.5%**
10-YEAR COMPOUND DIVIDENDS PER SHARE GROWTH: **20.5%**

		2008	2007	2006	2005	2004	2003	2002	2001	2000
Revenues (Mil)		6,718	6,001	5,406	4,872	4,262	3,625	3,012	2,602	2,289
Net Income (Mil)		1,148	1,017	778	644	586	454	346	272	221
Earnings per share		2.78	2.44	1.89	1.57	1.43	1.12	0.88	0.67	0.55
Dividends per share		0.33	0.22	0.11	0.11	0.09	0.07	0.05	0.04	0.035
Price	high	74.9	76.9	55.9	56.3	57.7	42.7	33.8	31.3	28.9
	low	35.4	54.9	39.8	39.7	40.3	29.9	21.9	21.7	12.2

CONSERVATIVE GROWTH

Sysco Corporation

1390 Enclave Parkway □ Houston, TX 77077–2099 □ Phone: (281) 584–1458 □ Website: www.sysco.com
□ Listed: NYSE □ Ticker symbol: SYY □ S&P rating: AA- □ Value Line financial strength rating: A++

Financial Highlights, Fiscal Year 2008

Sales grew 7 percent year/year, identical to the previous year's gains. Sysco now has thirty-eight consecutive years of sales growth. Operating income grew 10 percent, a decline from the previous year's 14 percent.

Cash from operating activities grew 13.8 percent over 2007, helping to fund a number of cost-cutting initiatives while maintaining margins.

Net earnings grew 10 percent to a record $1.1B, while per-share earnings grew 13 percent to $1.81, as the company repurchased nearly 17 million shares of stock. Dividends rose 14 percent to $.82/share.

Company Profile

Sysco was founded in 1969 with the goal of becoming a national food-service network. By 1977, the company had become the leading food-service supplier in North America, a position they have retained for over thirty years. They conduct business in over 100 countries.

Most people are unaware of just how many times during the day they cross paths with Sysco's products and services. As the continent's largest marketer and distributor of food-service products, Sysco operates 150 distribution facilities across the United States and Canada. Their eighty-four Broadline facilities supply independent and chain restaurants and other food preparation facilities. They have seventeen hotel supply locations, sixteen specialty produce facilities, fifteen SYGMA distribution centers (specialized, high-volume centers supplying to chain restaurants), twelve custom-cutting meat locations, and two distributors specializing in the niche Asian food-service market.

The company also supplies the lodging industry with guest amenities, equipment, housekeeping supplies, room accessories, and textiles.

These distribution facilities provide over 360,000 different food and related products to over 400,000 restaurants, hotels, schools, hospitals, retirement homes, hotels, and other locations where food is prepared to be eaten on the premises or taken away.

Sysco is by far the largest company in the food-service distribution industry. The company estimates that they serve about 16 percent of a $231B annual market. In sales, Sysco dwarfs its two chief competitors, U.S. Foodservice and Performance Food Group,

Reasons to Buy

Sysco keeps margins high by selling products under its own label, a strategy it began a year after its founding. It saves on national advertising and passes some of the savings along to its customers. Its private-label business carries an estimated 24 percent gross margin, or 10 percent more than it earns on national brands. This is a very healthy figure in the food industry.

As tough as the current economic conditions are for Sysco, they are likely even worse for Sysco's far smaller competitors. This may create a number of attractive buying opportunities for the company, perhaps expanding both its product lines and its geographical coverage. For example, in 2008 the company acquired Austin Tatum, a hotel amenity supplier based in Hong Kong.

Another example: Sysco announced in March 2009 that they had acquired their first broadline distributor outside North America, paying an undisclosed amount for Irish food-service supplier Pallas, which in FY2008 generated approximately $200M in revenues.

The company recently completed its implementation of a Transportation Management System, which has so far resulted in increased efficiencies both inbound and outbound: forecasting and inventory management has improved, truck turnaround is faster, cases per truck trip grew 1.6 percent, and their broadline fleet drove nearly 10 million fewer delivery miles in 2008 due to the TMS initiatives.

In the past two years Sysco's two largest competitors were bought and taken private by private equity firms. Depending on how these acquisitions play out for the purchaser, this could result in either of two possible benefits to Sysco shareholders: If things go well, Sysco could become a target for a buyout or, if not, Sysco may be able to buy market share on the cheap as the holding companies (potentially) leave the business by divesting of the former competitors.

Reasons for Caution

As the economic decline continues, people are eating out less often and restaurants and hotels are buying fewer supplies and equipment. Value Line analyst George Niemond predicts a full-year decline in sales in earnings, the first for Sysco in thirty-eight years.

SECTOR: **Consumer Staples**
BETA COEFFICIENT: **.65**
10-YEAR COMPOUND EARNINGS PER SHARE GROWTH: **14%**
10-YEAR COMPOUND DIVIDENDS PER SHARE GROWTH: **17.5%**

	2008	2007	2006	2005	2004	2003	2002	2001	2000
Revenues (Mil)	37,522	35,042	32,628	30,282	29,335	26,140	23,351	21,784	19,303
Net Income (Mil)	1,106	1,001	855	961	907	778	680	597	454
Earnings per share	1.81	1.60	1.35	1.47	1.37	1.18	1.01	0.88	0.68
Dividends per share	.82	0.72	0.66	0.58	0.48	0.40	0.36	0.28	0.22
Price: high	35.0	36.7	37.0	38.4	41.3	37.6	32.6	30.1	30.4
low	20.7	29.9	26.5	30.0	29.5	22.9	21.2	21.8	13.1

AGGRESSIVE GROWTH

Target Corporation

1000 Nicollet Mall ▫ Minneapolis, MN 55403 ▫ Phone: (612) 370–6735 ▫ Website: www.target.com ▫ Fiscal year ends Saturday closest to January 31 of following year ▫ Listed: NYSE ▫ Ticker symbol: TGT ▫ S&P rating: A+ ▫ Value Line financial strength rating: A

Financial Highlights, Fiscal Year 2008

Target saw revenues increase only 2.5 percent in 2008, while comparable earnings fell 22.3 percent (negative 16.5 percent EBIT, or earnings before interest and taxes). Diluted EPS fell 14.2 percent. Operating margins and net margin were off 130 and 110 basis points (1.3 percent and 1.1 percent), respectively. The company repurchased 7.7 percent of its outstanding shares and raised dividends 15.4 percent.

The bulk of the decline was not due to bad product mix or declining customer visits or store cannibalization or even hurricanes, but rather bad credit card debt. The company experienced a record number of defaults on its company-owned RedCards—earnings on credit card operations fell 81 percent year over year.

Target was one of the few big box stores to carry all of their own credit card receivables. In May the company sold 47 percent of its credit card loan portfolio to JP Morgan for $3.7B. The sale, early in the year, would appear to have paid off well, as the company's credit card losses in late 2008 could have been much worse.

Company Profile

Target Corporation (formerly Dayton Hudson Corporation) was formed in 1969 through the merger of two old-line department store companies, Dayton Corporation and J. L. Hudson Company. In 1990, TGT acquired another venerable retailer, Marshall Field & Company. The Dayton's and Hudson's stores (once run separately, but later under the Marshall Field umbrella) were sold to Federated Department Stores in late 2004. Target operates nearly 1,700 stores, including 240 "Super-Targets," which also carry groceries.

Target is the nation's second-largest general merchandise retailer, specializing in large-store formats, including discount stores, moderate-priced promotional stores, and traditional department stores. Target stores are situated largely in California, Texas, Florida, and the upper middle west. Current retail space is about 225 million square feet.

In 2000, the company formed "target.direct," the direct merchandising and electronic retailing organization. The business combines the e-commerce team of Target with its direct merchandising unit into one integrated organization. The target. direct organization operates seven websites, which support the store and catalog brands in an online environment and produces six retail catalogs.

Target positions itself against its main competitor, Wal-Mart, as a more upscale and trend-conscious "cheap chic" alternative. The typical Target customer has a higher level of disposable income, which the company courts through its offerings of proprietary goods from a number of high-end designers. By and large, however, there is a great deal of commonality between the company's branded offerings.

The company's revenues come from retail sales and credit card operations. Although credit operations contributed only 2 percent of revenue in 2007, they accounted for 28 percent of earnings. In 2008, the numbers were 2 percent and 7 percent.

Reasons to Buy

Although profits lagged badly in 2008 and comps (comparable store sales) from 2008 through early 2009 are sliding, the company has taken positive steps to put these problems behind them. They have reduced their exposure to bad credit card debt through the JP Morgan deal, and they have significantly scaled back their expansion plans to a net increase of around 40 stores (versus 90 stores during 2008).

Target has some of the highest customer satisfaction numbers in the industry, and though comps and unit volume dropped year to year, per-unit selling price actually rose 2.3 percent over 2007. Price increases have carried Target through a tight economy, and they plan to leverage this with an increased percentage of store brands. They also plan to increase customer visits by expanding their grocery offerings.

Improved economic conditions should improve Target's market share. Trend data indicates that Target performs better than its competitors during periods of economic growth. As consumer confidence improves through late 2009–2010, we expect Target to get the larger share of consumer spending growth.

Reasons for Caution

Target is up against some very tough competitors in Wal-Mart and, to a lesser extent (due to a different product mix), Costco. Also, these two competitors are growing their international presence, while Target has none and has no plans for same. Target is tied more closely to the domestic consumer market, consumer confidence, and access to credit than either of its major competitors.

SECTOR: **Retail**
BETA COEFFICIENT: **1.05**
10-YEAR COMPOUND EARNINGS PER SHARE GROWTH: **18%**
10-YEAR COMPOUND DIVIDENDS PER SHARE GROWTH: **11%**

	2008	**2007**	**2006**	**2005**	**2004**	**2003**	**2002**	**2001**	**2000**
Revenues (Mil)	64,948	63,367	59,490	52,620	46,839	48,163	43,917	39,888	36,903
Net Income (Mil)	2,214	2,849	2,787	2,408	1,885	1,841	1,654	1,419	1,264
Earnings per share	2.86	3.33	3.21	2.71	2.07	2.01	1.81	1.56	1.38
Dividends per share	.60	0.56	0.42	0.38	0.30	0.26	0.24	0.22	0.21
Price high	59.6	70.8	60.3	60.0	54.1	41.8	46.2	41.7	39.2
low	25.6	48.8	44.7	45.6	36.6	25.6	24.9	26.0	21.6

Teva Pharmaceutical Industries, Ltd.

5 Basel Street ▫ P.O. Box 3190 ▫ Petach Tikva ▫ Israel 49131 ▫ Phone: (215) 591–8912 ▫ Website: www.tevapharm.com ▫ Listed: NASDAQ ▫ Ticker symbol: TEVA ▫ S&P rating: not rated ▫ Value Line Financial Rating: A

Financial Highlights, Fiscal Year 2008

Revenues grew 17.8 percent to $11.1B in FY2008, with earnings climbing 21.6 percent to $2.37B. Per-share earnings rose 20.2 percent to $2.86 despite an increase in the share base of 83 million shares (related to acquisitions). Dividends grew 25.6 percent but remain at a relatively low yield of 1.1 percent and are expected to remain at a relatively moderate yield level.

On December 23, 2008, Teva completed the acquisition of Barr Pharmaceuticals, a U.S.-based multinational generic pharmaceutical company with operations mainly in the United States and Europe (as Pliva), for approximately $4.6 billion in cash and 69 million American Depository Receipt (ADR) shares. Barr's net debt as of the acquisition date was approximately $1.5 billion.

Barr was the fourth-largest generic pharmaceutical manufacturer in the world. The acquisition of Barr enhances Teva's leadership position in the United States and expands its international presence, particularly in Central and Eastern Europe. The acquisition also provides Teva with growth opportunities in first-to-market generic positions in their core U.S. business and new capabilities in women's health care, including a strong proprietary product portfolio.

Company Profile

Teva was founded in Jerusalem in 1901 as a small wholesale drug business that distributed imported medicines loaded onto the backs of camels and donkeys to customers throughout the land. The company was called Salomon, Levin and Elstein, Ltd., after its founders. Teva Pharmaceutical Industries, Ltd., is now a global pharmaceutical company specializing in generic drugs. The company has major manufacturing and marketing facilities in Israel, North America, and Europe.

Teva's scope of activity extends to many facets of the industry, with primary focus on the manufacturing and marketing of products in Human Pharmaceuticals and Active Pharmaceutical Ingredients segments.

The Human Pharmaceuticals segment produces generic drugs in all major therapeutic realms in a variety of dosage forms, from tablets and capsules to ointments, creams, and liquids. Teva manufactures innovative drugs in niche markets where it has an R&D advantage.

Active Pharmaceutical Ingredients (API) competitively distributes to manufacturers worldwide as well as supporting its own pharmaceutical production. API offers raw materials used by drug manufacturers, including more than 190 different bulk chemicals or active ingredients for use in human pharmaceuticals. Teva's acquisition of Sicor added complementary API operations to its existing capabilities.

These activities account for 90 percent of Teva's total sales.

Reasons to Buy

Teva is now the largest player in the generic drug industry. Their large portfolio of pending approvals and the large value of the corresponding branded products (over $100B) gives Teva a strong pipeline, vital in the pharmaceutical industry. The company has also developed internally two unique medications, one to address certain forms of multiple scle-

rosis, and another which is used to slow the progression of Parkinson's disease. Finally, growth prospects are enhanced by biogenerics as regulatory hurdles are cleared.

The company is financially solid, with ample cash flow and credit for future acquisitions and funding of internal R&D.

Reasons for Caution

Teva's success is greatly affected by their ability to prevail in so-called "Paragraph IV" patent challenges—challenges to the exclusivity rights granted to the patent holder by the FDA. If successful at these challenges, Teva is granted an exclusive 180-day window in which to produce and market their generic form of the drug in the United States. As of February 2009, 128 of Teva's nearly 200 product applications to the FDA were Paragraph IV applications.

SECTOR: **Health Care**
BETA COEFFICIENT: **.60**
5-YEAR COMPOUND EARNINGS PER SHARE GROWTH: **27.0%**
5-YEAR COMPOUND DIVIDENDS PER SHARE GROWTH: **29.0%**

		2008	2007	2006	2005	2004	2003	2002	2001	2000
Revenues (Mil)		11,085	9,408	8,400	5,250	4,799	3,276	2,519	2,077	1,750
Net Income (Mil)		2,374	1,952	1,867	1,072	965	691	410	278	148
Earnings per share		2.86	2.38	2.30	1.59	1.42	1.04	0.76	0.53	0.29
Dividends per share		0.49	0.39	0.30	0.27	0.16	0.14	0.09	0.06	0.07
Price	high	50.0	47.1	44.7	45.9	34.7	31.2	20.1	18.6	19.7
	low	35.9	30.8	29.2	26.8	22.8	17.3	12.9	12.1	8.0

The TJX Companies, Inc.

770 Cochituate Road □ Framingham, MA 01701 □ Phone: (508) 390–2323 □ Fiscal year ends the last Saturday in January □ Listed: NYSE □ Website: www.tjx.com □ Ticker symbol: TJX □ S&P rating: A+ □ Value Line financial strength rating: A+

Financial Highlights, Fiscal Year 2008

TJX in 2008 experienced a growth in net sales of 4 percent, to $19B, with consolidated comps (comparable stores sales) increasing 1 percent. Net income from continuing operations was $915, and adjusted diluted earnings per share rose 4 percent to $2.01. Total store square footage grew 4 percent with a 123-store net increase.

In August 2008, the company announced the sale of its underperforming Bob's franchise (34 stores) to Versa Capital Management and Crystal Capital. The company raised $23M in cash through the sale, and incurred $15M in expenses in FY2008, or $.03 on a per-share basis.

Company Profile

The TJX Companies, Inc., is the leading off-price apparel and home fashions retailer in the United States and worldwide, with $19 billion in revenues in 2008, eight reporting businesses, and more than 2,500 stores. The company's off-price mission is to deliver a wide variety of quality, brand name merchandise at prices that are 20–60 percent less than department and specialty store regular prices, every day. Its target customer

is a middle-to-upper-middle income shopper who is fashion- and value-conscious and fits the same profile as a department store shopper.

T.J. Maxx, founded in 1976, is the largest off-price retailer of apparel and home fashions in the United States. T.J. Maxx offers brand name family apparel, giftware, home fashions, women's shoes, and lingerie, and emphasizes accessories and fine jewelry, at prices 20–60 percent below department and specialty store regular prices. T.J. Maxx, which operated 847 stores at the end of 2007, has further growth opportunities in the United States.

Marshalls is the second largest off-price retailer in the United States and was acquired by TJX in 1995. The Marshalls chain, operating 762 stores at the end of 2007, continues to grow in many markets across the United States.

Winners operates 191 stores in Canada and has grown into the leading off-price family apparel retailer in that country since it was acquired by TJX in 1990. Patterned after T.J. Maxx, Winners offers brand name family apparel, giftware, fine jewelry, home fashions, accessories, lingerie, and family footwear.

With its launch in 2001, Home-Sense introduced the home fashions off-price concept to Canada. Similar to HomeGoods in the United States, HomeSense offers customers a wide selection of giftware, home basics, accent furniture, rugs, lamps, accessories, and seasonal items with frequent inventory updates. At year-end 2005, HomeSense operated 71 stores with a typical store size of 24,000 square feet.

T.K. Maxx, a T.J. Maxx–like off-price apparel and home fashions concept, operates 221 stores in the United Kingdom and Ireland. T.K. Maxx has been very well received since its launch in 1994, and management sees the United Kingdom and Ireland supporting 300 stores in the long term.

HomeGoods, a chain of off-price home fashions stores, operates 289 stores in the United States. This chain operates in a standalone and superstore format, which couple Home-Goods with a T.J. Maxx or Marshalls. Ultimately, the company believes that the U.S. market could support 650 HomeGoods stores.

A.J. Wright, launched in 1998, operates similarly to the company's other off-price concepts, but targets the moderate-income customer. A.J. Wright operates 129 stores, with an average size of 26,000 square feet. Longer-term, TJX believes that the United States could potentially support 1,000 stores.

Reasons to Buy

A year ago at this time, TJX was a solid pick for 100 Best. Steady earnings, healthy margins, solid finances

. . . all the things that keep sound businesses sound. One year later, even after a hard reset in the worldwide economy, not much has changed at TJX. Revenues are basically flat, earnings are holding up well, and margins are steady or slightly improving due to cost reductions in early 2009.

In fact, given the squeeze on consumer income, TJX's prospects look even better. TJX's appeal is to consumers looking for brand appeal but who are willing to sacrifice some level of shopping experience for big everyday discounts, and discount retailers continue to draw while the upscale mall operators go begging for traffic.

TJX's international operations are growing at a faster rate than domestic businesses, owing at least partially to the novelty of the retailing concept. TJX is the first European operator offering deep everyday discounts on high-end labels, and comps in the European (and Canadian) stores were up an average of 14 percent last year. Given the wide-open market, this could be the first indications of a tremendous growth opportunity for TJX.

Reasons for Caution

A.J. Wright's has been operating at a loss. The company has been closing unprofitable stores, but the departure from the core concept that these stores represent and their relatively poor performance will merit attention in the coming year. Also, as top-line retailers and manufacturers adjust their production and inventory models, it could be relatively more difficult to source product to sell at deep discounts; the "sweet spot" for performance of this kind of store (low prices for strapped consumers, excess inventory widely available) may already be past.

SECTOR: **Retail**
BETA COEFFICIENT: **.85**
10-YEAR COMPOUND EARNINGS PER SHARE GROWTH: **15%**
10-YEAR COMPOUND DIVIDENDS PER SHARE GROWTH: **22%**

	2008	2007	2006	2005	2004	2003	2002	2001	2000
Revenues (Mil)	19,000	18,647	17,405	16,058	14,913	13,328	11,981	10,709	9,579
Net Income (Mil)	884	777.8	738	690.4	683.4	658.4	578.4	540.4	538.1
Earnings per share	2.01	1.66	1.63	1.29	1.34	1.28	1.08	0.97	0.93
Dividends per share	0.44	0.36	0.28	0.24	0.18	0.14	0.12	0.09	0.08
Price high	37.5	32.5	29.8	26.0	26.8	23.7	22.5	20.3	15.8
low	17.8	25.7	22.2	20.0	20.6	15.5	15.3	13.6	7.0

Tractor Supply Company

200 Powell Place ❑ Brentwood, TN 37027 ❑ Phone: (615) 440–4000 ❑ Website: www.tractorsupply.com ❑
Listed: NASDAQ ❑ Ticker symbol: TSCO ❑ S&P rating: A+ ❑ Value Line financial strength rating: A+

Financial Highlights, Fiscal Year 2008

Sales in 2008 totaled $3B, up 12 percent from 2007's total. Gross margin was down 120 basis points, or 1.2 percent, to 30.3 percent and net margin was down 90 basis points or 0.90 percent to 2.7 percent (recent average is about 3.7 percent). Net income fell 17.5 percent to $81.9M, while per-share earnings fell 9 percent to $2.22.

Comparable same store sales were up a slight 1.4 percent but total store returns were diluted somewhat by the new stores and were off 1.7 percent. Daily transactions were off 3 percent, but price increases drove average transaction value up 2.1 percent.

TSCO opened 91 new stores in 2009 and closed none. Since 2004 they have closed only four stores.

Company Profile

Tractor Supply Company is the largest operator of retail farm and ranch stores in the United States. They are focused on supplying the needs of recreational farmers and ranchers and those who enjoy the rural lifestyle, as well as tradespeople and small businesses. They operate retail stores under the names Tractor Supply Company and Del's Farm Supply. Their stores are located in towns outside major metropolitan markets and in rural communities. Representative merchandise includes supplies for pets and farm animals, equipment maintenance products, hardware and tools, lawn and garden equipment, and work and recreational clothing and footwear.

Tractor Supply stores typically range in size from 15,500 square feet to 18,500 square feet of inside selling space and additional outside selling space. As of December 27, 2008, they operated 855 retail farm and ranch stores in 44 states.

Del's Farm Supply operates 28 stores primarily in the Pacific Northwest, offering a wide selection of products (primarily in the horse, pet, and other animal category) targeted at those who enjoy the rural lifestyle. Del's stores currently range in size from approximately 2,000 to 6,000 square feet of inside selling space plus additional outside and covered/sheltered selling space.

They operate their own distribution network for supplying stores and in fiscal 2008 stores received approximately two thirds of their merchandise through this network. The six distribution centers are located in Indiana, Georgia, Maryland, Texas, Nebraska, and Washington, representing total distribution capacity of 2.9 million square feet. In 2008, the Waco distribution center was increased by approximately 347,000 square feet. No expansions are needed or planned for 2009.

Tractor Supply Company sells both at retail locations and online.

Reasons to Buy

TSCO serves a growing, specialized niche in geographies often un-served by other retailers. They carry a specialized mix of merchandise that occupies a broad space—part big-box hardware, part garden shop, and part feed store. Their unique target market nonetheless has broad geographic distribution, giving TSCO room for growth, and they plan to grow more than 10 percent a year, with a target of 1800 units.

TSCO carries a higher percentage of house brands than you would find at a typical hardware retailer. They earn higher gross margins on these products and build re-buy loyalty in the process.

Recognizing the distances some customers have to travel to get to a store, TSCO set up their e-commerce site in 2007 and has grown its offerings in 2008.

TSCO's 1Q2009 results were very good. Sales were up 12.8 percent over the previous quarter and comps were up 4.2 percent versus same quarter 2008. Gross margin for the quarter was 30.9 percent, up 60 basis points over 2008's average, and the company opened 28 new stores.

TSCO doesn't sell heavy equipment, such as combines and large tractors, but does sell the consumables and repair parts for these products, which carry high margins and continue to sell well during a slowing economy.

Reasons for Caution

TSCO's growth is bound to attract competition. The sooner they can build out to their target size, the better they will be able to protect margins.

SECTOR: **Retail**
BETA COEFFICIENT: **0.95**
10-YEAR COMPOUND EARNINGS PER SHARE GROWTH: **19.50%**
10-YEAR COMPOUND DIVIDENDS PER SHARE GROWTH: **Nil**

		2008	2007	2006	2005	2004	2003	2002	2001	2000
Revenues (Mil)		3,007	2,703	2,370	2,068	1,739	1,473	1,210	850	759
Net Income (Mil)		81.9	96.2	91.0	85.7	64.1	58.4	38.8	25.8	16.4
Earnings per share		2.19	2.40	2.22	2.09	1.57	1.45	0.99	0.71	0.47
Dividends per share		Nil								
Price	high	47.5	57.7	67.6	58.6	45.8	44/9	22.8	8.7	5.5
	low	26.7	35.1	38.8	33.2	30.2	14.7	8.4	2.1	1.6

UnitedHealth Group

9900 Bren Street ❑ Minnetonka, MN 55343 ❑ Phone: (952) 936–1300 ❑ Website: www.unitedhealthgroup.com ❑ Listed: NYSE ❑ Ticker symbol: UNH ❑ S&P rating: A- ❑ Value Line financial strength rating: A+

Financial Highlights, Fiscal Year 2008

UNH's revenues grew 8 percent year over year to $81.2B, primarily due to growth in the number of clients served in the Public and Senior Markets group and premium rate increases. Additional gains were due to the increased client base due to the Fiserv Health acquisition.

Adjusted net earnings fell 36 percent to $3.0B, however, due primarily to lower operating margin driven primarily by costs associated with acquisitions, the settlement of two class action lawsuits, and a change in business mix toward fee-based services. Operating margin fell 390 basis points or 3.9 percent to 6.5 percent.

In 2008, UNH acquired three smaller health insurers for a total of $4.2B—Fiserv Health, Inc.; Sierra Health Services, Inc.; and Unison Health Plans.

Company Profile

UnitedHealth Group is the parent company of a number of health insurers and service organizations. They are the second-largest publicly traded health insurance company in the United States, with over $81B in revenue reported in 2008.

The company operates in three basic segments: United Health Care, which sells health insurance plans to

companies and individuals; Ovations, which provides Medicare benefits; and AmeriChoice, which provides benefits to Medicaid clients. Taken together, these operations generated $73.6B in revenue in 2008, or approximately 90 percent of UNH's overall revenue.

The remainder of the company's revenue comes from their health services businesses, which consists of Optum-Health, Ingenix, and Prescription Solutions. OptumHealth is a comprehensive care management and services company targeted at end consumers. Ingenix provides clinical health-care data, analytics, research and consulting services to other health-care providers. Prescription Solutions is a pharmacy benefit management program.

Reasons to Buy

UNH provides insurance for some 70 million Americans. The scale of UNH's operation gives it tremendous leverage when negotiating for the services of health-care providers. Hospitals are strongly motivated to join UNH's network as doing so will provide assurance of steady referrals.

The company has been able to reduce expenses some $475M (annualized) and plans to accelerate cuts in the future. Also, first quarter 2009 showed year over year growth in revenue, although earnings are lagging somewhat.

Recent upturns in the unemployment rate has hit all health-care providers as employers trim the rolls of their group plans. UNH's recent acquisitions put it in good stead to accelerate growth when employment turns around.

Even if unemployment continues to erode the ranks of fee-based subscribers, UNH has nearly $8B in cash and solid capital and can continue to add top-line growth through acquisitions, at the cost of margin performance.

The company also plans to shore up share prices with a stock repurchase. Since 2006, they have reduced outstanding shares by 145 million and plan to buy back an additional 175 million shares through 2010, for a total reduction of approximately 25 percent in outstanding shares over four years.

Reasons for Caution

The Obama administration has taken on health-care reform with a mild vengeance. In particular, they have targeted private insurance plans that serve the Medicare Advantage healthcare programs, promising/threatening budget cuts. Medicare premiums generate some 40 percent of UNH's revenue, and funding cuts could certainly affect UNH's top line, but it's not clear that a) these cuts will be made, or b) at what level, or c) whether the care recipients can simply make up the difference. The reader will need to review this as the administration's plan gets fleshed out.

SECTOR: **Health Care**
BETA COEFFICIENT: **1.0**
10-YEAR COMPOUND EARNINGS PER SHARE GROWTH: **27.5%**
10-YEAR COMPOUND DIVIDENDS PER SHARE GROWTH: **23.0%**

		2008	2007	2006	2005	2004	2003	2002	2001	2000
Revenues (Mil)		81,186	75,431	71,542	45,365	37,218	28,823	25,020	23,454	21,122
Net Income (Mil)		2,977	4,654	4,159	3,300	2,587	1,825	1,352	913	705
Earnings per share		2.95	3.42	2.97	2.48	1.97	1.48	1.06	0.70	0.53
Dividends per share		.03	.03	.03	.03	.02	.01	.01	.01	.01
Price	high	57.9	59.5	62.9	64.6	44.4	29.3	25.3	18.2	15.9
	low	14.5	45.8	41.4	42.6	27.7	19.6	17.0	12.6	5.8

United Parcel Service, Inc.

55 Glenlake Parkway N. E. □ Atlanta, GA 30328 □ Phone: (800) 877–1503 □ Website: www.ups.com
□ Listed: NYSE □ Ticker symbol: UPS □ S&P rating: AA □ Value Line financial strength rating: A

Financial Highlights, Fiscal Year 2008

UPS's 2008 revenue grew 3.4 percent to $51.5B, while adjusted net income fell 18.1 percent to $3.6B, primarily due to a $548M goodwill impairment taken against UPS Freight, which continues to struggle.

Adjusted per share earnings fell 14.8 percent to $3.50, operating margin fell 250 basis points (2.5 percent) to 11.6 percent, and net margin fell 180 basis points or 1.8 percent to 7.0 percent. The company raised the dividend 8 percent to $1.77 and repurchased 53.6 million shares for $3.6B.

It was a tough year for most transportation and freight companies—fuel prices at record highs and the fourth quarter fall-off in revenues were a double blow to the bottom line.

Company Profile

UPS is the world's largest package delivery company, both in terms of revenue and volume, and a global leader in supply chain solutions. They deliver packages daily from 1.8 million customers to over 6 million recipients in over 200 countries. In 2008, nearly 4 billion pieces were delivered, or an average of over 15 million pieces per day.

Although their primary business is the delivery of packages and documents, they have extended their capabilities in recent years to address the breadth of services known as supply chain solutions, which includes freight forwarding, customs brokerage, fulfillment, returns, financial transactions, and repairs. The company provides supply chain services to customers in over 180 countries and territories. They are also a leading provider of LTL (less-than-truckload) transportation services.

The company maintains a fleet of over 100,000 vehicles, including over 1,800 alternative-fuel vehicles. The company also operated a fleet of about 570 aircraft (263 jets), making them the ninth largest airline in the world.

The company operates over customer 23,000 outlets, including the UPS Store, formerly Mail Boxes Etc., UPS Customer Centers, and other authorized outlets. The company also supports over 40,000 UPS Drop Boxes.

In addition to their traditional infrastructure, the company provides a number of online services that expand their core offerings. These include UPS.Com, which processes over 18 million tracking transactions every day. They also provide software for integration in the customers' own websites and ordering systems, and provide services for package tracking, pickups, drop-offs, transit times, and supply orders, as well as labeling and outbound shipment processing.

Reasons to Buy

The company is focused on the expansion of global trade. They target growth primarily in China, India, and Europe, taking advantage of falling trade barriers and developing consumer markets. The larger strategy is to expand the geographical coverage of the traditional small-package delivery business while growing the supply-chain services segment. The supply-chain business did well in 2008 (revenue up 6 percent, operating margin up 5 percent) and appears ready for continued growth in 2009–2010.

The outsourcing of supply chain management has been a boon for UPS, as they have been able to pitch their service as a key differentiator for companies in highly competitive industries with complex sourcing models.

The company has been diligent with regard to cost controls and reducing expenditures during the current downturn. Their liquidity entering 2009 should see them through several more quarters of reduced revenues.

Like FedEx, UPS has benefited from the departure of DHL from the domestic delivery industry. In particular, UPS was able to grow its express market share.

As of mid-2009, the company is trading at a 30 percent discount to its 2004–2008 average. This is a good opportunity to pick up shares in this well-run and universally well-respected company.

Reasons for Caution

The domestic freight business continues to be drag on earnings. Even at recent historic lows, the company trades at multiples in the low 20's. The company's growth potential is well-recognized.

SECTOR: **Transportation**
BETA COEFFICIENT: **.80**
5-YEAR COMPOUND EARNINGS PER SHARE GROWTH: **11.5%**
5-YEAR COMPOUND DIVIDENDS PER SHARE GROWTH: **15%**

		2008	2007	2006	2005	2004	2003	2002	2001	2000
Revenues (Mil)		51,486	49,692	47,547	42,581	36,582	33,485	31,272	30,321	29,771
Net Income (Mil)		3,581	4,369	4,202	3,870	3,333	2,898	3,182	2,425	2,795
Earnings per share		3.50	4.17	3.86	3.47	2.90	2.55	2.84	2.10	2.38
Dividends per share		1.77	1.68	1.52	1.32	1.12	0.92	0.76	0.76	0.68
Price	high	75.1	79.0	84.0	85.8	89.1	74.9	67.1	62.5	69.8
	low	43.3	68.7	65.5	66.1	67.2	53.0	54.3	46.2	49.5

United Technologies Corporation

One Financial Plaza ◻ Hartford, CT 06103 ◻ Phone: (860) 728–7912 ◻ Listed: NYSE ◻ Website: www.utc.com
◻ Listed: NYSE ◻ Ticker symbol: UTX ◻ S&P rating: A+ ◻ Value Line Financial Strength A++

Financial Highlights, Fiscal Year 2008

Earnings per share in 2008 climbed to $4.90, and net income of $4.7 billion increased 14.8 and 11 percent, respectively, from 2007 results. Revenues increased 7 percent, to $58.7 billion, including 5 points of organic growth, 1 point from foreign exchange, and 1 point from acquisitions. All operating segments experienced organic growth, with the exception of Carrier, which saw an organic decline of 1 percent year/year.

The company continued to reduce outstanding shares, buying back approximately 40 million shares, or 4 percent. Dividends rose 15 percent.

Company Profile

United Technologies provides high-technology products to the aerospace and building systems industries throughout the world. Its subsidiary companies are industry leaders and include:

- Pratt & Whitney—Large and small commercial and military jet engines, spare parts and product support, specialized engine maintenance and overhaul and repair services for airlines, air forces, and corporate fleets; rocket engines and space propulsion systems; and industrial gas turbines.

- Chubb—Security and fire protection systems, integration, installation and servicing of intruder alarms, access control and video surveillance, and monitoring, response, and security personnel services; installation, and servicing of fire detection and suppression systems.

- Hamilton Sundstrand—Aircraft electrical power generation and distribution systems; engine and flight controls; propulsion systems; environmental controls for aircraft, spacecraft, and submarines; auxiliary power units; product support, maintenance, and repair services; space life support systems; industrial products including mechanical power transmissions, compressors, metering devices, and fluid handling equipment.

- Sikorsky—Sikorsky designs and manufactures military and commercial helicopters; fixed-wing reconnaissance aircraft; spare parts and maintenance services for helicopters and fixed-wing aircraft; and civil helicopter operations.

- UTC Power—Combined heat, cooling, and power systems for commercial and industrial applications and fuel cell systems made by UTC Fuel Cells for commercial, transportation, and space applications, including the U.S. space shuttle program.

- Carrier—Heating, ventilating, and air conditioning (HVAC) equipment for commercial, industrial, and residential buildings; HVAC replacement parts and services; building controls; commercial, industrial, and transport refrigeration equipment.

- Otis—Designs and manufactures elevators, escalators, moving walks, and shuttle systems, and related installation, maintenance, and repair services; modernization products and service for elevators and escalators.

Nearly two-thirds of UTC's revenue came from international customers.

Reasons to Buy

UTC is having a rough go of things in 2009, as many of its end customers, particularly in the construction industry, are taking the brunt of the recession's effects. Sales at UTC will fall year over year and earnings will be down some 20 percent. UTC is undertaking a large and costly restructuring in 2009, using cash on hand to implement broad cost-cutting measures and (likely) to shore up the pension fund, which took a pounding last year.

Summing up the recovery picture at UTC nicely, Erik Manning of Value Line wrote on April 24, 2009: "The longer-term effects of the restructuring should begin to be realized in 2010. Management believes that it can cull about $1 billion from its cost structure if everything falls properly into place. If this is the case, UTX will likely return to profit growth next year. Its broad array of divisions gives it a leg up on its industrial brethren, and its growth engine will likely be firing on all cylinders well before its peers. This belief obviously assumes that some semblance of economic recovery begins in earnest as 2009 winds to a close. With that, we anticipate earnings may well jump 7 percent from the current year's depressed expectation, to $4.45."

What this should mean is a buying opportunity for the savvy investor. UTC is globally diversified, its customers are in resilient markets, and its brands are universally respected. If the investing market is slow to recognize the recovery potential, you should be able to pick up this quality issue at a bargain price. The recent dividend growth and share repurchase activity only adds to the appeal.

Reasons for Caution

About 25 percent of UTC's revenues are generated through residential housing. Should the domestic housing market remain in its current slump through the better part of 2010, Carrier will continue to be a drag on the top line.

SECTOR: **Industrials**
BETA COEFFICIENT: **0.95**
10-YEAR COMPOUND EARNINGS PER SHARE GROWTH: **15%**
10-YEAR COMPOUND DIVIDENDS PER SHARE GROWTH: **14%**

	2008	2007	2006	2005	2004	2003	2002	2001	2000
Revenues (Mil)	58,681	54,759	47,740	42,725	37,445	31,034	28,212	27,897	26,583
Net Income (Mil)	4,689	4,224	3,732	3,069	2,788	2,361	2,236	1,938	1,808
Earnings per share	4.90	4.27	3.71	3.03	2.76	2.35	2.21	1.92	1.78
Dividends per share	1.55	1.28	1.02	0.88	0.70	0.57	0.49	0.45	0.42
Price high	77.1	82.5	67.5	58.9	53.0	48.4	38.9	43.8	39.9
low	41.8	61.8	54.2	48.4	40.4	26.8	24.4	20.1	23.3

AGGRESSIVE GROWTH

Valmont Industries

One Valmont Plaza □ Omaha, NE 68154-5215 □ Phone: (402) 963–1000 □ Website: www.valmont.com
□ Fiscal year ends September 30 □ Listed: NYSE □ Ticker symbol: VMT □ S&P Rating: BB+ □ Value Line
financial strength rating: B++

Financial Highlights, Fiscal Year 2008

Revenues increased in 2008 roughly 8 percent over 2007. By the company's own analysis that was mostly due to increased selling prices to recover higher material costs. That said, the company did see unit volume increases, and demand was strong in all segments. The largest sales unit volume increases were in the Irrigation and Coatings segments.

As a result of higher materials costs and compensatory price increases, operating margins were roughly comparable to 2007 at a healthy 14.1 percent. Gross margins improved in the Coatings and the Utility segments. Selling, general, and administrative (SG&A) expenses increased for the fiscal year ended December 27, 2008, as compared with 2007, mainly resulted from increased sales activity, effects of acquisitions and divestitures, and foreign currency translation effects. All reportable segments contributed to the improved operating income in 2008.

Cash flows from operations were down in 2008 from $110.2 million to $52.6 million; this was attributed to increased accounts receivable and in inventories to handle increased sales volume and to manage and hedge against rapidly rising steel prices and delayed deliveries. These conditions should not repeat in 2009.

Company Profile

Largest segments include:

* The Engineered Support Structures (37 percent of revenue) segment manufactures and markets engineered metal structures and components

for the lighting and traffic, wireless communication, and international utility industries, as well as for other specialty applications. It offers steel and aluminum poles and structures to which lighting and traffic control fixtures are attached for a range of outdoor lighting applications, such as streets, highways, parking lots, sports stadiums, and commercial and residential developments.

- The Irrigation segment (30 percent) is probably best known and produces all sorts of equipment for large-scale agricultural irrigation. Higher farm prices produced a bit of a boom in 2008 that covered higher materials costs; the segment is a bit weaker this year as agricultural prosperity has subsided somewhat. This unit has significant overseas sales in the Pacific Rim, Middle East, and Brazil.

- The Utility Support Structures segment (23 percent) sells and services transmission substation and fabricated distribution pole structures made of steel and concrete to utility customers. The business is strong, and although much of 2008's improved performance was due to price increases to cover cost increases and to an acquisition, the backlog at year end 2008 doubled from 2007.

- The Coatings segment (6 percent) provides galvanizing and powder coating services for steel

for an assortment of customers. Margins improved in 2008 due primarily to lower zinc costs and operating efficiencies.

The company made several small acquisitions in 2007–2008 primarily in lighting and wireless structures businesses fitting into the ESS segment.

Reasons to Buy

Valmont is a solid and well diversified business. They are the dominant player in the major segments in which they operate. Although agriculture is down a bit recently, it's hard to bet against agriculture in the long term. Irrigation systems will be in demand as worldwide agriculture assumes greater importance. Utility infrastructure will benefit from the need to replace old equipment and improve the reliability of infrastructure. Lighting and wireless systems will also benefit from infrastructure spending programs. Finally, all of these businesses will play out well on the global stage as China and other nations spend on infrastructure improvements and agriculture.

The company was able to pass on steel cost increases; it's always a good sign when a company has pricing power. This company has relatively few strong or entrenched competitors in any of its businesses.

A significant part of the company's recent growth was from acquisitions, and that's always a bit of a concern, but these acquisitions seem to fit well into the company's portfolio and have not caused any loss of earnings growth or momentum; in fact, it has increased, an indication of synergy.

While the dividend is nothing to get excited about, it has been raised in each of the last eight years. This company appears to be well managed, and management appears to consider the interests of shareholders. The company recently had a positive credit watch from S&P, an indicator of strength in the wake of the economic crisis.

Reasons for Caution

Lower crop prices and an attenuation of the ethanol boom may cause a delay in some purchases of agricultural irrigation equipment, and public infrastructure investments may be eventually hurt by the weak state of public finances. Volatile prices for steel and other raw materials bring some question marks to margins and profitability, although the company has been successful recently in passing cost increases on.

The company's expansion, strong markets and good fortune have not gone unnoticed in the markets, and the share price has responded accordingly and is historically high, although the economic crisis produced some good buying opportunities in 2008 and 2009.

SECTOR: **Industrials**
BETA COEFFICIENT: **1.76**
10-YEAR COMPOUND EARNINGS PER SHARE GROWTH: **12.5%**
10-YEAR COMPOUND DIVIDENDS PER SHARE GROWTH: **7.0%**

	2008	2007	2006	2005	2004	2003	2002	2001	2000
Revenues (Mil)	1,907	1,500	1,281	1,108	1,031	837	855	872	846
Net Income (Mil)	132.4	94.7	61.5	40.2	26.9	25.9	33.6	28.7	30.4
Earnings per share	5.04	3.63	2.38	1.58	1.10	1.06	1.37	1.09	1.28
Dividends per share	0.50	0.41	0.37	0.34	0.32	0.31	0.28	0.26	0.20
Price high	120.5	99.0	61.2	35.3	28.0	24.3	25.5	20.7	21.7
low	37.5	50.9	32.8	21.3	19.3	17.7	14.1	12.1	13.9

Varian Medical Systems, Inc.

3100 Hansen Way ▫ Palo Alto, CA 94304–1030 ▫ Phone: (650) 424–5782 ▫ Website: www.varian.com ▫ Fiscal year ends on Friday nearest September 30 ▫ Ticker symbol: VAR ▫ Listed: NYSE ▫ S&P rating: B+ ▫ Value Line financial strength rating: A+

Financial Highlights, Fiscal Year 2008

Varian turned in another strong year of top- and bottom-line growth in 2008. Revenues grew 16.9 percent to $2.07B and income rose 23 percent to $295M. Operating margins rose 110 basis points, or 1.1 percent, to 21.8 percent, and net margin grew 10 points to 14.4 percent. Per-share earnings grew 24 percent to $2.61 and per-share cash flow rose 20.7 percent.

In spite of a major product introduction and recent acquisitions, the company exited the year with record working capital levels and negligible debt.

Company Profile

Varian Medical Systems is the world's leading manufacturer of integrated radiotherapy systems for treating cancer and other diseases; it is also a leading supplier of x-ray tubes for imaging in medical, scientific, and industrial applications. Established in 1948, the company has manufacturing sites in North America and Europe and in forty sales and support offices worldwide.

In 1999, the company (formerly Varian Associates, Inc.) reorganized itself into three separate publicly traded companies by spinning off two of its businesses to stockholders via a tax-free distribution. Since then, the company has significantly broadened its product and business offerings, acquired new businesses, and set records for sales and net orders.

The company has three segments: Varian Oncology Systems, Varian X-Ray Products, and Ginzton Technology Center.

Varian Oncology Systems is the world's leading supplier of radiotherapy systems for treating cancer. Its integrated medical systems include linear accelerators and accessories, and a broad range of interconnected software tools for planning and delivering the sophisticated radiation treatments available to cancer patients. Thousands of patients all over the world are treated daily on Varian systems. Oncology Systems works closely with health-care professionals in community clinics, hospitals, and universities to improve cancer outcomes. The business unit also supplies linear accelerators for industrial inspection applications.

Varian X-Ray Products is the world's premier independent supplier of x-ray tubes, serving manufacturers of radiology equipment and industrial inspection equipment, as well as distributors of replacement tubes. This business provides the industry's broadest selection of x-ray tubes expressly designed for the most advanced diagnostic applications, including CT scanning, radiography, and mammography. These products meet evolving requirements for improved resolution, faster patient throughput, longer tube life, smaller dimensions, and greater cost efficiency. X-Ray Products also supplies a new line of amorphous silicon flat-panel x-ray detectors for medical and industrial applications.

The Ginzton Technology Center acts as Varian Medical Systems' research and development facility for breakthrough technologies and operates a growing brachytherapy business for the delivery of internal radiation to treat cancer and cardiovascular disease. In addition to brachytherapy, current efforts are focused on next-generation imaging systems and advanced targeting technologies for radiotherapy. The center is also investigating the combination of radiotherapy with other treatment modalities, such as bioengineered gene delivery systems.

Reasons to Buy

The radiation therapy market evolves rapidly, and with the appearance of new techniques older equipment becomes obsolete. Staying ahead requires a healthy dose of R&D, and Varian has been at the forefront of research in oncology and treatment for over a decade. Their new RapidArc technology has done very well since its introduction in early 2008.

A new radiotherapy installation will cost on the order of $2–3

million, but Varian's product strategy is to permit leverage of existing equipment wherever possible. The RapidArc upgrade, for instance, costs only $400,000. Varian designs their products to also permit the upgrade of competitor's equipment, where the smaller incremental cost (versus the cost of a full new installation) creates opportunities for expansion of market share.

Varian is far and away the leader in radiation therapy equipment. They have 60 percent of the world market share and 67 percent of the U.S. market share.

Reasons for Caution

The $40 million acquisition of Accel Instruments cut into net income and operating margins. The company reported higher than predicted expenses to commercialize Accel's proton technology and expects to spend more on R&D than it had in 2007. In addition, proton therapy systems and proton accelerators are at least 50 times more expensive than Varian's conventional radiotherapy equipment, suggesting that orders will come mainly from publicly funded projects at irregular intervals. As a result, Varian expects the new acquisition to continue to decrease net income in 2008. In addition and like most other high-tech health-care companies, initiatives to reduce overall health-care costs and spending could hurt the company.

SECTOR: **Health Care**
BETA COEFFICIENT: **.90**
10-YEAR COMPOUND EARNINGS PER SHARE GROWTH: **10%**
10-YEAR COMPOUND DIVIDENDS PER SHARE GROWTH: **None**

		2008	2007	2006	2005	2004	2003	2002	2001	2000
Revenues (Mil)		2,070	1,777	1,598	1,383	1,236	1,042	873	774	690
Net Income (Mil)		295	240	223	207	167	131	946	853	
Earnings per share		2.31	1.83	1.65	1.50	1.18	0.92	0.67	0.50	0.41
Dividends per share		Nil								
Price	high	65.8	53.2	61.7	52.9	46.5	35.7	25.7	19.3	17.8
	low	33.1	37.3	41.1	31.6	30.8	23.7	15.8	13.5	7.1

GROWTH AND INCOME

Verizon Communications, Inc.

140 West Street □ New York, NY 10007 □ Phone: (212) 395–1000 □ Website: www.verizon.com □ Listed: NYSE □ Ticker symbol: VZ □ S&P rating: A □ Value Line financial strength rating: A+

Financial Highlights, Fiscal Year 2008

Verizon's revenues grew 4.2 percent to $97.4B primarily due to strong growth in their Domestic Wireless segment. This segment grew revenues 12.4 percent over 2007 due mainly to a large increase in data revenues (up 44.2 percent over 2007). Operating income from the Domestic Wireless segment was $14B, an increase of 15.7 percent.

Wireline revenues decreased 1.9 percent primarily due to lower demand for and use of basic local services, although the company added over 650,000 net new broadband connections, including 956,000 net new FiOS connections. Operating income from the Wireline segment declined year-over-year by 11.1 percent to $3.9B.

No surprise, then, that in March 2009, Verizon announced plans to sell its local wireline operations in rural areas of 14 states to Frontier Communications for $8.6B, consisting of $5.3B of Frontier stock and $3.3B in cash and securities.

Overall, Verizon's earnings grew 5.6 percent to $7.24B. Dividends rose 8 percent, and the company repurchased 30 million shares, or 1.1 percent of its outstanding stock.

On January 8 2009, the company announced that it had completed its acquisition of Alltel from Atlantic Holdings for $28.1 billion. The acquisition makes Verizon Wireless the largest wireless carrier in the United States, in terms of subscriber count, which at the time was 83.7 million customers. The company said the purchase would expand its wireless network coverage to nearly the entire U.S. population.

Company Profile

The company operates two main segments: Domestic Wireless, which provides wireless voice and data services; and Wireline, which provides voice, broadband data and video, Internet access, long-distance, and other services, and which also owns and operates a very large global Internet Protocol network.

The Wireline segment also supplies Verizon's Fiber-to-the-Home (FiOS) broadband data infrastructure. One of Verizon's largest investments, FiOS provides very high bandwidth, easily surpassing DSL and even cable. Over this network, Verizon can provide HD video stream, high-speed data, and voice simultaneously.

The Domestic Wireless segment is served by Verizon Wireless, which is a joint venture between Verizon Communications, Inc., and Vodafone. Verizon Communications owns a 55 percent share in the business, and Vodafone 45 percent. Verizon Wireless is now the largest carrier in the United States.

Reasons to Buy

Verizon's partial divestiture of its rural, low-speed wireline services is a good thing. Copper wireline's operating expenses are high, its pricing structures are often regulated (depending on the state), and it doesn't fit at all into Verizon's longer-term plans, which include fiber-optic broadband (FiOS) delivered to the home. The FiOS rollout is very capital intensive, and money that could be spent deploying a pipe that delivers as much as $150 per month in revenue per address to Verizon is instead being used to maintain hundreds of miles of copper that brings in

as little as $10 per month. Easy math, and expect continued divestiture announcements from Verizon as credit markets firm up.

When TPG and Goldman Sachs took Alltel private last May they paid 9.2 times earnings, whereas Verizon picked them up for just under 8 times earnings. They also get the best coverage in the nation and potential tie-ins with the new customer base. Good deal for Verizon.

Verizon's win at the 700MHz spectrum auction last March gives them additional bandwidth for their current network and positioning it for the roll-out of the next generation of very high-speed wireless infrastructure (LTE). They spent $9.6B for this spectrum, and if they can keep their lead in subscriber base through the LTE roll-out, should be in a position to capitalize handsomely.

The 5 percent dividend yield is a big plus.

Reasons for Caution

Verizon cannot proceed as quickly as it would like with FiOS rollout, as local and state regulatory agencies are not paid to move quickly, but deliberately. And the longer it takes, the more territory they may lose to competitors such as Comcast and AT&T.

SECTOR: **Telecommunications Services**
BETA COEFFICIENT: **0.7**
10-YEAR COMPOUND EARNINGS PER SHARE GROWTH: **0.5%**
10-YEAR COMPOUND DIVIDENDS PER SHARE GROWTH: **1.5%**

	2008	2007	2006	2005	2004	2003	2002	2001	2000
Revenues (Mil)	97,354	93,469	88,144	74,910	71,283	67,752	67,625	67,190	64,707
Net Income (Mil)	7,235	6,854	6,021	7,151	7,261	7,282	8,361	8,391	8,101
Earnings per share	2.54	2.36	2.54	2.56	2.59	2.62	3.05	3.00	2.92
Dividends per share	1.78	1.65	1.62	1.62	1.54	1.54	1.54	1.54	1.54
Price high	44.3	46.2	38.9	41.1	42.3	44.3	51.1	57.4	66.0
low	23.1	35.6	30.0	29.1	34.1	31.1	26.0	43.8	39.1

CONSERVATIVE GROWTH

Vulcan Materials Company

1200 Urban Center Drive □ Birmingham, AL 35242–2545 □ Phone: (205) 298–3191 □ Website: www.vulcanmaterials.com □ Listed: NYSE □ Ticker symbol: VMC □ S&P rating: BBB □ Value Line financial strength rating: B++

Financial Highlights, Fiscal Year 2008

Sales increased 9.7 percent in FY2008 to $3.65B, but earnings fell 59.3 percent to $191M. Net margins fell 890 basis points (8.9 percent) to 5.2 percent, and operating margins fell 620 basis points (6.2 percent) to 21.8 percent. Cash flow was down 23 percent, and long-term debt rose 40 percent to a record $2.15B (versus a 10-year average in the $600M range).

As was the case for most infrastructure-related companies, Vulcan did not have a good 2008 and early 2009 was looking even worse, but hope came riding in from Washington in the form of the Economic Recovery and Reinvestment Act of 2009 stimulus package.

Company Profile

Vulcan Materials is the nation's largest producer of construction aggregates and a major producer of asphalt and ready-mix concrete. Construction materials consist of the production, distribution, and sale of construction aggregates and other construction materials and related services. Construction aggregates include crushed stone, sand and gravel, rock asphalt, and re-crushed concrete. Aggregates are employed in virtually all types of construction, including highway construction and maintenance, and in the production of asphaltic and Portland cement concrete mixes. Aggregates also are widely used as railroad ballast.

Vulcan operates primarily in the United States. In the most recent year, aggregates accounted for 65 percent of net sales. From 331 aggregates production facilities and sales yards, the company shipped a record 204 million tons to customers in twenty-two states, the District of Columbia, and Mexico. Vulcan's top ten states accounted for 85 percent of total aggregates shipments. Besides its aggregates business, the company produces and sells asphalt and concrete in California, Texas, Arizona, and New Mexico.

Customers for Vulcan's products include heavy construction and paving contractors; residential and commercial building contractors; concrete products manufacturers; state, county and municipal governments; railroads; and electric utilities.

Customers are served by truck, rail, and water networks from the company's production facilities and sales yards. Due to the high weight-to-value ratio of aggregates, markets generally are local in nature, often consisting of a single metropolitan area or one more counties or portions thereof when transportation is by truck alone. Truck deliveries account for about 85 percent of total shipments.

Reasons to Buy

Vulcan is a strong infrastructure reinvestment and stimulus package play.

From the company's Annual Report: "The American Recovery and Reinvestment Act of 2009 (the Act) was signed into law on February 17, 2009 for the purpose of creating jobs and restoring economic growth through, among other things, the modernization of America's infrastructure and the enhancement of its energy resources. Since the Act is expected to generate significant construction spending, demand for our products should increase. The Act allocates $27.5 billion for highways and bridges. Also, construction activity will increase due to spending allocated to the following areas: $1.1 billion for airports; $8.4 billion for mass transit; $8.0 billion for high speed rail; $4.6 billion for the Army Corps of Engineers; $6.0 billion for water and sewer projects; $4.2 billion for United States Department of Defense facilities; $6.4 billion to clean nuclear weapon sites; $6.0 billion to subsidize loans for renewable energy; $20 billion for renewable energy tax incentives; $6.3 billion to states for energy efficiency and clean energy grants; $8.8 billion for the renovation of schools; and $6.6 billion for a first time homebuyer credit of $8,000."

It's a long laundry list, and Vulcan should be one of the biggest beneficiaries of, and one of the companies most dependent upon, the stimulus package. Obviously, this piece of legislation could not have come at a better time for Vulcan, whose primary markets have all been dramatically affected by the recession.

Reasons for Caution

The slow deployment and uncertain targeting of stimulus funds is a concern. Also, in anticipation of renewed activity (and in order to pay down debt), the company issued 13.2 million shares of stock in June 2009, netting $521M but diluting existing shareholders.

SECTOR: **Materials**
BETA COEFFICIENT: **1.30**
10-YEAR COMPOUND EARNINGS PER SHARE GROWTH: **6.0%**
10-YEAR COMPOUND DIVIDENDS PER SHARE GROWTH: **11%**

	2008	2007	2006	2005	2004	2003	2002	2001	2000
Revenues (Mil)	3,651	3,328	3,342	2,895	2,454	2,892	2,797	3,020	2,492
Net Income (Mil)	191	451	468	388	261	223	190	223	220
Earnings per share	1.74	4.54	4.69	3.73	2.52	2.18	1.86	2.17	2.29
Dividends per share	1.96	1.84	1.48	1.16	1.04	0.97	0.94	0.90	0.84
Price high	84.7	128.6	93.8	76.3	55.5	48.6	50.0	55.3	48.9
low	39.5	77.0	65.8	52.4	41.9	28.8	32.4	37.5	36.5

AGGRESSIVE GROWTH

Walgreen Company

200 Wilmot Road ▫ Mail Stop 2261 ▫ Deerfield, IL 60015 ▫ Phone: (847) 914–2972 ▫ Fiscal year ends August 31 ▫ Website: www.walgreens.com ▫ Listed: NYSE ▫ Ticker symbol: WAG ▫ S&P rating: A+ ▫ Value Line financial strength rating: A+

Financial Highlights, Fiscal Year 2008

Walgreen Company reported its thirty-fourth consecutive year of record sales and earnings, a record matched by only one other *Fortune* 500 company. Earnings were $2.15B on sales of just over $59B, representing increases of 5.7 and 9.8 percent, respectively. The bulk of the revenue gains came from new outlets, as same-store sales increased only 4 percent year/year.

The company maintains its strong pharmacy orientation, with prescription drugs accounting for 65 percent of sales. Nonprescription drugs added another 10 percent, while "front end" (general merchandise) sales accounted for 25 percent. Dividends increased from $.33/share to $.40/share. Earnings/share grew 6.9 percent.

The company increased its outlet count by 937 in 2008, which included traditional retail outlets and workplace locations added in the acquisitions of I-Trax and Whole Health Management.

The company issued a $1.3B five-year note (A+ rating) for the repayment of short-term debt and for "general corporate purposes."

Company Profile

Walgreen Company is the nation's second largest drug store operator. As of April 30, 2009, they operate 6,783 drug stores in 49 states and Puerto Rico, as well as an additional 715 health-care facilities (worksite/home care facilities, specialty pharmacies) operated by its Take Care Health Systems subsidiary. They lead the chain drug store industry in sales and profits.

Founded in 1901, Walgreens today has 237,000 employees. The company's drug stores serve more than 4.4 million customers daily and average $8.3 million in annual sales per unit. That's $747 per square foot, among the highest in the industry. Walgreen has paid dividends in every quarter since 1933 and has raised the dividend in each of the past twenty-six years.

Competition from the supermarkets has convinced Walgreen that the best strategy is to build stand-alone stores. Since the rise of managed care, many pharmacy customers now make only minimal co-payments for prescriptions, removing price as the major differentiator among drug outlets. That leaves convenience as the major factor in choosing a pharmacy. The free-standing format makes room for drive-thru windows, which provide a quick way for drug store customers to pick up or drop off prescriptions.

On the other hand, the company's stand-alone strategy is more expensive. Walgreen insists on building its units on corner lots near an intersection with a traffic light. Such leases normally cost more than a site in a strip mall.

Home meal replacement has become a $100-billion business industry-wide. In the company's food section, Walgreen's carries staples as well as frozen dinners, desserts, and pizzas. In some stores, expanded food sections carry such items as fruit, and ready-to-eat salads.

Reasons to Buy

Walgreen has grown steadily and profitably through a combination of organic growth and opportunistic acquisitions. In the past few years this growth has quickened considerably—at one point they were opening a new location every sixteen hours. In 2009, the company has decided to moderate this level of expansion and concentrate on cost-cutting and improved profitability.

For example, recent store data indicates that 35 percent of the average store's SKUs account for only one percent of sales volume. Consequently, the company plans to significantly reduce the number of SKUs as part of a broader physical redesign of its existing layout. Other cost-cutting measures focus on more efficient prescription fulfillment and delivery methods. In total, the company expects to net $1B in cost reductions with improved profitability by the end of 2010.

The recent rapid growth and the emphasis on cost-cutting should not warn off investors, as the company is in solid financial shape. Long-term debt service amounts to only 9 percent of working capital (including the $1.5B bond issue), and operating margins are at a record high 7.3 percent. Walgreen is investing in itself so as to exit the current recession well-positioned for continued growth.

Reasons for Caution

Walgreen's cost-cutting initiatives will create a near-term drain on capital and reduced profitability before the benefits begin to accrue. Expect earnings per share to decrease near term, probably at least until the second half of 2010. There is also a risk that the drug store/convenience store genre is getting oversaturated, especially as suburban expansion wanes.

SECTOR: **Consumer Staples**
BETA COEFFICIENT: **.75**
10-YEAR COMPOUND EARNINGS PER SHARE GROWTH: **16.5%**
10-YEAR COMPOUND DIVIDENDS PER SHARE GROWTH: **9.5%**

		2008	2007	2006	2005	2004	2003	2002	2001	2000
Revenues (Mil)		59,034	53,762	47,409	42,202	37,502	32,505	28,681	24,623	21,207
Net Income (Mil)		2,157	2,041	1,751	1,478	1,360	1,176	1,019	886	756
Earnings per share		2.17	2.03	1.72	1.52	1.32	1.14	0.99	0.86	0.74
Dividends per share		.40	0.33	0.27	0.22	0.18	0.15	0.15	0.14	0.14
Price	high	39.0	49.1	51.6	49.0	39.5	37.4	40.7	45.3	45.8
	low	21.3	35.8	39.6	38.4	32.0	26.9	27.7	28.7	22.1

Wells Fargo & Company

420 Montgomery Street □ San Francisco, CA 94163 □ Phone: (415) 396–0523 □ Website: www.wellsfargo.com □ Listed: NYSE □ Ticker symbol: WFC □ S&P rating: AA+ □ Value Line financial strength rating: A

Financial Highlights, Fiscal Year 2008

As one might expect, 2008 was pretty much a throwaway year for Wells Fargo. The numbers are awful, and (unfortunately) fairly tell the story. Earnings were off 67 percent, to $2.66B, a level not seen in well over ten years. Return on total assets was off 86 percent. Long term debt was up 169 percent, and Loan Loss Provision was up 223 percent to $16 billion. If there's a highlight it's that their name is still on the door and the doors are still open.

On December 31, 2008, Wells Fargo acquired Wachovia Corporation in a stock-swap transaction valued at $12.5B to Wachovia shareholders. Wachovia was one of the nation's largest financial services companies, and being based in North Carolina, gives Wells a better presence in the eastern half of the United States.

Company Profile

Wells Fargo & Company is a diversified financial services company, providing banking, insurance, investments, mortgages, and consumer finance from more than 11,000 offices and other distribution channels across North America.

As of December 31, 2008, Wells Fargo had $1.3 trillion in assets, loans of $865 billion, deposits of $781 billion, and stockholders' equity of $99 billion. Based on assets, they are the fourth-largest bank holding company in the United States. They have over 281,000 employees, or "team members," as they are called by the company.

With the addition of Wachovia, Wells' profile in the industry has changed considerably. Here are some of the revised industry rankings for Wells Fargo as of April, 2009:

- #1 in U.S. banking stores
- #1 in small business lending
- #1 in mortgage originations
- #1 in middle market commercial lending
- #1 in agriculture lending
- #1 in commercial real estate lending
- #1 in commercial real estate brokerage
- #1 in bank-owned insurance brokerage
- #2 in banking deposits in the United States
- #2 in debit cards
- #2 in foreign exchange sales
- #3 in retail brokerage (21,889 financial advisors)

Reasons to Buy

Probably more than any other stock in this book, Wells is the example of "it's not about where the puck has been recently, it's about where it's going." Banks of all types and sizes got punished for profligate lending, and the worst of them are no longer around or have been in a severe downsizing mode. Wells pulled through because they were just a bit more conservative than most, and made some moves early on to avoid the worst of the credit crunch.

So where is Wells going? Indications point upward. They were trading below 8 in early 2009, and as of June they are solidly in the mid 20s. Their 5-year high is a split-adjusted 45, so they've rebounded nicely and have more than doubled their assets with the Wachovia deal. Wells has emerged from past banking downturns (as in 1990–91) quite well.

Despite the unprecedented contraction in the credit markets, Wells continues to lend to worthy customers. Wells made $106 billion in new loan commitments during 2008 to consumer, small business, and commercial customers and originated

$230 billion of residential mortgages. During fourth quarter 2008, their average core deposits grew 31 percent (annualized) over the prior quarter, and their cross-sell set records for the tenth consecutive year—their average retail banking household now has 5.73 Wells products.

As of February, Wells has the highest credit rating given to U.S. banks by Moody's ("Aa1") and Standard & Poor's Rating Services ("AA+").

Reasons for Caution

Of the $446 billion in loans acquired in the Wachovia deal, $94 billion were determined to be "credit-impaired," with a fair value of $59 billion. Wells has a year to revise these numbers up or down, as appropriate, so a final tally on the quality of the assets will not be made known until sometime after January 2010; there is some risk of negative surprises as these facts become known.

The healthy dividend may be at risk.

SECTOR: **Financials**
BETA COEFFICIENT: **1.25**
10-YEAR COMPOUND EARNINGS PER SHARE GROWTH: **8.5%**
10-YEAR COMPOUND DIVIDENDS PER SHARE GROWTH: **15.0%**

		2008	2007	2006	2005	2004	2003	2002	2001	2000
Loans (Bil)		843.8	344.8	306.9	296.1	269.6	249.2	192.8	168.7	157.4
Net Income (Mil)		2,655	8,060	8,480	7,670	7,014	6,202	5,710	3,423	4,026
Earnings per share		0.70	2.38	2.49	2.25	2.05	1.83	1.66	0.99	1.17
Dividends per share		1.30	1.18	1.12	1.00	0.93	0.75	0.55	0.50	0.45
Price	high	30.5	38.0	37.0	32.4	32.0	29.6	27.4	27.4	28.2
	low	7.8	29.3	30.3	28.8	27.2	21.7	19.1	19.2	15.7

APPENDICES

Appendix A
Online and Discount Brokers

These are just some of the most popular, easily accessible online and discount brokers in the United States. While all of these brokerages allow for DIY investing, many also provide investing advice and guidance for those who want these services. Discount brokers that offer walk-in, face-to-face assistance in addition to their automated trading services are noted.

Bank of America
www.baisidirect.com
800-926-1111
Easy trading for self-directed investors, both online and through their Intellibroker touchtone service. Also offers full-service investing.

Charles Schwab
www.schwab.com
800-435-4500
High volume and low prices from one of the biggest of the brokerage houses. Local branches located throughout the United States.

E*TRADE Financial
www.etrade.com
800-786-2575
High volume, very popular site with low prices. Walk-in branches in several states.

Fidelity
www.fidelity.com
800-544-6666
Recently rated best online broker by *Kiplinger's*. Many investor centers located throughout the United States.

Marquette De Bary Company
www.debary.com
800-221-3305
Oldest discount broker in New York City.

Regal Discount Securities
www.regaldiscount.com
800-786-9000
Offices in the Chicago area.

Scottrade
www.scottrade.com
800-906-7268
Has more than 400 walk-in branches throughout the United States.

Sharebuilder
www.sharebuilder.com
866-590 -7629
A service of ING Direct.

TD Ameritrade
www.tdameritrade.com
800-669-3900
More than 100 local branch offices nationwide.

Tradex Brokerage Service

800-231-6455
No online trading thus far. Offices in the Houston area.

USAA Brokerage Services

www.usaa.com
800-531-8343
Services are offered to current and former military personnel and their families.

Vanguard Brokerage Services

www.vanguard.com
800-992-8327

Zecco

www.zecco.com
877-700-7862 (only during standard business hours)
Offers only online trading at this time.

Appendix B
Investment Publications

There are dozens of publications that can be very helpful to investors. These financially oriented newspapers, magazines, and newsletters offer valuable insights about the markets, including stock tips, mutual fund rankings, and in-depth articles with a more educational angle. Publications can be a good place to get investing ideas, but you must still do your own research and analysis and make sure an investment fits well in your portfolio before you make any purchase decision.

Subscription prices listed are those posted on the publications' websites as of April 2009 and may represent special or limited-time offers. To help you decide which publications are the most useful to you before you shell out the money for a long-term subscription, visit your local library. Among other resources, you can gain valuable insight about investing from the following:

The Wall Street Journal
800-568-7625
www.wallstreetjournal.com

Published by Dow Jones and Company, the *Wall Street Journal* is a leading global newspaper with a focus on business. Founded in 1889, the newspaper has grown to a worldwide daily circulation of more than 2 million readers. In 1994, Dow Jones introduced the *Wall Street Journal Special Editions*, special sections written in local languages that are featured in more than thirty leading national newspapers worldwide. The *Wall Street Journal Americas*, published in Spanish and Portuguese, is included in approximately twenty leading Latin American newspapers. The *Wall Street Journal* offers one-year print-only subscriptions for $119, one-year online subscriptions for $104, and a combination one-year print and online subscription for $140.

Barron's
800-975-8620
www.barrons.com

Barron's is also known as the *Dow Jones Business and Financial Weekly*. With its first edition published in 1921, *Barron's* offers its readers news reports and analyses on financial markets worldwide. Investors will also find a wealth of tips regarding investment techniques. One-year print-only subscriptions are $99, a one-year print plus online subscription runs $149, and a one-year online-only subscription costs $79.

Investor's Business Daily
800-459-6706
www.investors.com

Founded in 1984, *Investor's Business Daily* is a newspaper focusing on business, financial, economic, and national news. The publication places a strong emphasis on offering its readers timely information on stock market and stock market–related issues. The front page of each issue provides a brief overview of the most important business news of the day. It's published five days a week, Monday through Friday, and you can get a one-year subscription for $295, which includes full access to its website. The strictly online edition, called eIBD, offers annual subscriptions for $235 or monthly subscriptions for $28.95 per month. A one-year subscription to the daily print edition and eIBD is $365.

Forbes
800-888-9896
www.forbesmagazine.com

Forbes magazine is a biweekly business magazine for "those who run business today—or aspire to." Each issue contains stories on companies, management strategies, global trends, technology, taxes, law, capital markets, and investments. A one-year subscription, or twenty-six issues, is $59.95, and that comes with complete access to its real-time website.

Money
800-633-9970
http://money.cnn.com

Money is a monthly personal finance magazine from Time-Warner publications, covering such topics as family finances, investment careers, taxes, and insurance. Each issue includes tips, advice, and strategies for smart investing. The magazine also features other related matters like finding cheap flights, buying a home, and preparing for tax season. It also offers a substantive annual mutual fund guide. A one-year subscription, or thirteen issues, is $14.95.

BusinessWeek
888-878-5151
www.businessweek.com

This weekly publication comes jam-packed with comprehensive coverage of both the U.S. and global business scenes. From the economy to politics to how both impact stock prices, *BusinessWeek* provides in-depth market analysis and incisive investigative reporting. A twelve-week subscription costs $12 and a fifty-week subscription is $46, including online access.

Fortune
800-621-8000
www.fortune.com

Every month, *Fortune* magazine, a Time-Warner publication, offers analysis of the business marketplace. The publication's annual ranking of the top 500 American companies is one of its most widely read features. *Fortune* has been covering business and business-related topics since its origins in 1930. A one-year subscription, or twenty-five issues, is $19.99.

Smart Money
800-444-4204
www.smartmoney.com

Smart Money, a monthly personal finance magazine, offers readers ideas for investing, spending, and saving. The publication also covers automotive, technology, and lifestyle subjects, including upscale travel, footwear, fine wine, and music. One-year subscriptions are $11, and two-year subscriptions cost $18.

Kiplinger's Personal Finance
800-544-0155
www.kiplingers.com

One of the most respected names in financial publications, *Kiplinger's* offers investing ideas, updates on companies, insider interviews with top financial experts and fund managers, and very detailed listings of the best-performing mutual funds in a wide range of categories. One-year subscriptions cost $12 for either the print or digital edition.

ValueLine Investment Survey
800-634-3583
www.valueline.com

A weekly publication available at most libraries and through subscription, it offers ratings, reports, opinions, and analysis on about 130 stocks in seven or eight industries on a weekly basis. Approximately 1,700 stocks in about ninety-four industries are covered every thirteen weeks. CD-ROM subscribers can also purchase an expanded version containing reviews of 5,000 stocks. A thirteen-week trial subscription, which includes full online access, costs $75; a one-year subscription costs $598.

Appendix C
Investment Websites

The Internet has made an unparalleled impact on the world of investing. The web has significantly affected the manner in which business is conducted worldwide. It has taken the information once found buried in the business sections of newspapers and made it easily accessible to investors at all levels. Add to that a vast array of software, as well as investment websites designed for the investment professional, and you have a whole new world of investing, literally at your fingertips.

A majority of the major financial institutions and nearly all of the major brokerage houses offer their own websites. The most comprehensive of the many websites offered by major investment firms include the following:

www.invescoaim.com
www.americancentury.com
www.fidelity.com
www.franklintempleton.com
www.iShares.com
www.invescopowershares.com
www.prudential.com
www.wellsfargoadvantagefunds.com
www.vanguard.com

Historical information, fund holdings, performance updates, fund profiles, information on fund managers, libraries of articles and general information, and even glossaries and investor tips can be found on various websites. Needless to say, the investor tips and how-to information can lean in favor of the funds offered by a fund family. You usually won't find the virtues of REITs or advantages of muni bond funds discussed by a fund family that doesn't handle them. Nevertheless, you will get a lot of overall information at the websites of financial institutions.

Home in on the specific areas that you are looking for, such as tax-free investments, socially responsible investing (try *http://coopamerica.org*), or information on particular funds. This will narrow down your search and reduce your time spent online, since some websites are loaded with promotional material and hype or are simply confusing with numerous bells and whistles.

There are dozens of sites on the Internet devoted to investing and investment advice. Some will give you an overall picture of investing as a whole, and others will focus on a particular area. The list on the following page includes just a sampling of the many investment-related websites available:

Bloomberg

www.bloomberg.com

Bloomberg's online financial news and information site, with real-time streaming quotes.

Bondtrac Financial Information

www.bondtrac.com

If you're looking for bond information and the latest in bond offerings, this site should be of help.

CCH Financial Planning Toolkit

www.finance.cch.com

This website offers expert advice on financial planning and investing, including free planning tools and financial calculators.

CNN Money

www.money.com

The CNN Financial News Network offers a site with an extensive amount of information about U.S. and global markets.

Co-Op America

http://coopamerica.org

Describes how to integrate social investing into your financial plan and portfolio.

Dogs of the Dow

www.dogsofthedow.com

Gives you the lowdown on the stocks in the Dow Jones, from historical information to the latest quotes, plus news and updates.

Dow Jones Business Directory

www.dowjones.com

Offers you a comprehensive listing of all sorts of financial sites on the web, even reviewing many of them.

The Green Money Journal

www.greenmoneyjournal.com

Advice and information especially for green investors.

The Global Investor Directory

www.global-investor.com

As the name indicates, this site provides access to a plethora of international investing information, including performance information on worldwide alternative and emerging markets.

Hoovers Online

www.hoovers.com

Gives you the scoop on more than 32 million companies, from IPOs to industry profiles.

Investopedia

www.investopedia.com

This website is jam-packed with articles, tutorials, and investment calculators, all designed to help you become an even better investor.

Investor Guide

www.investorguide.com

Offers a long list of subjects, with plenty of information and tons of links.

MarketWatch

www.marketwatch.com

This financial site has information on stocks, bonds, mutual funds, the economy, and more, plus charts and commentary.

The Mutual Fund Investor's Center

www.mfea.com

Helps you gather all the information you need to select the mutual funds.

Moody's

www.moodys.com

The place to go for bond ratings (including a downgrade watchlist) and authoritative reports on credit trends and corporate finance.

Morningstar

www.morningstar.com

One of the most comprehensive investing websites on the Internet, you'll find information about mutual funds, ETFs, bonds, stocks, and options; a veritable wealth of information.

The Motley Fool

www.fool.com

Provides a wide variety of information, including a lot of investing basics, in plain clear language.

Investing in Bonds

www.investinginbonds.com

Legislative and statistical information, research, prices, and more, all tailored for bond investors.

Quote.com

www.quote.com

Up-to-the-minute quotes from numerous markets, along with analysis and commentary.

Reuters

www.reuters.com

Offers all the latest financial news you need, from one of the most trusted sources in the world.

U.S. Government Investment and Tax Information

www.treasury.gov

The government's website for government investments and tax information, plus news on the U.S. and world financial markets.

U.S. Securities and Exchange Commission

www.sec.gov

Information on corporations, brokerage houses, SEC policies, and news, as well as a place for individual investors to learn about current fraud investigations and personal fraud protection (including reporting suspected instances of investment fraud).

Treasury Direct

www.easysaver.gov

The U.S. Treasury Department's site designed to help you invest in government bonds, even by using direct deposit, to make saving and investing very easy.

Yahoo Finance

www.finance.yahoo.com

From personal financial tutorials to streaming real-time quotes, this site offers lots of advice to novice investors.

Zack's Investment Research

www.zacks.com

A research site with market commentary and information.

INDEX OF STOCKS
BY CATEGORY

Aggressive Growth

- Air Products
- Apache Corporation
- Apple Baxter
- Boeing Company
- CarMax
- Caterpillar, Inc.
- Cintas
- Costco Wholesale
- Deere & Company
- Dover
- eBay
- Emergen
- EnCana Corporation
- Fair Isaac
- FedEx Corporation
- Fluor
- FMC Corporation
- Goodrich
- Harris Corporation
- Hewlett-Packard
- Honeywell
- Iron Mountain
- Lowe's
- Marathon Oil
- McDonald's
- Medtronic
- Monsanto
- NIKE
- Patterson Companies
- Paychex
- Peet's
- Perrigo
- Raytheon
- Ross Stores
- Schlumberger
- Sigma–Aldrich
- St. Jude Medical
- Staples
- Starbucks
- Stryker
- Target Corporation
- Teva Pharmaceutical
- TJX
- Tractor Supply
- UnitedHealth
- Valmont
- Varian
- Vulcan Materials Co.
- Walgreen

Conservative Growth

- Archer Daniels Midland
- Becton, Dickinson

Campbell Soup

Clorox

Coca-Cola

Colgate-Palmolive

C.R. Bard

CVS/Caremark Corporation

Dentsply Int'l

Ecolab

General Dynamics

W.W. Grainger

Hormel Foods

Illinois Tool Works

International Business Machines

International Paper

Johnson Controls

McCormick & Co.

Norfolk Southern

Northern Trust

PepsiCo

Praxair

Procter & Gamble

Sysco Corporation

3M Company

United Parcel

Growth & Income

Abbott Laboratories

Alexander & Baldwin

AT&T

Chevron

ConocoPhillips

Diebold

Dominion Resources

DuPont

Entergy

ExxonMobil

FPL Group

General Mills

Heinz

Johnson & Johnson

Kellogg

Kraft

Lubrizol

Southern Co.

United Technologies

Verizon

Wells Fargo

About the Authors

Peter Sander (Granite Bay, CA) is an author, researcher, and consultant in the fields of personal finance, business, and location reference. He has written twenty-three books, including *Value Investing for Dummies, What to Do When the Economy Sucks, 101 Things Everyone Should Know about Economics,* and *Cities Ranked & Rated.* He is also the author of numerous articles and columns dealing with investment strategies. He has an MBA from Indiana University and has completed Certified Financial Planner (CFP®) education and examination requirements.

John Slatter (Essex Junction, VT) has a varied investment background and has served as a stockbroker, securities analyst, and portfolio strategist. Slatter has written hundreds of articles for such publications as *Barron's* and *Better Investing* as well as for brokerage firms he has worked for, including Hugh Johnson & Company and Wachovia Securities. His books include *Safe Investing, Straight Talk about Stock Investing,* and eleven prior editions of *The 100 Best Stocks You Can Buy.*